THE BOOK OF ASSASSINS

THE
BOOK OF
ASSASS NS

A BIOGRAPHICAL
DICTIONARY FROM
ANCIENT TIMES
TO THE PRESENT

GEORGE FETHERLING
RESEARCH ASSOCIATE CHRISTOPHER MARTIN

CASTLE BOOKS

This edition published in 2006 by
CASTLE BOOKS ®
A division of Book Sales, Inc.
114 Northfield Avenue
Edison, NJ 08837

This edition published by arrangement with and permission of
John Wiley & Sons, Inc.
111 River Street
Hoboken, New Jersey 07030

Previously published in Canada by Random House Canada under the title
A Biographical Dictionary of the World's Assassins

This publication is designed to provide accurate and authoritative information in regard to the subject matter provided. It is sold with the understanding that the publisher is not engaged in rendering professional services. If professional advice or other expert assistance is required, the services of a competent professional person should be sought.

ISBN-13: 978-0-7858-2181-6
ISBN-10: 0-7858-2181-3

Printed in the United States of America

CONTENTS

ACKNOWLEDGEMENTS

This book would not have come about without research tips and advice from Tim Brook, translation assistance from Stefano Cossu, Cathy Hanson and Ralf-Dieter Schindler and editorial criticism from Cynthia Brouse, William Davies, Rhona Sawlor and Daniel Williman. Special thanks to the supportive and unflappable Anne Collins, who made the project possible.

INTRODUCTION

There are many thousands of books on particular assassinations and on the subject in general, but nearly all of them deal with the victims, not the perpetrators. This is overwhelmingly the case even in the roomful of volumes on the John Kennedy assassination, the instance in which the most attention has been paid to the presumed killer or the hunt for substitute suspects. Until now, however, there has been no single reference book solely on assassins themselves, in various periods and countries, for the convenience of students, researchers, historians, criminologists, psychologists and general readers interested in true crime. This is ironic in a sense, because a certain kind of assassin, as the reader will see quite readily, kills in order to be ensured a place in history, only to be rejected by the historical record in the chaos that the killing sets in motion.

Ask yourself this question: Who killed the Archduke Ferdinand in 1914, thus igniting the First World War, in which ten million people died and twenty million were wounded and which redrew the map of Europe, dealt the *coup de grâce* to European colonialism, made the United States a world power—and led inevitably, unstoppably, to the Second World War? That person, arguably one of the most influential of the twentieth century, survived until 1918 but his name has been forgotten by all but a few. (You'll find the answer by consulting *Franz-Ferdinand* in the Index of Victims at the end of this book.) Similarly, who carried out Stalin's orders and killed Leon Trotsky at his well-guarded compound in Mexico City in 1940? This was surely one of the most important events in the rise and fall of communism, the world's numerically dominant political system for much of the twentieth century. The person's name is not generally remembered though he lived until 1978. For that matter, who killed Rasputin and then lived on until 1967? Then there are acts of assassination as little known as the people who perform them. How many recall now that, a decade before he was gunned down in Memphis in 1968, a young Dr. Martin Luther King was very nearly assassinated in New York during a book signing?

This encyclopedia will answer such questions and tell such tales, and many more besides. I can't resist pointing out some of history's most infamous assassins turn out not to have been assassins at all. Lucrezia Borgia is often referred to as an assassin but in fact never attempted to kill anybody (unlike her brother Cesare, who was probably the most prolific assassin of the Italian Renaissance, one of the great boom periods in assassination). Yet the world has not been without its female assassins, of whom the most notorious is Charlotte Corday, who killed the French political writer Jean-Paul Marat in the Revolutionary period and actually inspired later women to kill or try to. Because the women assassins are so interesting and so contrary to our preconceived ideas about gender, I have let them make up ten per cent of this book (an artificially high figure) and include women who have made attempts on the lives of people as different as Adolf Hitler and Andy Warhol.

This leads to a related point. The greater the variety of assassins, the more diverse the targets. Sakamoto Ryoma, the founder of what became Mitsubishi Corporation, was an assassin. Alexandr Ulyanov led a failed conspiracy to kill the czar of Russia and was executed, thus provoking his younger brother, V.I. Lenin, to a life of communist agitation. Although most of the people identified in the Index of Victims are political or religious figures or social activists (for such is the nature of power and the reaction against it), the book also includes three professional criminals, two singers, two actors and one each of the following: fashion designer, banker, publisher, explorer, playwright, industrialist, radio talk show host, famous philosopher, retailer, visual artist, tennis star and professional baseball player.

As we know, assassination sometimes seems to run along dynastic lines, as with the American Kennedys, of course, but also the Gandhi family of India. Indira Gandhi and her son Rajiv Gandhi (both prime ministers—and no relation to M.K. Gandhi) were assassinated, while Indira's other son, Sanjay, died in a suspicious plane crash. Surely two of the most bizarre stories in this book concern President Ferdinand Marcos of the Philippines and his wife Imelda. The former rose to power through being an assassin; the latter courted public sympathy after being attacked by an assassin—whom she beat off with one of her famous pairs of shoes. Then there are people who, through political longevity and a lack of inhibitions about making dangerous enemies, are assassination prone. As no even remotely accurate figures about the number of attempts on Fidel Castro have come to light, Charles de Gaulle of France must serve as the record holder, having survived thirty-one documented assassination attempts (in all of which together he suffered only a scratch).

You get the idea. This book is both a ready reference and one in which to browse, or to read cover to cover as a study of the assassin personality. It has no political subtext. It is a collection of biographical stories, most of them hard come by, of individual assassins living in many ages and places. To use the book effectively, however, readers must take a moment to consider a few questions, such as the one that first led me to the study of the subject: the matter of

ASSASSINATIONS IN DIFFERENT CULTURES

The concept of assassination is not deeply rooted in English-speaking countries. As readers, we are left to guess at the reasons for this. Assassinations, we might venture, are more likely to take place in cultures where political instability has been the rule and are less frequent in societies where parliamentary government has a lengthy, unbroken history. Certainly such notions have some meat on them. Assassination, as the term is understood today, is never the act of an individual in authority killing someone who is powerless (that would be *execution*). Assassination, rather, occurs when a powerless or comparatively powerless person, or one seeking power, deliberately kills the powerful. In terms of social class and position, an assassin must kill *up* and not *down* to distinguish himself from the common murderer.

As regards political instability, however spontaneous the act itself, conditions leading up to assassination tend to be long-standing ones: injustices that have become ingrained, grievances that finally have boiled over as murder or attempted murder—or symbolic murder. This kind of assassination is most likely to be a feature of those places that are administratively fragmented, such as Japan at the beginning of the Meiji or Italy before its unification by Garibaldi and others. As for democracy, its presence certainly lowers the incidence of assassination—up to but not beyond the point at which democracy turns into American-style populism, in which the elected officials are expected to mingle with the populace on equal terms. Looking at the subject historically, the student can see that states undergoing a profound structural change, be it a revolution or the transition from monarchy to republic, often reached a point at which assassination almost seemed to be an expected part of the process. There were occasions, some of them covered in this book, when an assassin considered his act of violence to be a speeded-up version of a referendum, just as an explosion, when viewed by a chemist, is nothing more than a too-fast burning of fuel in an enclosed space.

Despite all this, the English-speaking countries, the United States in particular, have certain distinctions in the field. For example, to kill a celebrity as though in an attempt to steal his or her fame appears to be an idea largely confined to the wealthiest nations (though it seems remarkably similar to aboriginal and primitive beliefs about the hunter assuming the power of the prey). It's an idea that is likely to spread as globalization increases the reach of American pop culture. Another largely American addition to assassination lore has been official fear of the crazy lone gunman, the disenfranchised outcast or recluse whose popping up cannot be predicted and whose action cannot be explained. One of the most criticized portions in all twenty-six volumes of the *Report* of the Warren Commission on the assassination of President John F. Kennedy (Washington, 1964) has been the background paper by Allen Dulles, the former director of central intelligence whom Kennedy had fired, tracing the development of this archetype in American society. Dulles's purpose clearly was to support the assertion that Lee Oswald, the person named in the findings as Kennedy's killer, fit such a historical pattern: an idea that is now widely disputed, even discredited. But Dulles's wide-ranging overview was basically correct; ironically, his appendix is one of the most accurate and valuable components of the commission's conclusions.

In any event, what can be said for certain is that the United States leads the way in writings about the subject of assassination. To suggest that the literature is vast is almost comic understatement. Since the Warren *Report* and its ideological opposite, Mark Lane's prescient and groundbreaking work *Rush to Judgement*, published in 1966, perhaps as many as three thousand books on the first Kennedy assassination have been published in the United States. And of course this by no means indicates how long the bibliography would be that included other American books on other assassinations or on assassination in general, much less all the studies published in other countries. Which leads to the matter of

THE NOMENCLATURE

The word *assassin* shares origins with the Arabic *hashīsh*, which originally meant dried herbs or fodder but came to refer to the drug now known in the West as hashish or hash. The name assassin was applied to any member of the religious sect, a splinter group of Ismaili Muslims, who, beginning in the late eleventh century, were thought to take the drug prior to committing their acts of mayhem and terrorism. The most cogent discussion of this may be found in *The Assassins* by Bernard Lewis (London, 1967), though there are a number of other less scholarly works on the subject by writers such as Colin Wilson (*The Order of Assassins: The Psychology of Murder*, London, 1972). Lewis argues convincingly that Crusaders brought the word back from Syria to Europe, where it became corrupted as *assassin* and took on its present meaning—or rather, its modern meaning. Dating the transition is difficult, but a hired killer was hanged in England in 1242 for making an attempt on the life of Edward I "after the manner of the Assassins." In any event, such phrases as "attempted assassin" and "would-be assassin" were until recently so many redundancies. Far into late Victorian times, *assassin* meant anyone who even tried to kill a public official or head of state or other person in authority, and *to assassinate* meant to make an attempt on the life of another; whether the attempt succeeded or failed was not within the province of the word to indicate. For instance, this is the sense in which Thomas Jefferson, then the American minister in France, used the term in 1785 when, in a letter to Abigail Adams, the spouse of his colleague in London, he complained that British newspapers "teem with every horror of which human nature is capable. Assassinations, suicides, thefts, robberies, and, what is worse than assassination, theft, suicide or robbery, the blackest slanders!" More than a century later, the word was still being used, and understood, in the same way.

The first American president to be assassinated was Andrew Jackson, in that, in 1835, Richard Lawrence made an attempt on his life that failed. Today we assume that the first president to be assassinated was Abraham Lincoln, because the attempt was successful. But *assassination* would have applied to John Wilkes Booth's efforts even if Lincoln had incurred a non-lethal wound. Pinpointing when the meaning of the word changed cannot be done with absolute precision, though the alteration can be narrowed down to a period of a few years. In 1881, James A. Garfield, the twentieth president of the United States, was shot by a human curiosity named Charles Guiteau. *Assassination* was the word applied from the beginning even though Garfield was merely wounded on July 2 and did not die until September 19. (The attempt on Garfield is the leitmotif of Clint Eastwood's 1992 film *The Unforgiven*, which takes place between the time of Garfield's wounding and the date of his death, and in which the characters speak throughout of "the assassination" rather than of the attempted assassination: a rare instance of Hollywood sensitivity to the subtle evolution of the English language.) By the time President William McKinley was shot in 1901, *assassin* and *assassinate* had assumed their present implications of fatality. When the former president Theodore Roosevelt was shot and seriously wounded in 1912, his assailant was an "attempted" assassin. The same type of shift in meaning seems to be underway today with regard to *suicide*, which once meant any attempt at self-assassination or any person committing such an act, whether successfully or not. Now the term *para-suicide* is used in clinical circles for those who try to kill themselves and fail. Perhaps this distinction will take hold in lay language as well.

Comparing English with some other European languages in this regard also might be useful. In Italy, where assassination as an instrument of policy goes back to the Roman Empire, when it was common practice, the noun *assassino* refers specifically to someone who kills a politician or other public personality. *Assassinio* (assassination) and *assassinare* (to assassinate) are used a little less strictly, especially outside legal circles. In Spanish, both *asesinato* (assassination) and *asesinar* (to assassinate) are supposed to refer to the death of *un personaje importante*, but the verb is now used in the media, the popular newspapers especially, to refer to any type of murder—of anyone, by anyone. French remains more pure, with *assassin* (the killer of a personage), *assassiner* (the verb) and *assassinat* (the noun referring to the act). In German, the terminology differs. By placing the words *das* (or *auf*) *Attentat* before the word *Mord*, one distinguishes an attempted assassination from a successful one.

But putting aside such questions of philology, what do people generally mean by the term *assassination* now? Nearly every book one consults on the subject offers a slightly different answer. The definition used here may be called middle-of-the-road: a criminal event in which someone not so prominent as the intended victim at least tries to kill the other person for reasons that have to do with the victim's renown or power, whether real or largely symbolic. A political motive is not always the same as a partisan one: John Hinckley, Jr., who ended up trying to kill Ronald Reagan, set out originally to kill Reagan's political opposite, Jimmy Carter, and presumably would have been equally happy with either trophy.

There is a relation to be noted between intent and effect. Sometimes assassins will claim that they were merely trying to warn (or startle or frighten) the victim. In some of the instances researched for this compilation, such claims might be true. But they were discarded in selecting the subjects for these miniature essays. Instead, I have stuck to the intent-effect rule that one or both of the following conditions must be met before an unpleasant incident can truly be considered an assassination: 1) the assassin must have been intending to kill the victim, or 2) although the assassin may not have intended to kill, his or her actions could have caused death. A case like that of John William Bean, who made an attempt on Queen Victoria in 1842, *is* considered an assassination, because although Victoria was perfectly safe, Bean, in his insanity, really did think his pistol was a lethal weapon even though it was loaded with tobacco rather than lead. A case such as that of Günter Parche, who attempted to kill the athlete Monica Seles in 1993, is considered an assassination because, although Parche claimed that he intended to wound, he stabbed her in such a way that easily might have caused death.

In any case, this book certainly does not glorify assassins. Most of the subjects, as will be seen, led pathetic, barren lives. What it attempts to do rather is to salvage from obscurity the schematic and anecdotal outlines of their biographical existence. The intention is basically the same as that of John Aubrey, the seventeenth-century English antiquary, in assembling the book now popularly known as *Brief Lives*. No one would claim that this work is so important as Aubrey's, but they share an impulse.

THE TYPOLOGY

of assassination is another concern that springs naturally from work on a project such as this. In studying hundreds of assassins of various cultures and eras, many more than legal concerns and the economics of publishing have allowed us to include, my research associate and I have come up with a method by which virtually any assassin may, for convenience' sake, be classified.

Type 1 assassins, the most common in the ancient world and indeed in most recorded assassinations until the Renaissance in Europe, were men who deposed rulers in order to assume the position themselves, or women who killed (often their husbands or sons) in order to get one of their children or someone else whom they loved on the throne. Naturally, this type of assassination has been in decline since the diminishing of the monarchy but is still seen in Latin American and African nations where usurping the power of a dictator tends to be comparably simple once the dictator is dead, usually with at least the tacit support of the local military or some First World power. In spite of the fact that Type 1 assassinations tend not to take place in countries with stable systems of government, nearly every US vice-president who has become president on the violent death of his superior has been rumoured to be an example of this variety.

Type 2 assassins are the most under-reported group: the mercenary killers. They are professionals who usually kill at long range and in the expectation of escape. Relatively few of these are included in this book (exceptions are Vlada the Chauffeur, Balthazar Gerard and Charles Harrelson), because these professionals are trained in evasion and escape and are rarely brought to justice. Type 2s were grotesquely common in earlier epochs, when their deeds were openly acknowledged and rewarded. The contemporary equivalent are assassins retained by various governments. Comparatively few of these are included in this encyclopedia either, because I have made the decision to deal only with individuals rather than to write speculative entries on such organizations as the KGB or the CIA. Under the heading Type 2, I include only those instances in which one government worker is given the assignment of assassinating a worker of some other government, for whereas individuals in the private sector must kill *up* in order to qualify as assassins, the public sector may assassinate laterally, with someone in a government bureau or agency killing his or her opposite number on the other side of the ideological fence, as was common during the Cold War.

Government-sanctioned assassination raises any number of ethical and moral concerns quite beyond the simple question of murder. Why do citizens of a particular country believe that their government is actually invested with moral authority when someone is assassinated in their name? And might there not be cases in which they would be correct to think so? As early as the 1930s, there were attempts on the life of Adolf Hitler (virtually all by German military personnel, who knew him better than his distant enemies). How can we say in this instance that the taking of a human life, had any of the plans succeeded, would not have benefitted humankind (though this is precisely the debate that kept the British general staff from carrying out an attempt on Hitler)? I leave the answers to specialists in these matters; I merely pose the questions. In any case, the attempts on Hitler were not mercenary in nature, but I believe that in most assassinations of such political figures the motivation is as likely to be mercenary as ideological or even political. Professional peace-time intelligence agents ordered to kill a foreign leader do so because they draw salaries for their jobs as a whole, positions for which a rudimentary sense of patriotic duty is required. The editorial principle in this reference work generally has been to ignore (sometimes this was painful) assassinations such as those of Ngo Dinh Diem of South Vietnam for whom we have not even a putative individual shooter, while at other times, as logic seemed to dictate, to include the story of a political assassination under the name of the known ringleader or mastermind rather than that of the person who actually pulled the trigger. In both cases, the wish has been to keep the book focused on assassins themselves rather than on victims.

Type 3 assassins are the most unusual in North America but the most common in modern Europe. They are the people whose motives are ideological or religious. Until the sixteenth century, the latter was more common than the former, but the change was slow. Also, there have been periods, particularly in the Middle Ages and the Renaissance, when such distinctions required a fine eye. With the rise of proletarian politics in the nineteenth century, regicides and similar crimes were likely to be based in feelings related to class and politics. When presented with a Type 3 assassin, many societies appear determined to prove the individual is insane rather than acting out of political belief. Consider the case of Oscar Collazo, who attempted to kill US president Harry Truman and who American authorities desperately tried to show was insane while so many genuinely insane American assassins were tried as criminals. A similar case in Japan involved an attempt on Emperor Hirohito. Of course, many authorities classify defendants as insane on the basis of their political beliefs (see the entry on Byron De La Beckwith) but being clinically insane does not necessarily prohibit a person from being an ideologue as well. In ancient Rome, the assassin was never considered insane but the victim was. In the case of some emperors, they indeed were.

Type 4 assassins may be characterized as those who attack celebrities because of their fame, perhaps hoping that by doing so they will become more famous than their victims. The phenomenon is comparatively recent. Virtually all such assassins come from countries with highly developed economies, particularly the United States, Britain, France, Germany and Japan. As with the other categories, the boundaries of Type 4 are not perfect or exclusive. But as a generalization one can say that Type 4 assassins are what the psychiatric community calls CMI (certifiably mentally ill). An example would be Mark David Chapman, who killed John Lennon.

Type 5 assassins act as they do seeking personal revenge, a rather small group but one that seems to exist in all eras and venues. Examples are John Felton, Hamud Mohamed Hamud and Henriette Caillaux. The victims of Type 5 assassins seem to range, in decreasing order of frequency, from those who have killed friends or family members of the assassin to those who have denied the assassin a rise in rank or status to those who have signed a death warrant for the assassin.

Of the well over two hundred cases studied in this book, Lee Oswald is the only one who might conceivably qualify for membership in all five categories, if all the theories about his actions were somehow true.

ARCHETYPES AND STEREOTYPES

abound in the study of assassins and assassinations. The assassin of the ancient world is depicted as a scheming person (as often a woman as a man) who resorts to poison or other treachery to remove a rival to her or his own twisted ambitions. Although the wording sounds a bit harsh, this picture is more accurate than later stereotypes. Most assassins prior to 1500 are Types 1 and 2. Many female assassins were in fact working to put their sons on the throne, whereas most male assassins were either trying to take the throne themselves or were mercenaries working for someone who they expected to be the next monarch.

Links are obvious between assassin stereotypes and archetypes on the one hand and the weapons or methods used on the other. For centuries, no other means of assassination was more despised than poison, because it was considered the choice of female assassins, unmanly and cowardly by its nature. No doubt it also was hated because it was so often effective—more so than we are ever likely to know. In later eras, when killing at a distance became easier, poison fell out of favour, though in modern times poison has often been considered by government agencies. For the purposes of this book, any attempt to kill the potential victim with a fatal disease is considered a poisoning. Strangulation and beating the victim to death have remained far less common than poisoning—except, in the case of strangulation, with regards to Roman emperors and Russian czars. Other changes in fashion can be traced to advances in technology. With the exception of the Yamaguchi case in Japan in 1960, the sword has been out of style among assassins since the invention of gunpowder, when use of the long blade was limited mainly to military officers and persons of rank. Japan must be considered separately, however, because the mystique of the samurai makes the sword the weapon of choice among nationalist zealots. Surprisingly few accounts appear to exist of persons being assassinated by archers, whereas knives have been by far the commonest weapon and the longest-lived. One of the earliest assassins in this book—Brutus, who led the murderous attack on Julius Caesar in 44 BCE—used a knife. So did one of the most recent, Michael Abram, who stabbed the singer George Harrison in 1999. Only pistols have rivalled knives as weapons of assassination, as they are easy to conceal and are even more deadly than knives at close range. Shoulder weapons, being more difficult to hide, are used mainly in assassinations involving the military, terrorist groups and intelligence agencies and by professional freelance assassins: in short, by people who fire from a great distance in the hopeful expectation of getting away with their crime. Anastasio Somoza the younger, of Nicaragua, was killed in 1980 with a bazooka, surely a singular case. Then, of course, there are bombs, once so beloved by editorial cartoonists depicting assassins and their ways.

Method or weaponry is closely related to gender. The nineteenth-century assassin was likely a male. Or rather, although there are many female assassins in this period, they are usually ignored by those who subscribe to the stereotype of the unshaved, dishevelled, quiet and foreign-born anarchist who throws a spherical round black bomb with a sputtering fuse (the cartoon-type) while shouting "*Vive l'anarchie!*" regardless of his native tongue. The truth is that anarchism, as a philosophical and political movement growing up in reaction to industrial capitalism, was at its zenith in the last decades of the nineteenth century, the era of anarchist thinkers as different as Bakunin and Kropotkin. For a time anarchism did indeed include a faction dedicated to "propaganda by the deed": the use of individual acts of violence to advance their views. That this minority was soon denounced or abrogated by serious anarchists did not stop the spread of the stereotype, particularly in Britain and America, where it carried heavy nativist and anti-Semitic overtones. During this period, the press and the authorities tended to label all politically or socially motivated assassins as anarchists, even when many were clearly Marxists, the anarchists' polar opposite. The world has now forgotten that a splinter group within the violent anarchist minority favoured destroying buildings rather than individuals, as though in anticipation of the neutron bomb. An example is a French anarchist named Martial Bourdin, who planned to blow up the Royal Observatory at Greenwich on February 15, 1894, but was killed when his bomb exploded prematurely. The incident inspired Joseph Conrad to write his novel *The Secret Agent* (1907). Type 3 assassins from this period were usually fairly stable and well-educated, but often poor.

In the twentieth century—"the American century"—assassins have tended to be described as loners, awkward outsiders, overly attached to their mothers perhaps and secretly hating their fathers. In this period when Freud had displaced science just as science had displaced religion, the assassin was viewed as someone who had transferred his Oedipal complex to one of the leaders of his country. Having lived a pointless life of little acknowledged success, he decided to kill in order to gain publicity, the substitute for achievement. When applied to US assassins, this description is often somewhat (but only somewhat) accurate. In the rest of the world, it seldom obtains. The truth of this stereotype might be said to decrease the farther one travels abroad from the headquarters of CNN in Atlanta.

As for government assassination conspiracies, another traditional US preoccupation, the stereotype seems to overwhelm the reality and yet clearly fills a psycho-cultural need. That John Wilkes Booth led an elaborate if somewhat bumbling conspiracy to kill Abraham Lincoln there was never any doubt. Yet stories rose about plots by the federal government, usually under the leadership of Edwin M. Stanton, the war secretary, to suppress the truth. Some theories linked the Catholic Church to Lincoln's death, others the Freemasons. Available evidence on government attempts to assassinate foreign leaders shows that the efforts are largely futile, even silly. Government agencies are more skilled at undertaking domestic assassinations. Indeed, many of the dictators killed since the end of the Second World War were obviously murdered by government insiders. This, however, should not blind us to the rule that truly successful assassinations are the ones that are not detected. Also, there is a strange double standard at work here, especially as regards the United States. One reason the mythology of the lone-nut assassin looms so large in the American imagination is that the reality of it is precisely what the authorities fear the most. Despite the FBI's much-vaunted system of computer profiling, the sheer stumblebum anonymity of an Arthur Bremer, the man who shot George Wallace, makes his movements all but impossible to detect, much less forecast. Such people, unlike the professionals, have no expectation or desire to escape. Therein lies their danger, one that applies to celebrities as much as to public officials. The singer Joni Mitchell was said to avoid live performances for many years because she feared assassination on stage. In Britain, Germaine Greer, who was attacked in 2000 by a teenaged female student, confided to the press that "the off chance some nutter is going to pick me off" is a fact with which she must learn to live. By comparison, a conspiracy is by its very nature a committee: less efficient than an individual, prone to leave evidence behind, relatively easy to infiltrate.

THE LITERATURE OF ASSASSINATION

is rife, particularly in North America, with publications in the vernacular or folk tradition. The field is one in which cranks, crackpots, eccentrics and obsessive amateur investigators have felt free to indulge their pet theories. Occasionally one does find among such books a work of private-sector scholarship at its most worthwhile, but these are comparatively few. They are also distinct from the works of professional scholars, such as Peter Dale Scott, one of the most significant experts on conspiracy theories and the author, in particular, of *Deep Politics and the Death of JFK* (Berkeley, 1993), probably the most profound work on the environment in which the first Kennedy assassination took place. Scott labours in a tradition that finds its inspiration in classic texts such as *The Paranoid Style in American Politics and Other Essays* by Richard Hofsteader (New York, 1965) and has been carried on more recently by a number of others, such as *The Seventies Now: Culture as Surveillance* by Stephen Paul Miller (Durham, North Carolina, 1999) and *Empire of Conspiracy: The Culture of Paranoia in Postwar America* by Timothy Melley (Ithaca, New York, 2000). In fact, such broadly analytical works about political traits conducive to a culture of assassination research, few though they are, are easier to identify than the relatively small number of truly worthwhile books on assassination itself.

In the course of delving into this literature and subliterature, my research associate and I have become aware of a number of signals that suggest that a work falls below the level of quality needed to be first rate or even acceptable. We have also laboriously assembled a list of works that are easy to recommend, however specialized they may be.

One almost infallible sign of a dubious work on assassination history is reaching back to the Bible to describe Cain or even Judas as an assassin, whereas the former committed simple fratricide out of jealousy and the latter was a stoolie. The free use of racial or cultural stereotypes as motives is another such sign. An example might be the phrase "hot Latin temper" in discussing Latin American assassination (when in fact deposed Latin American heads of state are far more likely to be exiled than assassinated). This sort of characterization is particularly common in writings about assassinations in Second and Third World countries by British and American historians of the past.

Another sign of impending disappointment for the discriminating reader is an author's suggestion that assassinations never bring about fundamental change, whether for better or for worse. This statement is associated with Benjamin Disraeli, the British prime minister, reacting to news of Abraham Lincoln's murder. Claiming that all assassins are insane is another such sign. One could say that Type 3 and Type 4 assassins, who know that they will be apprehended or killed and may even wish for it, are not fully integrated personalities, but this must be weighed against the self-sacrifice, in theory not much different from that of religious martyrs, of those who are prepared to die for their beliefs. But then social mores so often take precedence over logic. If an eighteen-year-old boy joins the army when his country is at war and knowingly risks his life to kill other boys his own age in the enemy camp, even though none of them had anything to do with the causes or conduct of the war, he is considered a hero. If he decides instead to kill the person who actually started the war, he is considered the lowest form of life imaginable (one definition of assassin easily found in the early literature). To say that assassination never solves anything is itself to solve nothing. There have been many assassinations that made conditions worse in a political entity and there have been many assassinations that have meant cruel dictators were replaced by less cruel ones. No doubt the conspirator and the lone gunman have contributed about equally to both outcomes. To say that assassination never solved anything is as inaccurate as saying crime never pays. Or that all assassins come to a bad end. Obviously much depends on the culture and the atmosphere in which the crime takes place. In Japan in the 1930s, numerous assassins received average sentences of fifteen years in prison and served between four and five years. And of course Type 2 assassins are rewarded for their work (in such cases as those of the brothers Aleksei and Grigorii Orlov, quite handsomely) while Type 1 assassins reap the benefits of power. After metabolizing hundreds of books about assassinations in various languages, my research associate and I suggest that the chances of an alleged assassin being acquitted in court are about five per cent. The best defence against conviction is to have been French and a woman before 1930.

One final tendency to be mentioned is that of romanticizing the victim. A king such as Henri III of France, whose enemies went so far as to accuse him of cannibalism, still comes down to us as a benevolent figure. Assassination revisionism was a prominent feature of Western historiography during the Cold War period. A dictator who was on good terms with the West was therefore a champion of freedom and democracy, though he may have used secret police to kill dissidents. Such rulers were often targets for assassination, and once dead were likely to be mourned as fallen statesmen. Many members of the 1960s generation cling to the theory that if John Kennedy had lived there would have been no full-scale war in Vietnam. But they would do well to consider how common similar speculation has been about so many romanticized victims of the more distant past. Such romanticizing of victims is related to the less common romanticization of perpetrators, in some cases through the use of polling techniques and other statistical measures of popularity. Polls suggest that at least sixty per cent of the American people now believe that Lee Oswald, if he participated in the killing of John F. Kennedy, did not act alone.

The procedure used in *A Biographical Dictionary of the World's Assassins* has been to read, where possible, the contemporary accounts of the assassinations discussed, usually in newspapers, manuscripts or reports, and then to compare these to the published books on the subject. The most useful of these books—reflecting, again where possible, a variety of opinion and interpretation—have been listed at the end of each entry as resources. Of all the works consulted, a number recur fairly often, and these are listed here as representing, in our opinion, the most thoroughly researched and trustworthy cream of assassination literature, even though some of the titles are, as you will see, rather specialized in scope. The books are:

• ***Royal Murders: Hatred, Revenge, and the Seizing of Power*** by Dulcie M. Ashdown (Stroud, Gloucestershire, 1998), which is far and away the most thoroughly and carefully researched book on the assassination of European monarchs. The author seems to have worked hard to track down whatever information can be found about the assassins themselves, though the book contains many incidents that the present work, with its different criteria, would not consider assassinations. Ashdown's interest is generally before the twentieth century. The first edition is preferred to the revised one of 2000, in which the focus is looser.

• *Encyclopedia of Assassinations* by Carl Sifakis (New York, 1991) describes more than four hundred assassinations from round the world in pieces of a few hundred words each. Because Sifakis is writing about assassinations rather than those who perform them, a large number of his entries give little or no biographical information on the assassins, though he generally records the accused assassin's name when he can. The book is an excellent starting point.

• *Assassination: The Politics of Murder* by Linda Laucella (Los Angeles, 1998) dwells on fascinating assassination plots, passes few if any moral judgments on particular assassinations (though she covers sixty-six of them in detail) and provides quite a lot of biographical information on assassins.

• *Political Assassinations by Jews: A Rhetorical Device for Justice* by Nachman Ben-Yehuda (Albany, New York, 1993) is an excellent source for assassinations by Jews in Europe before the Second World War. Because the emphasis is on the assassin as much as on the victim, the book offers excellent biographical information, at least in its first half. In the latter portion, when the focus shifts to Palestine, the author displays a tendency to avoid mentioning assassins' names. Still, an invaluable piece of true scholarship.

• *Assassination: A Special Kind of Murder* by Willard A. Heaps (New York, 1969) takes an extremely hard line when it comes to the difference between assassination and murder. For example, Heaps defines all of the suspects the present book considers Type 1 assassins as simple murderers instead. The work is accurate and not geocentric, as it deals with numerous assassinations in Latin America, Asia, Africa and the Middle East.

• *Assassination in America* by James McKinley (New York, 1975) is useful in that it deals heavily with assassins of presidential aspirants such as Huey Long, Robert Kennedy and George Wallace as well as with presidential assassins: that is to say, with Type 4 personalities.

• *Assassination and Political Violence: A Report to the National Commission on the Causes and Prevention of Violence* by James F. Kirkham, Sheldon G. Levy and William J. Crotty (New York, 1970) is largely a gathering of statistics attempting to prove that America has more assassinations than any other country. The figures and methodology may be debatable (the authors claim that there were no assassinations in China during the Qing Dynasty), but the book is virtually unique in listing hundreds of US assassinations down to the level of local judges and sheriffs. In contrasting the US situation with those elsewhere, it also provides leads on assassinations in various other parts of the world.

• *Killing No Murder: A Study of Assassination as a Political Means* by Edward Hyams (London, 1969) is highly unusual, in that Hyams argues that some victims of assassination got what they deserved at the hands of persons who, by their actions, made the world a better place. That is to say that, using our typology, he deals almost exclusively with Type 3 assassins. This is in no sense an extremist work, merely one that, in some instances, goes public with carefully considered conclusions that other historians would hesitate to commit to print. He does not take sides—yet his description of Umberto I of Italy, for example, is so harsh that one is left to marvel that only three people tried to kill him. Because he concentrates on motive, Hyams provides quite a bit of biographical information on the assassins.

• *The Politics of Assassination* by Murray Clark Havens, Carl Leiden and Karl M. Schmitt (Englewood Cliffs, New Jersey, 1970) seems almost a reaction against Hyams. The book considers ten case studies to offer the thesis that assassination rarely if ever brings about real change.

• *Political Murder: From Tyrannicide to Terrorism* by Franklin L. Ford (Cambridge, Massachusetts, 1985) surveys assassination through the ages, emphasizing the different types of assassins in various eras and cultures. A sound narrative history of the subject.

Such are some of the necessary works in the wide field of assassination studies (a minor academic discipline on a growing number of campuses). I only hope that the fundamentally different book you are now holding is worthy to be put alongside them, for writing it has taught me just how elusive, difficult and complex the whole subject is, from the standpoints of history, criminology and psychology—and how fascinating, too.

ABRAM, Michael (b. 1966), attempted to kill George Harrison (b. 1943), the former member of the twentieth century's most famous singing group, the Beatles. At approximately 3:00 a.m. on

December 30, 1999, Harrison and his wife Olivia were awakened by the sound of broken glass at their home at Henley-on-Thames, about forty kilometres from London. Harrison went downstairs to investigate while his wife called the local police station located four hundred metres from the estate. When Harrison found the intruder, Michael Abram, Abram stabbed him in the chest with a twenty-centimetre knife. Harrison tried to escape up the stairs to wait there until police arrived, but Abram followed him and attempted to stab him again, cutting and slashing at his victim repeatedly. When Olivia Harrison appeared, Abram began attacking her as well, in a struggle that would continue for several minutes. Eventually, Mrs. Harrison struck Abram squarely on the head with a heavy brass lamp and her husband then held the attacker until police arrived.

Although the wounds to Mrs. Harrison were no more than minor cuts and bruises, the initial attack on the singer had partially collapsed his left lung and had come dangerously close to severing the superior vena cava, a vein that carries blood from the head and upper body to the heart. Yet Harrison was in good spirits, mentioning to his doctor that he was sure that the event had not been a simple burglary and that Abram "certainly wasn't auditioning for the Traveling Wilburys" (a band that Harrison had helped to form some years after the breakup of the Beatles). Harrison's recovery would take several weeks, but he checked out of hospital within a few days and convalesced in Ireland.

Michael Abram, a former heroin addict with a long history of mental problems, apparently believed all recorded music lyrics literally. He also wore a Walkman almost constantly, playing music to drown out the voices in his head. His mother had been trying to get him psychiatric treatment, as he had been diagnosed as suffering from drug psychosis. He was informed that his symptoms of insanity would disappear if he stopped using heroin. In fact, Abram had been off heroin for over seven months before the attack on Harrison but his madness had worsened.

Initially Abram had been obsessed with the pop group Oasis. But after being informed that Oasis's music was strongly influenced by the Beatles, he became obsessed with them instead. Known as "Mad Mick," Abram had been telling acquaintances that the Beatles were witches and that they were evil. He became obsessed with killing a Beatle even though he had no previous history of violence.

Harrison's estate was known to local residents as Fort Knox owing to the heavy security measures Harrison had put in as a result of the assassination of his former Beatles colleague John Lennon by a crazed fan and various death threats he himself had received. The home, built by an eccentric millionaire solicitor in the nineteenth century, featured motion detectors, razor wire, guard dogs, powerful lights and video cameras but also elaborate hedges and stone gargoyles, which provided enough cover for Abram to approach a cellar window and thus gain entry. Abram's mother blamed the attack on the British National Health Service. "Nothing gets done," she said. "The system is totally and completely useless. If they had listened to me and Michael [her husband, Abram's father] over the last six months this would have never happened." Michael Abram was found to be insane.

ACCIARITO, Pietro Umberto (1871–1943), attempted to assassinate the Italian king Umberto I (1844–1900) on April 22, 1897, as the monarch attended a horse race in Naples being run in honour of his twenty-ninth wedding anniversary. A crowd of well-wishers was on hand, as well as his fatal ill-wisher, who approached the royal carriage, producing a knife. When Umberto saw the weapon, he stood up and moved far enough away in the carriage that Acciarito could not reach him. Acciarito tried to stab Umberto anyway, but his knife struck harmlessly against the vehicle. Acciarito then proceeded to carve a letter A and a cross in the side of the carriage. In the panic and commotion that followed, Acciarito calmly walked from the scene. He was finally apprehended fifty metres away. The king, not wanting to appear shaken by the event, attended the races as scheduled.

Pietro Acciarito was born in poverty. His father, Camilo Acciarito, who worked as a doorman, was proud of the fact that his birthday was the same as Umberto's and that his son's middle name was Umberto. As an adult, Acciarito became a blacksmith and operated a small shop of his own. Although poorly educated, he was a supporter of radical politics, but he was not a member of any political group. He did, however, have a strong hatred of the upper classes, a fact about which he was quite vocal. He also showed what would today be considered signs of clinical depression.

On April 20, 1897, he shut his blacksmith shop and informed his father that this would be the last time they would see each other. When his father asked if he was planning to emigrate or commit suicide, Acciarito replied that he would find out soon enough as he was off to the racetrack. Acciarito's father then contacted the police and told them to be prepared for an attack on Umberto at the races. When Acciarito was arrested, he was asked why he had attacked the king. His response was that the king seemed willing to give twenty-four thousand lire to a horse (the purse from the race that day) but nothing to the poor. Convinced that he was part of an anarchist conspiracy, police interrogated and tortured Acciarito to force him to betray accomplices. But in the end they arrested only Acciarito's friend Romeo Frezzi because Frezzi had a photograph of Acciarito in his home. Frezzi died under interrogation three days later. The initial verdict on Frezzi's death was that he had committed suicide by banging his head against the cell wall. A second investigation was concluded by stating that Frezzi had died of a stroke. When both explanations were disputed, a third investigation was undertaken; it found that Frezzi had jumped six metres to his death.

The Frezzi affair was the centre of mass protests against police brutality. The officers responsible for Frezzi's interrogation were soon transferred. The police then forged a letter from Acciarito's girlfriend saying that she was pregnant and later informed Acciarito that they would release him to be with his girlfriend if he would name his co-conspirators. Acciarito named five men who were all quickly arrested. At their trial, Acciarito's five supposed accomplices were found not guilty as the only evidence against them was Acciarito's statement made under extreme duress. Acciarito, however, was found guilty of attempted regicide and sentenced to life imprisonment. While in solitary confinement, he went insane. He was then transferred to the same asylum as the assassin Giovanni Passannante, where he lived out the remainder of his life. The same eugenicists who examined Passannante's brain concluded that because Acciarito's head was oval-shaped, he was predisposed to assassination.

RESOURCE: *Giovanni Passannante. La vita, l'attentato, il processo, la condanna a morte, la grazia 'regale' e gli anni di galera del cuoco lucano che nel 1878 ruppe l'incantesimo monarchico* by Giuseppe Galzerano (Scalo, 1997).

ADLER, Friedrich (1879–1960), assassinated Karl von Stürgkh (1859–1916), prime minister of Austria, on October 21, 1916, as the victim was dining at the Hotel Meissl & Schadin in Vienna, as was his custom. Adler was himself a political figure as secretary of the Austrian Social Democratic Party (SDP), which had been founded by his father, Viktor Adler. But the younger Adler was not present that evening in order to eat. Walking to von Stürgkh's table, he produced a pistol and shot the prime minister three times in the back of the head while shouting "Down with tyranny! We want peace!" Von Stürgkh died instantly and Adler was apprehended at the scene.

Karl von Stürgkh's administration had moved Austria during the war years from a constitutional monarchy (at least in theory) to a dictatorship. Von Stürgkh's censorship of foreign newspapers was so strict that not only was it illegal to possess newspapers published by enemy nations but also those from allied nations such as Germany. During the war, von Stürgkh was determined not to allow dissent. As a result, he refused to call parliament on the grounds that some parliamentarians were against the war and would speak out against it. He refused to meet with delegates from the SDP even when the party offered to support the war effort. Friedrich Adler, whose father had been jailed repeatedly for his political views in the past, decided to stop von Stürgkh's dictatorship at all costs. Knowing von Stürgkh's routine well, he found it a simple matter to be waiting for him with a pistol in his pocket.

Although Karl von Stürgkh was not a popular figure at the time of his death, his reputation improved considerably thereafter. Emperor Franz-Joseph, speaking from his own death bed, declared that the killing of von Stürgkh was a greater loss than any battle could bring. The Social Democrats denied all responsibility and condemned Adler for his actions. Adler's trial, however, helped the assassin's reputation. The intelligent and articulate Adler gave a masterful defence of himself and his actions. But the court was not in sympathy and he was sentenced to death. The new emperor, Charles I, commuted Adler's sentence to life imprisonment.

With the war in its final days, Austria released a large number of political prisoners. Among the pardoned men was Adler, who had served less than two years. Adler returned to political activities. Resuming his post with the Social Democrats, he organized several workers' councils, but his political skills were not equal to his father's. Adler eventually became secretary-general to the Second Internationale. When the Nazis threatened to annex Austria, Adler began making plans to leave the country. He eventually made his way to the United States, where he remained for the duration of the war. When peace came, Adler returned to Europe to live out his remaining years in Switzerland.

RESOURCE: *The Passing of the Habsburg Monarchy 1914–1918* by Arthur May (Philadelphia, 1966).

AGCA, Mehmet Ali (b. 1959), attempted to assassinate Pope John Paul II (b. 1920) on May 13, 1981, as the pontiff was being driven around Rome's St. Peter's Square in an open Jeep-like vehicle nicknamed the Popemobile, which he stopped now and then to give personal blessings to some of the crowd of ten thousand. The Holy Father was on his third orbit of the square when Agca stepped from the crowd and, from less than six metres away, opened fire with a 9-mm Browning semi-automatic pistol. The pope was struck twice, one bullet grazing a hand and arm producing little more than superficial wounds, the other bullet lodging in his abdomen. Agca dropped his pistol and turned to escape when he was knocked to the ground and subdued by Suor Letizia, a large and robust nun. Letizia shouted, "Why did you do it?" To which Agca responded, "Not me, not me." Agca was held until police arrived. The pope was rushed to the Gemelli Clinic, which has a special section reserved for papal medical emergencies. His blood pressure was falling rapidly and his pulse was almost undetectable. Just before surgery, last rites were administered to the unconscious patient. Although his situation was grave, John Paul had been lucky. The second bullet had not shattered on impact as it was supposed to. Also, in a pattern that duplicated almost exactly that of the bullet that entered US president Ronald Reagan only weeks earlier, it missed the aorta by millimetres. The pope's surgery lasted over five hours and the doctors removed almost two feet of the victim's intestines. In spite of losing sixty per cent of his blood to internal hemorrhaging, the pope survived.

Mehmet Ali Agca was born in the shantytown of Yesiltepe, just outside Malatya, Turkey. His family's situation worsened with the death of his alcoholic father when Agca was only seven. Agca was forced to work from a very young age selling water at the local train station. Intelligent and industrious, he managed to continue his education in spite of his circumstances.

While attending Malatya's Teachers' Training High School in 1975, he became affiliated with the Grey Wolves, a right-wing, anti-Western terrorist group affiliated with the National Action Party. In 1979, while attending Istanbul University, Agca was arrested for his involvement with the assassination of Abdi Ipekci, the editor of the leftist newspaper *Milliyet*. Agca pleaded guilty to the murder and insisted, in spite of eye-witness testimony, that he had acted alone. Within a month of his arrest, Agca had escaped from prison, simply walking out wearing an army uniform that had been smuggled into his cell. He left a letter for *Milliyet* declaring that the pope's impending visit to Turkey was intended to erode Islamic unity and that John Paul II would be killed if he entered the country. Agca did not attempt to kill the pope on his visit to Turkey, but at about the same time the informant who had fingered Agca in the editor's assassination was murdered.

A report prepared by the Vatican following the shooting stated that after his time in prison Agca left Turkey and travelled to more than twenty countries between 1979 and 1981. His time abroad apparently included training by the Palestinian Liberation Organization. Evidence also pointed to the conclusion that Agca had four confederates the day the pope was shot to help him make his escape. When Agca was apprehended at the scene, the others dispersed; only one was ever located.

Agca's motives have been the subject of much speculation, as was the question of who financed his travels and activities. Rumours suggested that the order to assassinate John Paul was probably issued by the Bulgarian secret service, though the exact nature and extent of Bulgarian involvement have never been determined. Some speculate that the Bulgarians were merely carrying out orders for the Soviet Union through the KGB. For his part, Agca, after serving about ten months of his life sentence, began to talk about Bulgarian involvement in the affair. His statements led to the arrest of three Bulgarians and four Turks. The trial of these conspirators, however, broke down when Agca rose in court and declared loudly, "I am Jesus Christ. In the name of the omnipotent God, I announce the end of the world. No one, neither the Americans nor the Soviets, will be saved. There will be destruction." The chief prosecutor, whose case relied completely on Agca's testimony, said,

"When he starts speaking of facts, he is very believable." Agca changed his testimony from implicating the Bulgarians to placing the blame for the attempt on members of a secret Italian Masonic lodge and Italian intelligence. After nine months of such farce, all the defendants were acquitted for want of evidence. Agca remains the only person incarcerated for the attempt to kill the pope.

John Paul II, as is traditional for popes who have survived assassination attempts, visited Agca in his cell to forgive him for the attack. The two men chatted in Italian for twenty minutes. As the pope was leaving, Agca kissed his hand and declared to the press, "The pope knows everything." The pope's own theory was that the attack was the work of Islamic forces, not communists. He also believes that he was saved through a miracle performed by the Virgin of Fatima whose feast day is May 13, the date of the attack. "One hand fired," the pope declared, "and another hand guided the bullet." Mehmet Ali Agca remains imprisoned in Italy. When the pope visited the shrine of Fatima in Portugal in 2000, he finally revealed the so-called third secret of Fatima, as given by the Virgin Mary to three children in a 1917 vision. The third secret was that there would be an attempt on the pope's life in 1981. In June 2000, Italy's president granted clemency to Agca, who thereupon resumed serving a ten-year sentence for the assassination of the newspaper editor.

RESOURCES: *His Holiness: John Paul II and the Hidden History of Our Time* by Carl Bernstein and Marco Politi (New York, 1996). *To Kill the Pope* by Tad Szulc (New York, 2000) is a novel inspired by the Agca affair.

AGRIPPINA THE YOUNGER (16–59 CE) assassinated Claudius (10 BCE –54 CE), the man who became emperor of Rome by using his physical liabilities, such as lameness and stuttering, to convince previous emperors that he was feeble-minded. While others in line for the throne were being assassinated, Claudius survived because it was felt that he was not a threat to their rule; with the death of the Emperor Caligula (12-41 CE), the Praetorian Guard declared Claudius his successor, whereupon he was revealed to be an intelligent albeit deviant person.

While Claudius was not so insane as his nephew Caligula, he was capable of great cruelty. When he discovered his wife, Messalina, was plotting against him, he had her executed, as well as all the men she had slept with while they were married: the total numbered in the hundreds.

Afterwards Claudius compelled the senate to change the laws concerning incest so that he could marry his niece, Agrippina. Incest was nothing new to her. She was the sister as well as the former wife of Caligula.

Once married to Claudius, Agrippina was determined to see her son fathered by Caligula, Ahenobarbus (later renamed Nero—37–68 CE), become Claudius's heir. Claudius, however, favoured his own son, Britannicus, by his former wife, Messalina. Agrippina improved Nero's position by having Claudius adopt him. She also had Nero marry Claudius's daughter Octavia, making Nero Octavia's cousin, brother and husband. As Claudius grew old and frail, he began to have second thoughts about his succession and appeared ready to remove Nero from the line of succession in favour of Britannicus. At that point, Agrippina decided that Claudius would have to be eliminated. She consulted with Rome's most infamous poisoner, Locusta, and bought poisoned mushrooms that she later put into Claudius's stew. In one account, the mushrooms did their work and Claudius died the evening after eating them. In others, Claudius began to recover from the poisoning and had to be further treated by Agrippina and her physician. In either case, Claudius was succeeded by Nero, who within a few years decided that his mother must go. Nero had tired of Agrippina and wanted to eliminate her.

Agrippina saw Octavia as an ally as well as a stabilizing influence on her mad son. Nero knew his mother was too wise in the ways of poison for him to try that method. In 59 CE, he tried to sabotage her ship so that she would appear to have drowned. When Agrippina survived the sinking, Nero dispatched troops to execute her. When the soldiers approached Agrippina, she is reputed to have requested they stab her in the womb that had produced Nero. The troops granted her request.

RESOURCE: *Agrippina: Sex, Power, and Politics in the Early Empire* by Anthony Barrett (New Haven, Connecticut, 1996).

AIZAWA Saburō (1889–1936) assassinated General Negata Tetsuzan (1884–1935), chief of Japan's Military Affairs Bureau, an intelligence agency. Aizawa Saburō, an army lieutenant colonel, entered Negata's office in the War Ministry in Tokyo. The general was behind his desk speaking to the head of Tokyo's military police about maintaining discipline. Aizawa drew his sword and attacked. Wounded, Negata tried to flee through a door when Aizawa pounced again, piercing the general in the back and killing him. Aizawa then proceeded to the office of his friend General Yamaoka Jūkō; Aizawa had been wounded in the struggle, and Yamaoka bandaged the attacker's hand as the military police arrived. As Aizawa was being escorted out of the building, General Yamashita Tomoyuki approached the group, shook Aizawa's good hand and thanked him for killing Negata.

Aizawa was a member of the radical right Kōdōha Faction, also called the Imperial Way Movement or the Young Officers' Movement. The primary motive for the assassination was the fact that Negata belonged to the Toseiha (Control Faction), which favoured democratic government over a militaristic one loyal to the emperor. Negata had replaced a Kōdōha general as head of Military Affairs. The previous November, the Kōdōha Faction had fallen into disgrace when plans for a *coup d'etat* were revealed, though Kōdōha members claimed that the Toseiha had fabricated the charges. Nevertheless, many Kōdōha officers were demoted, including the head of Military Affairs. To the Kōdōha, Negata was the main figure behind the demotion and transfer of Kōdōha officers. On July 19, 1935, Aizawa gained an appointment with Negata. He advised Negata to resign. Negata reacted by ordering Aizawa transferred to Taiwan. On the day of the assassination, Aizawa was supposed to be preparing for his new assignment.

Aizawa's public trial quickly became a circus. With a large faction of the army behind it, and considerable public support from rightist civilians, the defence attempted to put the government on trial for the struggle between military factions that eventually led to Negata's death. Even the prosecution agreed that Aizawa was defending the emperor and Japan by his actions. Thousands of letters begged the court for Aizawa's release, many of them written in blood. In one extreme case, the writer also enclosed two of his own fingers as a sign of support. When the events of the February 26 Incident (an attempt by the Young Officers to overthrow the government) halted the proceedings, the trial was cancelled, with no verdict given.

In April 1936, a new trial commenced. Unlike the previous one, it was a court martial conducted in secret. With no distractions, the court soon found Aizawa guilty and sentenced him to death. On July 3, 1936, Aizawa was executed. Although Aizawa had paid for the assassination with his life, the Kōdōha would win out. The defence minister resigned in disgrace immediately after the assassination. His successor, although considered neutral in the dispute between the two factions, in fact tended to side with the Kōdōha. Within a few years, the Young Officers had the government they had wished for.

RESOURCE: *The Young Officers and the February 26, 1936 Incident* by Ben-Ami Shillony (Princeton, 1973).

AKBAR, Said (d. 1951), assassinated Liaquat Ali Khan (1895–1951), prime minister of Pakistan, on October 16, 1951, as the latter was about to give a speech at a public meeting in Rawalpindi. The politician had just mounted the podium and had barely begun to speak when Said Akbar, who was sitting in the audience on the left side of the podium, stood and fired twice. The first bullet severed Ali Khan's aorta. Ali Khan's last words were *"Khuda Pakistan Ki Hifazat Kare"* ("May God Preserve Pakistan"). The prime minister was rushed to hospital, where, despite massive blood transfusions and emergency surgery, he died within a few hours. Akbar was grabbed by another member of the audience after his second shot, and a third shot was fired in the struggle. Akbar was then gunned down by a policeman. Members of the Muslim League National Guard ran the assassin through with their ceremonial spears; Akbar died on the scene.

Said Akbar was the son of Babrak, the leader of the Zandran tribe in Khost, a southern province of Afghanistan. The Zandran had been fighting the Afghan government for some time when Babrak fell in battle, at which point leadership passed to Akbar's brother, Mazarak. When the tide turned against the Zandran, Mazarak and Said fled to India, where they were offered asylum. The two men and their families were given a house and an allowance by the Indian government, but they were forced to agree not to leave their home in Abbottabad without official permission. Shortly after arriving, Said requested a separate home for his family as he was not getting along with his brother. The request was granted.

According to his wife, Akbar began to have dreams which he interpreted as visions. He became deeply religious, spending most of his days praying, fasting and reading the Koran. According to his young son Dilawar, whom Akbar had taken with him to the assassination, the Sultan Mahmud Ghaznavi appeared in one of the dreams and instructed Akbar to kill Ali Khan because "Ali Khan was a bad man who must go to hell for his sins" (from the official government inquiry into the assassination). While this theory has been disputed because of inconsistencies in the boy's story, papers on Akbar's person when he was killed indicated that he did favour a Pakistani invasion of Kashmir. Ali Khan, wishing to preserve peace between the two new nations, had refused to challenge

India's authority over Kashmir. Although Akbar, being Afghani, was not particularly interested in Indian-Pakistani politics, being a devout Muslim made the question of control of the predominantly Muslim state a religious rather than a political issue.

On October 14, 1951, Akbar, in violation of his agreement with the Indian government, left Abbottabad for Rawalpindi, taking with him two thousand rupees and a pistol. Authorities later would trace the money to see if Akbar had been paid to carry out the killing, but no evidence was found to support this theory. After the shooting, Akbar's son walked away from the scene without being detected. Having no way to get home, however, Dilawar lived on the streets until the authorities realized who he was. The official government report of the assassination mentioned a wide range of motives for the killing, but could not specify one in particular; it did, however, condemn police and the Muslim League National Guard for not taking the assassin alive.

RESOURCE: *The Assassination of Mr. Liaquat Ali Khan: Report of the Commission of Enquiry* (Karachi, 1952).

ALVES, Darli (b. 1934), masterminded the assassination of the Brazilian labour leader Francisco "Chico" Mendes (1944–1988). Like his father before him, Mendes was a rubber tapper, a person who extracts latex sap from rubber trees in the Amazonian rainforest. The source of considerable wealth in the late nineteenth and early twentieth centuries, Brazil's rubber industry fell on hard times following the invention of synthetic rubber substitutes and the transplanting of rubber trees to Southeast Asia. During the boom times, the so-called rubber barons amassed incredible fortunes while the tappers eked out a bare existence; the tappers were poor, uneducated and usually at the mercy of the landowners. Mendes had one advantage over many of the others in that from an early age he had had a mentor who taught him to read and write and allowed him to listen to short-wave radio.

In 1964, the Brazilian government was overthrown in a military coup. Radio Moscow reported it as a CIA-backed plot to subvert a liberal government; just as predictably, Voice of America called the event a triumph of democracy over communist fellow-travellers. As a Brazilian, Mendes knew what the new government was really like, and, as a result, came to sympathize with the anti-American view. This in turn eventually led him to become a socialist. In 1975, Mendes founded the Union Movement in his home region of Acre. In 1979, he helped to establish the Workers' Party and in 1985 formed the National Council of Rubber Tappers to fight for better working conditions.

By then, the question of the future of Brazil's rainforests was receiving international attention: with a surging population and a declining rubber industry, the government had opened up the area for deforestation and the creation of new ranch land. Although much of the world was aghast at the erosion of the rainforest, a new class of Brazilians, the wealthy ranchers, kept domestic opposition in check. Mendes realized that the rubber tappers, who quite naturally depended on the forest for their livelihood, could utilize environmental movements throughout the world to keep the forests from being destroyed. He preached the benefits of "extractive reserves": the idea that keeping the forest intact could provide an economic resource that would boost Brazil's economy and please environmentalists internationally. Mendes travelled throughout the United States speaking of the economic benefit of environmentalism. Because he spoke only Portuguese, a translator was needed; because the audience was American, references to organized labour and socialism were not translated. Chico Mendes received the Global 500 award from the United Nations Environmental Program as well as the entrepreneur Ted Turner's Better World Society Environment Award.

Because of his success as an activist on the world stage, Mendes made many powerful enemies at home, including Alves, a wealthy ranch owner. In 1988, Mendes led the Xapuri Rural Workers' Union in a successful effort to stop Alves from deforesting an area that was later made into a reserve for rubber tappers. In addition, Mendes was pressuring Brazilian justice officials to enforce a court order for the arrest of Alves for the murder of a labourer in 1973. Police corruption and a tradition of wealthy landowners not being prosecuted for murdering workers made the task nearly impossible. Nevertheless, as talk about the possible elimination of Mendes began among members of the Democratic Rural Union (UDR), a political group founded by the landowners, Alves was quick to volunteer to kill the troublemaking rubber tapper.

On December 22, 1988, Mendes was in his kitchen with two untrained bodyguards appointed by the authorities. The bodyguards had only one pistol between them. Mendes walked outside to take a shower in the outdoor bathhouse. Within seconds of his leaving, a shotgun blast was heard and Mendes staggered back into the kitchen with nearly thirty pellets in his chest; he fell to the floor and died. The two bodyguards jumped through the window and escaped into the forest. Within minutes, reporters began arriving; their timing indicated that they had been tipped off. Later, witnesses claimed that several landowners had begun parties to celebrate the death of Mendes hours before the event. International attention forced the authorities to prosecute the case, and several national officials were brought in to take charge for fear that locals would be in the pay of the assassins. Still, the investigation probably would not have achieved any results but for the fact that Alves, along with his brother Alvarino and his son Darcy (who had actually done the shooting), turned themselves in. The assassins showed no remorse. Darli Alves revelled in the worldwide attention he received and regaled the press with stories of his sexual prowess (he had had five wives, more than a dozen mistresses and claimed to have fathered more than thirty children). Darli and Darcy Alves were sentenced to twenty years' imprisonment each: the first instances in Brazilian history of landowners being jailed for killing a worker. In 1993, when the world media had lost interest in the plight of rubber tappers, the two Alves men escaped; Darli Alves was not recaptured until 1996, Darcy the following year.

Today, the Chico Mendes Extractive Reserve protects almost one million hectares of forest. Brazil, haunted by negative attention and concerned about the question of tying environmental protection to international trade policy, hosted the Earth Summit in Rio de Janeiro in 1992. Darcy and Darli Alves are still in prison. Brazilian officials have announced that they will not be allowed to escape again.

RESOURCE: *Into the Amazon: Chico Mendes and the Struggle for the Rainforest* by Augusta Dwyer (Toronto, 1990).

AMIR, Yigal (b. 1970), assassinated Yitzhak Rabin (1922–1995), the prime minister of Israel, on November 4, 1995. As Rabin was walking to his car after addressing a peace rally in the Kings of Israel Square in Tel Aviv, he was approached from behind by Amir, who produced a 9-mm Beretta pistol loaded with dumdum bullets and fired three times from point-blank range. The first two shots struck Rabin in the back; the third missed and wounded a bodyguard. At first many of the officers near Rabin believed that the shots were blanks, as they had been told to expect a security test involving an actor posing as an assailant. But the shoulder wound of the injured bodyguard proved that this was a real attack. Rabin was bundled into his car, but crowds blocking the street meant that the trip to hospital took much longer than necessary, and Rabin's situation was grave by the time he arrived. Although rushed to the operating room, he died less than ten minutes later. Back at the crime scene, Amir had been apprehended, even though some security personnel were still certain that what they had heard was a drill. When news from hospital reached them, Amir was arrested for murder.

Amir was born to a poor Orthodox family who had immigrated to Israel from Yemen. As a teen, he became ultra-Orthodox, and was said to be hard-working, diligent and an extremist on religious and political matters. While his classmates were avoiding military service, he volunteered for a five-year Hesder program that combined combat training and religious scholarship. He was an excellent soldier. He became known as someone who could be counted on to volunteer for extra duty.

In 1992, Amir worked for the Liaison Bureau, which sent scholars into Russia to teach Hebrew (and possibly to spy); he spent three months in Riga. Returning to Israel, he enrolled at Bar-Ilan University near Tel Aviv. At about the same time, Yitzhak Rabin was concluding negotiations with the Palestinian Liberation Organization for peace in Israel. The famous handshake between Rabin and the PLO leader, Yasser Arafat, on the lawn of the White House in Washington infuriated many Israelis, including Amir, who attended classes taught by Dr. Uri Milstein, the author of a biography harshly critical of Rabin. (In later editions of the book, Milstein mentions that Amir was a student of his, but he places blame for the assassination on Rabin himself, making the point that as the prime minister was also minister of security, the responsibility for lapses in security lay with him.) Amir came to believe that the only way to stop the perceived giveaway of land along the West Bank, a key issue in Israeli-Palestinian talks, was to "take down" (his own words) Rabin and the former prime minister Shimon Peres in order to bring about, he hoped, a government headed by the right-wing Benjamin Netanyahu. Amir made such speculations with his brother, Hagai. Their early discussion centred on a possible bombing; later, Hagai, who wanted most of all to escape after the assassination, tried to obtain a sniper's rifle to shoot Rabin from a great distance. In the end, Yigal decided that the mission could be accomplished only by a lone gunman with a pistol at close range.

On the night of the rally, Amir waited for his chance in the VIP car park. The fact that neither he nor about twenty other unauthorized persons were removed from what was supposed to be a secured area does indeed indicate that the Shin Bet, the internal security service responsible for the prime minister's safety, was not operating efficiently. Amir's defence at his trial was based on his interpretation of Jewish tradition, citing, among others, Maimonides, who had called for the elimination of collaborators. To Amir, anyone who advocated relinquishing territory in the West Bank was a candidate for retribution. Amir later said that he was merely intending to paralyze Rabin in order to keep him from signing the Oslo Agreement.

Although only the Amir brothers were brought to trial, three other suspects were charged originally, leading to the spread of conspiracy theories in which the Shin Bet or its external equivalent, the Mossad, were involved—theories ruled out by the authorities less than three weeks after the shooting. Many viewers of Yigal Amir's televised trial were distressed by his lack of remorse, his constant smiling and his open-mouthed gum-chewing; some demanded that he be kept behind a screen so they would not have to look at him.

The court found the Amir brothers guilty. Hagai was sentenced to twelve years in prison for conspiracy. As to Yigal, as Israel imposes the death penalty only on Nazi war criminals, he was sentenced to life imprisonment, plus another eleven years for wounding the bodyguard and endangering the lives of others. Yigal Amir began serving his sentence in 1996. In 1998, a young woman friend of the jailed killer was convicted of knowing his intentions but failing to report them to the authorities. At the same time, she was acquitted of aiding Amir in obtaining weapons illegally.

RESOURCES: *Shalom, Friend: The Life and Legacy of Yitzhak Rabin*, ed. David Horovitz (New York, 1996); *Murder in the Name of God: The Plot to Kill Yitzhak Rabin* by Michael Karpin and Ina Friedman (New York, 1998); *The Rabin File: An Unauthorized Exposé* by Dr. Uri Milstein (Jerusalem, 1999). The conspiracy theory is upheld by Barry Chamish in *Who Killed Yitzhak Rabin?* (Venice, California, 1998).

AN Chung-gun (1879–1910) was the Korean nationalist who, while in what is now northeastern China, in 1909 assassinated Ito Hirobumi (b. 1841), the "resident general" of Korea during its period as a Japanese protectorate following the Russo-Japanese War of 1904–1905. By 1908, Ito and his political masters in Japan had imposed a puppet emperor as well as a puppet prime minister and had disbanded the Korean army. In reaction to such events, a number of former military men and Korean nationalists had formed militia groups, known as Righteous Armies, with members often recruited through Protestant schools and professing to be Christians (in some cases, in an attempt to garner favour in Europe and America). The Righteous Armies clashed with Japanese troops between 1907 and 1909; the uprisings were suppressed harshly.

On October 26, 1909, Ito was en route to Moscow to discuss plans for full annexation by 1910. He was to change trains in Harbin for the long trip on the Trans-Siberian Railway. Surrounded by his aides and Russian diplomats as well as by Russian security agents, Ito was approached by An, a former Righteous Armies officer. An wore western clothing, which created the impression among the Russian security officers that he was Japanese. Producing a pistol, An shot Ito three times; one of the bullets pierced the liver and Ito died fifteen minutes later. An was executed on March 25, 1910. Some have suggested that Ito's assassination was the final pretense for Korea's full annexation, which took place later that year, but the annexation had already been decided on in Japan before Ito's death. In spite of his reputation among Korean nationalists, Ito was a moderate who personally opposed full annexation.

RESOURCES: *Korea: Tradition and Transformation—A History of the Korean People* by Andrew C. Nahm (Elizabeth, New Jersey, 1988); *A History of the Korean People in Modern Times, 1800 to the Present* by Robert T. Oliver (Cranbury, New Jersey, 1993).

ANCKARSTROM, Jacob Johan (1762–1792), was the killer in a conspiracy to assassinate Gustavus III of Sweden (1746–1792, reigned from 1771) while the king was attending a masked ball at the Royal Opera House in Stockholm on March 16, 1792. Although Gustavus was wearing a mask, he was instantly recognizable because the mask hid only half his face, revealing the disfiguring effects of a childhood accident. The large number of medals he was wearing also left no doubt as to his identity. Early in the evening, the king had been handed a note telling him that his life was in danger, but having been threatened before, he ignored the warning. As he mingled with the crowd, a masked figure approached him and said, "Good evening, fair mask." The phrase was an agreed-upon signal amongst the conspirators. At that point, Anckarstrom shot the king in the hip with a pistol. As he fell, Gustavus cried out, "I am wounded! Arrest him!" But an immediate arrest was impossible. Not only were the conspirators masked, they were also crying out "Fire! Fire!" to spread confusion. Reacting quickly, the king's guards sealed the exits and declared that nobody would be allowed to leave. They soon discovered two pistols and a dagger on the floor but no indication of who had brought them. Gustavus was ushered away and despite the ablest medical treatment died of gangrene less than two weeks later.

Anckarstrom, a former guards officer, opposed Gustavus's military policies, which included making peace with Russia (on terms Anckarstrom found humiliating to Sweden) and preparing to go to war against revolutionary France. His opposition to the king soon became maniacal, and he became involved with a group of nobles who had their own reasons for wishing Gustavus dead. Early in his reign, Gustavus had reduced the power of Sweden's nobility in favour of parliament, though he later devalued parliament and became autocratic. The conspirators believed that Gustavus's assassination would lead to full-scale rebellion by the military and nobility. But although he was not particularly popular during most of his reign, Gustavus gained wide sympathy during the thirteen days he lay dying. Yet many in authority feared that punishing the nobles involved in the plot might indeed lead to the uprising for which conspirators (who were quickly arrested, despite their escape from the scene) were hoping. As a result, Anckarstrom alone was punished. After a brief trial, he was executed by torture.

RESOURCE: *Gustav III og Stockholm* by Godfed Hartmann (Copenhagen, 1974).

ANGIOLILLO, Michel (1871–1897), assassinated Antonio Cànovas del Castillo (1828–1897), the prime minister of Spain, on August 9, 1897, when Cànovas and his wife were on holiday at Santa Agueda in the Basque mountains, an area known for its mineral springs. While on a walk, the Cànovases were approached by Angiolillo, who produced a pistol and shot the prime minister repeatedly until he was dead. Mrs. Cànovas, witnessing her husband's death, cried out "Assassin!," to which Angiolillo replied, "I'm not an assassin, I am an avenger" before running off.

Angiolillo was born in Foggia, Italy, and was introduced to anarchism while in the military. Becoming a convert to radical politics earned him rebuke by the army, and he served the remainder of his tour in a disciplinary company. After his discharge, he worked as a typesetter until his views brought him to the attention of the authorities. In April 1895, he was sentenced to eighteen months in prison for "subversive activity" (distributing pamphlets).

After being released, he decided to leave Italy, and he travelled to France and Belgium before arriving in England. While in England, Angiolillo read that Cànovas of Spain had launched a campaign of persecution against anarchists after a bombing incident at a religious procession in Barcelona. Cànovas ordered mass arrests and torture to learn the names of anarchists involved. The result was four anarchists executed by garrotting and seventy-six sent to prison for the bombing. Incensed, Angiolillo returned to Spain with one purpose, to kill Cànovas. Although Angiolillo escaped the scene of the shooting, he was arrested within a few days. At his short trial, he attempted to defend himself on the grounds that he was merely executing a tyrant. He quoted St. Thomas Aquinas to demonstrate that such killing was justifiable. The court disagreed. On August 19, 1897, Angiolillo was garrotted.

RESOURCE: *Cànovas* by José Luis Comellas (Madrid, 1965).

ARAMAKI Taisuke (1895–?), who had been secretary-general of the Taika Kai (Great Reconstruction), a Japanese nationalist group forced to disband by the American occupation forces in 1946, stabbed Kishi Nobusuke (1896–1987) six times in the thigh at a reception at Kishi's official residence on July 14, 1960, only a few hours after Kishi had resigned as prime minister. The reception was being held to honour Kishi's successor, Ikeda Hayato. Kishi's life was not in danger as a result of the attack but he was hospitalized for twelve days after losing a considerable amount of blood. Aramaki, who was seized immediately after the attack, pleaded guilty but showed no remorse for his actions. His defence was that he had attacked Kishi to "make him reflect on his maladministration," a statement that was probably an indictment of Kishi's pro-American stance. Aramaki was sentenced to two years' imprisonment.

RESOURCE: *Nationalism and the Right Wing in Japan: A Study of Post-War Trends* by Ivan Morris (London, 1960).

ARNOLD, Samuel Bland (1834–1906), one of the persons tried and sentenced to prison in the Abraham Lincoln assassination conspiracy, maintained his innocence and, towards the end of his life, after years of embittered silence, published his memoirs, hoping to exonerate himself in the eyes of history. Born in the District of Columbia, Arnold served briefly as a Confederate soldier early in the Civil War before being discharged on medical grounds; he later worked as a civilian employee of the Confederate government. By the latter part of the war, he was living in the border state of Maryland, a hotbed of intrigue and espionage, the geographical middle ground between the warring capitals of Washington and Richmond.

In September 1864, he was summoned by John Wilkes Booth, an old schoolmate, who introduced him to the other conspirators in what was originally a plan to abduct Lincoln, first from a theatre, later from a carriage, and hold him hostage until the North released Confederate prisoners of war. In order to hasten the collapse of the Southern war effort, the North, which had by far the larger pool of personnel from which to draw, had suspended the practice of exchanging prisoners. Arnold, who engaged in the discussions out of patriotic motives rather than mercenary ones, thought Booth's plans impractical, but agreed to play his assigned role, which consisted largely of keeping arms and horses at the ready.

When the final abduction scheme failed, Arnold quit the conspiracy and took work on April 2, 1865, as a shop clerk in Old Point Comfort, Virginia. "This ended my connection with the conspiracy," he wrote in old age, "and I heard nothing further from it nor from any of the parties connected therewith." He was thus far from Washington when Booth killed Lincoln at Ford's Theater in that city on the evening of April 14, an event he learned of the following morning. Searching Booth's possessions, authorities discovered letters between the two men.

Arnold was arrested on April 17. He and seven others went on trial before a military commission. Four were hanged; Arnold and three others were sentenced to prison and served time at the infamous Fort Jefferson in the Dry Tortugas, a place whose brutality his memoir describes in detail. After a general pardon in 1869, he went into seclusion in rural Maryland. His manuscript entitled "Lincoln Conspiracy and the Conspirators," written mostly in the 1890s, was acquired by the Baltimore *American* and serialized in that and other major newspapers in

1902–1903. Arnold died of "galloping consumption" in Baltimore and was buried in Greenmount Cemetery in that city, where the family plot containing John Wilkes Booth may also be found.

RESOURCE: *Samuel Bland Arnold—Memoirs of a Lincoln Conspirator*, ed. Michael W. Kaufman (Bowie, Maryland, 1995).

ASHU, Mustafa (1930–1951), was a tailor's apprentice who assassinated King Abdullah Ibn Hussein of Jordan (1882–1951) on July 20, 1951. Abdullah, along with his grandson Hussein, entered the al-Aqsa Mosque in the Jordanian-held Old City of Jerusalem when a *shaykh* (sheik) came forward to pay homage to the king, whose guards parted to let him pass. Just then Ashu pushed his way past the *shaykh* and fired a single shot, striking Abdullah in the head. The king was dead before he hit the floor. Abdullah's bodyguards returned fire recklessly. Not only was Ashu shot to death but more than twenty other worshippers were killed and another hundred wounded.

Ashu, a native of Jerusalem, was involved with a group of Palestinian activists from his neighbourhood. Along with the Old City, Abdullah had seized the West Bank of the Jordan River during Israel's war of independence in 1948–1949. Most of the Arab world had earmarked the West Bank for a Palestinian homeland, but Abdullah's goal was to expand Jordan to take in all of the former British mandate of Palestine. When he realized that he could not conquer Israel by force, Abdullah entered into secret negotiations with it. Details of these talks were leaked to radicals in Egypt and the former Palestine. When word reached members of Ashu's group, they decided to act.

Jordanian negotiations with Israel died with Abdullah. Police quickly rounded up the other conspirators. Ashu's neighbourhood *qabaday* (boss), Abid Ukah, along with a cattle breeder, a butcher and a café owner, were quickly tried, without a chance to give testimony, and executed. The group was described as "professional terrorists and assassins," but no record of any previous terrorist activity was produced. Abdullah al-Tall, formerly Jordan's military governor in Jerusalem, and the person who revealed the existence of the secret negotiations with Israel, fled to Cairo, where he made known his participation in the plot against Abdullah. Egypt refused to extradite him to Jordan.

Some have speculated that the authority behind Abdullah's assassination came from Egypt, but a lack of evidence, along with Egypt's refusal to co-operate with the investigation, brought the subject to an end. Abdullah was succeeded by his son Talal, but within a year Talal, due to mental instability, was forced to abdicate in favour of his own son, Hussein.

RESOURCE: *Man Qatala al-Malik Adb Allah?* by Nasir al-Din Nashashibib (Kuwait, 1981).

ATZERODT, George Andrew (1842?–1865), a native German who earned an exiguous living painting carriages and repairing their wheels, became a member of the plot to abduct Abraham Lincoln for the simple reason that he owned at least one small boat tied up at Port Tobacco, Maryland, on the Potomac River, which separates Washington, DC, and Maryland from Virginia and the Confederacy. He was recruited for the conspiracy in January 1865 by John Surratt, a far more important member of the group, and a Confederate agent named Thomas Harbin. When in March 1865, the plan, led by John Wilkes Booth, proved a wild failure, Atzerodt's involvement, and that of his co-conspirators, was simply transferred to Booth's self-sanctioned plot to assassinate Lincoln instead of kidnapping him.

Atzerodt met with Booth and others at the Herndon House, a hotel near Ford's Theater in Washington, at 8:00 p.m. on April 14, 1865, the date of Lincoln's shooting. Atzerodt was given the important chore of assassinating the vice-president, Andrew Johnson, while Lewis Powell, a.k.a. Lewis Payne, was to kill William H. Seward, the secretary of state. In a confession read by his counsel at the trial (as well as a later confession written in his cell and also in an interrogation transcript that came to light again only in the 1980s), Atzerodt truthfully denied even making an attempt on Johnson (whereas Powell did indeed wound Seward). In fact, Atzerodt, the only one of the conspirators who insisted on being paid for his services, is reliably reported to have drunk away his fee and then pawned the revolver he had been issued.

The war department's reward circular dated April 20, putting a $25,000 bounty on his head, indicated that Atzerodt was "sometimes called Port Tobacco." He was captured at the house of a female acquaintance about thirty-five kilometres north of the Kirkwood Hotel in Washington, where a search of his room revealed weapons and other incriminating evidence. Atzerodt thus became one of eight civilian prisoners, following Booth's death on the run, to be tried by a military commission in May 1865. Like Powell, he was represented by William E. Doster, a former provost marshal of the District of Columbia. On June 30, all were found guilty; four, including Atzerodt, were sentenced to hang. The execution took place on July 7 in Washington, and Atzerodt, like the others, was buried under the stone floor of a warehouse on the grounds of Old Arsenal Prison. On March 4, 1869, as his term was expiring, President Johnson ordered the bodies exhumed and returned to their families. Of all the inner circle of Lincoln conspirators, Atzerodt consistently has been held in the lowest esteem by historians of the assassination, with Booth's granddaughter, Izola Forrester, calling him a "clumsy, slow-thinking ferryman" and Lloyd Lewis describing him as a "squat, unbathed gnome" and "a cartoon of an assassin, humped, simian, fawning, with hair that hung and whiskers that straggled."

RESOURCES: *Myths after Lincoln* by Lloyd Lewis (New York, 1929; reprinted as *The Assassination of Lincoln: History and Myth*, [Lincoln, Nebraska, 1994]); *Beware the People Weeping: Public Opinion and the Assassination of Abraham Lincoln* by Thomas Reed Turner (Baton Rouge, Louisiana, 1982); *The Lincoln Murder Conspiracies* by William Hanchett (Urbana, Illinois, 1983); *April '65: Confederate Covert Action in the American Civil War* by William A. Tidwell (Kent, Ohio, 1995).

AUDISIO, Walter (a.k.a. Colonel Valerio) (1909–1973), assassinated Benito Mussolini (1883–1945), the ruler of Italy. On April 28, 1945, Colonel Valerio, an Italian Communist Party operative, along with three other men, approached a farmhouse near Como. Inside, the former fascist dictator Benito Mussolini was being held by Italian partisans who had apprehended him four days earlier as he attempted to flee the country. When Valerio and his men arrived they argued with the partisans, who were not communists and resented their prize being taken from them. Nevertheless, Valerio won out and entered the house, informing Mussolini that he was about to be rescued. Mussolini was sceptical, but his mistress, Clara Petacci, begged him to go with Valerio as it was their only chance to escape. Mussolini finally agreed, and Valerio took Mussolini and Petacci to a villa near the town of Azzano. Once there,

Valerio declared: "By order of the general headquarters of the Corpo Volontari della Liberta [Volunteers for Freedom Corps] I am required to render justice to the Italian people." Valerio then tried to fire his machine pistol, but the weapon jammed. He then produced a revolver, but it too failed to fire. Finally, Valerio grabbed a machine pistol from one of his men and shot Mussolini five times in the chest. Valerio then shot Petacci. Mussolini and Petacci both died instantly.

Although the identity of Colonel Valerio remained a mystery for a few years, the Italian Communist Party later revealed that Colonel Valerio was in fact Walter Audisio, one of its members. Audisio was from a middle-class family and was trained as a bookkeeper. In 1929, he joined the army, where he was exposed to communist ideas. In 1931, he became a member of the party and three years later was arrested for distributing communist literature. He was sentenced to exile on the island of Ponza, where many political dissidents were sent during Mussolini's rule. In 1935, he was removed from Ponza after participating in a riot on the island and transferred to the notorious Poggioreale prison in Naples. Four years later, due to illness, Audisio was released after renouncing communism. He worked as a bookkeeper until resuming political activity in 1942, then went underground.

In 1943, he organized a clandestine partisan group, the Brigate Garibaldi, which was part of the umbrella group the Corpo Voluntari della Liberta, and was given the code name Colonel Valerio. He worked closely with Allied intelligence during the liberation of Italy. When news of Mussolini's escape became known, the communists feared that if he was captured by the Allies, he would become the centrepiece of the war-crimes trials that must surely follow the end of hostilities. Such an outcome, they feared, could lead in turn to widespread prosecution of Italians and possibly Allied occupation for many years. Killing Mussolini before the Allies could get him, they reasoned, would eliminate such dangers.

After the shooting, the bodies of Mussolini, Petacci and fifteen other fascists were thrown into a van and taken to Milan, where they were dumped in the Piazzale Loreto, the same spot where fifteen hostages had been killed by the Nazis a year earlier. The next day the bodies were arranged in a row. Passersby began kicking and spitting on the corpses. Eventually, Mussolini and Petacci were hung upside down from a girder. Petacci's dress fell past her ears until one woman climbed up on a box and secured the dress to the dead woman's ankles.

Mussolini and Petacci were buried in paupers' graves in Milan's Musocco Cemetery on May 1. In 1946, Mussolini's corpse was taken to the Capuchin monastery cemetery in Cerro Maggiore. Mussolini was moved again, in 1957, to his family's vault at the Cassiano Cemetary in Predappio. After the war, Audisio used his fame as the man who killed Mussolini as a stepping-stone to political office. He sat as a Communist member of the legislature from 1948 to 1963, when he was elected to the senate, where he remained until his retirement in 1968.

RESOURCE: *Duce! The Rise and Fall of Benito Mussolini* by Richard Collier (London, 1971).

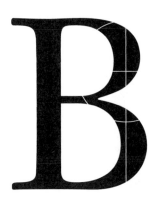

BABINGTON, Anthony (1561–1586), a former page in the court of Mary Queen of Scots, conspired to assassinate Mary's Protestant rival, Elizabeth I of England (1533–1603, reigned from 1558), in what is known as the Babington Plot, most dramatic of all the conspiracies to remove Elizabeth from the throne and re-establish Catholicism. Babington made his way from Scotland to London in about 1579 and cultivated the friendship of fellow Catholics at Elizabeth's court. Within a year he co-founded a secret society aimed at protecting the Jesuit order. Later he travelled on the European mainland to make contact with individuals sympathetic to the imprisoned Mary. One of them was Fr. John Ballard, a former Cambridge scholar and diplomat. Ballard had gone to Rome in 1584 in the company of Anthony Tyrrell (1552–1610?), a rogue priest and freelance spy (and a descendant of Sir James Tyrrell, the supposed assassin of the two princes [Edward V and Richard, Duke of York] in the Tower of London). Fr. Ballard and Tyrrell gained the pope's approval of a plan to assassinate Elizabeth. Ballard recruited Babington to organize the details. Before the plot could be put into motion, however, its outline became known to Sir Francis Walsingham, Elizabeth's spymaster, to whom Babington was then betrayed by Ballard. When apprehended, Babington, in an effort to save himself, betrayed the others in turn. He later escaped and assumed a disguise, only to be recaptured. Both he and Ballard were tortured on the rack and then executed. Mary's own execution followed revelation of her complicity in the plot.

RESOURCE: *Plot for the Queen: The Babington Plot* by Margaret J. Miller (London, 1936).

BARDO, Robert (b. 1970), assassinated Rebecca Schaeffer (1965–1989), a television actress, in Los Angeles on July 17, 1989. Earlier in the day Bardo rang the doorbell of her apartment. When she came to the door (the building intercom was not working), he handed her a fan letter and walked away. Returning some time later, Bardo again rang Schaeffer's bell. This time when she came to answer the door, Bardo shot Schaeffer in the chest. The bullet shattered on impact, ripping Schaeffer to shreds; she died within minutes.

Bardo was the product of a dysfunctional family. His father, a career military man, was an alcoholic who was abusive when drunk; his mother was clinically paranoid; one of his brothers was a sadist who beat Bardo and forced him to drink urine. Because of his father's career, the Bardos moved from city to city almost annually. As a result, Bardo's mental problems went undiagnosed until his teen years. At thirteen, when he was living in Tucson, Arizona, teachers noticed Bardo's anti-social tendencies. He had begun writing letters dealing with murder and suicide to a female teacher. Attempts to persuade Bardo's family to allow psychiatric counselling were unsuccessful. Bardo also began writing to Samantha Smith, a young girl who had gained international fame by writing to Soviet president Mikhail Gorbachev. Later, when Smith died in a plane crash, Bardo was convinced that he had willed the tragedy to happen.

He was not unaware of his problems. On a form he brought home from school requesting his parents' permission to begin therapy, Bardo wrote: "Help, this house is Hell. I'm going to run away again. I can't handle *it* anymore. Please help. Fast." His parents, however, refused to accept the fact that their son was severely disturbed. They contended that his actions were simply a phase in his development. In 1985, Bardo was placed in a foster home, but his parents soon had him returned to them. Bardo was also hospitalized at a psychiatric centre. Once again, his parents forced his release. Shortly afterwards, Bardo dropped out of school and began to work as a janitor.

In 1986, he became obsessed with Schaeffer, the co-star of a situation comedy entitled *My Sister Sam*. To Bardo, Schaeffer became the personification of purity and innocence. He wrote her a fan letter, receiving in return a form-written postcard describing his letter as "the nicest, and most real" letter she had ever received. What was, in most cases, a bit of insincere flattery that pleased her fans, seemed to Bardo a signal that the two of them were fated to be together. He travelled to Hollywood to be with her, but was refused entry to the studio. Feeling betrayed, he returned to the studio carrying a knife and once again was denied admittance.

For the next year or so, Bardo turned his attention to two teenaged singing stars, Debbie Gibson and Tiffany. But in 1989, after seeing Schaeffer in the film *Scenes from the Class Struggle in Beverly Hills*, Bardo became convinced that Schaeffer had to die. In the film, Schaeffer, who had played virginal roles up until then, had a nude scene and was shown having sex with one of her co-stars. To Bardo, the attempt by Schaeffer to play a more adult role was the ultimate betrayal. His former symbol of purity and innocence was now "a worthless fucking whore." Realizing that another attempt to locate Schaeffer at the studio would end in failure, Bardo engaged a detective agency to find Schaeffer's home address. He returned to Hollywood with his letter, a copy of *The Catcher in the Rye* (his way of honouring Mark David Chapman, the killer of John Lennon) and a .357 Magnum loaded with hollow-nosed bullets (again, like Chapman).

After the shooting, Bardo returned to Tucson where he turned himself in. After being extradited to California, Bardo was prosecuted by the assistant district attorney, Marcia Clark, who would act as chief prosecutor in the O.J. Simpson murder case. Clark contended that Bardo's history of mental instability was a hoax to attempt to avoid being punished for his act. Bardo's defence attorney agreed to forgo trial by jury on the condition that his client be spared the death penalty. The judge eventually gave Bardo the harshest sentence he could, life imprisonment with no chance of parole.

RESOURCES: *Star Stalkers* by George Mair (New York, 1995); *If You Really Love Me: A Psychiatrist's Journal of Erotomania, Stalking, and Obsessive Love* by Doreen Orion (New York, 1997).

BASTIEN-THIRY, Jean-Marie (code names "Germain" and "Didier") (1927–1963), was a principal in the Organisation de l'armée secrète (OAS) who frequently attempted to assassinate President Charles de Gaulle of France (1890–1970). On August 22, 1962, de Gaulle, his wife, his chauffeur and a car full of secret service agents were driving from his residence, the Elysée, to Colombey. On the avenue Petit-Clamart, the limousine was ambushed by twelve men with automatic weapons. Well over one hundred rounds were fired on de Gaulle's car, but only a dozen actually entered the vehicle (two others striking the bulletproof tires). Astoundingly, no one was killed or hurt in the attack. The only injury related to it came when de Gaulle cut his finger when brushing broken glass off his coat. When commenting on his miraculous escape sometime later, de Gaulle was heard to remark, "They shot like pigs." The OAS was a group composed primarily of French military men and white French Algerians (*pied-noirs*) determined that Algeria remain a French colony. The OAS realized that without de Gaulle, who had been moving towards Algerian independence since the 1950s, the territory would likely remain French. The attack on the avenue Petit-Clamart, however, was neither their first nor last attempt to kill de Gaulle, though by summer 1962, French Algeria was a lost cause. In a referendum, Algeria's predominately non-white population had voted overwhelmingly for independence, which was proclaimed on July 1.

The *pied-noirs*' fears that the Algerian majority would terrorize the white minority after such a declaration proved well founded. Before the year was out, over three hundred *pied-noirs* were kidnapped and executed and more than three hundred thousand ethnic French had resettled in France. To the OAS, the death of Charles de Gaulle would not restore Algeria as a French colony, but at least would exact revenge for the perceived abandonment.

In May 1962, French security had arrested the leader of the OAS, André Canal (code name "the Monocle"), causing the Algerian section of the OAS to collapse. Command passed to a group known as "the old General Staff," commanded by Lieutenant Colonel Jean-Marie Bastien-Thiry, an air force engineer who helped design internationally recognized ground-to-ground missiles. He had been a supporter of de Gaulle in the 1950s, but became committed to de Gaulle's assassination over the Algerian question. Under Bastien-Thiry, the OAS attempted to kill de Gaulle no fewer than five times between September 5, 1961, and August 22, 1962. On the first of these dates, a 120-kilo bomb made of butane gas, one kilo of TNT and forty-five kilos of plastic explosive was buried in a sand pile near the Pont-sur-Seine. The plan was to detonate the bomb as de Gaulle's car passed by, while several gunmen with automatic weapons sprayed the vehicle to ensure that everyone was dead. But the operative in charge of the bomb lost his nerve. On September 8, as de Gaulle's car passed by again on the return trip, the TNT set off the butane igniter but the main charge of plastic explosives neglected to work. De Gaulle's car was engulfed in flames, but de Gaulle's chauffeur drove through without stopping. Later investigation showed that the *plastique*, which dated from the Second World War, failed owing to its age. Bastien-Thiry and his men tried again on June 23, 1962, when de Gaulle was scheduled to attend a wedding at Rebrechien, near Orleans. An ambush was prepared on the road to the celebration. Bastien-Thiry had obtained an invitation to the wedding and waited there for news of the attack. But plans were thwarted when de Gaulle decided to travel by helicopter rather than automobile. Two days later another ambush was attempted at the Meudon Wood; this time police discovered one of the conspirators' cars, and the assassins were forced to flee just minutes before de Gaulle's car arrived.

On August 8, 1962, de Gaulle was scheduled to drive to the airport to receive Dwight D. Eisenhower, the former US president. Bastien-Thiry and his men were waiting across from the Boucicault *métro* station, intending to drive alongside and open fire. De Gaulle's chauffeur, however, used an alternate route to the airport. When the assassins realized what had happened, they drove at top speed to catch up to the president. As the lead OAS car was about to pull up alongside de Gaulle's vehicle, a civilian commuter squeezed into the space between them. Choosing not to fire on innocent bystanders, the OAS operatives scrapped the mission and waited until the ambush at Petit-Clamart, following which French police mounted a massive hunt for OAS assassins. Although none of the conspirators the police arrested could name Bastien-Thiry (he was known to most OAS operatives as "Didier"), police obtained enough clues to narrow the search down until Bastien-Thiry was the only remaining suspect.

On September 17, 1962, Bastien-Thiry was arrested in his home. In spite of advice from the OAS that he leave the country, he decided to stand trial, and freely admitted his role in the assassination attempts. Assassinating de Gaulle, he stated, was a case of tyrannicide rather than regicide, citing St. Thomas Aquinas's declaration that tyrannicide was not a sin. He further compared his actions to Colonel von Stauffenberg's attempt to kill Adolf Hitler in 1944. Finally, in an apparent reversal of his previous statements, Bastien-Thiry declared that Petit-Clamart had been only an attempt to kidnap de Gaulle. Court observers felt that this change in tactics cost Bastien-Thiry any credibility he may have had. On March 4, 1963, Bastien-Thiry was found guilty of conspiring to assassinate de Gaulle and sentenced to death.

Many OAS leaders had been sentenced to death only to have their sentences commuted to life imprisonment by de Gaulle. In the case of Bastien-Thiry this did not happen. Some have suggested that de Gaulle became incensed at Bastien-Thiry's allegations against him. Others have claimed that de Gaulle felt personally betrayed by Bastien-Thiry, a man whom he had presented with a medal for his work in missile design. Still others suggest that de Gaulle was appalled that the assassins had fired on his car knowing his wife was also inside. It has even been suggested that de Gaulle was disgusted with Bastien-Thiry because he was not actually present at the attack in Petit-Clamart (Bastien-Thiry had signalled that de Gaulle was coming, but had stayed behind). But the most likely explanation came from de Gaulle himself: "The French need martyrs. They should choose them well. I could have given them one of those idiot generals [in the OAS]. I gave them Bastien-Thiry. They can make a martyr out of him, if they want to, when I'm gone. He deserves it." On March 11, 1963, Jean-Marie Bastien-Thiry, clutching his rosary and seemingly at peace, was taken to the prison courtyard and executed by firing squad. He immediately became a martyr among anti-Gaullists. The bullet-riddled car in which de Gaulle rode on August 22 is now on exhibit at the Musée Charles-de-Gaulle at Lille. The Trianon café across from the attack site had been sprayed with stray bullets; it was renamed Le trianon de la fusillade. In all, Charles de Gaulle survived at least thirty-one separate assassination attempts between 1944 and his resignation in 1968. De Gaulle would die, peacefully, in front of his television.

RESOURCES: *Objectif de Gaulle* by Pierre De Maret and Christian Plume (Paris, 1973); *De Gaulle* by Brian Crozier (New York, 1973); *Charles de Gaulle, le souverain 1960–1970* by Jean Lacouture (Paris, 1984).

BAVAUD, Maurice (1916–1941), attempted to assassinate German chancellor Adolf Hitler (1889-1945). On November 9, 1938, Bavaud sat in a reviewing stand in Munich waiting for Hitler to pass by as part of a parade. Bavaud had in his pocket a 6.35-mm Schmeisser pistol with which he had been practising. A Swiss and a devout Catholic, Bavaud had left technical school, where he was studying to be a draughtsman, in order to enter a seminary at Saint Ilan in Brittany. While studying for the priesthood, he fell in with an anti-Semitic conservative group led by Marcel Gerbohay, who claimed to be the son of Czar Nicholas II and believed that Hitler should immediately invade the USSR. A suggestion exists that Gerbohay told Bavaud that he should implore Hitler to invade Russia and that he should be killed if the request was refused. But this evidence came from Bavaud himself after weeks of torture and therefore cannot be wholly believed. A more likely possibility is that Bavaud felt that Hitler must be eliminated because of the Nazis' perceived persecution of German Catholics. That Bavaud saw German imperialism as a threat to Swiss independence is another possibility.

On October 9, 1938, Bavaud embezzled six hundred Swiss francs and travelled to Germany, where he thought it best to portray himself as an admirer of Hitler's. A copy of the French edition of *Mein Kampf* (Bavaud did not read or speak German) and a book of Hitler's speeches were among his meagre possessions. While visiting relatives in Germany, Bavaud expressed his admiration of Hitler and his hope of actually seeing him while he was in the Fatherland. On October 21, Bavaud arrived in Berlin, where he purchased his pistol and several rounds of ammunition and inquired about meeting Hitler in Berchtesgaden. When Bavaud realized that it would take a ruse to get close to Hitler, he drafted a forged letter of recommendation from the French National Socialist leader, Pierre Taittinger. The text stated that Bavaud had a letter for the Führer that had to be delivered personally. Bavaud also prepared an empty envelope with Hitler's name on it. But when Bavaud heard of the memorial parade in Munich, he travelled there instead and purchased a seat in the front row of the reviewing stand. Bavaud believed if Hitler passed on the same side of the street as the stand that he would be within range. If Hitler marched on the other side then Bavaud was ready to jump from the stand and run close enough to the chancellor to get a good shot. What Bavaud hadn't counted on was the fact that Hitler (who passed on the far side) would be guarded by members of the SS who lined up two abreast in front of the platform to prevent anyone from trying what Bavaud planned to do. Dejected, Bavaud watched helplessly as Hitler went past.

Later, returning to his first plan, Bavaud took his letters and his pistol to the "Braune Haus" in Munich where Hitler was staying. SS guards in front of the building refused to allow him to pass but promised to make certain that Hitler saw the document. Bavaud refused and left. By now, Bavaud's stolen funds were virtually exhausted. To conserve what remained, he purchased a rail ticket that covered only half of the trip from Munich to Berchtesgaden. The conductor called police when he discovered that Bavaud was travelling without a proper ticket; when police realized that Bavaud was a foreigner, they turned him over to the Gestapo. A quick search revealed the letters and the pistol. Bavaud was arrested for attempting to assassinate Hitler, who became obsessed with the case. He had long known that he was a target for assassins, and the lone-gunman assassin was the most likely to succeed.

Unlike the Elser case, this arrest could be prosecuted secretly. No publicity of any kind was allowed. Bavaud was interrogated, tortured, and tried and condemned without official notice. Under torture, Bavaud gave the Gestapo the name of Gerbohay, whom he believed to be safe from prosecution as he was still in France. But when the Germans invaded France in 1940, Gerbohay was arrested and shot. Bavaud himself was kept alive for some time as Hitler was determined to find as many co-conspirators as possible. When they realized that Bavaud had acted alone and was not put up to the job by foreign elements, the Nazis quietly executed him on May 14, 1941, by guillotine.

Although the Bavaud affair was conducted entirely in secret, one aspect of the case had an impact on all Germans. Because Bavaud was Swiss, Hitler, who called Bavaud "that Swiss waiter," banned the performance of the play *William Tell* on the grounds that William Tell was a Swiss revolutionary. The ordinance even prohibited the use of "songs and pithy sayings" from the play or the book on which it was based.

RESOURCE: *Tell 38* by Rolf Hochhuth (Hamburg, 1979).

BEAN, John William (b. 1825), a hunchbacked dwarf standing about 1.05 metres tall, was the third man to attempt to assassinate Queen Victoria (reigned 1837–1901). On July 3, 1842, just a few weeks after a previous attempt on Victoria's life by John Francis, Bean pointed a pistol at Victoria. Although he fired, the queen was in no real danger as the pistol was loaded with a combination of paper and tobacco, with just enough powder to make a noise. Bean escaped in the confusion and police arrested every hunchbacked dwarf in London until he was found. He was judged to be insane and his death sentence was commuted to eighteen months' imprisonment. After this, the second attack on Victoria that year and the third in three years, the authorities felt that something had to be done to discourage insane would-be assassins. Figuring that the reason for attacking the queen was the desire for publicity the attacks and trials for high treason produced, they decided to reduce the penalty for attempting to assassinate the queen from a capital crime to a high misdemeanour, punishable by seven years' imprisonment or transportation to a penal colony after flogging. Nevertheless, Queen Victoria would be targeted no fewer than four more times over the next four decades—by William Hamilton (May 19, 1850); Robert Pate (June 27, 1850); Arthur

O'Connor, the grandnephew of the Irish nationalist Feargus O'Connor (February 29,1872); and Roderick McLean (March 2,1882).

RESOURCE: *Victoria: The Young Queen* by Monica Charlot (Oxford, 1991).

BECKWITH, Byron De La (1920-2001), was the convicted assassin of the American civil rights martyr Medgar Evers (1926–1963), field secretary of the Mississippi chapter of the National Association for the Advancement of Colored People (NAACP). Just after midnight on June 12, 1963, Evers was returning to his home in Jackson, Mississippi. As he got out of his car, carrying an armload of sweatshirts printed with the slogan "Jim Crow Must Go," he was shot in the back by someone firing an aging Enfield 30.06 rifle. Evers managed to crawl to his front door. His family, assisted by neighbours, loaded him into a station wagon and drove him to University Hospital in Jackson, where he died soon afterwards.

Mississippi was torn by racial strife during this period; Evers had been receiving death threats for some time before the shooting but refused to accept transfer to a safer region. Mississippi, which led the fifty states in lynchings, was known as a jurisdiction in which a white could expect not to be prosecuted for the murder of a black. Despite this, local police made a thorough investigation, and the murder weapon, with a fingerprint on it, was found hidden in some honeysuckle vines a short distance from Evers's driveway. The rifle's scope was traced to Byron De La Beckwith of Greenwood, Mississippi. Eyewitnesses remembered a man driving a white Plymouth Valiant with a whip antenna asking directions to the Evers home on the night of the shooting; Beckwith owned such a vehicle (the radio antenna was to receive calls when he was in the field, in his capacity as a manure dealer). When the fingerprint on the scope was matched with those in his military file, Beckwith was arrested.

Byron De La Beckwith was a product of the nineteenth-century Southern aristocracy who often mentioned with pride that his grandmother was a friend of Varina Davis, wife of Jefferson Davis, president of the Confederate States. Since then the clan had fallen on hard times. Beckwith's father, an alcoholic, philanderer and gambler, left his family poor when he died. His son was eight at the time, and twelve when his mother, who was reputed to suffer from mental illness, died of cancer. Beckwith was reared by his bachelor uncle in a home without women. An indifferent scholar, Beckwith dropped out of school in 1942 to enlist in the Marine Corps, in which he excelled, being noted as an excellent marksman. He received the Purple Heart and an honourable discharge at the end of the Second World War. While a marine, Beckwith married a WAVE who returned with him to Mississippi after the war. By all accounts, Beckwith was an abusive husband, and he and his wife would marry and divorce three times. Like his father, Beckwith was an alcoholic. His binges often led to violence.

He always shared his family's racist views—as an adolescent he admired the Ku Klux Klan—but by the late 1950s became even more radical in his attitudes. He began carrying a gun to church to protect the institution from African-Americans and joined the White Citizens' Council (WCC) even though he considered the group to be "soft" on race. The WCC came to Beckwith's aid after his arrest and raised money for his defence; it also began, surreptitiously, to harass the witnesses against him. Beckwith was not worried about going on trial for murder. In 1955, Emmett Till, a fourteen-year-old black youth from Chicago, had been brutally murdered in Mississippi for whistling at a white woman. His killers were acquitted in court. Two months later, the killers confessed their guilt in an interview in *Look* magazine, with no repercussions.

At Beckwith's first trial, in 1964, the defence countered the prosecution's eyewitnesses with three police officers who swore that Beckwith was in Greenwood, some 154 kilometres from Jackson, when the shooting took place. Beckwith confirmed that the gun was his but claimed it had been stolen. The trial ended in a hung jury. The fact that Beckwith wasn't acquitted outright by the all-white jury surprised many Mississippians. A second trial also resulted in a hung jury. Beckwith returned home to a hero's welcome, as prosecutors saw the futility of trying to convict Beckwith under Mississippi justice until public attitudes shifted—a process that took thirty years.

Beckwith was a member of the White Knights of the Ku Klux Klan, a particularly radical splinter group, and at many Klan meetings he would admit to killing Evers, always receiving an ovation. The FBI had infiltrated the Klan and in 1973 alerted local authorities that Beckwith had a bomb and was planning to destroy the headquarters of the Anti-Defamation League, a Jewish organization, in New Orleans. In Louisiana, where juries of five persons are permitted instead of the usual twelve, Beckwith, in 1974, was found guilty in front of a jury of five African-American women of transporting dynamite illegally and sentenced to five years in prison. He served three years, kept in isolation, because, as the killer of

Medgar Evers, his life was in danger. While thus incarcerated, Beckwith boasted frequently of killing Evers.

After his release, Beckwith returned to Mississippi to live in poverty in a trailer. By 1991, prosecutors believed that they finally could try him successfully in the Evers case. Modern methods of photo enhancement positively placed Beckwith's car in Jackson on the night Evers was killed. Although nearly thirty years had passed, most of the state's witnesses were still alive. In addition, the prosecution had obtained letters from Beckwith to his first wife showing motive for the murder and his affiliation with the Ku Klux Klan. These facts, together with Beckwith's constant confessions out of court, proved sufficient to gain a conviction. On February 6, 1994, one day short of the thirtieth anniversary of the end of his first trial, Beckwith was found guilty of the murder and sentenced to life imprisonment. Beckwith died in January 2001.

RESOURCES: *Ghosts of Mississippi: The Murder of Medgar Evers, the Trials of Byron De La Beckwith, and the Haunting of the New South* by Maryanne Vollers (Boston, 1995); *Portrait of a Racist: The Man Who Killed Medgar Evers?* by Reed Massengill (New York, 1997); *The Ghosts of Medgar Evers* by Willie Morris (New York, 1998).

BELLINGHAM, John (b. 1772?), the first and so far only person to kill a British prime minister (although plots were to be hatched against Winston Churchill, by the Nazis, and attempts were made on Margaret Thatcher and John Major by the IRA). At 5:15 p.m. on May 11, 1812, Bellingham shot Prime Minister Spencer Perceval (1762–1812) in the lobby of the old House of Commons. Perceval's last words were, "Oh, I am murdered." A large-calibre ball had struck very near the centre of his heart. Bellingham was apprehended by other politicians in the crowd, and although he was described as agitated, he offered no resistance, saying only, "I am the unfortunate man." Later he added: "My name is Bellingham. It is a private injury. I know what I have done. It was a denial of justice on the part of the Government." The prisoner, who was found to have a second, larger pistol with a detachable barrel in a hidden pocket of his breeches, was the subject of an inquiry within hours of the event. The proceedings revealed that Bellingham was a timber merchant from Liverpool who had been arrested near Archangel in Russia in 1804 after a merchant ship in which he was a partner was lost off that coast. Neither the Russians nor the British would compensate him, nor would Lloyd's, with which the ship was insured. On returning to England, Bellingham had taken his case from one official to another, seeking redress; Perceval had been the last to refuse him. Following the hearing, Bellingham was taken outside, where a populist mob cheered and applauded him, and was committed to Newgate pending trial, which took place on the fourth day after the shooting. Bellingham was convicted and sentenced to death. The trial revealed that he had been plotting the murder for eight years, that he had practised with his pistols on Primrose Hill each day for a fortnight before the event, and that he had spent the earlier part of the fateful afternoon touring museums with his landlady, until excusing himself "to buy a prayer book." In a remark to be echoed by assassins down through the years, he also said he had "never found my mind so tranquil as since this melancholy but necessary catastrophe." Parliament, in its grief, voted a pension of £1,000 per annum for Perceval's widow and £50,000 to be held in trust for his children and their descendants. In time, the money devolved as a lump onto Perceval's great-grandson Edward (later Sir Edward) Marsh (1872–1953). Marsh, who was Churchill's private secretary for twenty-five years, used the windfall to patronize two generations of British painters and poets.

RESOURCE: *A Biography of Edward Marsh* by Christopher Hassall (1959).

BENNETT, George (d. 1880), the disgruntled former boiler-room engineer at the Toronto *Globe* (since 1936 the *Globe and Mail*), fatally wounded the paper's founder, George Brown (1818–1880). Brown was also a founder of the Liberal Party who put aside his dislike of John A. Macdonald to help bring about Confederation in 1867. Bennett, whose origins are obscure, faced three savage obstacles in nineteenth-century Toronto: he was a Roman Catholic, an alcoholic and a poet. The second of these led to his downfall, as he was dismissed from the newspaper on February 5, 1880, for being drunk on duty. Bennett appealed to Brown for reinstatement but to no avail. He sank into inebriated despair that vacillated between suicide and murder. In the end, the second won out, and on March 25 he told the proprietor of the hotel where he lived that he was "going to Leadville"— that is, was carrying a loaded revolver. At about 4:30 p.m. he called on Brown in the editor's office, asking for a reference. Brown refused, an argument ensued and Bennett withdrew his pistol. He and Brown scuffled for a moment and Brown was shot in the thigh. Bennett pleaded not guilty to a charge of shooting with intent to kill. Brown suffered blood poisoning, which developed into gangrene, and died on May 9 after terrible suffering. On May 11, Bennett was charged with murder and tried and convicted on June 23. His lawyer, Nicholas Flood, the former London barrister and dashing foreign correspondent who had come to Canada for adventure and later founded the Regina *Leader* (for which he secured a death-cell interview with Louis Riel on the eve of his hanging), could not save Bennett from the gallows. At his execution the following month, Bennett said, "I was in liquor or I would not have done it."

RESOURCE: *Brown of the Globe* by J.M.S. Careless (2 vols., Toronto, 1959, 1963).

BERTON, Germaine (1902–1942), assassinated Marius Plateau (1886–1923), general secretary of the French royalist newspaper *L'action française* and leader of the political movement Camelots du Roi, on January 22, 1923, after meeting him at his office, supposedly in order to reveal inside information on France's anarchist and communist parties. Plateau's organization always was interested to learn when and where communists were meeting so that it could violently disrupt leftist gatherings. Berton had been seeking an audience with the royalist leader Léon Daudet but settled for Plateau, his assistant. The meeting was not fruitful and Plateau ended it prematurely, turning to open the door for his guest. While his back was to her, Berton shot five times with a revolver, striking him twice. Plateau was dead on the floor within minutes, whereupon Berton turned the weapon on herself but succeeded only in giving herself a grazing wound across the chest. Police escorted her to hospital where she recovered quickly.

Germaine Berton was a member of the labouring classes who became involved with anarchist organizations after the death of her father in 1919. Her fellow radicals found her extreme outspokenness made her difficult to work with. At the time, the French anarchist movement was split on the question of whether political violence advanced or hindered the anti-authoritarian cause. Berton sided with the Individualists, whose belief in political violence estranged them from mainstream anarchism. She was determined to exact revenge on the royalists after being attacked at a rally by the Camelots du Roi, royalist bully boys who inflicted a serious wound to her shoulder with a sabre. Berton was also determined to avenge the assassination of Jean Jaurès, the Socialist Party leader assassinated in 1914 by a rightist, Raoul Villain, whom the courts had acquitted. Following her attack on Plateau, she was imprisoned for nearly eleven months before being brought to trial, and passed the time writing an essay on Charlotte Corday, the assassin of Jean-Paul Marat in 1793. Outside, the Camelots du Roi bombed left-wing newspapers.

Her trial, which began in December 1923, quickly turned into a circus. The galleries were packed every day with radical leftists and rightists in roughly equal numbers, and extra security was needed to keep the spectators from fighting amongst themselves. Berton never denied that she had killed Plateau. Indeed, she declared on several occasions that her only regret was that she had been unable to kill Daudet as well. Her defence centred on three points: 1) that if the courts had acquitted a rightist (Villain) for assassinating a leftist (Jaurès), then to punish a leftist for killing a rightist would show political prejudice; 2) that because the Camelots du Roi, and Plateau himself, advocated political violence, her dealing with them violently was appropriate; and 3) that because France was a republic and the royalists advocated a return to the monarchy, she was actually a French patriot, trying to preserve the republic. After a five-day trial, the jury acquitted Berton of all charges, an announcement that elicited loud cheers and equally loud cries of outrage in the courtroom. Newspapers worldwide were aghast that "the Girl Anarchist" had been found not guilty.

The trial is also remembered because it produced a love story that mirrored "Romeo and Juliet." Philippe Daudet, the son of Berton's original target, attended court every day and over the course of the trial became more and more enamoured of the defendant. By the end, he announced that he was in love with her. In 1924, Philippe showed up at the offices of the anarchist newspaper Le Libertaire and, using an assumed name, volunteered to join the cause. He was instantly recognized and just as quickly shown the door. Despondent that he could not become an anarchist, he killed himself with a pistol outside the prison where Berton had been confined. Berton, who wore a locket containing two newspaper photographs of Philippe Daudet, then took poison while sitting on the young Daudet's fresh grave, but was found in time and revived. In spite of their mutual strong feelings, Berton and Daudet actually had never spoken to each other.

Berton seems to have been prone to depression and displayed suicidal tendencies. In 1942, the Vichy government announced that she had killed herself with a drug overdose, which may quite easily have been true. André Breton, the French surrealist, followed the case closely and was disappointed by Berton's acquittal, as he believed that it diminished her actions.

RESOURCE: *Revolution of the Mind: The Life of André Breton* by Mark Polizzotti (New York, 1995).

BET ZOURI, Eliahu (1922–1945), assassinated Walter Edward Guinness, Baron Moyne (1880–1944), Britain's minister resident in the Middle East. On November 6, 1944, Lord Moyne, his secretary, his driver and his aide-de-camp were driving from Moyne's office in Cairo to his home. As they stopped at the gate, two men were loitering outside: Eliahu Bet Zouri and Eliahu Hakim (1927–1945). The car passed the gate and pulled up in front of the house. When the car stopped, Bet Zouri and Hakim vaulted over the wall and ran towards the vehicle. As they approached, both men produced revolvers and told the passengers not to move. Hakim shot Moyne three times. Moyne's final words before losing consciousness were, "We have been shot." He died later that day. The victim's driver moved towards Hakim to protect the baron but Bet Zouri shot him three times as well, and he too died soon after. The two assassins then jumped over the fence again and mounted bicycles they had hidden in the shrubbery.

Eliahu Bet Zouri was born in Palestine to a Russian immigrant father and a Sephardic mother. He had blond hair and blue eyes. Fluent in Hebrew, Arabic, English, Italian, French and Ladino (the Sephardic dialect of Castilian), he could easily pass as a European. His upbringing was difficult as the family was poor and his parents' mixed marriage the source of a great deal of tension. As a boy, Bet Zouri noticed that in the frequent clashes between Jewish settlements and Arabs, the British tended to treat the Jewish defenders as though they were equally as guilty as the Arabs. This, along with many other persecutions of the Jews while the British ruled the region, made Bet Zouri hate Europeans and become an activist. In school in Tel Aviv, Bet Zouri was noted as a troubled student who obtained high marks; while there he joined the National Cells, a Jewish nationalist debating society.

In 1939, the British government produced a White Paper on Jewish settlement in Palestine that called for immigration of no more than fifteen thousand Jews a year over the next five years and no Jewish immigration at all thereafter except with Arab consent. Palestine would become an Arab nation. The fact that the Holocaust was soon to begin in Nazi Germany made the White Paper, and the Balfour Declaration that followed it, particularly tragic. The Balfour Declaration, which essentially made the recommendations of the White Paper law, set off a series of riots in Palestine. One of the rioters was Eliahu Bet Zouri. In 1943, Bet Zouri joined the Stern Gang, so called after its founder, Avraham Stern. Bet Zouri's European looks and flawless English enabled him to impersonate a British officer, a talent that proved handy when transporting weapons, as it was illegal for Jews to possess firearms.

In 1944, the Sternists resolved to kill Harold MacMichael, the British high commissioner. MacMichael was not only pro-Arab, but shared the Nazis' attitude towards Jews. MacMichael had turned back to Nazi-controlled waters several ships carrying Jewish refugees; the passengers were almost surely killed in the Holocaust. Yet despite several attempts, including separate tries by Eliahu Bet Zouri and Eliahu Hakim, MacMichael survived to leave the Middle East and return to Britain. With MacMichael gone, the Sternists turned their attention to Lord Moyne. Early in 1944, an agent for German officials had met with Moyne and offered to exchange one million Jews from the death camps for ten thousand trucks. Moyne's response was, "What would I do with one million Jews?" This flippant comment cost one million Jews their lives.

To insure the success of the attempt on Moyne, two members from separate cells were chosen for the mission: Hakim, who had shown coolness under fire in several instances, and Bet Zouri for his intelligence and ability to impersonate a European. Ironically, the two Eliahus had never met, even though they unknowingly had participated in assignments together. Hakim, in 1940, had personally witnessed the explosion of the SS *Patria*, whose passengers blew themselves up rather than return to Nazi territory after the British refused to let 1,700 Jewish refugees land: an event that made the young Hakim a dedicated Jewish nationalist soldier. He joined the British Army so he could steal and transport weapons. He later deserted, but he kept his uniform for undercover missions. When Hakim was told that he had been chosen to kill Moyne, he responded that he was filled with pride: "That I, I should have been chosen." Hakim began to study Moyne's movements and reasoned that killing him near his home would lessen the chances of harming innocent civilians. There was considerable debate among Sternist leaders about using Bet Zouri, for he was a valuable agent and the chance of his escaping seemed slighter. But when Bet Zouri was sounded out about his participation, he responded with as much enthusiasm as Hakim: "This is for me! I must be the one! I must go!" Using papers taken from a soldier on leave, Bet Zouri travelled from Palestine to Egypt to meet Hakim. The two men hired bicycles and investigated possible escape routes while another agent continued to monitor Moyne's movements. At the end of October 1944, Moyne flew to Athens to meet with Anthony Eden. To the Sternists, he seemed to have vanished. The two Eliahus worried that somehow the plan had been discovered and that Moyne had been removed for his own protection. But Moyne returned and resumed his regular routine. The assassins were relieved but knew that they should act quickly. After the killing, the two assassins might have escaped except for an Egyptian policeman on a motorcycle who passed by and immediately noticed the bodies in the driveway. A brief chase ensued with the officer fired upon by Bet Zouri. Both Eliahu Bet Zouri and Eliahu Hakim were captured.

Strangely, the trial that followed produced a rare show of Arab-Jewish unity. British rule did not sit well with the Arabs, although British policy favoured them over the Jews. The fact that the two young men had killed a British official created a wave of sympathy for the assassins, and the two Eliahus were treated with the utmost care and civility in prison. Security around them was tight, out of fear that they would be liberated by their supporters. Although both men attempted to refuse counsel, the finest lawyers at the Egyptian bar were hired to defend them. Hakim was told to plead his youth (he was only seventeen at the time of the assassination); he refused. Both were advised to claim that they killed Moyne only because they were threatened with death by the Sternists if they did not succeed. The two Eliahus were infuriated by the suggestion, as it was the same excuse offered by the Nazis who had assassinated Walter Rathenau. They refused to plead insanity.

Bet Zouri did cause a disturbance in court by insisting that the trial be conducted in Hebrew. He made this demand in fluent Arabic but continued to speak Hebrew during the trial: a fact that delayed proceedings until a translator could be found. When Bet Zouri decided that the translator was not accurate enough, he began to speak in English and directed his comments to the American and British reporters in the courtroom.

Both men pleaded guilty with premeditation to the murder, but denied attempting to murder the Egyptian policeman, explaining that the shot was merely to frighten the officer. Bet Zouri did express his regrets over the killing of Moyne's driver. He claimed that he did not want to kill the driver, but his training had kicked in and he fired three times, as was standard procedure among the Sternists. When Bet Zouri was informed that even though he was popular, both he and Hakim would surely be executed if they did not seek mercy, he replied: "Some men live short lives in which nothing significant happens. That is a tragedy. But to live a short life which includes a deed for one's motherland...that is a triumph...if it must be so, I am happy to give my life, for I know our nation will benefit by our deed." The Egyptian court was more than willing to let the defendants express their hatred of the British, but when Bet Zouri began to speak on Jewish nationalism, the court attempted to silence him and confiscated all writing instruments from the press so that his words would not be recorded. Nevertheless, members of the press gathered and exchanged mental notes on the day's proceedings, which were published over the objections of both the Egyptians and the British. Ironically, some of the most pro-Zionist statements made during the trial were by the Arab lawyers hired to defend the Jewish assassins. In the end, both men were found guilty and sentenced to hang. In 1945, Egyptian president Ahmad Mahir had been assassinated. While public opinion remained high for the two Eliahus, this later act of assassination was distasteful to the Egyptian people. On March 23, 1945, Eliahu Bet Zouri and Eliahu Hakim were executed.

RESOURCE: *Palestine to Israel: From Mandate to Independence* by Michael J. Cohen (London, 1988).

BOGROV, Dmitri (1887–1911), a Russian revolutionary, shot and killed Prime Minister Peter Stolypin at Kiev on September 1, 1911: one of the last major Russian assassinations of the pre-Bolshevik era. Stolypin was a moderate who, during the failed revolution of 1905-1907, had told radicals from the floor of the Duma, "You will not intimidate us." This and his efforts at silencing the revolutionaries made him enemies who persisted in their hatred once peace had been restored. Bogrov, a solicitor's clerk and the son of assimilated Jews with non-specific leftward leanings, was one of these. In 1906, he joined a group of anarchist-individualists in Kiev, declaring, "I am my own party." A friend remembered him this way: "He always laughed at 'good' and 'bad'. Despising conventional morals, he developed his own, whimsical and not always comprehensible." The proof of this was when he became a police informer, receiving as much as 150 rubles a month, which fed his addictive gambling. He saw no contradiction in this behaviour but earned the rightful suspicion of his colleagues, who imagined that he obtained the funds by embezzlement. On August 16, 1911, a radical emissary informed him that his colleagues intended to accuse him of treason publicly and then kill him, suggesting that Bogrov could redeem himself only by committing a striking act of terrorism. He was given a deadline of September 5. He considered Kiev's police chief as a target but found him unworthy. Later he entertained the notion of killing Czar Nicholas II himself, but feared that act might lead to pogroms. Then he settled on Stolypin, whom other assassins had already plotted to kill in 1906 and again the following year. Giving his police handler false information to divert official resources elsewhere, Bogrov began stalking the prime minister. His chance finally came during intermission at a performance of Rimski-Korsakov's opera *Tale of Tsar Saltan* at the Municipal Theatre. He fired two shots. Stolypin expired saying, "I am happy to die for the Czar" and blessing the emperor with the sign of the cross. More than ninety security agents were present in the theatre and Bogrov was arrested almost at once. Stolypin died of his wounds on September 5. Bogrov was found guilty and was hanged on the night of September 10/11.

RESOURCE: *Thou Shalt Kill: Revolutionary Terrorism in Russia, 1894–1917* by Anna Geifman (Princeton, New Jersey, 1993).

BONHOEFFER, Dietrich (1906–1945), an internationally renowned German theologian, was hanged by the Nazis for his role in the 1944 attempt on the life of Adolf Hitler (1889–1945), the best known and most nearly successful of the numerous plots against the Nazi leader. Bonhoeffer studied conventional Protestant theology at German universities but increasingly became identified with the Swiss theologian Karl Barth (1886–1968), an early foe of Hitler's. He served as a pastor in Barcelona in 1928–1929 before resuming studies at the New York Theological Seminary in 1929–1930. He then returned to pastoral work in London between 1933 and 1935 while also teaching in Germany. During this last period especially, he never was far from the centre of religious developments in his native country.

Within a year of Hitler's assumption of power in 1933, Bonhoeffer was one of the original signatories of the Barmen Declaration, establishing the Confessional Church as an alternative to existing German Protestantism, which was increasingly sympathetic to the Nazi regime. By 1935 he was part of an underground anti-Nazi seminary, where he met his future biographer and editor Eberhard Bethge (1910–2000), who married Bonhoeffer's niece. When war was declared, Bonhoeffer worked for military intelligence, forming part of an anti-Hitler cell within the organization. In 1942, he travelled to Sweden to make a secret report to the Allies about the brewing conspiracy against Hitler, but he was betrayed; he was arrested in April 1943 after his return to Berlin. He was first imprisoned, then sent to the Flossenburg concentration camp. Thus Bonhoeffer was not among those rounded up in mass arrests after the 1944 attempt on Hitler, because he was already in custody. But the Nazis were certain of his involvement. He was hanged by the Gestapo days before the camp was liberated by Allied troops. For a time, suspicion extended to Bethge as well, but he managed to survive and to carry on Bonhoeffer's ideas long after the war, until his mentor became, posthumously, one of the most widely known and influential Christian thinkers of the century.

RESOURCES: *Widerstand und Ergebung* by Dietrich Bonhoeffer (1951, trans. Eberhard Bethge as *Letters and Papers from Prison* [New York, 1955]); *Dietrich Bonhoeffer: Man of Vision, Man of Courage* by Eberhard Bethge (New York, 1970).

BONNIER DE LA CHAPELLE, Fernand (1922–1942), assassinated Jean Darlan (1881–1942), a French Vichyite admiral, on Christmas Eve 1942 after being admitted to Darlan's headquarters at the Palais d'Été in Algiers on a pass issued by Darlan's staff. While Bonnier was waiting for Darlan to arrive, guards at the scene left the building. As Darlan and his aide approached the admiral's office, Bonnier shot Darlan twice with a pistol. An aide who struggled with the gunman was shot in the thigh. Finally, two guards who apparently had not been alerted to what was going to happen that day came in and arrested Bonnier. Darlan was taken to his car and rushed to hospital where he died soon afterwards. Bonnier was a French patriot who, at great personal risk, had participated in anti-Nazi demonstrations in Paris in November 1940. He travelled via

Gibraltar to North Africa where he joined the Free French forces after finding that he could not go to Britain and there make contact with Charles de Gaulle, who was headquartered in London at the time. Once in Algeria, Bonnier became infuriated with Darlan's collaboration with the Nazis. Darlan suppressed anti-Nazi demonstrators, sometimes fatally, and rewarded the killers of French patriots. When the Allies landed in Africa in 1942, Bonnier joined demonstrations supporting them, while Darlan, sensing political change, became an Allied supporter.

Bonnier was not alone in finding such hypocrisy intolerable. A group of like-minded French patriots began plotting Darlan's death. One plan called for a hundred men to fire on Darlan's car and then disperse, but the scheme was quickly shelved in favour of a lone gunman ambushing Darlan in his office. Bonnier was provided with travel papers under the name Mornard but was apprehended before he could flee to Tangier as planned. Although he obviously had help, Bonnier insisted that he had acted alone. He said he killed Darlan "to bring justice to a traitor who stood in the way of the union of France." He was tried, convicted and sentenced to death by a military court all within twenty-four hours of Darlan's murder. He was executed by firing squad on December 26, 1942—only to have his sentence annulled posthumously.

The day before the assassination, the Abbé Cordier heard Bonnier's confession and had absolved Bonnier in advance; the abbot later pleaded with the court for Bonnier's life (even though Bonnier's name had not been released). In all, thirteen men were arrested as conspirators in the Darlan assassination but the other twelve were released without being charged. The Allies were quick to declare Darlan's assassination the work of Nazi operatives. Darlan himself, however, had long assumed that he would be killed by the British. He is quoted as saying, "If I survive to my natural death, it will prove that the British have more scruples, or fewer means of action, than once upon a time." Others believe that the Darlan assassination was masterminded by Gaullists in North Africa.

RESOURCES: *Le secret de Darlan 1940–1942: Le vrai rival de De Gaulle* by Pierre Ordioni (Paris, 1974); *L'affaire Darlan: L'instruction judiciaire* by Albert Jean Voitvriez (Paris, 1980).

BOOTH, John Wilkes (1839–1865), the man who shot and killed US president Abraham Lincoln in 1865, has lingered in history as a figure of almost mesmerizing curiosity—a magnet for contrarian opinion and conspiracy theory—for precisely the same reason as Lee Oswald. By being themselves assassinated before they could be put on trial, they were denied the opportunity to refute, confess, explain or even describe their actions. Both were secretive young men by nature, but history has left them enduring mysteries whose lives are examined and guessed at endlessly.

Booth was the youngest member of a pre-eminent American theatrical family. His brother was Edwin Booth (1833–1893), considered in the US as perhaps the finest Shakespearean actor of his day; their English-born father was Junius Brutus Booth (1796–1852), who spent his last thirty years in the United States, famous as a tragedian, notorious as a drunkard and an extreme eccentric. John Wilkes Booth, named after the eighteenth-century English radical and called "Wilkes" by his intimates, was by no means the failed actor that he is sometimes claimed to have been. His fame may never have encroached on that of his elder brother, but he was a well-known public personality, photographs of whom could be purchased as souvenirs. As for his talent, it can be judged only through the eyes of his contemporaries. Watching Booth's turn in the title role of *Richard III* at the Union Theater in Leavenworth, Kansas—said to be the most important house between St. Louis and Sacramento—a reviewer in the Leavenworth *Daily Times* wrote on December 24, 1863, "We have never witnessed a more thrilling representation of deceit, hate, revenge and ambition."

The date illustrates how Booth continued his career during most of the war rather than give expression to his fierce Southern patriotism by being part of the military. Some historians have read guilt into this decision. Others have seen it as proof that he used his profession as a cover for covert work in the Confederate cause. There is some evidence of the latter, what with Booth's numerous trips to the Confederate capital at Richmond and his meetings with the Confederate States representatives in Canada. His feelings grew stronger as the war went on and prospects for an independent Confederacy grew weaker. The turning point was probably Lincoln's election to a second term in 1864. Booth can be seen in a photograph of the crowd surrounding Lincoln reading his second inaugural address; some even believe that they can spot the faces of the other principal conspirators.

The weight of evidence shows overwhelmingly that the Confederate government gave at least tacit approval to Booth's plan, in the last few months of the war, to abduct Lincoln and hold him in exchange for badly needed Confederate prisoners of war incarcerated in the North—this after discovery of the Dahlgren Plot, a Union plan that included the proposed assassination of the Confederate States president, Jefferson Davis, and his cabinet. The choice of Booth was clever only in that Booth was able to move about freely, northward or southward, trading on his fame; but it was ill-advised in that, for all his hair-tonic charisma, he was without leadership ability. He surrounded himself with incompetent hero-worshippers such as David Herold, Michael O'Laughlin and George Atzerodt. Like his contemporary Walt Whitman, Booth required the adulation of young working-class males (though for different reasons). His friends, however, tended to let him down. So that there should be no doubt that his was a righteous conspiracy, Booth, on the afternoon of the shooting, wrote a two-page letter naming his colleagues and setting out his reasoning behind the whole affair. He entrusted the manifesto to John Matthews, a fellow actor, to deliver to the editor of the *National Intelligencer* the next morning. Once he heard of the murder, Matthews opened the letter, read it with horror and destroyed it.

Matthews had a small part in Tom Taylor's *Our American Cousin*, a play being performed at Ford's Theater. Although written as recently as 1858, the comedy about transatlantic misunderstanding was already something of a chestnut. The final performance of the engagement at Ford's, a benefit to be held on Good Friday, April 14, 1865, was to be the one-thousandth for its star, Laura Keene, a popular actress of the day who was, to say the least, associated with the lead role. Booth had appeared in two plays at Ford's since the beginning of the year and was so familiar a figure there that he used the theatre as his mailing address. Picturing him seems a fairly easy matter. One sees the dark, good-looking and sometimes slightly inebriated matinee idol with feelings of inferiority and a genuine desire to hasten the end of the war, on terms favourable to the South, by snatching Lincoln. One sees a highly—the word is unavoidable—theatrical personality, whose theatricality turns to histrionics as the dream of abduction falls apart and ultimately becomes a question of murder instead. His actions come down to us as a proof that opportunity and means are more important than motive (as tends to be true of American assassinations), a reminder that some crimes just seem to happen, propelled by events that their perpetrators cannot stop because they cannot control themselves. As the novelist Don DeLillo writes in *White Noise* (New York, 1985): "All plots tend to move deathward. This is the nature of plots. Political plots, terrorist plots, lovers' plots, narrative plots, plots that are part of children's games. We edge nearer death every time we plot. It is like a contract that all must sign, the plotters as well as those who are the targets of the plot."

There were more than a thousand patrons already seated when the Lincolns and their party arrived about a half hour into the first act, which began at 8:00 p.m. A large number of them would record, in police statements, depositions, articles, letters and interviews, what they saw and heard that evening. The final such reminiscence was made by the last surviving witness as recently as 1954. The accounts given within hours or a day of the shooting tend to agree on specific details; the greater the distance in time from the events of that evening, the more widely the facts disperse, like the pellets in a shotgun shell. Sticking with the earliest and most reliable testimony, one can catch the sequence of events.

When the Lincolns appeared, the performers paused; the orchestra played and the crowd rose to its feet. Eyewitnesses suggest there was one guard with the presidential party, but, legends to the contrary, his identity, orders and exact whereabouts never have been established. During the second act, at approximately 10:15 p.m., Booth, who had been bolstering his resolve with brandy at a saloon next door, entered the theatre dressed in black and was greeted by the doorman. The two shook hands and conversed. Booth watched a bit of the play. During Act III, Scene II, a point at which a big laugh could be expected, he entered the door that gave onto the dress circle and from there climbed the steps to the first balcony, where the presidential box was located. A Union captain gave him an inquisitive look, which Booth returned with an unspoken request to enter, presumably to offer his regards to the chief executive. Booth presented his calling card to a guard, messenger or usher outside the box, who was to relay it to Lincoln. Booth then entered the small room separating the corridor from the box itself and the door closed behind him. He carried a twenty-centimetre dagger and a percussion pistol, one of a pair bearing the name of the maker, Henry Deringer of Philadelphia. This was not a weapon that could be hidden in the palm of the hand, for Deringer's name had not yet come to mean the tiny weapon favoured by professional gamblers and fascinating ladies (assuming an additional r in the process). Booth's was a larger, heavy weapon of .44 calibre. As Harry Hawk, momentarily alone on stage, uttered the uproarious line ("Well, I guess I know enough to turn you inside out, old woman, you damned old sockdologizing mantrap"), Booth fired into the back of the president's head at virtually point-blank range. The ball, now preserved at the

Walter Reed Army Medical Center Museum in Washington, entered behind the left ear, passed through the brain and lodged in back of the eye on the opposite side. Major Henry R. Rathbone, accompanying the president and the first lady along with his fiancée, struggled with Booth amid a cloud of black-powder smoke, but Booth slashed him with his knife and jumped to the stage less than gracefully, catching one spur in a Treasury Department flag decorating the outside of the box. Ascertaining the distance jumped is difficult, as the theatre was gutted in 1866 (not to be reopened until 1968), but the answer is probably between three and four metres. He may have injured himself but he probably did not break his left leg in the process; the fracture later set by Dr. Samuel Mudd was likely incurred in a riding accident during the subsequent getaway. Still holding the dagger (having dropped the pistol), Booth ran across the stage, calling out the state motto of Virginia, "*Sic Semper Tyrannis*" ("Thus be it ever to tyrants"): a phrase dating from the American Revolution. On this matter, however, the testimony is unusually divided, with a number of the most reliable witnesses contending that these words, and perhaps also "The South is avenged!", were uttered from the box, before the jump. Mrs. Lincoln screamed, "My husband is shot!" Major Rathbone shouted, "Stop that man!" Pandemonium broke out as Booth disappeared amid the rapid click of hooves on paving bricks. Lincoln was carried to a private home across the street, where the death watch was presided over by Edwin M. Stanton, the secretary of war, and included, at various times, Mrs. Lincoln, who finally had to be led away, and the Lincolns' son, Robert, a Union captain at the time.

Abraham Lincoln died at 7:22 the following morning, without regaining consciousness. His wallet was found to contain only nine newspaper cuttings and a Confederate five-dollar banknote. Mrs. Lincoln never recovered from the trauma and spent the rest of her life in seclusion—finally, in an asylum, committed there by Robert Lincoln who, shortly before his death in 1925, burned a considerable number of his late father's personal papers, provoking the suspicions of conspiracy students not yet born.

Booth, trapped in a blazing outbuilding on a Virginia farm, chose to die fighting rather than surrender. Although the detachment of federal cavalry that had found him had orders not to shoot him, Sergeant Boston Corbett did so, using a pistol, administering a wound similar to that Booth inflicted on the president. Corbett became a celebrity and went mad, eventually castrating himself. Other lives were ruined as well.

Public opprobrium forced Edwin Booth to retire from the stage. (In his memoirs *Every Man in His Time* [New York, 1974], the Hollywood director Raoul Walsh, who as a young actor in 1915 played John Wilkes Booth in D.W. Griffith's *The Birth of a Nation*, recalled the elderly Booth visiting his parents' home and admiring a bronze casting of human hands and asking whose hands they represented—only to be told that they were Lincoln's.)

Unlike Lincoln, John Wilkes did not immediately lose consciousness once shot in the head, and was removed to the front porch of the nearby farmhouse, where he asked the soldiers to show him his hands, which he could not raise by himself. "Useless, useless" were his last words. He was buried in an unmarked grave, but later his remains were allowed to be removed to the Booth family plot in Maryland. Legends that Booth escaped capture and disappeared down the American rabbit hole have persisted to the present day. In earlier generations, they were furthered by the exhibition, in carnival sideshows and similar venues, of the mummified corpse said to be Booth's (now in a private collection).

The existence of a diary kept by Booth when he was on the run—a disjointed series of notations written out of sequence in a printed journal for the year 1864—was revealed publicly only during the trial of John H. Surratt, a co-conspirator, in 1867, by which time the pages dealing with the assassination itself had disappeared. Since then, despite professional preservation techniques, the diary has deteriorated physically almost to the point of being unreadable. The FBI reviewed its contents as recently as 1977.

The assassination plunged America into unprecedented mourning, but elsewhere the reaction was less profound. A crowd of American expatriates in Rome first heard the news while standing near the Forum and decided among themselves that the event was evidence of growing political maturity in their homeland.

RESOURCES: The first book about the assassination, *The Life, Crime and Capture of John Wilkes Booth* by George Alfred Townsend (New York, 1865), appeared while the conspirators were on trial; the first by a participant in the investigation was *History of the United States Secret Service* by the guileful Lafayette C. Baker (Philadelphia, 1867). The first serious attempt at sorting out the facts did not come until the centenary of Lincoln's birth; this was *The Death of Lincoln: The Study of Booth's Plot, His Deed and the Penalty* by Clara Laughlin (New York, 1909). The most prevalent conspiracy theory, the one involving evil doings by Edwin M. Stanton, did not materialize until publication of *Why Was Lincoln*

Murdered? by Otto Eisenschiml (New York, 1937). It is a work that has often been debunked but which continues to exert an influence, especially on writers of fiction, ranging in quality from G.J.A. O'Toole's *The Cosgrove Report* (New York, 1979) at the high end to Benjamin King's *A Bullet for Lincoln* (Gretna, Louisiana, 1993) somewhat lower down. Eisenschiml's book provoked an outpouring of works with differing viewpoints and additional information, including *John Wilkes Booth, A Memoir* by Booth's sister Asia Booth Clarke (New York, 1938—published posthumously) and *This One Mad Act—The Unknown Story of John Wilkes Booth and His Family* by the assassin's granddaughter, Izola Forrester (Boston, 1937). In fact, the period 1937–1940 was an especially fertile one in Booth studies, a time that also saw *The Man Who Killed Lincoln: The Story of John Wilkes Booth and His Part in the Assassination* by Philip Van Doren Stern (New York, 1939) and the first publication of Edwin Booth's letters, *The Last Tragedian—Booth Tells His Own Story*, ed. Otis Skinner (New York, 1939), as well as *The Great American Myth* by George S. Bryan (New York, 1940). More recent books of special importance include *The Mad Booths of Maryland* (Indianapolis, 1969); *The Lincoln Murder Conspiracies* by William Hanchett (Urbana, Illinois, 1983), a level-headed and thorough work that critiques the key earlier titles; *Assassin on Stage: Brutus, Hamlet and the Death of Lincoln* by Albert Furtwangler (Urbana, Illinois, 1991); *We Saw Lincoln Shot: One Hundred Eyewitness Accounts*, ed. Timothy S. Good (Jackson, Mississippi, 1995); and *"Right or Wrong, God Judge Me": The Writings of John Wilkes Booth* ed. John Rhodehamel and Louise Taper (Chicago, 1997).

BORGIA, Cesare (1475?–1507), an outstanding personage of the Italian Renaissance and the illegitimate son of Pope Alexander VI, ordered the assassination of his brother-in-law, Alfonso of Bisceglie (1481–1500), duke of Aragon. On July 15, 1500, Alfonso was walking across St. Peter's Square in Rome on his way to his home at the Palace of Santa Maria when five men disguised as pilgrims made their way towards him, begging for alms. As they approached, they produced swords and began to stab the duke, who, drawing his own blade, tried to defend himself but soon fell to the street. As the assassins prepared to drag him off to a group of accomplices, friends of Alfonso appeared and drove away the attackers. Miraculously, Alfonso survived.

That Cesare Borgia was behind the attack was well-known. The plotter's father was a Spaniard named Rodrigo who changed his name to Borgia in order to advance through the Italian hierarchy, a process aided by bribery, intimidation and worse. As pope, the elder Borgia used his position to enrich the Borgia family, his reign being known for its extreme corruption and ruthless brutality, even by the standards of the day. But his lack of ethics paled in comparison to his son's.

Cesare Borgia might be regarded as the greatest assassin of all time. His career as such probably started with the unexplained murders of his brothers Juan and Jofre. Before their deaths, Cesare had been earmarked to follow his father into the church. With no significant religious training, and even less interest in religious affairs, Cesare was made bishop of Pamplona and was later a cardinal. Through a combination of assassination and strategic marriages, he expanded the papal empire throughout Italy.

In 1498, Borgia decided that Alfonso of Aragon, who was a possible heir to the throne of Naples, should marry into the Borgia family. As bait to the seventeen-year-old duke, Borgia offered his beautiful sister Lucrezia (1480–1519) in marriage. This was not the first astute marriage for the young woman. In 1493, she had wed Giovanni Sforza of the powerful Milanese family. When Cesare allied the Borgias with the kingdom of Naples against Milan, Giovanni fled for his life. Later Alexander annulled the marriage on the preposterous grounds that in four years the marriage had not been consummated.

Here one might note that Lucrezia Borgia, often referred to as the "notorious female poisoner," never assassinated anyone. Her reputation as a poisoner was the result of spurious charges by Alexander's successor, Julius II, and the play *Lucrezia Borgia* by Victor Hugo. A more accurate title, one that was a common description of her during her lifetime, was "the greatest whore in the history of Rome." She had a seemingly unending series of lovers, including, perhaps, her brother Cesare. Others marvelled at Lucrezia's ability to "fall madly in love with whomever Cesare told her to." Lucrezia was devoted to her husband Alfonso. Once he had survived the attack in St. Peter's Square, Lucrezia took charge of his recovery, even to the extent of preparing all of his meals herself to ensure they were not poisoned.

But Cesare was not to be stopped. After marrying himself into the French royal family, Borgia decided that Alfonso was no longer needed. When he learned that the attack by the sword-wielding pilgrims had failed, Borgia was heard to say, "What is not done at lunch can be done at dinner." About a month later, Borgia, accompanied by five hand-picked men, entered the duke's bedchamber while Lucrezia was away and strangled him.

Although assassination had become commonplace during the reign of the Borgias, the thought of strangling a wounded man in his bed engendered hostility among officials throughout the Vatican. A story was quickly put about that Alfonso had died by falling out of bed and hitting his head. When that was disproved, a story went round that the duke had shot at Cesare with a crossbow while outside in the garden. The conclusion was therefore that Cesare entered the building with five armed men and strangled the duke in his bed in an act of self-defence. Alexander decreed a complete and full investigation of the matter, then promptly put the whole affair out of his mind. Cesare Borgia would never be prosecuted, much less punished, although his reputation was sullied even further. The Venetian ambassador to the Vatican was quoted as saying: "Every night, four or five murdered men are discovered, bishops, prelates, and others. So that all Rome trembles for fear of being murdered by the duke." Although the exact tally was undoubtedly exaggerated, the level of fear the Borgias inspired cannot be underestimated.

The fall of the Borgia family began with a mosquito. In 1503, a malaria epidemic swept through Rome. Among its victims were Alexander and Cesare. Although Cesare survived, his father did not. Without papal power to back him up, Borgia's ambitions were thwarted. He was imprisoned by Julius II. After escaping a fortress in Spain, he went to France, where he still had allies. He was killed in battle at Navarre in December 1507. The Basque king, John d'Albret, had the inscription over Borgia's grave read: "Here, in a scant piece of earth, lies he whom all the world feared." Alexander and Cesare had an admirer who documented many of their deeds in his masterwork of political science: *The Prince* by Nicolo Machiavelli.

RESOURCE: *The Borgias* by Clemente Fusero, trans. from the Italian by Peter Green (London, 1972).

BRADY, Joseph (1856–1883), along with Tim Kelly (1862–1883), assassinated the two leading British civil servants in British-ruled Ireland. On May 6, 1882, Lord Frederick Cavendish (1836–1882), who had just been sworn in as chief secretary for Ireland, was walking in Dublin with

Thomas Henry Burke (1829–1882, permanent secretary for Ireland from 1869) when they were surrounded in Phoenix Park by Brady, Kelly and eleven other members of the Invincibles, a splinter group of the Irish Republican Brotherhood, the nationalist society popularly called the Fenians. Brady stabbed Burke in the back with a long surgical knife; Burke died immediately. Alarmed, Cavendish attempted to repel Brady with an umbrella but Brady stabbed him repeatedly, while Kelly cut Burke's throat to make sure he was dead. Although the English press assumed that Cavendish was the intended target, Burke was the figure whom Brady had marked for death; the killing of Cavendish was an unearned dividend.

The murders arose ultimately from the English occupation of Ireland, which had reduced the Catholic majority to the status of near serfs by denying them the right to own land. Until 1881, Protestant landowners were free to exploit their Catholic tenant farmers unhindered. That year the government in London introduced a reform measure, the Land Bill, which established land courts to ensure fair rents, security of tenure and the free sale of leases. Unfortunately, the measure came at the same time as the Coercion Bill, which allowed English authorities in Ireland to deal with civil agitation as they saw fit, making English rule there more authoritarian than ever. As a result, "agrarian murder," as the assassination of landlords and officials was called, increased after 1881.

The Invincibles were one part of this reaction. They called for the assassination of all English officials in Ireland, as well as that of all "castle rats" (Irish officials loyal to the English). They particularly despised Burke because, as an Irishman, he was the biggest castle rat of all. Following the assassinations, Westminster passed the Prevention of Crimes (Ireland) Act, which gave police virtually unlimited powers while suspending the juridical system in Ireland. After several weeks' intensive investigation, police, through the use of informants, identified Brady, Kelly and the other Invincibles responsible for the deaths of Burke and Cavendish. Brady, Kelly and three others were hanged in 1883.

RESOURCE: *Killing No Murder: A Study of Assassination as a Political Means* by Edward Hyams (London, 1969).

BREMER, Arthur (b. 1950), shot and crippled George C. Wallace (1919–1998) on May 15, 1972. Wallace, the governor of Alabama, was seeking the Democratic Party nomination for the presidency of the

United States and was campaigning in Maryland for the upcoming primary. After speaking at a shopping centre, Wallace began shaking hands with supporters. Bremer, wearing a jacket covered with Wallace campaign buttons, shot the candidate five times with a .38-calibre revolver, hitting him in the chest, arms and abdomen; he was wrestled to the ground by security agents. Wallace (who won the Maryland primary) recovered from the attack but was paralyzed from the waist down for the remainder of his life. Bremer was the fourth of five children, an isolated young man who had made few friends. He claimed that one factor in his decision to attempt to kill an important figure was that he had lost the love of his life, fifteen-year-old Joan Pembrick. But Pembrick claimed that she barely knew Bremer, as they had dated only a couple of times before Bremer's behaviour caused her to end the relationship. Bremer's first intended target was the incumbent president, Richard M. Nixon, whom he stalked during Nixon's official visit to Canada in early spring 1972.

Bremer felt that Canadian security might be lax enough to allow him access, but he was disappointed to find that Nixon's protection would make a serious attempt extremely difficult. Bremer, who admired Sirhan Sirhan, the killer of Robert Kennedy in 1968, decided to choose an easier target and began to pose as a Wallace supporter after rejecting the notion of assassinating Senator George McGovern, the liberal Democratic candidate. Much of the information on Bremer's motives and plans comes directly from his diary. In it, Bremer declared that he was "as important as the start of WWI. I just need the little opening & a second of time."

By contemporary US standards, his trial, lasting five days, was a model of brevity. Judge Ralph Powers was about to leave on holiday and decided that the case would not be allowed to delay his plans. Bremer's psychiatric evaluation was marred by the fact that his Rorschach test results were so much like Sirhan's that it was more than possible that Bremer had merely mimicked Sirhan's responses, which he had read about. Bremer's diary, which he predicted would contain "the most closely read pages since the scrolls in those caves," was entered into the record, and some of the entries drew laughter from spectators, which their author found humiliating. In his final statement to the jury, Bremer stated: "It was said that society needs protection from people like me. Looking back on my life, I, uh, would have liked it if society had protected me from myself." The jury deliberated for just over an hour before finding him guilty. He was sentenced to sixty-three years' imprisonment and is currently confined at the Maryland Correctional Institution in Hagerstown.

Bremer's story was the inspiration for Martin Scorsese's 1976 film *Taxi Driver*, which later inspired John Hinckley to attempt to kill President Ronald Reagan. George Wallace eventually served two more terms as governor of Alabama. A self-avowed racist and segregationist before the shooting, Wallace was a changed man after the attempt on his life. He became racially tolerant and a born-again Christian; he even wrote Bremer, forgiving him for the attack.

RESOURCE: *An Assassin's Diary* by Arthur H. Bremer (New York, 1972).

BRESCI, Gaetano (1869–1900), was an anarchist who assassinated Umberto I of Italy (1844–1900) on July 29, 1900. A silk-weaver by trade, born in Prato, Bresci emigrated from Italy to the United States, settling in Paterson, New Jersey. An anarchist circle in that heavily industrialized city drew unwanted attention from police in 1900 to a possible attempt on the life of President William McKinley. The rumours were taken especially seriously as recent attempts had been made on the Prince of Wales and the ruler of Persia. Local police were particularly suspicious of Italian-born anarchists, twenty-six of whom were arrested that August. Indeed, the concern was national, and security around McKinley was increased. But, in fact, the Italian threat ran in the opposite direction, as Bresci, returning to Italy, killed the king, who was attending a gymnastics competition at the Palestro Sports Grounds in Monza in order to present awards to the winners. After the tournament, Umberto was mounting his carriage when Bresci, who carried one pistol and had another hidden under the stands, fired thrice. All three bullets hit Umberto: one in the throat, another in the ribs and the fatal one in the heart. Umberto died within minutes. Bresci was immediately apprehended at the scene.

Like many radicals, Bresci evinced hatred of Umberto after the monarch suppressed workers' rights. A letter Umberto had sent to a general in Milan praising him for the brutal way he had dealt with striking workers in May 1898 was a clear signal that the king was a bloodthirsty despot who had to be removed. Bresci proclaimed himself the emissary of the anarchists of Paterson, inspired by two unsuccessful attempt on Umberto in 1878 and 1897. The Paterson anarchists apparently drew lots to determine who would travel to Italy to perform the deed. Bresci won and practised his marksmanship while the other members of his cell raised money for the trip. When questioned, Bresci claimed that he had acted alone with no outside help. Some anarchists later disavowed him and his actions. He was quickly convicted and sentenced to death and, after refusing to appeal, was executed.

RESOURCE: *Gaetano Bresci: La vita l'attentato, il processo e la morte del regicida anarchico* by Giuseppe Galzerano (Salerno, 1988).

BRUNETTI, Luigi (1828–1849), assassinated Count Pellegrino Rossi (1787–1848), prime minister of the Papal States, on November 15, 1848, as the count was ascending his carriage to travel to the legislative assembly. Rossi had just taken his seat when the conveyance was surrounded by between twenty and thirty young radicals, one of whom, Brunetti, jumped in and stabbed him in the neck with a dagger. Rossi fell into the street where he bled to death in minutes. Brunetti was the son of Angelo Brunetti (1800–1849), a wine dealer who at one time had been a loyal communicant of the church but was, by the time of the democratic uprisings of 1848, a secular republican. All Italy at the time was caught between the forces of Italian unity and nationalism and the conservative elements that favoured papal rule. The elder Brunetti had once assisted the papacy by throwing immense parties for the peasants where he would give away a great deal of his inventory of wine. These events were considered helpful in keeping the masses under control. But his beliefs changed by mid-decade. Gone were "the politics of conviviality." Pope Pius IX, desperately looking for a means to retain power while pacifying opposition forces, appointed Rossi, a former law professor who was considered a moderate, to the prime ministership. True to the assessment of him, Rossi sought compromise between conservatives and republicans. He failed, however, to find a middle course, and secret societies began to flourish which, although radically at odds with one another, concurred on one point: the need to kill Rossi.

Thus Luigi Brunetti grew up in a politically charged environment. Along with a cell of like-minded republicans, he decided to undertake the assassination. Rossi's unpopularity is evident in the fact that the act was accomplished in front of many eyewitnesses who refused to attempt to intervene. The police (who also hated Rossi) conducted an investigation that failed to find the assassins. Within days, Rome was in revolutionary turmoil. The pope, realizing that he would be next if he remained, fled Rome for Naples, and a Roman Republic was established. Elections were held and Angelo Brunetti won a seat in the assembly.

The Roman Republic, however, was soon to fall. Pius IX contacted the kings of France, Spain and all other loyal Roman Catholic nations, whose nobility saw the experiment in Rome as a threat to the monarchy everywhere as well as to their faith. With Rome besieged by French, Spanish and Austrian forces, the republican government attempted to negotiate a peace agreement but without success. On July 1, 1849, the same day that it approved its constitution, the Roman Republic collapsed and the city was occupied, and Pius IX returned to establish an authoritarian regime. Angelo and Luigi Brunetti fled in disguise and were later apprehended in Austrian territory when a supposed supporter turned them in for the price on their heads. On August 10, 1849, Angelo, Luigi and Lorenzo (Angelo's second son, aged 15) were executed by firing squad for having taken part in the republican uprising. By 1854, the situation in Rome had stabilized to the point where an actual investigation into Rossi's assassination could be undertaken. Witnesses finally began to tell what they knew, and Luigi Brunetti was revealed as the assassin. Further testimony cleared Angelo Brunetti as the instigator of the murder when it was learned that the father was shocked and angered that his son had committed the deed.

RESOURCE: *Pio IX e la rivoluzione Romana del 1848* by Domenico Demarco (Modena, 1947).

BRUTUS, Marcus Junius (85–42 BCE), assassinated Julius Caesar (102-44 BCE) on the Ides of March 44 BCE as Caesar made an appearance at the Roman senate. Caesar had attempted to cancel his appointment that day as he was feeling ill, but was persuaded to appear by one of the collaborators in his assassination—a group whose numbers are put between twenty-three and sixty. As Caesar made his way to the senate, he was given a note warning him of the impending attack, but passed the note to a slave, intending to read it later. When informed that the note was extremely important and should be looked at immediately, he had it returned to him but still did not read it; the warning was on his person when he died.

Arriving at his destination, Caesar was approached by a senator, Tillius Cimber, with a petition, at which moment the other conspirators surrounded him. Tillius Cimber grabbed Caesar's robe and tore it open from the neck. This was the signal that the other conspirators had been awaiting. The first senator aimed his dagger for Caesar's throat, but instead struck him a glancing blow to the chest. Caesar began to struggle against his attackers. Receiving several wounds, he fought off the assailants even when he was virtually blinded as the blood from a head wound poured into his eyes. He did, however, see the attacking form of Marcus Junius Brutus, whereupon, according to many reports, Caesar said, in Greek, *kai su teknon* ("You too, my child"). Thus the body of evidence does not support Shakespeare's assertion that Caesar's last words were "Et tu Brute." The other senators advanced on Caesar again and stabbed him repeatedly, during which process many also stabbed one another. In the end, Caesar died after being pierced more than twenty times.

Brutus had been recruited into the conspiracy by his brother-in-law Gaius Longinus Cassius (d. 42 BCE). Plutarch's account of his life influenced the depiction of Cassius familiar to us from Act 1, Scene II of Shakespeare's *Julius Caesar*: "Yond Cassius has a leane and hungry looke, he thinkes too much: such men are dangerous." Brutus, by comparison, was, in Shakespeare's view—again, influenced by much older sources—"the noblest Roman of them all": an idealist. Both men had fought on the side of Pompey the Great, Caesar's rival (and son-in-law), but were later forgiven and became close associates of Caesar. Cassius had been trying to recruit conspirators against Caesar and realized that Brutus would be a key acquisition. Brutus's family was descended from the Brutus who had led the revolt against the last of the Roman kings in the sixth century BCE. What's more, his reputation would doubtless aid in the recruitment of others.

There were many reasons among the conspirators for wishing Caesar's death. Caesar had been planning to leave Rome on March 18 to engage in a campaign in the east to capture Parthia, pacify Scythia and conquer Germany; the conspirators knew that if he were victorious, as every Roman assumed he would be, he would become unstoppable. Also, rumour suggested that Caesar planned to move the capital to Alexandria to be closer to his lover, Cleopatra of Egypt. What's more, Caesar had banned the practice of senators imposing extra taxes on the provinces for their own benefit. In addition, republican elements realized that a return to the republic was impossible as long as Caesar ruled. Caesar himself never claimed the title of king or emperor; since abolishing the monarchy five hundred years earlier, Rome was sensitive to the question of monarchs. But Caesar's rule was obviously dictatorial.

For his own part, Brutus had another, far more personal reason for killing Caesar. At about the time of Brutus's conception, Caesar had been the lover of Brutus's mother. Although his mother neither confirmed nor denied Brutus's paternity, Caesar himself considered Brutus his son, so that Brutus, proud of his family name, was forever dogged by the rumour that he was illegitimate. Although Caesar had been his mentor and had given him honours and titles, Brutus could not stand the controversy about his parentage. In light of this, the fact that Caesar called him "my child" as he was dying takes on special significance, as does the fact that Brutus stabbed Caesar in the groin.

After Caesar's death, the wave of republican sentiment that many of the senators had been hoping for did not materialize. The public was aghast at the actions of the conspirators. The very day after the killing, Cassius and Brutus addressed the senate on the reasons for acting as they did, and the senators sat completely silent during their addresses. Clearly, the conspirators had made no plans for a coup. In practical terms, they erred in sparing the lives of Caesar's closest associate, Marcus Antonius (82?–30 BCE), and his adopted son, Octavius Gaius. One of the conspirators had engaged Marcus Antonius in conversation outside the senate that day so he would not be present during the assassination. After Caesar's death, Marcus Antonius disguised himself as a slave and escaped Rome lest the conspirators recognize their mistake but returned on March 17 to address the senate, where he was received far more warmly than the two leading assassins had been. Marcus Antonius took control of the situation, pardoned the conspirators and announced that there would be no inquest, but the speech he made at Caesar's funeral incited the populace against the assassins even further. Angry mobs attempted to burn the homes of the conspirators, many of whom, including Brutus, fled the city for their lives. Civil war soon broke out with troops faithful to Marcus Antonius engaging forces loyal to Cassius and Brutus. After their armies had been broken by Marcus Antonius's men, Cassius and Brutus both committed suicide. Cassius had himself killed by his freed slaves and Brutus fell on the sword of a friend. Marcus Antonius was later succeeded by Octavius Gaius who subsequently adopted the name Augustus.

RESOURCES: *Architect of the Roman Empire* by T. Rice Holmes (Oxford, 1928); *The Ides of March* by Naphtali Lewis (Toronto, 1985); *Caesar* by Christian Meier (London, 1995).

BUICA, Manuel (1877–1908), was the assassin of Carlos I of Portugal (1863–1908, reigned from 1889), the monarch who stepped up his country's colonial adventures in Africa while suppressing republican sentiment at home. Examples of the latter include appointing the dictatorial João Franco as prime minister, suppressing freedom of speech, exiling dissidents to Africa and indeed (in 1907) suspending the constitution. As a result, an illegal revolutionary movement grew. Among its members was Buica, a former sergeant of cavalry and, since 1900, a teacher in Lisbon. Buica was an expert marksman who had competed in many shooting matches. On February 1, 1908, Carlos and the rest of the royal family made their way from the railway station to the palace. En route, Buica emerged from the crowd, jumped onto the royal carriage and discharged three shots at the monarch, killing him. At the sound of gunfire, Carlos's two sons, Crown Princes Luis and Manuel, drew their own pistols and returned fire. Buica turned his aim towards Luis, hitting him three times as well. Buica was then fatally shot, either by police or by one of the princes. A second assassin, Alfredo Costa, was also shot and killed, along with at least one bystander. The carriage rushed to a nearby arsenal, where Crown Prince Luis died soon afterwards; Prince Manuel was slightly wounded. At first, anti-republican reaction was brutal. Republican parliamentarians, who had enjoyed immunity from persecution for their views, were arrested, and Buica's two children (one aged seven, the other only three months) were detained as conspirators. But within a few days a spirit of moderation prevailed. A coalition of pro-monarchist parliamentarians was formed. Prime Minister Franco resigned and entered voluntary exile and there was a general liberalization. Carlos's surviving son, Manuel, was crowned Manuel II.

RESOURCE: *O Rei Dom Carlos (1973–1908) factos inditos do seu temp factos inèo* by Julio de Sousa e Costa (Lisbon, 1943).

BUSSCHE, Axel von dem (1919–1993), conspired to assassinate Adolf Hitler (1889–1945), the chancellor of Germany. Hitler was well aware of the possibility of his own assassination, but while he could understand being shot at by fanatics, communists, Catholics or Jews, he did not suspect, until the bomb attack of July 20, 1944, a conspiracy against him within the German army. Captain Axel von dem Bussche was one of those conspirators. On the surface, he seemed the ideal soldier. He had been awarded the Iron Cross first and second class as well as the German

Cross in Gold and the Knight's Cross. He also had been decorated for being wounded in the invasion of France, where he had lost a thumb. Despite his heroism on the battlefield, however, Bussche was opposed to Hitler and Nazism; many others loyal to their vows as members of the German army felt the same. One night, while Bussche and a few fellow officers were drinking, one member of the group pulled his revolver and shot a hole through the forehead of the regiment's official portrait of Hitler. Rather than report the dissident officer's actions, the others present also shot the portrait, so none of them would be at liberty to report the incident.

Bussche's feelings towards Hitler turned towards assassination after an incident at Dubno airfield in Ukraine in autumn 1942. There Bussche saw the mass shooting of some five thousand Jews. Whatever loyalty he felt to Hitler as the supreme commander was abrogated by the barbaric policy towards Jews. Thereafter, Bussche began making discreet attempts to find fellow conspirators. In October 1943, he met with Claus von Stauffenberg to discuss the assassination. The obvious answer, a pistol attack by a lone gunman, was discarded as neither man at that time enjoyed any sort of access to the Führer. What's more, Hitler was rumoured to be wearing body armour at all public appearances. A bomb, then, seemed the only hope.

Hitler had ordered the designing of new uniforms, particularly for winter fighting in Russia. He was expected to inspect the prototypes personally before mass production began. Bussche, as a decorated war hero who also possessed the blond-haired, blue-eyed look of the Nazi archetype, was an ideal candidate to model one of the uniforms. Rejecting the silent time bombs that the British had been dropping over Germany for use by the underground, Bussche instead chose a German grenade fuse attached to one kilogram of explosives. The British bomb had a ten-minute fuse while the German-designed fuse would detonate in just under five seconds. Bussche decided to disguise the hissing noise that the German weapon would produce by coughing loudly after setting the fuse, then grab Hitler and hold him securely until the bomb went off, killing them both. All was in readiness, except for the fact that Hitler had not chosen a specific date to inspect the uniforms. In the meantime, von Stauffenberg set in motion the plans for a coup to follow immediately on the assassination so that a non-Nazi government could be established to sue for peace from the Western Allies. Just when plans seemed to be ready, an Allied bombing raid destroyed the uniform prototypes and the demonstration was cancelled until new uniforms could be produced.

Bussche, his chance postponed, returned to the Russian Front. When the ceremony was rescheduled for January 1944, Bussche's superior officer, who was not part of the conspiracy, refused to allow Bussche to return to Germany for a trivial matter such as modelling uniforms for Hitler. A few days later Bussche was severely wounded and lost a leg. He was still in hospital on July 20, 1944, when von Stauffenberg planted another bomb, which nearly succeeded in killing Hitler. At that point, Bussche ate his address book, page by page, in order to keep it out of Gestapo hands. Although not apprehended for his participation in the plot against Hitler, Bussche was not out of danger, as his own bomb was still in his kit. Unable to leave hospital to dispose of this incriminating evidence, he carried the bomb from hospital to hospital until he was released towards the end of 1944 and could throw it in a lake. Axel von dem Bussche survived Hitler, the war and nearly all of the other conspirators against Adolf Hitler.

RESOURCE: *Widerstand, Staatsstreich, Attentat 1933–1945: Der kampf der Opposition gegen Hitler* by Peter Hoffmann (Munich, 1970).

BYCK, Samuel (1930–1974), attempted to hijack an airplane to crash into the White House in a bid to kill US president Richard M. Nixon (1913–1998). On February 22, 1974, Byck shot and killed an airport security guard with a .22-calibre pistol. He then boarded Delta flight 523 leaving Washington for Atlanta, shot the co-pilot and tried to force the pilot to take off. In addition to his pistol, Byck had a gasoline bomb that would have exploded on impact. He grabbed a female passenger and threw her into the cockpit and told her that she was to help the pilot fly the plane. The pilot refused to comply with Byck's requests and radioed for help. Security agents surrounded the plane on the runway and began firing into the cockpit. Byck was struck in the stomach and chest. When he fell to the floor, Byck shot himself in the head, dying instantly.

Byck was the eldest of three brothers. He served briefly in the US Army, receiving training in weapons and explosives. He later married and was the father of four; he worked as a tire salesman and applied for a $20,000 loan from the Small Business Administration to open his own tire business. He then admitted himself to a psychiatric hospital for treatment for anxiety and depression. Diagnosed as manic-depressive, Byck was still in hospital when he was informed that his loan application had been turned down. After this, he became hostile towards the Nixon administration. He gave $500 and some tires to the Black Liberation Army. He also supported George McGovern for the presidency in 1972. In October of that year, Byck was investigated by the Secret Service when they learned that he had been telling people that Nixon had to be killed. Byck's psychiatrist stated that Byck might say such things, but that he would never actually try to kill the president. At about the same time, Byck's wife threw him out of the house, and his hatred of the government increased. He became intrigued by a mass-murderer named Mark ("Jimmy") Essex who had shot to death six people from the top of a Howard Johnson's motel in New Orleans before being killed by police. Byck was drawn to the story because before his attack Essex had scrawled "Kill pig Nixon and all his running dogs." In the margin of a newspaper article that he had clipped about Essex, Byck wrote, "I'll meet you in Valhalla, Mark Essex—OK! SAM BYCK." The Secret Service once again questioned Byck when his wife reported him missing after he had left a note indicating that he planned to attend Nixon's inauguration. After speaking to them, Byck was admitted to the Philadelphia General Hospital for psychiatric evaluation. He was released at about the same time his divorce was finalized. On Christmas Eve 1973, Byck paraded in front of the White House in a Santa Claus suit with a sign that read: "Santa sez, ALL I WANT FOR CHRISTMAS IS MY CONSTITUTIONAL RIGHT TO PEACEABLY PETITION MY GOVERNMENT FOR A REDRESS OF GRIEVANCES." On the other side was the simple sentiment "Impeach Nixon."

By the beginning of 1974, Byck began what he called Operation Pandora's Box. He used a tape recorder to enunciate his plan as well as his reasons for it. Byck sent copies of the tape to an assortment of well-known personalities he apparently felt he could trust to release his version of the story after the event. The list included Jonas Salk and Leonard Bernstein. Byck claimed to be a terrorist; he denied that he was insane. In the end, Richard Nixon was in no actual danger from Byck's attempt as the plane never left the ground. But Nixon would not serve out his term, as he was brought down by the Watergate scandal—another of the reasons Byck had mentioned for wishing to kill Nixon.

RESOURCE: *American Assassins* by James W. Clarke (Princeton, 1982).

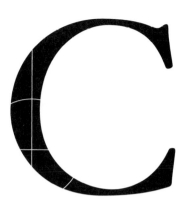

CÁCERES, Ramón (1866–1911), assassinated Ulises Heureaux (1845–1899), president of the Dominican Republic, on July 26, 1899, when Heureaux was in Moca discussing the nation's financial crises with merchants and creditors. Heureaux's regime was notable for the debt it amassed. The president taxed merchants excessively and floated numerous loans in other countries to accumulate a large personal fortune at the expense of the nation. As he was meeting with an official of the local office of the Hacienda Department, he was accosted by Cáceres and his accomplice, Jacobito Lara, aged sixteen. The two assassins fired pistols at the president repeatedly. Heureaux reached for his own revolver, but his right hand had been mangled in a war-related injury several years earlier, so that when he was finally able to draw his weapon, he fired wildly, killing a nearby beggar. At that point, one of the assassins' shots struck Heureaux in the mouth and entered the brain, killing him instantly.

Although Heureaux's bankrupting of the Dominican economy provided much of the motivation behind the conspiracy, Cáceres had an additional reason to act as he did, being the son of Manuel Cáceres (1838–1878), an influential member of the previous government headed by General Buenaventura Báez. During the turmoil that had brought down the Báez government and ushered in the Heureaux era, Manuel Cáceres had been assassinated—on the orders of Heureaux, many believed. Ramón was twelve at the time and not particularly interested in politics. Throughout his teen years, he devoted himself to agriculture, particularly to breeding cattle. His cousin, Horatio Vásquez, a friend since boyhood, was a political activist, and realizing the value of recruiting the son of Manuel Cáceres, he politicized him at every opportunity. Vásquez was the first to tell Cáceres about Heureaux's involvement in his father's murder. Cáceres pledged revenge. At some point in the 1890s, Cáceres joined a revolutionary movement, the Junta Revolucionaria de Jóvenes. Although its members were all in favour of removing Heureaux, opinion was split on whether it was more ethical to work for revolution or to plot Heureaux's assassination. For Cáceres, however, there was no question. He not only wished Heureaux assassinated but was determined to fire the fatal bullet.

In spring 1899, a new member of the group appeared after returning from exile in France. Ramón Lara had been in contact with a group of Dominican revolutionaries in Paris who were followers of exiled leader Juan Isidoro Jiménez. Lara quickly united the rebels on the side of assassination. When volunteers were needed to undertake the task, two appeared: Cáceres and Lara's son Jacobito. The remaining rebels took up positions outside Moca to ambush Heureaux should the two assassins fail.

After the assassination, the spontaneous revolution that many assassins expect after their deed actually did take place. Rebel groups emerged from underground and the status quo dissolved overnight; a new government was formed with Cáceres as war minister. Elections were soon called, and Jiménez, now back from Paris, was elected president with Vásquez his vice-president. Questions about succession soon split the new government. Cáceres resigned and formed an army to unify the country. Jiménez founded a rival movement. A third force took shape and attempted to enlist Vásquez as its leader. When Vásquez refused to join, this movement united with Cáceres. A civil war, now known as the War of Disunion, broke out. Through his former contacts as war minister, Cáceres was supported by the Dominican navy. In the end, the United States selected Cáceres as president. He himself was assassinated in 1911. Between 1916 and 1924 the country was under US military occupation.

RESOURCE: *Naboth's Vineyard: The Dominican Republic 1844–1924* by Sumner Welles (Mamaroneck, New York, 1966).

CAILLAUX, Henriette (1877–1943), assassinated Gaston Calmette (1858–1914), editor of the influential Paris newspaper *Le Figaro*, over a scandal that had romantic as well as political undertones. On March 26, 1914, Caillaux was ushered into Calmette's office and asked him, "Do you know why I am here?" When Calmette responded that he had no idea, Caillaux withdrew a Browning automatic pistol from her fur muff and shot Calmette six times. When newspaper staff tried to apprehend her, she shouted, "Do not touch me, I am a lady." Caillaux waited until police arrived and then insisted that she be allowed to surrender herself, travelling to the station in her chauffeur-driven limousine. Caillaux was the wife of Joseph Caillaux (1863–1944), former prime minister of France and leader of the Radical Party.

Although the Caillaux were wealthy and socially prominent, the Radicals had infuriated the upper classes by calling for an income tax. *Le Figaro*, which was bitterly opposed both to the Radicals and income taxes, began a series of articles belittling Joseph Caillaux's character. Calmette had admitted that he was attacking Caillaux's private life because there was nothing to attack in his record as a politician. To Mme Caillaux, Calmette's worst act was publishing a thirteen-year-old letter (signed *Ton Jo*—"Your Joey"—and known thereafter as the *Ton Jo* letter) that Caillaux had written to his mistress, who later became his first wife. The second Mme Caillaux felt that if there were no legal means of stopping the humiliating attacks on her husband, she must take matters into her own hands. On the morning of March 16 she purchased the fatal pistol and spent an hour learning its use and practising at the gun dealer's target range.

Her trial, which began in July 1914, was among the many described as "the trial of the century." France was weeks away from becoming embroiled in the Great War, but Mme Caillaux dominated the front pages of French newspapers. Several witnesses testified to having seen her commit the crime, but the question of extenuating circumstances made the outcome far from a foregone conclusion. The defence argued that, as a woman, a creature of emotion and passion, the defendant was not responsible for her action. The prosecution argued that the killing was premeditated and deliberate and that the prisoner, although a woman, had acted in a completely unladylike fashion. French newspapers were divided in their support, with those on the political left depicting Caillaux as a victim of persecution by *Le Figaro* and Calmette, and those on the right describing her as a cold-blooded killer. The jury eventually acquitted Caillaux of murder. Yet the damage to her husband's public life had been done. Although he was to serve as finance minister in various coalition governments, his chances of ever again being prime minister were dashed.

RESOURCES: *L'affaire Caillaux: Ainsi finit la Belle Époque* by Paulette Houdyer (Les Sables-d'Olonne, 1977); *Death of an Editor: The Caillaux Drama* by Peter Shankland (London, 1981); *The Trial of Madam Caillaux* by Edward Berenson (Berkeley, California, 1992).

CASERIO, Sante Ieronimo (1873–1894), assassinated Sadi Carnot (1837–1894), the president of France (and son of the scientist who developed the second law of thermodynamics) on June 24, 1894, after Carnot delivered a speech at an exposition at Lyon. As he proceeded to his carriage, Carnot informed security that they should allow onlookers the opportunity to approach him. One of the onlookers was Caserio, an Italian anarchist who had once wanted to become a priest. When he was within arm's-length of the president, he produced a fifteen-centimetre dagger from within a rolled-up newspaper and plunged it into Carnot's stomach while shouting, "*Vive la revolution, Vive l'anarchie!*" Carnot died a few hours later.

Sante Ieronimo Caserio was born in Motta Visconti, near Milan, the eighth of nine children. His father operated a ferry service. As a young man, Caserio had few friends although he was known for being outgoing. His family was too poor to pay for his education and at ten he began working in a bakery; he was still employed at such work when a co-worker introduced him to anarchism. Two years later, on May Day, Caserio was arrested for distributing anarchist literature. After serving eight months in jail, he decided to leave Italy. After a short stay in Switzerland, he moved to France, where he found a job in a bakery in what is now Cora Sète near Montpellier. Soon after arriving in France, he joined Les coeurs de chêne, a French anarchist group. At an anarchist convention in Switzerland, Caserio learned that Carnot would be appearing in public in Lyon. Carnot had angered French anarchists by refusing to commute the death sentence of August Vaillant, who had thrown a bomb (one that caused little harm) into the chamber of deputies in 1893. Vaillant had been executed. Caserio was also inflamed by Carnot's persecution of Italian immigrants in France.

After the stabbing, Caserio was immediately apprehended. While in custody he was beaten until his face was severely swollen and he had lost three teeth. At his trial, he dismissed his lawyer for trying to enter a plea of insanity. Caserio's father had been committed to an insane asylum some years before, but Caserio pointed out that his father's "madness" was a result of pellagra, contracted through poor nutrition. Caserio accepted full responsibility for his actions, claiming that he acted as he did because the elites of France were responsible for the poverty of the lower classes. After a two-day trial, a jury found Caserio guilty. Still unrepentant, he was led to the guillotine on August 16. His last words were "*Vive l'anarchie.*"

RESOURCE: *L'anarchiste et son juge: À propos de l'assassinat de Sadi Carnot* by Pierre Truche (Paris, 1994).

CHANG in-Hwan (1875–1930), a Korean nationalist during the period 1905–1910, when Korea was a Japanese protectorate, fatally shot Durham White Stevens, a vocal American supporter of the Japanese regime on the peninsula, on March 23, 1908. Stevens (1851–1908) had been a paid adviser to the Japanese administration in Korea as well as a Japanese government spy when he returned to America for a speaking tour in support of the Japanese occupation. Stevens's position mirrored US policy towards Korea at the time, as Washington hoped that by supporting Japan, it would encourage Tokyo to tacitly endorse expansion of American influence in China. Stevens was anathema to the many Korean nationalists living in the United States, and on March 22 he was physically assaulted by four Koreans in San Francisco. The following day, as he was about to board a train for Washington, Stevens was approached by Chang, a member of the nationalist group Taedong Pogukhoe (the Great Unity Fatherland Protection Society), and another man, Chon Myong-un. The pair demanded that Stevens recant his statements. When Stevens refused, Chon began to beat him. As Stevens attempted to flee, Chang produced a revolver wrapped in a handkerchief and fired three times. One shot pierced one of Stevens's lungs, the next struck him in the groin (and the third accidentally hit Chon). Stevens was taken to hospital where doctors pronounced his condition as good and announced that the patient would recover shortly. But Stevens died two days later. Chang showed no remorse. In a statement released the day after the shooting and published in the *New York Times* and elsewhere, he declared: "I shot him because he was the main factor in the Japanese reign of bloodshed and oppression in Korea, and because he, as the head and adviser of the regime, was responsible for the deaths of our fathers, mothers, and brothers in Korea." When Chang heard of Stevens's death, he was jubilant. He was sentenced to twenty-five years but was released from prison on April 11, 1924, after serving almost two-thirds of his sentence.

RESOURCES: *The Koreans in America: 1882–1974* by Hyung-chan Kim (Dobbs Ferry, New York, 1974); *The Korean Diaspora: Historical and Sociological Studies of Korean Immigration and Assimilation in North America,* ed. by the same authority (Santa Barbara, California, 1977).

CHAPMAN, Mark David (b. 1955), assassinated John Lennon (1940–1980), the singer-songwriter and former member of the Beatles, outside the Dakota Apartments in New York City on December 8, 1980, at the end of a day during which the men's paths already had crossed twice. The first time, at about 11:00 a.m., Chapman was engrossed in reading J.D. Salinger's 1951 novel *The Catcher in the Rye*; on the second occasion, early in the evening, Chapman had Lennon autograph a copy of his latest album, *Double Fantasy*. Finally, at about 9:30 p.m., Chapman arrived at the building to wait for his prey, who appeared approximately fifteen minutes later. As Lennon walked past, Chapman pulled a .38-calibre revolver loaded with hollow-tipped bullets and shot Lennon in the back five times. Lennon died in minutes. Chapman sat on the ground and resumed reading *The Catcher in the Rye* until police arrived.

Chapman was born in Decatur, Georgia. His father was physically abusive towards his mother, and from an early age Chapman attempted to intervene to stop the beatings. From about age ten, Chapman began to see and hear what he described as "the Little People," a kingdom of small beings visible only to him. Chapman, who was their benevolent king, would play Beatles music for them. Yet at other times, to vent his frustration, Chapman would imagine that he was massacring his subjects.

The Little People and the Beatles appeared in Chapman's life at about the same time. Chapman played *Meet the Beatles* over and over, and learned to play the guitar like his idol, Lennon. By the time he was fourteen, Chapman, like Lennon, began using drugs, particularly marijuana and LSD. At one point he ran away to Miami where he met with other self-described hippies and worked in a carnival. This was also the period that Chapman first read Salinger's novel, the story of Holden Caulfield, a frustrated teenager on the verge of a nervous breakdown.

Chapman soon returned home and became a born-again Christian, whereupon his opinion of Lennon changed. Chapman felt the Lennon song "Imagine" was communistic and that Lennon's remark a little less than a decade earlier that the Beatles were "bigger than Jesus" was nothing short of blasphemy. Chapman would play guitar for his fellow Christians and would sometimes perform a parody of "Imagine" containing the line "Imagine John Lennon is dead." While Chapman would remain a Christian to various degrees, his "Jesus Freak" period lasted only a couple of years.

Unlike many other assassins, Chapman was an outgoing and gregarious fellow. Wherever he ventured, in either the hippie world or the

Christian one, he went to great lengths to gain acceptance. Denis Mee-Lee, a psychiatrist who examined Chapman before the assassination, said: "He tried hard to give a good impression, to please, and to be helpful. But his approach to getting along with people was to be 'too nice'. I felt it covered up a lot of anger." During his Jesus Freak phase, Chapman became involved with the YMCA, first as a volunteer, later as a counsellor and assistant program director. At the YMCA he was known as "Captain Nemo" and was a favourite among children, with whom he was particularly skilled. He taught guitar and also performed skits with his friend Michael McFarland. Chapman described their act as "a clean version of the Smothers Brothers."

In 1975, Chapman joined the YMCA's international program and was sent to Beirut during the civil war. When the YMCA pulled out of Beirut a few weeks later, Chapman was dispatched to Arkansas to help Vietnamese refugees. He later worked briefly with autistic and mentally ill children, but he was a failure in that field. Nor was Chapman a success with women. In 1975, he became engaged to Jessica Blankenship and followed her to Tennessee, where they both enrolled in Covenant College. But after one semester Chapman dropped out and returned to Georgia, their engagement at an end.

In 1976, Chapman found work as a security guard, a job in which he became extremely isolated from other people, as assignments mostly involved working at night in empty facilities. He suffered a nervous breakdown and travelled to Hawaii for the purpose of committing suicide. While there, he rented a car and purchased a length of vacuum cleaner hose, which he attached to the exhaust pipe, placing the other end inside the vehicle and sealing the windows. He then started the engine and prepared to die of carbon monoxide poisoning. But the hose melted off the exhaust pipe and the attempt failed. Chapman then checked himself into a psychiatric hospital where, within two weeks, he was offered a job. He was found to be excellent with the patients and he began to learn Japanese to help with those of Japanese heritage. While planning a trip to Asia, Chapman met and became involved with Gloria Abe, a Japanese-American woman five years older than himself. They married on June 2, 1979. At about the same time, Chapman's parents divorced. Chapman experienced a desire to kill his father, whom he felt had not provided an adequate settlement for his mother. Late in 1979, Chapman left the hospital and resumed work as a security guard. His emotional state worsened and he began drinking and binge-eating. At about this time, the Little

People from his childhood returned. Chapman quit his job, signing out on his last day under the name "John Lennon"; he gave his wife a copy of *The Catcher in the Rye* inscribed "To Gloria from Holden Caulfield." He became a househusband, much the same way that Lennon had done. After reading *John Lennon: One Day At A Time* by Anthony Fawcett, Chapman became furious with Lennon. The book claimed that Lennon's earlier phase of protesting against war was a sham, that Lennon cared only for money. *The Catcher in the Rye* expresses Holden Caulfield's rage against "adult phonies." To Chapman, Lennon was the biggest phoney of them all and therefore deserved to die; he began to fantasize about killing his former hero. On October 9 (Lennon's birthday), Chapman announced to his wife that he was going on a trip to London: a lie to cover up his real intention of going to New York City to murder Lennon. At the end of the month, Chapman purchased a .38-calibre revolver, a type of weapon with which he was familiar from his security-guard training. On October 30, Chapman arrived in New York and staked out the Dakota but did not see Lennon at this time. Also, he discovered that he had not brought any ammunition for his gun and that purchasing bullets in New York was extremely difficult. He travelled to Georgia to visit old friends and buy hollow-tipped cartridges. Back in New York, he still did not see Lennon, and on November 12 he went again to Hawaii, where his mental condition continued to deteriorate. He began to make threatening and harassing phone calls, at one point ringing the Ili Kai Hotel in Honolulu and reporting that he had planted a bomb in the building. With his marriage in tatters and his mind obsessed with killing Lennon, Chapman returned to New York a final time on December 6. While there, he purchased a copy of *Playboy* featuring an interview with Lennon and a new copy of *The Catcher in the Rye*, the Lennon album and a small poster from the film *The Wizard of Oz* (Chapman had always identified with Dorothy, a child lost in a strange land). He also patronized a prostitute who happened to be wearing a green dress like the prostitute in *The Catcher in the Rye*. Before leaving his room on December 8, Chapman created a display for police when they searched the premises: an eight-track tape of Todd Rundgren (often considered a rival of Lennon's), the *Oz* poster, his passport, a Bible open to the Gospel According to John and photos of himself interacting with Vietnamese children. When arresting him for Lennon's murder, police took extreme measures to prevent Chapman being killed by hysterical Lennon fans. Chapman claimed: "The child killed John Lennon. He killed him. To be important. To be somebody." Chapman explained that his mind was controlled by a small child as well as a "fake" adult. He was taken to Bellevue Hospital for psychiatric examination where doctors declared him fit to stand trial in spite of a stew of mental disorders including, but not limited to, depression, schizophrenia and narcissism. Chapman believed the shooting would make him the Holden Caulfield of his generation. He carried *The Catcher in the Rye* with him wherever he went and even called up the publishers, Bantam Books, and told them to expect an increase in the book's sales. Chapman entered a guilty plea to second-degree murder and was sentenced to twenty years' to life imprisonment. Since then he has been at the Attica state prison. He is in protective isolation as he receives hundreds of death threats each year. Chapman was denied parole twice in 2000. Chapman is a believer in what he called by the Jungian term *synchronicity*, pointing out that Lennon wrote the song "Helter Skelter," which influenced the Manson family to kill Sharon Tate whose husband, Roman Polanski, directed the film *Rosemary's Baby*, which used exterior shots of the Dakota, where John Lennon was killed. Or that Lennon played a benefit concert for the families of the victims of the Attica prison riots in 1972 and recorded a song called "Attica State" with the Plastic Ono Band.

RESOURCES: *Let Me Take You Down: The Mind of Mark David Chapman, the Man Who Killed John Lennon* by Jack Jones (New York, 1992); *The Mourning of John Lennon* by Anthony Elliot (Berkeley, California, 1999); *Lennon in America, 1971–1980* by Geoffrey Giuliano (New York, 2000). See also the documentary film *The Murder of John Lennon* by Marc de Guerre and Rachel Low (2000).

CHASTEL, Jean (1574–1594), attempted to kill Henri IV of France (1553–1610, reigned 1589–1610). On December 27, 1594, Chastel stalked Henri while the king was returning from Picardy and, along with his entourage, stopped in at the Hôtel de Schomberg in Paris, near the site of the present Louvre, to pay a visit to Gabrielle d'Estrées, his mistress. Chastel stood behind two noblemen until they began to bow down to the monarch. Realizing that Henri's jerkin would deflect a knife blow, Chastel aimed for the king's throat but instead cut Henri's lip and broke one of his teeth. During the confusion several bystanders were apprehended before the king identified Chastel as his assailant. A Jesuit scholar and student of the law, Chastel was a tormented man who had had an *affaire* with his sister but lied in confession when asked if he had committed incest; both of these deeds, he felt, would damn him to everlasting torment. He became convinced that only by killing Henri and subsequently being executed could he atone partially for his sins.

Henri had converted to Catholicism as a condition for entering Paris and annexing it to his realm, but he was still awaiting papal absolution, without which the Jesuits refused to acknowledge his conversion—a conversion whose sincerity may be judged by Henri's famous statement that "Paris is worth a mass." Official reaction to the Jesuit stand was to attempt to expel all Jesuits from France. A motion to do just that had been presented to the Paris parliament, and was narrowly defeated. To Chastel, the effort to try to exile the Jesuits was clear proof that the king was a heretic. Under torture, Chastel admitted that he had studied philosophy under a Jesuit priest named Fr. Gueret. From this point, the questioning turned from his motives to alleged Jesuit incitement to assassination. Evidence against the Jesuits was no more than circumstantial, but was enough to provoke their persecution. Fr. Gueret was brought in to be tortured. In spite of the skill and brutality of the torturers, he denied any knowledge or approval of Chastel's acts. Papers found in the possession of Fr. Jean Guignard showed that he had written approvingly of the assassination of Henri III by Jacques Clement in 1589. Despite the lack of a formal charge against him, Fr. Guignard was hanged for his writings. Sending children to be taught by Jesuits, even outside France, became a criminal act. Paris voted to exile all Jesuits, as did Rouen and Dijon. Yet Bordeaux and Toulouse refused to follow suit.

Punishment for Chastel, in spite of his poor showing as an assassin, set the precedent for future regicides. The hand he used to stab the king was burned off with sulfur and the flesh was torn from his body with red-hot tongs. A mixture of molten lead, resin, wax and sulfur was poured into his wounds. Then he was drawn and quartered. Chastel's family was exiled from France for nine years. After their return they were forbidden to enter Paris or any of its surrounding towns. The family home was destroyed. In its place, a stone pyramid was erected with an inscription on each side telling the story of "the most wicked, most detestable parricide attempted against the King's person." In 1603, Henri IV lifted the ban against Jesuits in France. He was later assassinated by François Ravaillac.

RESOURCE: *L'assassinat d'Henri IV 14 mai 1610—Le problème du tyrannicide et l'affermissement de la monarchie absolue* by Roland Mounhier (Paris, 1964).

CH'EN Yu-liang (1320–1363) assassinated Hsu Shou-hui (d. 1360), emperor of the rebel kingdom of T'ien-wan, China. The declining years of the Yuan dynasty (1279–1368), like the end of most Chinese dynasties, was marked by rebellions and the foundation of breakaway states. T'ien-wan was established in 1351 by disciples of the monk P'eng Ying-yu. The religious sect chose Hsu Shou-hui, formerly an itinerant peddler, as leader, on the basis of a number of signs interpreted by its wise men; the fact that Hsu is described as big and imposing might have been an additional factor. Under Hsu, the state of T'ien-wan grew quickly as Yuan forces were defeated time and again before pulling out of the region altogether. Although large, T'ien-wan was never well administered, partly because government officials, both Chinese and Mongol, refused to work for the insurgent state. Indeed, the most fierce resistance to T'ien-wan expansion came from local officials who defended to the last man every city and town under their control.

One of the few officials to become a rebel was Ch'en Yu-liang, a former fisherman whose intelligence and hard work enabled him to pass the examinations to become a civil servant. Finding such labour unexciting, he joined the rebellion in 1351 and obtained a command position in the military, where he flourished and soon had a large following of his own. His position was enhanced when Ch'en assassinated Ni Wen-chun, an army rival. In order to consolidate his power, Ch'en also killed Chao P'u-sheng, another potential threat. By 1359, Ch'en was the second most powerful person in T'ien-wan, next to the emperor. Ch'en established headquarters in the city of Chiang-chou. Late that year, Hsu announced that he would move his court there from Han-yang, against the wishes of his subordinate Ch'en Yu-liang. As Hsu and his entourage approached Chiang-chou, men loyal to Ch'en attacked the imperial party, killing all of Hsu's retainers, taking Hsu prisoner and assuming control of the state.

By this time, T'ien-wan's opposition came not from the Yuan government nor from loyalist local officials but rather from rival breakaway states. Chief among these was the kingdom of the rebel leader Chu Yuan-chang. In June 1360, Ch'en defeated Chu at T'ai-p'ing. With his chief competitor defeated, Ch'en felt that he had no reason to keep Hsu alive any longer and had his men beat the former emperor to death. After the assassination, Ch'en renamed his kingdom Han and took the title of emperor (his imperial title was Ta-i or Greatly Righteous Emperor).

After Ch'en assumed the throne, his fortunes began to decline. Chroniclers point to the fact that the succession ceremonies took place during a thunderstorm as a sign of Heaven's displeasure. Chu Yuan-chang massacred Ch'en's troops at Lung-wan and Ch'en was forced to flee the battlefield. Chu pressed his offensive and Ch'en's forces fought a defensive battle that led Chu's troops to the very gates of the Han capital. In 1361, Ch'en was forced to abandon Chiang-chou. In June 1363, Ch'en attempted to besiege the city of Hung-tu with virtually his entire army; the siege was lifted by a relief column under Chu himself. In October 1363, with his troops starving, Ch'en attempted to break through Chu's lines and lead his troops to the Yangtze River. In a skirmish with Chu's forces, Ch'en was shot by an arrow and killed. What was left of Han passed to his son Ch'en Li, but within six months the kingdom of Han ceased to exist.

RESOURCE: *The Glory and the Fall of the Ming Dynasty* by Albert Chan (Norman, Oklahoma, 1982).

CHEROZAMSKY, Vlada (a.k.a. Vlada Georgiev, Stoyanov, Dimitriov, Suk, Kerin, Keleman, Velichko and Vlada the Chauffeur), assassinated Alexander I (1888–1934) of Yugoslavia and Louis Barthou (1862–1934), the French foreign minister, on October 9, 1934, when Alexander arrived in Marseilles on a royal visit to France. Alexander was met by Barthou and escorted to a large open touring car built before the First World War. The motorcar was to travel the city's streets at about eight kilometres an hour. Shortly after it set out, Vlada the Chauffeur, a Bulgarian hitman working for Croatian nationalists employed by Italian fascists, dashed out from the crowd lining the street and jumped onto one of the vehicle's running boards. Pulling a pistol, he shot Alexander twice; the king died within minutes. Barthou, realizing what was happening long before security did, flung himself over the king's body and received one wound in the arm. At that point, the police began to react. The first gendarme to approach Vlada was shot in the stomach, but a cavalryman on the scene rode up to Vlada and began slashing away with a sabre. A confederate of Vlada's was supposed to be throwing bombs into the crowd by that point in order to create confusion and allow Vlada time to escape, but the accomplice lost his nerve and fled; Vlada tried to rouse him by firing into the crowd, killing two bystanders in the process. A police officer then shot Vlada in the head, and the crowd surged forward to kick and tear at the body of the killer, now lying dead in the street. Barthou was taken slowly (the motorcar had a top speed of only thirty-two kilometres an hour) to hospital. Barthou bled to death that day, due to medical incompetence.

Vlada the Chauffeur (even the name Cherozamsky is in some dispute) was a professional. Beyond that relatively little is known of him. He was virtually illiterate and was certainly cold-blooded in the way he dealt with his chosen profession. "Killing a man," he once remarked, "is nothing more to me than uprooting a tree." Born and reared in Bulgaria, he was on the run from authorities there for a number of assinations.

Vlada was introduced to Ante Pavelich, leader of the Croatian nationalist group the Ustacha, who realized the usefulness of such a man and hired him to be his personal bodyguard. The Ustacha, although officially a Croatian nationalist organization, had little support among Croatian nationalists in Yugoslavia, who considered it a group of fascist thugs and possibly nothing more than a puppet of a foreign power. Yet the Ustacha did enjoy financial support from Croatian nationalists overseas and the fascist government of Italy under Benito Mussolini. The latter provided the Ustacha with false passports and safety within its borders. The Allied nations had promised Italy a piece of the territory that would make up Yugoslavia as a condition of that nation's entry into the First World War, though the pledge was forgotten when the war ended. Mussolini vowed to gain by coercion or force that which he had been denied at Versailles. Thus, to Italy, any action that undermined the new nation of Yugoslavia was good for Italian ambitions.

Alexander had been trying to unify and rule a region that had been split by ethnic and religious conflicts for centuries. To promote that aim, Alexander had suspended the constitution and ruled Yugoslavia as a military dictator. To the Croat Ustacha, the Serbian Alexander was the biggest obstacle to Croatian independence; to Italians, Alexander was the biggest obstacle to their planned conquest of Yugoslavia. Although the Italians already had placed a bounty on the king's head, Alexander's meeting with the French foreign minister provided an additional incentive for an assassination attempt.

Louis Barthou was an avowed anti-fascist. One of the few foreign officials who had read *Mein Kampf* by Adolf Hitler, he was convinced that the major European powers needed to put aside their differences and unite against the fascist menace. He had been negotiating with the Soviet Union to that end. A pact between France and the USSR would thwart imperialist ambitions for both Italy and Germany. (In spite of what the Germans had to gain from the shooting, there is no evidence of their involvement.) The Italians saw killing Alexander and Barthou in one blow as vital to their self-interests and provided Pavelich and his co-conspirators with weapons, money and papers; the Ustacha did the rest.

Alexander was succeeded by Peter I, still a young boy. Prince Paul, Alexander's cousin, acted as regent. Under Paul, the constitution was re-established, and Yugoslavia continued to deal with the problems of foreign aggression and internal conflicts, with mixed success. After the assassination, France broke off talks with the Soviet Union. French rightists always had opposed dealing with the communists, and after Barthou's death the foreign ministry in Paris was less inclined to worry about fascism.

Although Vlada himself was killed on the scene, two members of the Ustacha were arrested while trying to leave France. They were sentenced to life imprisonment. Ante Pavelich, however, managed to escape to Italy unscathed. After the German occupation of Yugoslavia in 1941, Pavelich became leader of a puppet Croatian state. After the war, he was forced to flee, eventually ending up in Argentina, where he died in 1959.

RESOURCES: *Atentatut v Marsiliia: Vlado Chernozemski zhivot otdaden na Makedoniia* by Mitre Stamenov (Sofia, 1993); *The Turning Point: The Assassination of Louis Barthou and King Alexander I of Yugoslavia* by Allen Roberts (New York, 1970).

CHING Ch'ing (1370?–1402) planned to assassinate the Yung-lo emperor (1360–1424, reigned 1402–24), third ruler of the Ming dynasty (1368–1644). On September 12, 1402, the emperor called for palace guards to search the robes of his censor-in-chief, Ching Ch'ing. Many have speculated that the emperor noticed a furtive look on Ching's face. Others have suggested that the emperor's spies had informed him that Ching should be searched that day. What is more likely, however, is simply that the emperor had Ching under close observation since usurping imperial power from his brother, the Chien-wen emperor. In any case, the search revealed a concealed dagger. Thus caught, Ching readily confessed his plan to assassinate the emperor as an act of revenge for usurping the throne. As he was explaining his actions, Ching burst into a tirade of abuse towards the emperor. The emperor ordered the guards to remove all of Ching's teeth to silence him. Defiant until the end, Ching spat a mouthful of blood onto the emperor after his teeth had been smashed in. The emperor, now enraged, ordered Ching executed on the spot.

Little is known of Ching Ch'ing's past before he appeared at the palace for examination in 1394 except that his real surname was probably Keng but that it had been listed as Ching through clerical error. Ching received the second-highest score in the exams that year and was assigned to the prestigious Hanlin Academy, where he further distinguished himself as an outstanding scholar. He was appointed to the court censorate in 1398 by the first Ming emperor, the Hung-wu emperor. After a brief period in prison as the result of a scandal, he was pardoned by the emperor and sent on a mission to investigate tea smuggling on the Sichuan-Shanxi border. After this, and a brief period as prefect in Chin-hua, Chekiang, he was appointed censor-in-chief by the Chien-wen emperor, whose reign was brief (1398–1402).

From the beginning, the new emperor was opposed by his half-brother Chu Ti. During their struggle, Ching declared on several occasions that he would never work for the usurper Chu Ti, who had been born the fourth son of the Hung-wu emperor but whose mother was a lowly courtesan. To Ching, Chu's low birth disqualified him from ever obtaining the throne. But when the usurper defeated his half-brother and ascended the throne, Ching Ch'ing seemed more than willing to take up his old duties for the new regime. What appeared to be hypocrisy was actually a ruse to get close enough to the new emperor in order to kill him.

After Ching's execution, the emperor ordered the corpse be skinned, stuffed with straw and hung at the main palace entrance. The emperor also ordered the execution of all Ching's relatives, by either blood or marriage. As a final act of vengeance, the emperor had every man, woman and child of Ching's native village put to death. A legal term that emerged from this vendetta, translatable as "melon-vine tendrils guilt," refers to the extension of guilt by association. Folk myths sprang up round Ching. The most famous stated that Ching's ghost stalked the palace after his death, reprimanding the emperor until the maddened ruler ordered that the assassin's corpse be ground to pieces. In 1645, with the Ming dynasty reduced to a small kingdom in the southern region of

China, Ching Ch'ing was rehabilitated as a heroic figure who remained loyal to the Chien-wen emperor to the end. He was honoured with the posthumous name Chung-lieh.

RESOURCE: *The Usurpation of the Prince of Yen 1398–1402* by David B. Chan (San Francisco, 1976).

CHING K'o (d. 227 BCE) attempted to assassinate Cheng (reigned 246–210 BCE), the king of Ch'in, in modern-day China. The era of Chinese history between 453–221 BCE is known as the Warring States Period. It followed the Chou dynasty, whose erosion over a period of centuries gave way to a large number of small kingdoms marked by civil war and shifting alliances, facts which precluded any one kingdom from conquering China. In 246, however, a young prince, Cheng, ascended the throne and began a campaign against his rivals. Utilizing military tactics learned from the Northern Barbarians (the Hsiung-nu), the Ch'in overwhelmed the kingdoms of Sung, Lu, Chou and Wei and appeared to be unstoppable. The remaining major kingdoms (Han, Ch'u, Chao, Yen and Ch'i) searched for a means to stop the aggressive Ch'in, who appeared to have more in common with the Hsiung-nu than with the Chinese.

The solution seemed to appear in the kingdom of Yen with the arrival of Ching K'o in 237. A native of Wei, Ching was equally well-known for his scholarship and his swordsmanship (and also for his love of alcohol). After failing to obtain work at the court of Wei, he travelled throughout China seeking a court position. Arriving at Yen, he found a kingdom living in terror of the much larger and stronger Ch'in. Fan Wu-chi, a Ch'in general who had had a falling-out with his king, fled for his life to Yen, where he had been granted asylum. Now Ch'in was feared to be planning an invasion to capture and execute Fan. Ching K'o suggested that Fan could be used as part of a plot to assassinate Cheng. If Fan's head were presented to the Ch'in king as a peace offering, assassins might be able to get close enough to Cheng to kill him. Without its ruler, the plotters reasoned, the Ch'in kingdom would be plunged into chaos and the remaining kingdoms, particularly Yen, saved from capture. Historians of the period declared that when Fan heard of the plan, he willingly slit his own throat so that his head could be used. Ching suggested that an offer be made to Cheng that would include the kingdom of Yen as well as Fan's head. A large map of Yen was obtained to show the Ch'in king the territory. The map was particularly vital to the plan as it would conceal the weapon, a razor-sharp dagger coated in poison, which was tested several times before Ching set out. In each case, even though the test subjects were barely scratched by the poisoned blade, death was swift.

With the dagger, the map and Fan's head, Ching arrived at the Ch'in palace and presented expensive gifts to the palace counsellor, Meng Chia, a favourite of Cheng's. Meng obtained for Ching K'o an audience with the Ch'in king. When Ching was ushered into the throne room, he presented the king with Fan's head and the map of Yen. As Cheng unrolled the map, the dagger fell out. Ching took the knife in his right hand and seized the king's sleeve with his left. But before Ching could drive the weapon home, Cheng pulled away, tearing his sleeve, and fled the assassin. Ching chased him through the throne room while Cheng's retainers looked on. According to Ch'in law, possessing any sort of weapon in the king's presence was illegal. Therefore no one else in the room was armed except for Cheng and Ching. For lack of anything else to do, the court physician, Hsia Wu-chu, threw his medicine bag at the assassin. Although Cheng had his sword at his side, the scabbard was too tight to allow him to draw the blade easily. Cheng had many armed guards one floor below the throne room, but they would not come unless the king summoned them personally. Cheng panicked and did not call his guards. As the assassin chased the king around the room, Cheng finally managed to draw his sword. He turned on his attacker and cut him several times while calling for his guards. Realizing now that he would never get near enough to cut with his dagger, Ching, in desperation, finally threw the knife at the king. He missed. Ching was now unarmed and, sinking to the floor, was killed by the guards. After the attack, Cheng rewarded Hsia Wu-chu for throwing his medicine bag, thus becoming the only retainer who tried to stop the attack, however futile the gesture. Cheng then turned to the kingdom of Yen in wrath. Within five years, Yen ceased to exist. The Ch'in would go on to conquer the remaining kingdoms by 221, unifying China for the first time in centuries. Once he had completed his task, Cheng adopted the title Ch'in Shih Huang-ti, "the First Emperor of China."

RESOURCE: *The Grand Scribe's Records, Volume VII: The Memoirs of Pre-Han China* by Ssu-ma Ch'ien, ed. William H. Nienhauser, Jr. trans. Tsai-fa Cheng, Zongli Lu, William H. Neinhauser, Jr. and Robert Reynolds (Indianapolis, Indiana, 1994).

CLÉMENT, Jacques (1567–1589), was the assassin of Henri III of France (1551–1589, reigned from 1574). On August 1, 1589, Clément, being in possession of a letter from the Count of Brienne, requested an audience with the king. When he was presented to Henri, who was sitting on the commode, naked except for a dressing gown over his shoulders, Clément told him that he had a secret message that was for the king's ears only. As Henri took the letter, he leaned forward to allow Clément to whisper the secret into his ear. Clément withdrew from the sleeve of his robe a long-handled knife and stabbed the king in the belly. Henri pulled the knife from his body and told the guards to kill Clément, who, accordingly, died within seconds. A physician was summoned. He judged the wound serious but not mortal. Henri died eighteen hours later.

The reign of Henri III was a time marked by religious warfare, and the monarch was faced with two rivals. The first was Henri, Duke of Guise, unofficial leader of the Catholic League (of which Henri III was nominal head, but the League soldiers were loyal to Guise). The second was Henri of Bourbon, the king's distant cousin, who was the leader of the Protestants. The one who occupied the throne was, in terms of military strength and general character, the weakest of the so-called Three Henris. Fearing the strength of the Catholic League, he dispatched a squad of trusted bodyguards to assassinate Henri of Guise, earning the condemnation of French Catholics. Priests declared that the king's subjects were no longer bound by their oaths of allegiance to him, and he was forced to flee predominantly Catholic Paris. In an unusual ceremony, a procession of small children in Paris marched from the Cemetery of the Innocents to the church of the abbey of Ste. Geneviève, each carrying a lighted candle. At the entrance to the church the children cast down their candles and trampled them underfoot to symbolize the king's excommunication.

If Henri III had angered French Catholics by ordering the assassination of Henri of Guise, he enraged them further by forming an alliance with Henri of Bourbon. Henri III had often been accused of being an atheist. The fact that he had massacred Protestants as head of the Catholic League, then joined with the Protestants against the League, indicated that his religious devotion was not nearly so strong as his sense of political expediency.

Jacques Clément was a Dominican born to peasant parents in the village of Sorbonne. Perhaps the kindest description of his mind was that "he was not particularly clever or robust." All of his life he had spoken of leading a revolution. His friends had nicknamed him *le capitaine*. He had told his fellow Dominicans that he had had a dream in which angels had come to him with flaming swords telling him that he was fated to kill the heretic Henri III. Still worried for his soul, he had asked a priest if it was a sin to kill the king. After being informed that killing Henri would please God, Clément began preparations for his attempt. In addition to the letter from the Count of Brienne, who was imprisoned in Paris at the time, Clément had obtained a passport from another Protestant prisoner. By late summer 1589, Henri III, with a combination of mercenary troops and soldiers loyal to Henri of Bourbon, had surrounded Paris and was encamped at Saint-Cloud, Navarre at Meudon. As Henri III lay dying, he called for Henri of Bourbon and confirmed him as his successor.

The death of Henri III lifted the siege of Paris. Church bells in the city rang out in triumph. Clément was unofficially declared a saint for ridding France of the heretic king. Clément's mother, who was living in Paris at the time, was honoured as the mother of a saint; such acclaim was too much for the woman, who apparently went mad a year later. The celebrations of Catholic Parisians would prove to be short-lived. Henri of Bourbon, now Henri IV, would prove to be a much stronger king than Henri III. Several years later, Henri would convert to Catholicism in an obvious ploy to gain Paris and proclaim the Edict of Nantes, granting religious freedom to Protestants. Henri IV ruled until he too was assassinated in 1610.

RESOURCE: *Les régicides: Clément, Revaillac, Damiens* by Pierre Chevallier (Paris, 1989).

COHEN, Yehoshua (1922–1986), a Jewish activist, assassinated the diplomat Count Folke Bernadotte (1895–1948), nephew of Gustav V of Sweden and the United Nations representative in the new state of Israel. On September 17, 1948, Bernadotte arrived in Israel charged with an important task but one that was considered virtually hopeless: imposing a cease-fire agreement and negotiating a peace treaty between the Palestinians and the Jews. Since being founded with such great hopes at the conclusion of the Second World War, the UN had come to seem almost impotent, what with its failure to stop the arms race between the United States and NATO on the one hand and the Soviet Union and the Warsaw Pact on the other. Yet the UN still harboured hopes of being able to impose a peace or negotiate a settlement between smaller powers; dealing with the volatile situation in the Middle East would be a test of its utility. While being driven from the airport in Jerusalem, Bernadotte was shot at by an Arab gunman, who fired only one bullet, which passed through the car's fender: an omen of shootings yet to come.

Bernadotte had been sent because of his excellent reputation in Israel; during the Holocaust, as chairman of the Swedish Red Cross, he saved an estimated twenty-thousand inmates of Nazi camps. His work in the Middle East, however, seemed to be supportive of Britain's position there, which was essentially pro-Arab. His challenge was that the Israelis intended to occupy all land between the Nile and the Euphrates, a goal that conflicted with the Arab aim of pushing the Israelis back to the sea. Bernadotte bravely, or foolishly, rejected the notion of extra security for himself, on the grounds that he wished no greater level of protection than the UN peacekeepers whom he wished to bring into the region. An attack on him seemed inevitable. Indeed, he did not live out a full day in Israel. At just past 5:00 p.m., less than seven hours after his arrival, Bernadotte's car was stopped by a Jeep parked sideways across the road in the Jewish portion of Jerusalem. The Jeep was occupied by four men wearing Israeli army uniforms, three of whom jumped out and opened fire on Bernadotte's car with Schmiesser machine guns. While one of the squad remained behind as getaway driver, two others perforated the tires and body with bullets and the fourth fired through an open window, killing Bernadotte and his French aide-de-camp, André Serot.

Major world powers accused one another of sponsoring the attack, the Soviets declaring that Bernadotte had been shot by British secret service agents, the United States accusing the Soviets of smuggling the assassins into Israel among a planeload of Czechoslovakian Jews days before the incident. The UN believed that the shooting was the responsibility of the government of Israel, while Sweden believed that their Bernadotte had been killed by Zionist terrorists. Responsibility for Bernadotte's assassination had been claimed by a previously unknown group calling itself Hazit Hamoledeth (Fatherland Front). In fact, the Swedes were correct. Hazit Hamoledeth was a false name; the assassins were members of Lohmey Heruth Israel (Lehi), otherwise known as the Stern Gang after its founder, Avraham Stern. Lehi was a Zionist terrorist group linked to the assassination of Lord Moyne in 1944. The attack on Bernadotte was led—and the fatal shots fired—by Yehoshua Cohen, known by all Sternists for his intelligence, resourcefulness and marksmanship.

Cohen helped to break the Lehi leader, Yitzhak Shamir, out of a British prison in Palestine in 1942, after the British clamped down on the Sternists and arrested almost the entire group. Before Shamir escaped, the seventeen-year-old Cohen, already underground after the British put a price on his head, was the highest-ranking Lehi member not in custody. He had also trained the operatives who assassinated Moyne.

In 1948, a low point for the Sternists, an arms cache exploded accidentally, effectively disarming the band. Since coming into being in 1947, the Israeli government had been pressing the Sternists to dissolve. With morale at its lowest point, Cohen believed that he needed to perform an act that would rally his fellow Sternists. Recruiting a reliable team, he obtained Bernadotte's travel plans from a double agent known as "Nimry" (Leopard), who later claimed that the itinerary he turned over was a false one. But Bernadotte had changed his own plans and inadvertently placed himself in danger. Cohen also secured the Jeep and uniforms. He was never apprehended or charged in the Bernadotte assassination, although many Sternists knew what his role had been. Cohen retired to found a kibbutz in the Negev desert, the one to which David Ben-Gurion, the former prime minister, retired in 1956. Only in 1988, two years after Cohen's death, was the truth revealed when the two remaining conspirators broke their silence on live television and named Cohen as the chief assassin.

RESOURCES: *Bernadotte in Palestine, 1948: A Study in Contemporary Knight-Errantry* by Amitzur Ilan (New York, 1989); *A Death in Jerusalem: The Assassination by Jewish Extremists of the First Arab/Israeli Peacemaker* by Kati Marton (New York, 1994).

COLLAZO, Oscar (1915–1994), was a Puerto Rican nationalist who, along with Griselio Torresola (1927–1950), attempted to murder US president Harry S. Truman (1884–1972). A metal polisher by trade, Collazo was a happily married man and the father of two children and stepfather of others (or rather a bigamist, because his divorce from his first wife was never finalized). He moved from Puerto Rico to New York City in 1932. He was self-educated. He met new arrivals from Puerto Rico and helped to educate them on life in America in general and New York in particular. He had been a member of the Puerto Rican Nationalist Party since the 1930s and an associate of its leader, Albizu Campos. Upset by the slow pace of the movements towards self-rule for his country, Campos was planning an uprising in Puerto Rico for October 28, 1950. To publicize the fact that Puerto Rico was an American possession and deserving of its independence, Collazo, along with his friend and fellow nationalist Torresola, decided to attempt to kill Truman. They had no real animosity towards Truman, who in fact had been slowly advancing the cause of self-rule, but they felt, nonetheless, that assassination of the president, unlike an attack on the governor's mansion in San Juan, would be necessary. Collazo had never fired a gun in his life, but Torresola, who had been purchasing weapons for the uprising, instructed Collazo on how to use a pistol. The two men also purchased new pinstriped suits for their trip to Washington, DC. In 1950, Truman was not living in the White House, which was undergoing renovations, but rather at Blair House, a guest residence nearby. Although security measures were in place, including at least twenty armed guards, Truman was much more vulnerable at Blair House than he would have been at the Executive Mansion.

On October 30, Collazo and Torresola arrived in Washington and checked into a downtown hotel separately and under assumed names. They later hailed a taxi and took a tour of the city, instructing the driver to show them Blair House. Truman's bedroom was on the second floor facing the street. He was so vulnerable that a grenade tossed from the pavement would have killed him easily. But neither man knew exactly where the president slept. Their plan, such as it was, was to overwhelm the guards outside and then burst into Blair House, find the president and shoot him. On November 1, Collazo approached the front entrance, pulled out a Walther P-38 automatic pistol, pointed it at the guard stationed at the door and pulled the trigger. Nothing happened. Collazo had forgotten to take off the safety. The guard, Donald Birdzell, moved towards Collazo, who finally discharged his weapon. But his shot was low, hitting Birdzell in the knee. Birdzell crawled away from the building, in order to draw fire away from the president. At that point, other guards began firing at Collazo, who got off several more rounds but struck nothing. The guards meanwhile hit Collazo several times, once in the chest. Torresola then approached the sentry box at the other side of the building, where he shot and killed the guard, Leslie William Cofflet (1910–1950), at close range. Before he fell, Cofflet shot Torresola in the head, killing him instantly. Truman, who had been napping before the shooting started, moved to the window to see what was happening before horrified Secret Service agents quickly ushered him away. The entire exchange lasted less than a minute.

Collazo survived his wounds and stood trial. In a reversal of the usual procedure in trials of this sort, the prosecution seemed intent on proving that Collazo was insane. Collazo, reasoning that an insanity plea was a way of downplaying the cause of Puerto Rican nationalism, refused to accept such a plea and outlined his cause in his trial. He was found guilty and was sentenced to be executed, but Truman, without comment, commuted his sentence to life imprisonment. Collazo was imprisoned until 1979, when President Jimmy Carter pardoned him as well as a group of Puerto Rican nationalists that had opened fire inside Congress in 1954. Collazo returned to Puerto Rico, where he died in 1994.

RESOURCE: *Assassination: The Politics of Murder* by Linda Laucella (Los Angeles, 1998).

CONRADI, Maurice (1896–1947), assassinated Vatslav Vorovsky (1871– 1923), a Soviet diplomat, on May 10, 1923, while the victim was dining at the Cecil Hotel in Lausanne. Vorovsky was in Switzerland to attend a peace conference on the Near East. With him at the table were his private secretary, Maxim Divilkovsky, and his press chief, Jan Arens. As they ate, they noticed a young man at a corner table, drinking heavily, chain-smoking and talking to himself. At 9:10 p.m., the man they observed, Maurice Conradi, stood up and approached the Soviets' table. Producing a revolver, Conradi shouted "That's for the communists" and shot Vorovsky through the head at close range. The bullet, which had been filed down to shatter on impact, pierced the diplomat's brain; Vorovsky was dead before his head struck the table. Conradi then fired a second shot to frighten the other two officials, but Arens leapt from his seat and tried to overturn the table to create a shield. Conradi shot Arens twice, hitting him in the stomach and shoulder. When Divilkovsky attempted to stop him, Conradi shot him twice as well. After the incident, Conradi was in high spirits, calmly walking into the ballroom next door requesting the band play "Åsa's Death" by Grieg. When he was told that Vorovsky was dead but his companions had only been wounded, Conradi said that Vorovsky had been his sole target and that he would not have shot the other two if they hadn't resisted. Police arrived twenty minutes later, and Conradi surrendered without a struggle. As he was led away, he apologized to the hotel management for any inconvenience.

Conradi was born of Swiss parents in St. Petersburg. His family owned a candy and gelatin factory in Russia, and his upbringing was a moneyed one. He received a private-school education and was studying chemical engineering when war broke out in 1914. Being of Swiss extraction, Conradi was exempt from military service; nevertheless he volunteered for the Russian army, serving with distinction and winning several decorations including the Cross of St. George. After the Bolshevik Revolution in November 1917, he joined a White Russian army led by Colonel Mikhail Drozdovsky. The "Drozdovsty," as they were called, became famous for their nomadic existence. Travelling over 1200 kilometres through southern Russia, the group fought Austrians, Ukrainians and the Red Army. After defeat forced the remnants of the Drozdovsty out of Sevastapol, Conradi decided to take advantage of his parents' citizenship and went to Switzerland. Although fanatically anti-Bolshevik and somewhat anti-Semitic, Conradi belonged to no organized political groups, even though there were many political societies that would have welcomed someone with his background and beliefs.

In 1922, Conradi decided that he must assassinate a Soviet official, but his financial situation was so dire that he could not afford to journey anywhere where a Soviet official could be found. Purchasing a pistol also proved difficult. Conradi's salvation came from a former White Army officer, Arcadius Polunin, who thought highly of the young war hero and approved of his plan. Polunin supplied Conradi with the means to buy a pistol as well as expense money.

After Conradi was questioned, Polunin was also arrested for his involvement in the assassination. Their trial quickly turned into a circus. The defence moved the emphasis of the trial from an investigation of a murder to an examination of Soviet atrocities. Over the objection of the prosecution, outlandish statements were entered into the record, such as an allegation that the Soviet Union had nationalized all of its women. Under the laws of the time, the jury was composed of nine men. A guilty verdict could be returned if at least six of them found Conradi guilty of murder. Only five of the jurors felt the prisoners were guilty and so both Conradi and Polunin were freed. The prosecution, realizing that emotions, both within the courtroom and without, ran high in favour of the accused, declined to appeal. The Soviet Union was outraged by the verdict, describing it as an indication of an open season on Russian officials. The USSR reduced its diplomatic contingent in Switzerland to a bare minimum and Soviet-Swiss relations were strained for many years.

Conradi enjoyed a brief period of celebrity following the trial. In time, however, his drinking problem grew out of hand. He eventually joined the French Foreign Legion and then retired to Andeer, where he died penniless and nearly forgotten in 1947. Polunin left Switzerland immediately after the trial. He wound up in Paris in the service of Felix Youssoupov, the assassin of Rasputin.

RESOURCE: *Assassination in Switzerland: The Murder of Vatslav Vorovsky* by Alfred Erich Senn (London, 1981).

CORDAY, Charlotte (1768–1793), born Marianne Charlotte de Corday d'Armont, the assassin of the French revolutionary journalist Jean-Paul Marat (1743–1793), spent several years in a nunnery and was expecting to take her vows when such religious institutions were closed after the outbreak of the Revolution in 1789. In the aftermath of the Revolution, a power struggle began between the moderate Girondists, of whom Corday became a supporter, and the radical Jacobins. After the execution of Louis XVI in January 1793, Marat began to gather intelligence on the Girondists, leading to the group's downfall and persecution. Believing Marat the source of all the discord in post-revolutionary France, Corday resolved to kill him, feeling that whoever did so would be acting justly and would be seen as a hero. A studious woman, she was heavily influenced by accounts of Julius Caesar's assassination as well as by the biblical story of Judith, who, in the Book of Judith in the Apocrypha, saves the Jewish city of Bethulia by killing Holofernes, the general who besieged it.

On July 13, 1793, Corday, wearing her best frock, arrived at Marat's home in Paris claiming that she had vital information on Girondist activity in Normandy. Marat's servants tried to deny her access as Marat was taking one of the warm baths he used to alleviate an ulcerous skin condition (contracted during the revolutionary violence when he had been forced to hide in the Parisian sewers). Hearing the uproar, however, Marat asked that Corday be admitted to his bathroom, where he often received visitors and which in fact he used as his second office. Corday passed a few minutes answering Marat's questions about Girondist activity before suddenly producing a knife and stabbing him in the heart. Marat died within seconds. Corday probably believed that she herself would then be killed instantly, for inside her dress, near where she had concealed the weapon, she pinned a note addressed to the French people. In fact,

Corday was arrested without a struggle and swiftly put on trial. On July 19, 1793, she was executed by guillotine.

RESOURCE: *L'affaire Corday–Marat: Prélude à la terreur* by Jean Epois (Les Sables-d'Orlonne, 1980).

CUNANAN, Andrew Philip (a.k.a. Andrew Phillip DeSilva) (1969–1997), an American serial killer who terrorized the gay community, became an assassin when, on July 15, 1997, he shot the famous Italian fashion designer Gianni Versace on the steps of Versace's palazzo in the South Beach section of Miami. Cunanan, a Californian, the youngest child of an unhappy marriage, was an intelligent young hustler, capable of great charm, but also, as time went on, prone to overindulgence in pornography and violence. In San Diego on April 17, 1997, he killed Jeffrey Trail, a gay naval officer his own age whom he had known since 1992. Cunanan's weapon was a relatively unusual handgun, a .40-calibre Taurus Model PT-100. He murdered next on April 29; the victim was David Madson, an architect, killed near Minneapolis; again on May 3, when he shot Lee Miglin, a seventy-three-year-old Chicago real estate millionaire; and yet again on May 9, when he killed William Reese, the forty-five-year-old assistant curator of a Civil War cemetery in a remote part of New Jersey, by shooting him in the back of the skull while the victim knelt. By this time, a national manhunt for Cunanan was underway. Indeed, he had become one of the FBI's ten most-wanted fugitives.

Having completed his west-to-east drive across America, Cunanan turned south, towards Florida. Versace was about to unlock the front door of his home on Ocean Drive when Cunanan, wearing a tank top, shorts and a baseball cap, walked up to him and shot him from arm's-length. Nine days later, Cunanan was finally tracked to a Miami houseboat, where he committed suicide with his weapon rather than be taken alive.

RESOURCES: *Vulgar Flavors: Andrew Cunanan, Gianni Versace, and the Largest Failed Manhunt in U.S. History* by Maureen Orth (New York, 1999); *Three Month Fever: The Andrew Cunanan Story* by Gary Indiana (New York, 1999); *Undressed: The Life and Times of Gianni Versace* by Christopher Mason (New York, 1999).

CURRY, Izola (b. 1916), attempted to murder the American civil rights leader Dr. Martin Luther King (1929–1968) on September 20, 1958, when King was making an appearance at L. M. Blumstein, a department store in Harlem in New York City, to autograph copies of his first book, *Stride Toward Freedom*. As King was signing books and meeting with supporters, he was approached by Curry. She asked, "Are you Martin Luther King?" When King responded in the affirmative, she produced a steel letter opener, saying, "I've been looking for you for five years," and promptly stabbed him in the chest. Curry was apprehended immediately by store security, who found that she was carrying an automatic pistol. The letter-opener was sticking out of King's chest directly over the heart. Because of its position, the weapon was not removed until King could be taken to hospital, where a surgeon, Dr. Aubrey Maynard, discovered that its tip was resting against King's aorta. After performing the necessary surgery, Dr. Maynard declared that if King had so much as sneezed he would have bled to death within minutes. As it was, two of King's ribs had to be removed during the four-hour operation. King recovered after several weeks' rest.

Izola Curry was charged with felonious assault and possession of a firearm. At her hearing, she announced that she was charging King with "being mixed up with communists." She said, "I've reported the case to the FBI and it's being looked into." She also explained that she had stabbed King so that he would "listen to my problems, because I've been followed in buses and people have been making me lose my job." Basing his ruling partially on these statements, the judge ordered that Curry be taken to Bellevue Hospital for psychiatric assessment. She was found to be insane and was committed to the Matteawan State Hospital for the Criminally Insane. Several months after his recovery, King, while speaking in Memphis, read a letter that had been sent to him shortly after the attack: "Dear Dr. King, I am a ninth-grade student, and while it should not matter, I would like to mention that I am a white girl. I read in the paper of your misfortune and suffering. And I read that if you had sneezed you would have died. And I am simply writing you to say that I'm so happy you didn't sneeze!" King declared that he was happy he didn't sneeze as well.

Dr. Maynard, while finishing King's surgery, realized that it would be a simple matter for him to make King's scar resemble a cross. Because King was an ordained Baptist minister, Maynard thought the shape appropriate. After King's assassination in 1968, the autopsy showed that

King had a cross-shaped scar over his heart. To many of King's followers this was seen as a divine sign, but in fact it was a souvenir of the attempt on his life a decade earlier.

RESOURCE: *Symbols, the News Magazines, and Martin Luther King* by Richard Lentz (Baton Rouge, Louisiana, 1990).

CZOLGOSZ, Leon F. (1873–1901), fatally shot US president William McKinley on September 6, 1901, while the chief executive was attending, for the second day, the Pan American Exposition at Buffalo, New York. The president's guards were anxious about the size and enthusiastic volatility of the crowds. The presidential party entered the Temple of Music on the fairgrounds, followed by the other concert-goers, whom the authorities had shuffled into single file. McKinley, seated on a dais, shook the hand of each, as in a receiving line. Seven minutes into the process, while the orchestra played a Bach sonata as background, McKinley took the right hand of Czolgosz, who then, with his left, fired two shots from a short-barrelled revolver concealed in a white handkerchief, which caught fire in the process. Both bullets struck their target, who was taken by motorized ambulance to a makeshift hospital and operating room elsewhere on the grounds, which featured one of the first X-ray machines; but it was felt that the president's wounds were not serious enough to warrant using such an experimental device. After surgery, McKinley stayed at the home of John Milburn, president of the exposition.

Within moments, details of the crime had been flashed to newspapers nationwide by the Associated Press. When word of the tragedy reached the White House, a death-watch assembled spontaneously; it included Thomas Pendel, an aide who had experienced the sensation twice before, when he was part of the White House team awaiting word of James A. Garfield's fate in 1881 and a generation earlier, in 1865, when he was the first person at the Executive Mansion to hear the news of Abraham Lincoln's death.

Early reports were virtually unanimous in condemning Czolgosz, a clean-shaven and handsome young man, as a dark-hued foreign-born anarchist, motivated by madness and the prevailing anarchist peril. In fact, Czolgosz was born in Detroit, the fourth child in a family of ten. His mother died when he was twelve. His first job was working in a bottle factory when he was sixteen. He later found a better position in a wire

ASSASSINS A TO Z

mill, the scene of a bitter strike in 1893 that led him to become involved in radical politics. He was identified as a potential troublemaker, and so to regain his job after the strike he assumed the name Fred Neiman (translated "No Man").

In 1898, Czolgosz, a depressive, suffered a nervous breakdown, and retreated to the family farm near Cleveland, only a short distance from Canton, McKinley's hometown and official residence. In 1900, Czolgosz became obsessed with the assassination of Umberto I of Italy, collecting, reading and re-reading newspaper clippings of the event. As Fred Neiman, he contacted an anarchist club in Cleveland. His constant questioning of other members on proposed or imagined assassination plans led the local anarchist newspaper to publish a warning about him, suggesting that he was an infiltrator and possibly a government agent. On May 5, 1901, Czolgosz attended a lecture by Emma Goldman and later, in July, called on her in Chicago; Goldman was either suspicious of Czolgosz or simply unimpressed by him. Nevertheless, when she returned to her home in Rochester, Czolgosz followed her, and eventually settled in West Seneca, roughly midway between Rochester and Buffalo.

On August 31, he arrived in Buffalo, rented a room under the name John Doe and waited for McKinley to arrive in the city; on September 2, he purchased a .32-calibre revolver for $4.50. McKinley addressed a crowd of over fifty thousand, including Leon Czolgosz, three days later. Czolgosz planned to shoot him that day, but he found he was unable to get close enough. He then followed the president to Niagara Falls, where again he could not get a clear shot. McKinley's return to the fair in Buffalo would be Czolgosz's last chance. The first shot ricocheted off McKinley's breastbone and fell to the ground; the second entered the stomach, pierced the pancreas and one kidney and lodged in the back muscle wall. Czolgosz was immediately swarmed by guards. McKinley's immediate concern seemed to be for Czolgosz's well-being. His last statement in public was, "Don't let them hurt him." After a slight recovery, McKinley fell prey to gangrenous blood poisoning, dying in the early morning hours of September 14, his last words being "Goodbye—goodbye all." A forest ranger in the Adirondack Mountains had to track down the vice-president, Theodore Roosevelt, to tell him that he was now the commander-in-chief.

A lunacy commission pronounced Czolgosz fit to stand trial and he entered a guilty plea, which was rejected on the grounds that the laws of New York State at that time only allowed the death penalty for those who pleaded not guilty. Psychiatrists who examined him reported that Czolgosz said, "I don't believe in the republican form of government and I don't believe we should have any rulers. It is right to kill them.... I fully understood what I was doing [and] am willing to take the consequences." The trial lasted less than two days and the jury deliberated only thirty-four minutes before finding him guilty. He died by electrocution at 7:12 a.m. on October 29, less than two months after the crime. His last words were: "I killed the president because he was an enemy of the people—the good, working people. I am not sorry for my crime." Before Czolgosz was buried, authorities poured sulphuric acid into his coffin to dissolve his body. His tenuous connection to anarchism, the movement which in fact had shunned him, led Congress, in 1903, to enact a new law barring anarchists from the United States. Later, following the Great War, foreign-born American anarchists, such as Goldman and Alexander Berkman, were deported to Russia even though they were American citizens.

RESOURCES: *Assassination in America* by James McKinley (no relation) (New York, 1975); *American 1900: The Turning Point* by Judy Crichton (New York, 1998).

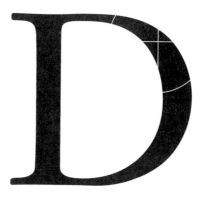

DAHLGREN, Ulric (1843–1864), a Union cavalry officer, altered the tone of the American Civil War in March 1864 by leading what is known to history as the Dahlgren Plot, a scheme to raid Richmond and assassinate the Southern president, Jefferson Davis, and his entire cabinet, as well as to free thousands of Union troops held as prisoners of war. Dahlgren, one of the youngest officers in the army to attain the rank of colonel, was the son of Admiral John A. Dahlgren, an ordnance expert after whom a type of cannon, the Dahlgren gun, is named. The younger Dahlgren, whose family were friends of Abraham Lincoln, had already lost a leg in the war. In the bungled terrorist operation, he lost his life. Confederate soldiers searching his body found written orders concerning the assassinations. The Southern high command was furious. General Robert E. Lee's response was: "The blood boils with indignation in the veins of every officer and man as they read the account of [Dahlgren's] barbarous and inhuman plot." In response, Davis authorized his secret service to rob banks, commit arson and undertake acts of sabotage in the North. The retaliatory campaign was largely unsuccessful, but it may well have created the atmosphere in which the Confederacy condoned the attempted abduction of President Abraham Lincoln, a plan that also failed and so turned into the private assassination plot by John Wilkes Booth.

RESOURCE: *The Dahlgren Affair: Terror and Conspiracy in the Civil War* by Duane Schultz (New York, 1999).

DAMIENS, François (1715–1757), attempted to assassinate Louis XV of France (1710–1774, reigned 1715–1774) on January 5, 1757, as the king and his entourage were preparing to move court from Versailles, which was impossible to heat during the winter, to the much warmer Trianon Palace. As the monarch was about to step into his coach, François

Damiens rushed past the guards and stabbed Louis in the chest with a penknife (one with two folding blades; Damiens used the shorter). At first Louis thought he had been punched, and even when, on looking down, he saw blood beginning to ooze from his coat, believed the wound was superficial. Damiens was seized within seconds of the event by the king's footman. A doctor on the scene was too timid to examine the king thoroughly and therefore ordered Louis to be bled, which of course made matters worse. Convinced now that he was about to die, Louis called for a priest to administer the last rites. He also confessed to his wife all of his marital infidelities. Eventually, the king's personal physician arrived; his quick examination proved that no arteries were severed nor any organ pierced. The doctor concluded that Louis was saved by the fact that he was wearing several layers of clothing against the cold. Fear arose that the blade Damiens had used had been dipped in poison, but swift interrogation of the prisoner showed that this was not the case. Louis rested for a few days, but he was never in any danger.

Damiens, born to a poor family, spent most of his life as a valet in wealthy households. He had a tendency, rare in that age, to change employers every few years; in one case he had been caught stealing from his master, a crime then punishable by death in France. He was also an alcoholic. At one time he had been a servant to a Jesuit institution that had attempted to cure him of his drinking problem; when the Jesuits failed, they released him from their service. Damiens also had a history of mental problems. Relatives' accounts suggest that he suffered from chronic depression. He was also known to bleed himself in a manner that can only be described as compulsive, and he was once committed to a house in Saint-Venant run by the Good Sons, an order that attempted to deal with mental illness.

After his arrest for the attempted assassination, Damiens was tortured extensively, as the authorities believed that he must have had co-conspirators. Their reasoning was based on the idea that a person of low birth would have neither the motive nor the ability to attack the monarch. The torture included the use of the Brodquin, a boot-like device that pulverized the bones in the leg as it was tightened. Under such torture, Damiens made several statements implicating former employers and landlords. He also described the assault as a warning and as the only means he could think of to induce the king to listen to the people rather than "heeding the pernicious advice of his ministers." Damiens was undoubtedly saying what he hoped his tormentors wished to hear. Another reason he gave for his actions was his indignation over his daughter's arrest in Paris during the "Children's Kidnapping Riot" of 1750—a statement that proved completely false as his daughter was in no way involved in that affair.

Judges at Damiens's short trial had two precedents from which to draw when deciding a penalty: the case of Jean Chastel, who had wounded Henri IV in 1594, and that of François Revaillac, who had killed him in 1610. Both were executed in as gruesome a manner as could be devised. The judges concluded that Damiens should be treated no differently. When the sentence was read, Damiens commented, "This day will be a sharp one." He was transported to a scaffold in a dung cart, then stripped and secured to the scaffold with iron shackles. His right arm was plunged into burning sulfur. His screams were reportedly audible for miles. His flesh was then torn from his body with red-hot pincers. A mixture of boiling wax, resin and lead was poured into all of the wounds except for those on his chest. He was then taken down and his limbs were tied to four strong horses that pulled in different directions. But instead of tearing the limbs from his body, the horses stretched them "to an astonishingly prodigious length." The surgeons on duty declared that the only way to properly draw and quarter him would be to sever Damiens's ligaments and tendons. This was done, and eventually one arm and one leg were torn from his body. Damiens was still alive. When the second arm and leg were pulled off, he finally died. His body parts were thrown onto a bonfire and burned for twelve hours, then his ashes were scattered to the wind. Damiens's brother was forced to leave France; his father, wife and daughter were allowed to remain but were forced to change their names to Guillemant. Damiens was the last French prisoner to be eviscerated and quartered.

RESOURCE: *The Damiens Affair and the Unraveling of the Ancien Régime* by Dale K. Van Kley (Princeton, New Jersey, 1984).

DASHEWSKI, Pinhas (1879–1934), a Zionist activist, although the child of an assimilated Jewish family, was outraged by events in Russia in April 1903, when Pavolaki Krushevan initiated the Kishinov pogrom, which saw perhaps fifty Jews murdered, several hundred more seriously injured and much Jewish property destroyed. Either with the endorsement of fellow Zionists in Keyov or acting on his own initiative, Dashewski decided that Krushevan must be punished. Dashewski arrived in St.

Petersburg in May and began to stalk Krushevan. Although he owned a pistol, Dashewski had no faith in his marksmanship and worried that if his hand shook he might shoot a bystander. He therefore decided to use a knife. On June 4, 1903, Dashewski attacked Krushevan and stabbed him in the neck. The wound, however, was little more than superficial. Dashewski immediately turned himself in and admitted that the attack was premeditated. He was sentenced to five years' hard labour but was released in 1906. Dashewski was rearrested after the revolution when he refused to denounce Zionism. He was sent to a Siberian prison where he died.

RESOURCE: *Political Assassinations by Jews: A Rhetorical Device for Justice* by Nachman Ben-Yehuda (Albany, New York, 1993).

DE BREM, Jean (1935–1963), was the assassin of Henri Lafond (1894–1963), chairman of the Banque de l'Union Parisienne. At 10:30 a.m. on March 6, 1963, Lafond had just entered his limousine when de Brem approached the car, pulled open the door and inquired, "Are you Monsieur Lafond?" When Lafond confirmed his identity, de Brem pulled a revolver and shot him twice in the chest. De Brem then turned his attention on Lafond's chauffeur, shooting him twice as well. Finally, de Brem shot Lafond one more time, in the head. Although there were many eyewitnesses, including the chauffeur who survived the shooting, a physical description of the assassin was not obtainable. De Brem wore bright red gloves during the shooting and witnesses could remember little beyond this fact, though one did mention that the shooter walked with a limp. Police concluded that the assassin was Georges Watin, an Organisation de l'armée secrète (OAS) assassin who was still at large. They were correct only to the extent that the killing had in fact been ordered by the infamous OAS.

Lafond had been playing a dangerous game. He was an adviser and friend of Charles de Gaulle, the French president, who had recently presided over the independence of France's former colony of Algeria. Yet Lafond also helped fund the group of white French Algerians (*pied-noirs*), army officers and students determined to assassinate de Gaulle over the Algerian issue. Jean-Marie Bastien-Thiry had led the most serious of these attempts. While Bastien-Thiry was awaiting sentencing for masterminding the most nearly successful of the many attempts on de Gaulle's life, an OAS operative met with Lafond at the latter's country club, insisting that Lafond use his influence with de Gaulle to commute Bastien-Thiry's impending death sentence. Lafond protested that he had no real influence on de Gaulle or the courts. He also reminded the operative that he had been quite helpful towards the OAS in the past, and was therefore taken aback by the intimidating manner of the demand. After a short heated argument, the operative threatened that "if Bastien-Thiry is sentenced to death, you will be shot." While the court was deliberating Bastien-Thiry's fate, the OAS was spying on Lafond's habits and movements. On March 4, 1963, Jean-Marie Bastien-Thiry was convicted and sentenced to death. Jean de Brem, a former second lieutenant in a colonial paratroop regiment, shot Lafond the following day.

De Brem was an idealist who had joined the OAS to protect the rights of white French Algerians. He was also originally recruited to drive one of the cars used in the Petit-Clamart affair, the attempt on de Gaulle's life for which Bastien-Thiry was arrested, but he had declined the mission. When he heard that the assassination attempt on de Gaulle had ended in failure, de Brem felt he deserved a portion of the blame as matters might have been different if he had participated. When he learned that there would be an attempt to intimidate Lafond, he volunteered to assassinate him as a way of making up for his failure at Petit-Clamart. The police never apprehended de Brem, their primary focus being the search for Watin. Yet on April 18, 1963, well over a month after the Bastien-Thiry execution and less than six weeks after the Lafond assassination, Jean de Brem was shot by the authorities. He and a fellow OAS member were in the act of stealing a car when accosted by police. De Brem pulled a revolver and exchanged fire with the officers. He shot and killed one of his adversaries before being shot in the head; he died instantly.

RESOURCE: *Objectif de Gaulle* by Pierre De Maret and Christian Plume (Paris, 1973).

DHANU (1970?–1991) assassinated Rajiv Gandhi (1944–1991), former prime minister of India, on May 21, 1991, while Gandhi made a late-night appearance at a rally near Madras when campaigning for the Congress (I) Party. Before his address to the crowd, Gandhi stopped to receive accolades from a crowd of female supporters. While Gandhi was receiving garlands from the women, Dhanu placed a sandalwood garland around the politician's neck, knelt at his feet, looked up at him while smiling and then exploded. Dhanu was wearing a denim girdle loaded with eight separate bombs packed with eighty grams of C4-RDX explosive and twenty-eight hundred 2-mm steel pellets. Although only six of the bombs actually went off, the force of the blast literally blew off Gandhi's face. The explosion also tore Dhanu's limbs and head from her body. In all, over a dozen people were killed when Dhanu, "the Human Bomb," as the press dubbed her, triggered the devices.

Dhanu was a member of the Liberation Tigers of Tamil Eelam (LTTE), also known as the Tamil Tigers. The LTTE had been fighting to secure a homeland in Sri Lanka. They are descended from Tamils who had been transported to the island by the British during India's colonial period and represent a Hindu minority in a nation dominated by Buddhist Sinhalese. During the administration of Gandhi's mother, Indira Gandhi, the Tamil Tigers, while never having the official support of the Indian government, were left alone to pursue their goal of a home-land on the north end of Sri Lanka. With the election of Rajiv Gandhi after his mother's assassination in 1984, such tolerance came to an end. Rajiv took a hard-line anti-Tamil stand, sending thousands of Indian "peacekeepers" to Sri Lanka. The LTTE army in Sri Lanka was decimated at a cost of thousands of Indian soldiers.

In 1989, a series of scandals brought down Gandhi's government. When its successor fell in 1991 and an election was called, Gandhi tried to regain his previous position. Realizing that once Gandhi returned to power, as all the polls suggested he would, his security would be so tight that assassination would be difficult, the LTTE leader, Villupillai Prabhakaran, dispatched four teams of Tamil Tigers to plan, arrange and carry out the act. The actual job of killing Gandhi was assigned to an agent named Sivarasan. Sivarasan's team consisted of himself, two photographers to film the assassination (photographing terrorist events being a trademark of the LTTE) and his cousins, Dhanu and Subha. Subha was on hand to back up Dhanu if for any reason she could not accomplish the task. An electronics expert designed the bomb belt. In a plan that was apparently lifted from the pages of Frederick Forsyth's novel *The Negotiator*, Dhanu was fitted with the bomb, over which she wore a salwar-kameez, a shape-less long shirt, which disguised the presence of the explosives.

Dhanu was willing to die for her cause. She had been raped by Indian soldiers during the occupation of Sri Lanka, a crime that led to her involvement with the LTTE. Before becoming a human bomb, she had been an assistant to Akila, head of the Women's Intelligence wing of the LTTE. On a dry run, the Tamils tested their ability to get close enough by attending a rally for Prime Minister V.P. Singh. When they encountered no difficulties, they were sure that their plan would not fail.

The explosion that killed Gandhi and Dhanu also killed one of the LTTE photographers. His camera, with ten photos of the events leading up to the assassination, was recovered by police. Identifying Sivarasan, who had escaped the scene with Subha, police began rounding up the Tamils responsible. Sivarasan's safe house was discovered and surrounded. Rather than give himself up, Sivarasan shot Subha and himself in the head. Many of the other conspirators took cyanide rather than be apprehended. Nevertheless, some twenty-six Tamils were arrested for participating in the assassination plans in one way or another. After a lengthy investigation and trial, all were condemned to death. On appeal to the Indian supreme court, nineteen were released and three had their sentences commuted to life imprisonment. But four were executed.

RESOURCES: *Assassination of Rajiv Gandhi* by Shashi Ahluwalia (Delhi, 1991); *Rajiv Gandhi's Assassination: A Blow to Democracy*, ed. K.L. Chanchreek (Delhi, 1991); *The Report of the Jain Commission into the Assassination of Rajiv Gandhi* (Delhi, 1991).

DIAZ, Juan Thomàs (1905–1961), was leader of the conspiracy to assassinate Rafael Leónidas Trujillo (1891–1961), president of the Dominican Republic. On the evening of May 30, 1961, Trujillo set off from Santo Domingo by automobile, intending to meet with one of his many mistresses at his farm near Ciudad Trujillo. Such occasions were the only ones on which he was known to travel without bodyguards. Instead, he carried a submachine gun by his side and his chauffeur was armed as well (although not trained in the use of his weapon). Just outside the capital, Trujillo's car was approached by two black Chevrolets. One of the seven occupants of the first car opened fire with a 12-gauge shotgun as the second car cut in front of Trujillo's driver, forcing the presidential vehicle to pull over to the side, in front of a third car that was blocking the road. Trujillo, who had been shot in the side in the opening salvo, ordered his chauffeur to leave the car and return fire. The chauffeur managed to wound two of the attackers before being shot five times (miraculously, he survived). Trujillo also left the car, but he was wounded so badly that he was unable to stand. Leaning over one of the car's fenders, Trujillo continued to fire on the assassins until he was cut down with more than twenty-seven bullets in his body. The attackers then repeatedly kicked the lifeless corpse and ripped one of the dictator's arms from its socket. The body was placed in the trunk of one of the attack cars. A search of the presidential limousine revealed a briefcase containing US$300,000. Taking the money, the attackers sped off.

The conspiracy to kill Trujillo probably involved more than twenty people. The leader of the group was Juan Thomàs Diaz, who descended from an old military family. After a short career in the civil service, Diaz joined the Dominican army in 1932 and quickly moved up in rank until he was a general. President Trujillo, who was despotic and cruel, used the country's secret police force, the SIM, as his own private army, and the Dominican economy as his source of income. By such methods he amassed a personal fortune in excess of US$800 million. He ruled through fear, and his abusive, bullying behaviour was as likely to be used on his friends as on his enemies. Trujillo publicly humiliated Diaz, beating him several times with his riding crop and stripping him of his rank. Some accounts say that Trujillo was furious with Diaz when he learned that Diaz had refused to torture captured insurgents. Other accounts speak of a personal matter concerning Diaz's sister, who had fled the country after attracting the dictator's attention. Most of the men implicated in the plot had once been close to the dictator. Diaz's cousin Modesto Diaz had run afoul of Trujillo when it was learned that Modesto had been acting sadistically, raping women at will and seizing others' property in Trujillo's name without approval (and without cutting in Trujillo on the spoils). The fact that a large group of fairly well-connected individuals were attempting to assassinate Trujillo was known to many Dominicans, but nobody informed on the plotters.

Although Juan Thomàs Diaz would not participate in the assassination itself, he was in charge of the attempt—and of the attempt afterward to survive. He purchased three automobiles for the ambush. Realizing that he would need cars fast enough to overtake Trujillo, he imported a mechanic from Spain who rebuilt the engines until the cars could easily travel at speeds over two hundred kilometres an hour. He also began to discuss with General José Romàn, secretary of state for the armed forces, the question of what to do with the SIM after the assassination. Romàn, who had no objections to killing Trujillo, in spite of the fact that his wife was Trujillo's niece, was concerned about moving against the dictator if the assassination failed. In the end, he promised to use the army to disarm the SIM, but only after he had personally seen Trujillo's corpse. The plan was that the body would be delivered to Diaz, who would show it to Romàn. But the assassins never took Trujillo's body to Romàn, a mistake that led to their downfall. By the time one of the assassins thought at least to tell Romàn that Trujillo had been killed, Romàn was already in the custody of the SIM, which soon picked up other conspirators as well. The agency also took the precaution of arresting friends and family of the accused. All men (women and children were mostly excluded), even those with no knowledge of the plot, were indiscriminately tortured, being stripped naked, beaten with clubs and pistols and shocked in the electric chair. Two prisoners were humiliated when a homosexual was brought in to force them into sexual activities, which were photographed. Every so often, Trujillo's son, Rhamadamès Trujillo, along with his friends, would come to the prison and beat the prisoners with riding crops, apply electrodes to their genitals and throw itching powder and red ants into their wounds. Diaz, who had been in hiding, was spotted at a restaurant. The assassin chief tried to escape but was eventually surrounded by more than a hundred SIM agents and killed in a gun battle outside a hardware store on Parque Independcia.

One of the few members of the conspiracy actually to be tried for his involvement was General Romàn. Because of his position, he was not tortured, except by means of sleep deprivation, but a court martial sentenced him to thirty years' imprisonment. He did not serve his sentence, for Trujillo's son Ramfis took charge of the prisoner after the trial and beat and tortured him constantly. When he tired of this, Ramfis ordered Romàn tied up and placed in the trunk of his car. Ramfis then drove Romàn to the Trujillo home, where he took the general to his firing range and showed him his father's gun. Trujillo's pistol was known throughout the Dominican Republic: a .357 Magnum mounted on a .44 frame. Starting at Romàn's feet and working his way up the body slowly, Ramfis shot the general fifty-three times, stopping on eight occasions to reload. The body was then placed in a burlap sack, which several dozen officers present were forced to stab. The body was taken to La Piscina, a favourite seaside dumping spot of the SIM, where it was thrown to the sharks. Eventually, without Trujillo's iron fist, the remaining Trujillistas were forced to leave the country. Today, a plaque marks the spot where Trujillo was assassinated. The simple inscription reads: "Gloria a la Gesta Liberatadora del 30 de Mayo."

RESOURCE: *Overtaken by Events: The Dominican Crisis from the Fall of Trujillo to the Civil War* by John Bartlow Martin (Garden City, New York, 1966).

DIMAHILIG, Carlito (1945–1972), attempted to assassinate Imelda Marcos (b. 1928), first lady of the Philippines, on December 7, 1972, when Mrs. Marcos was attending an awards ceremony in Manila. The awards were part of her National Beautification and Cleanliness contest. At the open-air ceremony, which was broadcast on live TV, one of the recipients, Carlito Dimahilig, left the lineup of prize recipients and attacked Mrs. Marcos with a bolo knife. Although the victim claimed that she had never received any martial arts training, her response to the attack mirrored a standard martial arts defence move: she folded her arms across her chest, covering her vital organs. Dimahilig slashed repeatedly at Marcos's arms, finally causing Marcos to fall backwards across a table, from which position she attempted to ward further blows using one of her many pairs of shoes. Congressman José Aspitas and Linda Amor Robles, secretary of the beautification campaign, then grappled with the assassin, only to suffer lacerations themselves. After what must have seemed an eternity, armed security guards, who had been standing well away from Marcos, began firing. Dimahilig died on the spot with two bullets in his back. Marcos was flown out by helicopter to a nearby hospital. The slash wounds on her arms required over seventy stitches. She also suffered tendon damage that would require further surgery.

Dimahilig was a geodetic engineer from Sinisian, a village about eighty kilometres from Manila. Acquaintances described him as quiet and shy; most who have written or spoken of the incident say that they believe his true target was the president, Ferdinand Marcos (1917–1989), who had suspended the constitution and imposed martial law less than three months earlier since which time he had been in seclusion. Hiding in the palace, he chose to send the first lady to public appearances in his stead. Others allege a conspiracy involving the president himself. Much is made of the fact that the usual security forces, under the command of a long-time Marcos loyalist, had been moved deliberately to the wings and were not in position to react quickly when the attack came. Opponents of the conspiracy theory point out that security did not want to be filmed by the TV cameras. Examination of the film, which was broadcast time and again on Philippines television over the next several days, showed the assassin appear to look over his shoulder before attacking, as though waiting for a signal, but the glance was not susceptible to conclusive evaluation.

Imelda Marcos recovered quickly from her attack, but wore her arm in a sling for many months—to gain sympathy, said her detractors. For normal daywear, she favoured a sling made entirely out of gold chain. For more formal occasions, such as the inauguration ball for Richard Nixon that she attended six weeks after the attack, she wore a sling encrusted with pearls.

RESOURCE: *The Rise and Fall of Imelda Marcos* by Carmen Navarro Pedrosa (Manila, 1987).

DINGANE (1795?–1840) assassinated Shaka (1788?–1828), king of the Zulus. When Shaka inherited the Zulu kingdom, Africans said, a person could walk from one end of it to the other in less than two hours; by the time Shaka died, the kingdom was the continent's largest, encompassing much of what is now South Africa. His ruthlessness in enforcing military discipline created a force that was widely feared and deadly in its efficiency. For example, soldiers carried large shields that could be used as weapons as well as for defence, and short *assagai* (spears), designed primarily for stabbing, replaced longer, lighter ones. But the factors that earned Shaka the nickname "Africa's Napoleon" were based on his personal fearlessness, as displayed in battles in which many of the tribes surrounding the Zulus were broken. Shaka ensured that there were few survivors and that those few became landless and nomadic and, ultimately, the victims of famine and chaos. Cattle, the source of wealth and prosperity for most tribes in the region, were slaughtered systematically.

Europeans who encountered Shaka were impressed by his intelligence, his size (estimates suggest he was nearly two metres tall and weighed in excess of a hundred kilos) and his desire to know more of the ways of Africa's foreign invaders. Shaka believed that if groups of his younger soldiers learned European military tactics, and his troops generally became familiar with European weapons, he would become invincible. Yet, however much he impressed Europeans, Shaka distressed many of his fellow Zulus with his legendary bad temper, which led to senseless massacres. On one occasion, when one of his armies was late sending reports of its progress, Shaka ordered all of the wives of those in the field to be arrested and randomly put to death. When his mother died in 1827, Shaka ordered executions throughout the kingdom so that all could share in his sense of loss.

The plot against Shaka was hatched by Shaka's aunt, Mkabayi, who was convinced that Shaka had actually poisoned his mother, her sister. Mkabayi soon brought Shaka's half-brothers, Dingane and Mhlangana, along with Shaka's head domestic servant, Mbopa, into the conspiracy. Shaka ordered his troops to advance to the north and sent Dingane and Mhlangana to accompany them. After marching two hours, Dingane and Mhlangana feigned illness and returned to Dukuza, Shaka's kraal. On September 22, 1828, Shaka received a delegation from the amaMpondo who bore a gift of crane feathers and otter skins. Shaka was displeased with the visitors for arriving late and met them in a filthy stockyard as a sign of his disrespect. He was accompanied by Mbopa, who had a stabbing *assagai* concealed in his clothing. Dingane and Mhlangana were hiding behind a fence watching their target. As Shaka berated the amaMpondo for tardiness, Dingane signalled to Mbopa to get rid of the emissaries. Mbopa shocked the Zulu king when he grabbed a club and drove off the amaMpondo, shouting and swearing at them. Dingane and Mhlangana then emerged from their hiding place and ran Shaka through with their *assagais*. Shaka is reputed to have said, "Children of my father, what is wrong?" before falling dead at his half-brothers' feet.

Shaka had no heir. Indeed, women carrying his child were customarily killed, because of his worries about potential rivals. The only reason that his half-brothers themselves hadn't been killed was that Shaka thought them harmless. Dingane, who was nearly the same size as Shaka, was known for being lazy; he owed his size to fat, not muscle; he so lacked ambition that dancing was the only strenuous physical activity in which he would engage voluntarily. Nevertheless, with no other heir to take control, and having by the very act of assassination exerted control, he became king.

Another version of Shaka's dying words holds that he used his last breath to tell his killers that if he died the whites would overrun the Zulu kingdom. The legend is merely a legend but the prediction, of course, was accurate. Dingane was an apathetic ruler who, after signing a treaty that ceded much of the kingdom to the Europeans, then sent troops to massacre the colonizers. Retribution against the Zulus was swift and merciless. After Dingane's troops were defeated at the Ngome River, which has since then been referred to by Zulus as the River of Blood, Dingane fled his kraal and set it afire. In 1840, he was defeated in battle by Mpande and forced to flee to Swaziland, where he was murdered by Swazi warriors. The Zulu kingdom then passed to Mpande, a puppet ruler of the encroaching Voortrekkers and others.

RESOURCE: *The Washing of the Spears: a History of the Rise of the Zulu Nation and Its Fall in the Zulu War of 1879* by Donald R. Morris (New York, 1965).

DOE, Samuel Kanyon (1950–1990), assassinated William R. Tolbert, Jr. (1913–1980), the president of Liberia, as part of a military coup. On April 12, 1980, Doe, along with nineteen co-conspirators, scaled the wall of Tolbert's mansion. Quickly overpowering Tolbert's guards, the rebels severed the phone line between Tolbert's suite and the military barracks, then broke down the door to Tolbert's quarters and disembowelled him. They then gouged out one of his eyes and fired three bullets into his head. Doe became president of the country later that day.

Samuel K. Doe was a high school early-leaver who, like his father before him, joined the Liberian army. Rising to the rank of master sergeant, he became involved with a group of other non-commissioned officers who believed that Tolbert must be eliminated. Tolbert's regime was marked by widespread corruption and economic problems. By the late 1970s, the price of staples, particularly rice, had skyrocketed, resulting in increased misery and hostility to the government. In addition, Liberia had a class system in which descendants of the indigenous population were discriminated against by the descendants of freed African-American slaves. Although Tolbert had been more accommodating of the indigenous peoples than his predecessors, he was still seen as a symbol of the nation-state's founding elite.

The day after the assassination, Doe (the country's first president of indigenous descent) also became chair of the People's Redemption Council, a group given the responsibility of trying members of Tolbert's administration. Although the charges were not always specified, the sentences were the same in all cases: thirteen defendants, including Tolbert's brother Frank, who was president of the senate, were executed. Doe claimed that his administration would be run for the benefit of all Liberians. Shortly after the coup, however, hostilities broke out between the Krahn tribe (to which Doe belonged) and the Mano and Gio tribes. Doe suspended the constitution and ruled as a dictator while the country underwent civil war. In 1990, Prince (a common first name in

Liberia) Johnson, a Gio tribesman and leader of the Independent Patriotic Front of Liberia, captured Doe and had him tortured to death on videotape. The video of Doe's death is readily available throughout West Africa.

RESOURCES: *The Africans* by David Lamb (New York, 1987); *The Liberian Civil War* by Mark Huband (London, 1998).

DUHAUT, Pierre (d. 1687), assassinated René-Robert Cavelier de La Salle (1643–1687), the French explorer who was the first European to locate the mouth of the Mississippi River. Typical of his type in the great age of European exploration, La Salle possessed a restless temperament that kept him from lingering in any one place for long. As a young man, he entered the Jesuit order but left to pursue his wanderlust. In New France, he became a seigneur and a fur trader, using the profits to help finance his voyages of discovery. In 1677, he returned to France to solicit Louis XIV's patronage to explore the Mississippi in the hope of discovering its mouth. Although he refused to assist financially, Louis gave his consent, allowing La Salle to establish forts in the newly discovered areas. In 1682, La Salle finally traced the Mississippi to its conclusion in the Gulf of Mexico after claiming all the lands along the way in the name of France (even though Spain already claimed the mouth of the Mississippi and the Gulf of Mexico—but not the majority of what is now Louisiana). He thus returned to Europe to great acclaim with new territory several times larger than France, lands which seemed rich enough for all.

In 1685, La Salle embarked on a second expedition with four ships and 280 men and women to further exploit his discoveries and to establish a fort at the great river's mouth. This second expedition was not a success. La Salle intended to sail to the mouth of the Mississippi from the Gulf of Mexico after a brief stop in Santo Domingo. Problems began almost at once, as when fever (possibly malaria) swept through La Salle's party, claiming several victims including La Salle himself. He convalesced in Santo Domingo, recovering fully, but he displayed a tendency to kill other casualties, who he believed were malingering.

While in Santo Domingo, La Salle stayed at a house rented by Pierre Duhaut, described in most sources as a wealthy merchant of high birth, in others as a former convict. Duhaut was in Santo Domingo to sell fabric and lace, which he did at no small profit. Food prices were extremely high there, and La Salle obtained a substantial loan from Duhaut to provision the expedition, on which Duhau and his younger brother would go along. Observers seem to have noted, however, that La Salle, always a harsh disciplinarian, became less than emotionally stable after his bout of sickness, flying into incoherent rages and displaying signs of what today might be described as paranoia. Nevertheless, he set off to complete his mission, though by this time syphilis was rampant among the crew.

Early in 1685, the expedition arrived at what is now Matagorda Bay in Texas. La Salle insisted that this was the mouth of the Mississippi and established Fort St. Louis nearby. The area was a natural breeding ground for disease and was surrounded by hostile aboriginals. The Europeans were so medically unskilled that the smallest cut quite often led to a slow and painful death once futile amputations were performed in an attempt to stop the spread of gangrene. The site of the fort was also home to several species of poisonous snakes that further thinned the ranks. Also, most of the supplies were lost when the lone remaining ship, which had no water on board but plenty of brandy, broke up on a sand-bar because of negligence by its drunken crew.

Duhaut became disenchanted with the whole affair. Not only was there no wealth to be found in the somewhat toxic New World, but La Salle, having struck out from his beleaguered fort, lost Duhaut's brother, Dominique, who was later slaughtered by the native inhabitants in revenge for being fired on. Duhaut began rallying the surviving members of the expedition to abandon the attempt to rediscover the Mississippi. La Salle quelled the dissent by a show of arms, and Duhaut, with a musket held to his head, agreed not to try to turn the survivors against their commander. Shortly afterwards, however, La Salle led another party into the wilderness including Duhaut, whom he abandoned just as he had abandoned Duhaut's brother earlier. Duhaut made his way back to Fort St. Louis after a remarkable solo trek that lasted over a month.

By then, La Salle understood that his position was untenable, and decided to strike out yet again, with twenty men, to find the Mississippi once and for all and follow it to New France, where he would resupply and rescue the remaining members of the expedition who would await their liberation at Fort St. Louis. He earlier had set aside a cache of Indian corn and now sent several men, including Duhaut, to retrieve it. The party found that the food had rotted due to seepage. With no other source of sustenance, Duhaut and others shot two buffalo and proceeded to begin smoking the meat. When La Salle learned of the change in plans, he sent his nephew, Moranget, to supervise the job. Moranget began berating the men for not smoking the meat to his satisfaction and for keeping the choicest pieces for themselves (although by convention this was the hunter's right). In retaliation, Moranget confiscated the entire store of meat. That night, while he slept, Moranget, as well as his servant and Nika, an aboriginal who had accompanied La Salle since his first expedition, were murdered by Duhaut and two accomplices. The killers realized that La Salle would have them executed as soon as he learned of their deeds.

The following day, March 19, 1687, La Salle appeared at the conspirators' camp to investigate the delay in the return of the men and provisions. Duhaut hid in tall grass and waited for La Salle to approach. When La Salle was within range, Duhaut fired his musket and shot him in the head. The explorer died within the hour. His body was stripped naked and thrown into the bushes to be consumed by wild animals. With La Salle dead, Duhaut proclaimed himself leader but decided that continuing to search for the Mississippi was foolhardy. He determined instead to lead his group back to Fort St. Louis and attempt to return to civilization through Spanish territory.

A former buccaneer who was in the party, a German who called himself James Hiems, demanded that Duhaut pay him the back-wages that La Salle owed him. When Duhaut refused, Hiems shot Duhaut in the face with a pistol, killing him instantly. Hiems then left the incompetent party and joined the native population. The few remaining Europeans decided to make one more try to escape via the Mississippi. By autumn, six survivors found their way to Fort St. Louis-des-Illinois. There they stayed until spring when they set out for Montreal, where they learned that their colleagues who remained behind at the fort had been massacred by the Spanish.

RESOURCES: *L'expedition de Cavelier de La Salle dans le Golfe du Mexique, 1684–1687* by Marc de Villiers du Terrage (Paris, 1931); *La Salle and the Discovery of the Great West* by Francis Parkman (Boston, 1869); *Cavelier de La Salle, ou, L'homme qui offrit l'Amérique à Louis XIV* by Anka Muhlstein (Paris, 1992); *River of Forgotten Days: A Journey down the Mississippi in Search of La Salle* by Daniel Spurr (New York, 1998).

DUMINI, Amerigo (1894–1966), assassinated Giacomo Matteotti (1885–1924), secretary of the socialist party of Italy, on June 10, 1924, while Matteotti was walking from his home to parliament. Matteotti was seized by four armed men and hustled into a waiting car. When word of his disappearance spread, fascist-controlled newspapers speculated that Matteotti might have taken a holiday without informing anybody while socialist newspapers assumed correctly that he had been killed by thugs working for the Fascist party under Benito Mussolini.

On August 16, Matteotti's remains were found in the woods of Quartarella. The leader of the group that had seized and killed him was, as his first name suggests, born in the United States. He spent his youth in St. Louis, where he was a petty thief with a streak of violence that led to charges of assault. Leaving America for Italy in 1916, he joined the army and fought in the First World War. His record as a soldier was exemplary. Wounded in action and twice decorated, Dumini was transferred to the special corps, the Arditi, where he distinguished himself further. After the war, he returned to gangsterism. Rabidly anti-communist, he became a fascist in 1921.

Mussolini's Fascists had many uses for someone with Dumini's background, and in October 1921 he commanded a group of five hundred to six hundred goons that attempted to sack the small town of Sarzana, which was seen as a communist stronghold. Local police, along with a large group of citizens, forced the attackers to disperse. In May 1922, Dumini set fire to a Communist meeting hall. This act led to a warrant for attempted murder, at which point Dumini was expelled from the Fascist Party, at least officially. He fled to Switzerland, remaining there until 1923, when he felt he could return to Italy safely, for by then his friends had seized power.

Two of his closest associates in the Fascist Party were Cesare Rossi, chief of Mussolini's press department, and Giovanni Marinelli, the party treasurer. Rossi had Dumini hired as a journalist at the Fascist newspaper *Corriere Italiano* even though Dumini was only semi-literate (and so was named circulation manager instead). In August 1923, Dumini was in trouble with the authorities again, this time for selling obsolete weapons to Yugoslavia. He was released and all charges against him were dropped due to Fascist Party pressure. Later that year he was sent to France with a squad of Fascists to beat French anti-Fascists and Italians who had fled Mussolini's Italy. By 1924, Matteotti, the brilliant, articulate and witty Socialist leader, had become a thorn in the side of the Fascist movement, embarrassing its members in parliament quite regularly. In particular, Matteotti attacked the government over the recent landslide election victory attributed to their control over the electoral process. Fascist newspapers had issued dark warnings that Matteotti should rein himself in. After an especially blistering attack against the Fascists on June 1, 1924, Matteotti said to a friend, "Now you can prepare orations for my funeral." Ten days later he was abducted. As Matteotti was being kidnapped, an eyewitness made note of the number plate of the automobile into which he saw the leader being hustled. The car was traced to Filippo Filippelli, the editor of *Corriere Italiano*. When Mussolini heard that the car had been identified, he was heard to exclaim, "Damn it, all they had to do was piss over the licence plate." When confronted by the police, Filippelli informed them that he had lent his car to Amerigo Dumini. When Dumini was apprehended, he claimed that they had picked up Matteotti only to talk to him. Somehow Matteotti had died while in the vehicle and the Fascists dumped his body in the forest out of fear. The story did not explain why Matteotti's body was found covered in stab wounds. Dumini revised the story, acknowledging that Matteotti was stabbed but that he, Dumini, could not have done the stabbing as he was behind the wheel at the time.

At their trial, Dumini and his three accomplices (one of whom the Fascists had ordered released from jail ten days before the kidnapping) were given five-year prison terms, even though the Fascist-controlled court could not actually determine who had killed Matteotti and ruled that the murder was not premeditated. Dumini, however, was released within a year. In fact, he served a longer sentence for an indiscreet remark. After being released, he was heard to declare, "If I deserve five years for killing Matteotti, Mussolini deserves thirty." For this, Dumini was returned to prison for fourteen months.

The scandal that the Matteotti assassination created nearly destroyed Mussolini's Fascist machine. United in outrage over the government's obvious role in the affair, the opposition walked out and formed a parliament of their own known as the Aventino, named for the hill of ancient Rome where the Roman plebeians had withdrawn after refusing to co-operate with the upper classes. Even moderate Fascists were appalled by the government's actions. Many members tore their party flashes from their sleeves. Within a few months, however, the furor had died down. With the opposition out of parliament, Mussolini was able to stifle dissent even more easily. The king, Victor Emmanuel, who always had been afraid of the Fascists, refused to condemn Mussolini for his actions, therefore giving the impression that he condoned them.

Eventually Mussolini's control over the police, army and government was secure enough that he could openly declare that he was indeed responsible for the Matteotti assassination. By that time there was no opposition left to attack him. There did remain, however, the problem of what to do with Dumini. After his release from prison, Dumini was given ten thousand lire and a farm. The farm went bankrupt soon afterward, whereupon Dumini appealed for more money, hinting that he had information that would embarrass Mussolini. Dumini's mother was given a "special" pension. In 1934, the Fascists gave Dumini another farm, this one in Libya. After Dumini went bankrupt a second time he was given a restaurant in Libya; it fared little better. When the Italians were forced to abandon Libya to the British, Dumini stayed behind to spy and engage in sabotage for the Italians. In March 1941, he was arrested by the British and sentenced to death, but he escaped to Italy.

From the end of 1941 until the end of the war, Dumini found a business at which he was relatively successful: receiving and selling stolen property. Yet this new profession had costs of its own, and Dumini spent the remaining war years in and out of prison. In 1945, while Italy was under Allied occupation, he was employed as a chauffeur for British officials. In 1947, he and the two surviving accomplices from the Matteotti kidnapping were retried for the crime. This time the assassins were sentenced to thirty years' imprisonment. In 1956, Dumini was released on grounds of ill health but lived another decade.

RESOURCE: *Il Delitto Matteotti: Affarismo e politica nel primo governo Mussolini* by Mauro Canali (Bologna, 1997).

DUNNE, Reggie (1898–1922), along with Joe O'Sullivan (1898–1922), assassinated Field Marshal Sir Henry Wilson (1854–1922), former chief of the Imperial General Staff and MP for North Down in Ulster, in London, on June 22, 1922. Sir Henry, in full dress uniform, had just unveiled a statue honouring railway workers who had perished in the Great War. As he was returning to his home, he was accosted by Dunne and O'Sullivan, each of whom had a revolver. Firing first, O'Sullivan discharged two shots, one of which struck the target, who turned and began to draw his sword. At that point the victim died when Dunne fired three times. The two killers attempted to get away on foot, but O'Sullivan was slowed by the fact that he had a wooden leg (having been wounded in France during the war). While escaping, the pair shot two policemen and a civilian, but were soon in custody.

Dunne and O'Sullivan were Irish Catholics born and reared in London. Both joined the British army and served with distinction. Only after the war did they become involved in the Irish Republican movement, joining Sinn Fein and the Gaelic League. Eventually they would help to revive the Irish Republican Army's cell in London, a group that Dunne would lead, while O'Sullivan gained a reputation for being willing to carry out executions. The London IRA was considered a farce by IRA groups in Ireland; as all IRA groups were, it was split by the Anglo-Irish treaty of 1921, which called for a free Ireland but also for the partitioning of the country, with the predominantly Protestant north to remain under British rule. Never particularly large or well organized, the London IRA fell into chaos.

The IRA had marked many political figures for assassination, but Sir Henry Wilson was a special case. An Irish Protestant, and rabidly anti-Catholic, he was blamed for the execution of Catholics in Northern Ireland. As a Conservative MP, he made the harshest anti-Catholic pronouncements on the Irish question of anyone in Westminster. He was a bigot who drew parallels between the Irish Republican movement and the Bolshevik Revolution. Dunne felt that the assassination was justified and warranted and that it might give the London group a certain respectability among IRA cells in Ireland. Dunne relied on the assistance of O'Sullivan, an old friend and one of the few members of the London IRA whom Dunne trusted. Armed with pistols that they had bought themselves, Dunne picked up O'Sullivan at work (he was employed at the labour ministry and performed the shooting during his lunch hour); the two of them then proceeded to Sir Henry's house at the corner of Eaton Place and Lyall Street to await their victim.

At Dunne and O'Sullivan's trial, neither was allowed to speak on his own behalf, but in a message smuggled out of prison Dunne described the killing as "ridding the human world of a scourge." In court, Dunne's only statement was made once he and O'Sullivan had been sentenced to death. When the judge concluded with the traditional words "May God have mercy on your soul," Dunne responded, "He will, my Lord." The two men were hanged on August 10, 1922.

Considerable speculation has suggested that the orders for Dunne and O'Sullivan came from Michael Collins, the first chairman of the

Irish Provisional Government and head of the Irish Republican Brotherhood, but the facts that the attempt was poorly conceived, that the weapons were provided by the assassins themselves and that there were no plans for a successful getaway all tend to dispute this assertion. Sir Henry Wilson's reputation was tainted a few years later with the publication of his diaries, in which the author reveals himself as a seriously deluded individual with fascistic tendencies.

RESOURCE: *Michael Collins and the Assassination of Sir Henry Wilson* by Peter Hart (*Irish Historical Studies*, November 1992).

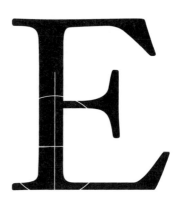

EARP, Wyatt (1848–1929), the legendary sometime peace officer of the American West and Southwest, is thought by many to have crossed the legal and moral line in what one admittedly anti-Earp newspaper called "the deep-dyed assassination" of Frank Stilwell (d. 1882). Stilwell was a stagecoach robber and one-time deputy sheriff of Cochise County, Arizona Territory, whose county seat was the notorious Tombstone. He is the person thought to have assassinated Earp's brother Morgan (1851–1882) and shot another brother Virgil (1853–1906), crippling him for life. These events took place in the months following the OK Corral gunfight of October 1881, in which the Earps and Doc Holliday bested the Clantons and McLaurys. Stilwell was a member of the Clanton criminal faction. On the night of March 19/20, 1882, Stilwell and at least one other person lay in wait for the Earps at Tucson, where Wyatt put the severely wounded Virgil and the body of Morgan on a train for California. Wyatt Earp saw Stilwell lurking in the shadows of the railyard and, by his own account, "let him have it [with a shotgun]. The muzzle of one barrel…was just below his heart. He got the second before he hit the ground." The coroner learned that Stilwell's liver and stomach were indeed full of buckshot but that other parts of the body had been superfluously riddled with pistol fire at point-blank range. Earp never returned to Tombstone but instead commenced his infamous vengeance ride in which he and a few associates tracked down and killed the other parties Earp believed responsible for the attacks on his brothers.

RESOURCES: *And Die in the West: The Story of the O.K. Corral Gunfight* by Paula Mitchell Marks (New York, 1989); *Wyatt Earp: The Life behind the Legend* by Casey Tefertiller (New York, 1997); *Inventing Wyatt Earp: His Life and Legends* by Allen Barra (New York, 1998). Stilwell's death is depicted in such films as Kevin Jarre's *Tombstone* and Lawrence Kasdan's *Wyatt Earp* (both 1993).

ELFRIDA (945?–1000) ordered the assassination of her stepson, the English king Edward the Martyr (963?–978). On March 18, 978, Edward rode to Corfe to visit Elfrida and his younger brother Ethelred. He was met by several servants from Elfrida's household, one of whom presented him with a cup of water. As the king drank, another servant took the king's right hand and appeared to be about to kiss it. Then another grabbed the left hand and pulled Edward from his horse. The king cried out, "What are you doing? Are you trying to break my hand?" As he fell, the king was stabbed in the stomach and fell dead. His body was buried in an unmarked grave in unconsecrated ground. Elfrida's motive for the assassination was to put Ethelred on the throne. When Elfrida married King Edgar they each had a son by a previous marriage. When Edgar died in 975, Elfrida tried to have her son Ethelred succeed him rather than Edgar's son Edward, citing Edward's volatile temper. The fact that Ethelred had no real claim to the throne did not enter into her plans, though the matter was of crucial importance to the Witan, who ruled that Edward had been proclaimed as Edgar's heir by Edgar himself. With Edward thus the king, Elfrida decided that the only way to clear the throne for Ethelred was through assassination. She invited Edward to visit her and instructed her servants to pull the king from his horse and stab him. Ethelred ruled England until his death in 1016, but his mishandling of the problem of Danish invaders would give him the infamous name of Ethelred the Unready.

RESOURCE: *Edward, King and Martyr* by Catherine Fell (Leeds, 1971).

ELSER, Johann Georg (1903–1945), a German cabinetmaker, electrician and general handyman, tried to kill Adolf Hitler (1889–1945) with a homemade bomb and nearly succeeded. As a communist, Elser saw the Munich Agreement, which ceded the Sudetenland to Germany, as a sure sign of impending war between Germany and Russia, a fate which only Hitler's death could prevent. On November 5, 1939, Elser placed a homemade time-bomb inside a wooden pillar in the beer cellar where Hitler had plotted to overthrow the Bavarian government in 1923, knowing that every year on November 8, the anniversary of the failed coup, Hitler would return to the beer hall to give a speech and reminisce with old party members. Hitler, who often failed to show up or left events earlier than planned in order to thwart would-be assassins, departed before the commemoration was over. Twelve minutes later, the bomb exploded, killing seven Nazis and wounding another thirty-three. Elser was captured at the Swiss border. After initially claiming that he had acted alone, he later admitted that he had been approached by two men, who did not identify themselves, and offered refuge abroad if the plan worked. The Gestapo used torture, drugs and hypnosis but could not obtain any more information. Infuriated that the Gestapo did not think him capable of plotting Hitler's assassination, Elser requested access to a carpenter's shop, where he recreated the explosive device. Hitler himself was convinced that Elser was an agent working for the British and insisted that the prisoner be kept alive until after the war when he could be used as the centrepiece of a war-crimes trial against British intelligence. Elser was imprisoned in Dachau where he was continually questioned, to no effect. On April 8, 1945, when it was apparent that Germany would lose the war, Elser was executed.

RESOURCES: *Plotting Hitler's Death: The Story of German Resistance* by Joachim Fest (New York, 1997); *Kill the Führer: Section X and Operation Foxley* by Denis Rigden (London, 1999).

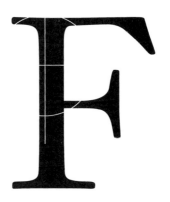

FAISAL, Musad Abdel Aziza (1947–1975), prince of Saudi Arabia, assassinated his uncle King Faisal (1905–1975, reigned from 1964) on March 25, 1975, during a celebration to mark the 1,405th birthday of the Prophet Mohammed. King Faisal was greeting a visiting delegation from Kuwait when he noticed Prince Faisal in the reception line. The king went to greet him, lowering his head so the prince could kiss the tip of his nose, as was the custom. The prince pulled a pistol from his robe and shot his uncle three times in the head, killing him instantly. Prince Faisal's motives for the shooting were based both on traditional beliefs and on a desire to modernize Saudi Arabia. In 1966, the prince's brother, Prince Khalid, was outraged by the king's decision to allow television in Saudi Arabia. Khalid was a fundamentalist who believed that the Koran specifically prohibits the projection of the human image. In order to stop what he considered blasphemy, Khalid and a group of armed extremists stormed the TV station. Khalid was killed by police. Prince Faisal blamed the king for his brother's death. But Prince Faisal was himself not a fundamentalist. He had been sent to attend university in the United States, where, in 1969, he was arrested for selling LSD and quickly released. In addition, Faisal wore his hair long in the American style and favoured western clothing. The young prince believed that the absolute monarchy in Saudi Arabia was preventing the nation from modernizing. Although he declared that the assassination was to avenge his brother, he also had obvious political reasons for his action. The assassination created difficulties for the legal community. On the one hand, the Koran was clear when it declared "A soul for a soul." On the other, a member of the royal family had never been put to death. If the courts interpreted the prince's deed as revenge within the royal family, then they would be powerless to prosecute him. In the end, a court ruled that Faisal was acting out of political motives and was therefore punishable by beheading. In front of a large crowd, he was taken to a public square and forced to his knees. An executioner with a golden sword decapitated the prince with a single stroke. His head was then placed on a stake and put on display before being buried in the wastelands. King Faisal was succeeded by his brother King Khalid.

RESOURCE: *Faysal al-qatil wa-al-qatil* by Abd al-Rahman Nasir Shamrani (Beirut, 1988).

FELTON, John (1595?–1628), assassinated the English nobleman George Villers, the first Duke of Buckingham (1592–1628). On August 23, 1628, Felton entered Buckingham's home in Portsmouth, a fairly easy task, as a naval expedition was being formed at the time and Buckingham, as lord high admiral, was besieged by applicants. Buckingham was speaking with a particularly short man, whom Felton leaned over in order to stab Buckingham in the chest with a tenpenny dagger. As he did so, Felton cried out, "May God have mercy on thy soul." The duke pulled the knife from his chest, took two steps towards Felton, then fell dead.

Felton was a commoner who had entered the Royal Navy in his early teens, advancing rapidly to lieutenant by the time he was twenty-five. His shipmates described him as morose and sullen and he was not particularly popular with his crews. In 1625, during the British campaign against the Spanish port of Cadiz, Felton earned the animosity of Sir Henry Hungate, a close friend of Buckingham; that this argument was the motive for Felton's later action is more than probable. By 1627, Felton had been recommended for command twice, by two different officers, but Buckingham refused him promotion. At one point, Felton pleaded with Buckingham personally, saying that without a captaincy he could not live. Buckingham is reputed to have suggested that Felton therefore hang himself.

Buckingham's career too was affected by a purely personal relationship, but with a far different result. When presented at court, Buckingham created quite an impression on James I, who was known for his cultivation of handsome men. The king gave Buckingham his rank and commissions. Buckingham's campaign against the Spanish was an unqualified disaster for England in terms of money and lost ships and manpower. Parliament requested that Buckingham be removed, but James, and Charles I after him, refused. Buckingham's influence during the last years of James's reign and the first years of Charles's was enormous. With an adversary such as Buckingham,

Felton realized his naval career was over. He resigned his commission and was soon reduced to poverty.

While searching for a scrivener to draft an appeal for his arrears of pay, Felton discovered a copy of a remonstrance by Parliament against Buckingham. This document, along with his own grievances, inspired Felton to plan Buckingham's assassination. Felton eventually collected many petitions and documents against Buckingham, including *The Golden Epistles*, a text written by Sir Geoffrey Felton (probably a distant relative). In August, Felton requested prayers for himself in a Fleet Street church as "a man disordered and discontented in mind." He also wrote out a sentence from *The Golden Epistles* stating that Buckingham was "cowardly and base and deserveth not the name of a gentleman or soldier that is not willing to sacrifice his life for the honour of his God, King or country." To this Felton added, "Let no man commend me for doing of it, but rather discommend themselves as the cause of it, for if God had not taken away our hearts for our sins he would not have gone so long unpunished." Felton placed this note in the lining of his hat, purchased the dagger and made his way to Portsmouth.

In the confusion after the assassination, Felton managed to leave the room. Someone, on seeing Buckingham dead on the floor, declared the assassination to be the work of a "Frenchman." Felton, in the next room, misheard "Frenchman" as "Felton" and, thinking himself caught, confessed his guilt. He was seized immediately. The death of Buckingham was a popular one indeed. The court sent a reprimand to Oxford University because patrons at a public house there began toasting the health of John Felton. When Felton travelled to London for trial, people lined the road to cheer him and wish God's blessings on him. Charles I, realizing that Felton was becoming a folk hero, had him executed quickly, without the usual pre-execution torture.

RESOURCES: *Buckingham, 1592–1628* by Mildred Ann Gibb (London, 1935); *Buckingham: The Life and Political Career of George Villers, First Duke of Buckingham, 1592–1628* by Roger Lockyer (London, 1981).

FIESCHI, Joseph-Marie (1790–1836), attempted to assassinate Louis-Philippe (1773–1850), king of France, on July 28, 1835, as Louis-Philippe rode in his carriage through Paris at the head of a military parade. As the monarch passed along the boulevard du Temple, a loud explosion was heard and the air was filled with bullets. The king turned to his companion and said, "This is for me." One ball grazed the king's head while another wounded one of the carriage horses. The king took the reins and rode off quickly while waving his hat in the air to let the crowd know that he was all right. A loud shout of "*Vive le Roi*" went up. The fusillade killed fourteen people and wounded twenty-two. Louis-Philippe, however, suffered no more than a bruise.

The unique device that had sprayed the street with lead was the brainchild of Joseph-Marie Fieschi, a petty thug and criminal. After a short time in the army, Fieschi, a Corsican, served ten years in prison for theft. He then moved to Paris and took a series of jobs, but returned to his chosen profession, crime. He later became a police informer but lost this position after being caught stealing silver.

In 1834, Fieschi met Pierre Morey and Theodore Pépin. Morey and Pépin were members of the banned republican organization the Rights of Man, and were strongly opposed to the reintroduction of the monarchy. Fieschi dreamed up an invention that he felt would aid them in their plans: a device operated by a single individual that would fire ninety rifles simultaneously. Morey told Fieschi that he didn't see the device, nicknamed "the infernal machine," as a weapon of warfare but rather as a tool for assassination. The republicans quickly worked out a plan to modify the machine (going from ninety guns to fifty and finally to twenty-five, because of financial limitations). Experiments were conducted with one of the conspirators, playing the king, riding past a building in which the conspirators had rented a room. At this point, plans began to break down. One of the conspirators, who had worked on the machine, a blacksmith named Victor Boireau, was an alcoholic. While in his cups he began speaking of the plot in public. Soon police were questioning him. He was quick to reveal the details of the plot, but police failed to stop it because they investigated the wrong street.

A further betrayal came from Morey. Realizing that twenty-five rifles firing simultaneously would create such noise and smoke that the police could locate the device at once, Fieschi, who would operate the machine, claimed that an assassin, having fired, could elude police easily by running from rooftop to rooftop. Morey had less confidence in Fieschi's ability to escape and therefore booby trapped the device so that it would explode once fired. This way, Fieschi would die and none of the other conspirators would be revealed. Morey's betrayal proved only slightly more effective than Fieschi's assassination attempt, for when the machine exploded, a piece of it struck him in the face. He was wounded and disfigured, but still alive. He then tried to escape but police caught him in a neighbouring house. Soon afterwards Pépin and Morey joined Fieschi and Boireau already in custody. The republicans were not without sympathizers. Pro-republican newspapers reported the event in a manner that suggested that the attempt was noble and its failure regrettable. This became the basis for the September Laws, a series of statutes designed to muzzle the press. Morey and Pépin were sentenced to death; Boireau was sentenced to twenty years in prison but was pardoned in 1850 and lived the remainder of his life in England. Fieschi got an extra penalty for being the one who actually fired the device: his thumb was cut off before he was sent to the guillotine.

RESOURCE: *Louis-Philippe* by Guy Antonetti (Paris, 1994).

FITZURSE, Reginald (d. 1173), a knight in the service of Henry II of England (reigned 1154–1189) was, along with William de Tracy, Richard Le Brito and Hugo de Morville, the assassin of Thomas à Becket (1118?–1170), a friend of the monarch who had been appointed archbishop of Canterbury as an ally, only to take a stand favouring the pope over the king at a time when the church and the Crown were competing for authority. After numerous conflicts with Becket, the king asked famously, "Will no one rid me of this meddlesome priest?" (maintaining later that the question was rhetorical). Fitzurse and his confederates took the statement as a call for Becket's death. Travelling from France to Canterbury, each by a different route, the four knights met at Saltwood on December 28, 1170, and proceeded together to Canterbury the next day. They approached Becket at his home on the afternoon of December 29, and began to argue with him. They demanded that Becket absolve the bishops whom he had excommunicated for participating in the coronation of Henry's son Richard and that he swear loyalty to the king. Becket refused, stating that his loyalty was to the church, which was a higher authority than the monarchy. The knights then left to don their armour and Becket went to the cathedral, where he refused to bar the door, feeling that Fitzurse would not desecrate the church by attacking him there. But the four knights forced an entry and again demanded that Becket comply with their demands. When Becket refused, Fitzurse gave the order to attack. The knights cut and slashed with their swords until Becket's head was sliced open and his brains spilled onto the floor.

Initially, the knights were proud of their service. Within days, however, outrage over the murder of England's highest holy man made them fugitives. They were excommunicated by the pope, and had to flee to Scotland, where they stayed for a year though they were shunned by all—to the extent, folklore insists, that Scots dogs would not eat the scraps from their table. Eventually the assassins gave themselves up to the king, who was also facing criticism for his role in the killing, but who felt he lacked authority to punish them for what was considered a crime against God. He therefore turned them over to the pope, who sentenced them to a term of fasting and fourteen years' banishment to the Holy Land as part of the Crusades. While it is generally assumed that all of them died in 1173, there is considerable evidence that Morville survived the Crusades and returned to England, where he died in 1204.

Public reaction against Henry was so fierce that in 1174 he did penance for his role in the assassination, walking barefoot in a pilgrim's gown and hair shirt through the streets of Canterbury to Becket's tomb, where he confessed and asked for pardon. He then bared his back and allowed every monk in the cathedral to lash him seven times.

Thomas à Becket was canonized in 1173 as St. Thomas of Canterbury, though his persecution by the Crown was not finished. In 1538, his bones were brought before the court of Star Chamber by order of Henry VIII and put on trial on a charge of treason and usurping papal authority. His remains were found guilty and burned.

RESOURCES: *The Development of the Legend of Thomas Becket* by Paul Alonzo Brown (Philadelphia, 1930); *The Turbulent Priest: A Life of St. Thomas of Canterbury* by Piers Compton (London, 1957).

FLEGENHEIMER, Arthur (a.k.a. Dutch Schultz) (1902–1935), conspired to assassinate Thomas E. Dewey (1902–1971), the district attorney of New York. Flegenheimer was a major kingpin of organized crime in New York City, controlling its beer market during much of the Prohibition period. After Repeal early in the Depression, he took over the illicit lottery known as the numbers racket; until then, betting on the last three digits of the total volume of shares sold that day on the New York Stock Exchange had been in the hands of small-scale operators in Harlem, primarily African-Americans. Flegenheimer unified the numbers operation by killing those who were not working for him.

As a personality, he was known for three traits. One, he was tight-fisted in money matters; people said of him that you could slander him or his mistress but if you stole a dollar from him you were dead; Charles ("Lucky") Luciano (1897–1962), top ruler of New York's Sicilian Cosa Nostra, called him the worst-dressed mob leader in America. Two, he was, unlike most other gangsters, a publicity-hound; Flegenheimer had chosen the name Dutch Schultz because he believed that it had a certain ring to it; as he himself said, "If I use the name Flegenheimer, nobody will print it in the papers"; some claimed that his only extravagance was two cents for a newspaper—and then only if he was mentioned. Three, he was distinctive in his ruthlessness, which was remarkable even by the standards of his milieu.

In 1935, in a meeting with Luciano and other organized crime leaders, Flegenheimer declared that Dewey, who was prosecuting mobsters with a zeal never before seen, must be killed. By this time, Flegenheimer, fearing arrest, had fled New York City and was directing his New York operations from Paterson, New Jersey. He pointed out to the other men assembled that Dewey would come after all of them eventually, but if Dewey were killed, the persecution would stop. Luciano vetoed the idea immediately. The Mafia, while having no problem with killing one another, knew if they began assassinating police or politicians that the retribution would be far worse than the pressure Dewey was applying. When turned down, Flegenheimer declared that he was going ahead with the attempt himself, and left the meeting.

He used operatives to track Dewey's movements, learning that each morning Dewey walked from his home to a nearby drugstore to place phone calls. Dewey used a phone booth because he suspected that his home and office telephones were tapped. A Flegenheimer operative was placed outside the drugstore with a small boy riding a velocipede. What appeared to be a father teaching a son to ride was in fact a stake-out team. Dewey was often flanked by bodyguards but tended to leave them outside the pharmacy while placing his calls. For a gunman in the shop to shoot Dewey and then walk out past the oblivious guards seemed a simple enough matter.

Flegenheimer's mistake was taking the mob hitman Albert Anastasia into his confidence. At the meeting with Luciano, Anastasia was the only person who supported Flegenheimer in his plan to kill Dewey, but his loyalties were with Luciano. When Anastasia told Luciano how far the plans had proceeded, Luciano decided that Flegenheimer had to be eliminated. On October 23, 1935, Flegenheimer was dining with three associates in a restaurant in Newark, New Jersey. Shortly after he excused himself to go to the toilet, three armed men burst into the restaurant. Two of them dispatched the men remaining at the table while the third checked the men's room for witnesses. Flegenheimer was shot at a urinal but staggered into the dining room, where he died.

His prediction about Dewey turned out to be correct. In 1936, Dewey, using not particularly legal means, convicted Luciano on prostitution and related charges that led to a sentence of fifty-four years' imprisonment. Luciano informed Dewey that it seemed to him that Dewey was being ungrateful for persecuting him when he had saved Dewey's life. At first Dewey was sceptical of the plot against him, but he went pale with recognition when Luciano told him about the father with a son on a bicycle. When Dewey was governor of New York State in 1946, he pardoned Luciano for services that the mob had performed for America during the Second World War, when it gathered intelligence, ensured that no spies worked on the New York docks and kept unions from striking. Luciano returned to Italy, where he lived out the remainder of his life. Dewey used his reputation as a crusading organized-crime fighter as a springboard to further his political career, gaining the Republican Party nomination for presidency twice (1944 and 1948).

RESOURCE: *The Mob* by Virgil W. Peterson (Ottawa, Illinois, 1983).

FORD, Robert Newton (1862–1892), the assassin of his colleague Jesse James (1847–1882), was so despised for his action that he was referred to on his victim's tombstone as "a traitor and a coward whose name is not worthy to appear here." Indeed, he was immortalized in one of America's most persistent folk songs as "that dirty little coward that shot Mister Howard" ("Howard" being the alias under which James was living at the time of his murder).

Jesse James and his brother Frank (1843–1915) were natives of Clay County, Missouri, who served as Confederate guerrillas during the Civil War—Jesse with William Quantrill, Frank with the almost equally notorious William ("Bloody Bill") Anderson. Following the cessation of formal hostilities, they transferred their raiding to the private sector, becoming the country's most infamous band of bank- and train-robbers, usually in association with the Younger brothers, to whom they were related. In fact, a strong sense of family runs through their entire story. In a raid on Northfield, Minnesota, in 1879, one from which the Jameses narrowly escaped, one Younger was killed and three captured, forcing the Jameses to accept new gang members with whom they did not share quite the same familial closeness.

In St. Joseph, Missouri, in 1881, Wood Hite, a cousin of the James brothers, was boarding at the home of Mrs. Martha Bolton. Hite had a rival for her attentions in an outlaw named Dick Liddil. Hite was killed with the help of Mrs. Bolton, who was the sister of Bob Ford and Charles Wilson Ford (1862–1884). Mrs. Bolton sought governor's pardons for both her siblings after Liddil turned state's evidence. Against the background of these events the Ford brothers became entangled with the Jameses.

In March 1882, when Jesse James, or Tom Howard as he had become, made a return visit to Clay County to see his mother, he was accompanied by Charley Ford, the newest gang member. Ford began pressing for his brother Bob to be admitted as well, which he was, reluctantly. In 1881, Missouri's governor, Thomas Crittenden, had posted $5,000 rewards for the James brothers, dead or alive. In April 1882, Jesse James robbed yet another Missouri bank. He did so unaware that his accomplices, the Fords, had made a deal to kill him in return for full pardons as well as the reward money. So it was that on the morning of April 3, 1882, in James's modest frame house at 1318 Lafayette Street in St. Joseph (since removed to another site), an unarmed Jesse James stood on the chair to straighten and dust a framed sampler that hung on one of the walls. The sampler read "In God We Trust." He was alone in the room with Charley and Bob Ford. The latter withdrew a pistol that James had given him as a gift—a Colt .45-calibre revolver, serial number 50432, with which Ford later would be proudly photographed—and shot him in the back of the head. As an autopsy revealed, the bullet entered at the occipital bone behind the right ear, travelling upwards through the brain to an area posterior to the left ear.

The Ford brothers were indicted on April 17, 1882. A jury found them guilty of first-degree murder and a judge sentenced them to hang. Governor Crittenden (who earlier in his career had made headlines by advocating that Charles Guiteau, the assassin of President James A. Garfield, be torn limb from limb) swiftly granted them full pardons, thereby ruining his political career. Whether the Fords received any of the reward money is less clear. What is certain is that the Fords were eager to defend their reputations even while trafficking in their notoriety.

In 1884, Bob Ford wrote to a St. Louis newspaper, denying that he had been promised a pardon or payment for killing Jesse James; he warned that "the man that calls me an assassin is a CONTEMTABLE [sic] SNEAK & if he wishes to resent it he will find me at the St. James Hotel in this city." Yet he and his brother performed in a stage presentation that dramatized the killing.

Charley Ford was found dead in a hotel room in Richmond, Missouri, an apparent suicide. Bob Ford moved farther west and ended his days running a saloon and gambling den in a tent in Crede, Colorado, a rough mining camp. There he was shot to death by Edward O'Kelly, a distant relative of the Jameses who until recently had been a peace officer in Crede. O'Kelly was convicted and sentenced to twenty years' imprisonment but was soon pardoned, to general acclaim. Frank James was tried for various crimes but never convicted. When Cole Younger, leader of the Younger clan, was finally released from Stillwater Prison in Minnesota in 1903, he and Frank James spent a brief time touring together on the theatrical circuit. Jesse E. James, the outlaw's son, became a corporate lawyer, explaining that there was too little money to be made practising criminal law. A nagging question about whether the body in the senior James's grave was actually that of the bandit was settled in the affirmative in 1995 by scientists who examined DNA samples.

RESOURCES: *I, Jesse James* by James Ross (New York, 1990); *Jesse James: The Man and the Myth* by Marley Brant (New York, 1998). Loren D. Estleman's novel *Billy Gashade: An American Epic* (New York, 1997), which purports to be a memoir by the author of the famous Jesse James ballad, brings both James and Ford to life with particular clarity and skill. *The Life, Times & Treacherous Death of Jesse James* by Frank Triplett (St. Louis, 1882; modern reprints) has often been called into question but remains the most generous source of contemporary information on the subject.

FRANCIS, John (b. 1822), the second of seven men who attempted to assassinate Queen Victoria (reigned 1837–1901), was a journeyman carpenter. He had two opportunities to shoot Victoria. On May 29, 1842, Victoria and Prince Albert were returning to Buckingham Palace when Francis stepped out of the crowd and pointed a pistol at their carriage. Albert heard the trigger snap, but there was no shot. The prince consort almost believed that he had merely imagined the incident, when a young man came forward and confirmed the attempt, further relating that the assassin had exclaimed: "Fool that I was not to have fired." Victoria and Albert decided to travel by carriage the next day to attempt to flush out the would-be assailant. The only precaution Victoria took was to leave her lady-in-waiting behind so that she would not be exposed to danger. On the return leg of the journey, while riding on Constitution Hill towards Buckingham Palace, in fact at almost exactly the same spot where Edward Oxford had attempted to shoot Victoria some two years earlier, Francis once again pointed a pistol, but this time he fired. And this time the route was lined by plainclothes police, one of whom was standing next to Francis when he discharged the weapon but missed his target. Francis was found guilty of high treason and sentenced to be hanged and quartered. This sentence was later commuted to life at hard labour and Francis spent the remainder of his days in Tasmania.

RESOURCE: *Royal Murders: Hatred, Revenge, and the Seizing of Power* by Dulcie M. Ashdown (Stroud, Gloucestershire, 1998).

FRANKFURTER, David (1909–1982), the assassin of Wilhelm Gustloff (1895–1936), leader of Switzerland's comparatively little-known Nazi Party, was born in Croatia, the son of a rabbi, and was involved in Zionist groups from an early age. In 1929, he enrolled in Leipzig University to study medicine. Once the Nazis came to power in Germany in 1933, Frankfurter observed first-hand the institutionalization of anti-Semitism, and left Germany to study medicine in Switzerland, whose own small Nazi movement was headed by Gustolff, who lived in Davos in the eastern part of the country. Frankfurter saw a potential Adolf Hitler in Gustolff and vowed to eliminate him, hoping that the assassination would send a worldwide message about the dangers of Nazism as well as ensure that Switzerland would remain free from official totalitarianism. On February 4, 1936, Frankfurt called at Gustloff's home and was shown into the study by his wife. When Gustloff entered to greet the visitor, Frankfurter drew a pistol and wounded him fatally. Frankfurter considered suicide, but eventually surrendered to police. He was convicted and sentenced to eighteen years' imprisonment. In 1946, however, he was pardoned as a result of the Nazi defeat and the mounting public evidence of the Holocaust.

RESOURCE: *Political Assassinations by Jews: A Rhetorical Device for Justice* by Nachman Ben-Yehuda (Albany, New York, 1993).

FRANKLIN, Joseph Paul (b. 1950), is that most unusual of creatures, the non-professional serial assassin, though he is known mainly for one particular shooting, his attempt on Larry Flynt (b. 1942), publisher of the American pornographic magazine *Hustler*. On March 6, 1978, Flynt was about to enter the courthouse in Lawrenceville, Georgia, where he was defending himself on charges of obscenity, one of a number of such actions against him in various jurisdictions across the United States. A sniper's bullet struck Gene Reeves, a local lawyer, in the arm, a second hit Flynt in the stomach. Flynt fell to the ground and lost consciousness. Within ten minutes an ambulance was rushing him to Gwinnett County Hospital, where a portion of perforated intestine was removed in order to halt Flynt's internal bleeding. Several transfusions were performed before he could be operated on again; in all, Flynt endured more than a dozen surgeries to save his life. Even though Flynt's spinal cord was intact, the bullet had passed through the bundle of nerves at the base of the spine called the *cauda equina* (horse's tail) and he would never walk again. Yet unlike those who have had their spinal cords severed, Flynt's nerve damage caused him excruciating pain for several years until further surgery was performed to cut the nerves. As a result of the pain, Flynt became addicted to prescription painkillers. The shooting of Flynt was one of more than twenty shootings by Franklin during a period of over three years, a spree that covered twelve states. Franklin was born James Clayton Vaughn, Jr. to an abusive family. His alcoholic father beat him severely while his puritanical mother was unable to show him maternal love. When he was eighteen, Vaughn sewed a swastika flash to his jacket and began frequenting neo-Nazi meetings. Soon afterwards he became active in the National Socialist White People's Party. At twenty-six, he joined the United Klans of America. By then, he had changed his name to Joseph Paul Franklin, taking the first two names from Adolf Hitler's minister of propaganda, Joseph Paul Goebbels, and the surname from Benjamin Franklin, the American diplomat of the Revolutionary period. Franklin quit the neo-Nazi and Klan groups after deciding that they were "soft." He believed that the time had come for direct action rather than for meetings, rallies and literature. He began planting pipe-bombs in synagogues and in the homes of prominent Jews. Later came a campaign of shooting people he perceived to be promoting "race-mixing." When Franklin saw a photo spread in *Hustler* depicting an interracial couple, he decided that Larry Flynt must die. The trial in Lawrenceville gave Franklin the perfect opportunity to wait from a secluded spot for his quarry to arrive.

Franklin has never been charged in connection with Flynt's shooting. He is currently on death row in Missouri convicted of several other murders. He has said that the attack on Flynt is one of his few regrets, as he has come to respect Flynt and "I was kind of deluded at the time and didn't know what I was doing." Franklin was portrayed by Jan Triska in Milos Forman's 1996 feature film *The People vs. Larry Flynt*.

RESOURCE: *An Unseemly Man* by Larry Flynt with Kenneth Ross (Los Angeles, 1996).

FRIZER, Ingram (1568?–1627), a creature of the financial and political demimondes of Elizabethan London, was the murderer—and most probably the assassin—of the playwright, poet and spy Christopher Marlowe (1564–1593), the author of such plays as *Doctor Faustus* and *Edward II* and a collaborator with other notable writers of the day, from Walter Ralegh to Thomas Nashe to (some believe) William Shakespeare (who actually quotes him in *As You Like It*). The specific details of Marlowe's death were unknown until the 1920s when Leslie Hotson discovered the long-lost report of the coroner's inquest. The document recorded how on the evening of May 30, 1593, Marlowe and three others—Ingram Frizer, Nicholas Skeres and Robert Poley—went to Mistress Bull's Inn, at Deptford, in southeast London on the Thames, to eat and drink. At least two of his companions, including Frizer, were, among other things, swindlers, while Poley was certainly an agent in the secret service of Sir Francis Walsingham, Queen Elizabeth's spymaster. According to the inquest findings, a scuffle took place over the bill and "it befell in that affray that: the said Ingrim [*sic*], in defence of his life, with the dagger aforesaid of the value of 12*d.* gave the said Christopher then & there a mortal wound over the right eye of a depth of two inches & to a width of one; of which wound Christopher Morley [*sic*] then & there instantly died."

The discovery of this manuscript provoked further scholarship on the incident, particularly by Samuel Tannenbaum, whose book *The*

Assassination of Christopher Marlowe argued that the killing was planned and that Ralegh was behind it. Later writers lay the blame at the feet of Mary Queen of Scots, among others. So numerous did the conspiracy theories become that Charles Norman, a later American biographer, was greeted with relief by readers when his own book refused to entangle itself in any such speculation. Far and away the most thorough and thoughtful truth-seeker is Charles Nicholl, who believed that Marlowe was probably recruited as a spy as early as 1585 while still a student at Cambridge and thrown into the world of "projections" (government- or Crown-sponsored conspiracies). As in most conspiracy studies, context and precedent are everything, and Nicholl wisely points out, for example, how "No account of the Elizabethan secret world…would be complete without [the story of the Babington plot, though it's] hard to say when the 'plot' took shape. In a sense it never did. There was a lot of wild talk—heads filled with wine, with dreams of Catholic rebellion, with an overheated, cultist devotion to the imprisoned Queen Mary—but what shape it had in terms of real action was largely provided by the government itself, whose agents infiltrated the conspiracy not so much to destroy it, as to encourage it. In the words of a priest named Davis, who was with [Anthony] Babington on the night before his capture, the plot was a 'tragedy', in which 'the chief actor and contriver' was Sir Francis Walsingham," a sinister figure indeed. As Anthony Burgess reminds us in his Marlowe assassination novel *A Dead Man in Deptford* (1993), Elizabeth herself referred to Sir Francis behind his back as "the Moor," because he had a dark complexion—and motives to match.

Tempting as it is to quote some of the more far-fetched inquirers into Marlowe's death, such as those who believe that the body buried in an unmarked grave in St. Nicholas Churchyard in Deptford is not his, prudence argues for quoting a bit more of Nicholl, who is easily the most subtle and thoughtful author to attempt to crack the puzzle. In the matter of Marlowe's poor choice of companions, there has long been the suggestion "that Marlowe's death involves these people because it is itself somehow part of the covert world which they all inhabit. There is a sense of closeness, a claustrophobia, in these repetitions and reappearances." In Nicholl's views, the participants are clearly "lying to conceal their involvement—and the involvement of ministers of the Crown…It is true that, whatever the cat's cradle of shared secrets and hidden antagonisms that binds these four men together, it would still be possible for two of them to have a foolish drunken spat over the bill, and for one of them to die for it. That was the Elizabethan way [but] absurdly complex projections and counter-projections were also the Elizabeth way—a way of life, a source of income, and for some a cause of death." In brief, "Marlowe did not die by chance, and he was not killed in self-defence. He had become an impediment to the political ambitions of the Earl of Essex, as these were perceived and furthered by secret operator....They had tried to frame him to get him imprisoned and tortured, to use him as their 'instrument' against Ralegh. They had tried all this and failed. He had proved elusive, a danger, a potential projector against them. His mouth—if it could not be made to say what they wanted it to say—must be 'stopped'... Marlowe's death was a *decision*. It was a point the day reached, by a process of dwindling options... a dirty trick, a rogue event, a tragic blunder."

Of Frizer, little is known beyond mention in a few public documents, such as conveyances, wills, lawsuits (enough of the last so that we know he was litigious by nature). He became sufficiently prosperous to lend money at interest on a professional basis, and he was a friend or associate of Marlowe's most important literary patron. After his arrest, Frizer was committed to Newgate but on June 28, 1593, four weeks after the stabbing, Queen Elizabeth granted him a pardon. He removed to Kent where he held minor offices and operated a small brewery.

RESOURCES: *The Death of Christopher Marlowe* by J. Leslie Hotson (Cambridge, Massachusetts, 1925); *The Assassination of Christopher Marlowe* by Samuel Tannenbaum (London, 1928); *The Muses' Darling* by Charles Norman (New York, 1946); *The Reckoning: The Murder of Christopher Marlowe* by Charles Nicholl (London, 1992).

FROMME, Lynette Alice ("Squeaky") (b. 1948), a former member of the Manson Family group of serial killers, attempted to assassinate US president Gerald Ford (b. 1913) on September 5, 1975, in Sacramento, California. On learning that Ford was appearing in the city, she put on a long flowered dress, a flowing red robe and a pair of sandals and strapped a .45-calibre automatic pistol to her leg. When Ford appeared before a crowd in front of the state capitol, Fromme pulled her pistol from beneath her robe and tried to fire, but although the weapon's clip contained four bullets, none was in the firing chamber. She was apprehended before she could pull the trigger a second time.

Fromme was born to a suburban family and as a child was a member of a dance troupe known as the Lariats that once appeared on the *Ed Sullivan Show*. Her nickname was "Red." She ran away from home as a teen and met the charismatic cult-leader Charles Manson on Venice Beach, near Los Angeles. In a famous exchange, Manson told her he was known as "the Gardener" because he tended to all the flower children. She joined his doomsday band of misfits, several of whose members, including Manson himself, were arrested for the Tate-LaBianca murders in 1969. During Manson's trial, Fromme was one of several female followers who shaved their heads and sat in front of the courthouse in a kind of vigil. She also appeared in the documentary film *Manson*.

After Manson was found guilty, Fromme lived with two other Manson disciples in Sacramento, devoting much of her time to writing protest letters to companies she considered major polluters. She also wrote threatening letters to the judge who had sentenced Manson to life imprisonment. Her original lawyer, Phil Shelton, claimed that Fromme did not intend to kill Ford, the empty firing chamber being offered as evidence of this point. Fromme had backed away at the last moment, Shelton asserted, because Ford reminded her of her father. Shelton also attempted to offer a plea of insanity as a defence, but was pulled off the case after Fromme refuted his explanations. Fromme was found guilty and is serving a life sentence. In 1979, she was moved to a maximum-security prison after attacking a fellow inmate with a hammer. In 1987, she escaped from a prison in West Virginia but was recaptured two days later. She is currently in a maximum-security institution in Texas where she is still, apparently, a disciple of Manson. The singer-songwriter Loudon Wainwright III once recorded a love song about her.

RESOURCE: *Squeaky: The Life and Times of Lynette Alice Fromme* by Jess Bravin (New York, 1997).

GALLAGHER, James J. (1852–
1913), an Irish-born labourer
on the municipal docks in New
York City, shot the mayor,
William J. Gaynor (1848–
1913), on August 9, 1910. The result was the most startling and infamous
assassination photograph ever seen by the public until the most gruesome frames of Abraham Zapruder's 8-mm motion picture of the John F.
Kennedy assassination were made available nearly fifty years later.

On the morning of the shooting, Mayor Gaynor, a former judge
with gubernatorial and even presidential ambitions, was in Hoboken,
New Jersey, standing on the foredeck of the German Lloyd liner *Kaiser
Wilhelm der Grosse*, preparing to depart on a European holiday. He had
given interviews and posed for press photographs. Gaynor exchanged
pleasantries with the president of Chile, a fellow passenger, and was
discussing matters with a number of New York office-holders when
Gallagher, whom witnesses described as unkempt, approached from
behind and shot the mayor below the right ear from about fifteen centimetres away, saying, "You took my bread and butter away; now I've got
you." The statement referred to the fact that Gallagher had been dismissed
from his job on the grounds of tardiness and insolence and had been
unsuccessful in getting the mayor and others to reinstate him. At that
very instant, William Warnecke of the *Evening World*, who had arrived
on the scene after his rivals from the other papers had left, tripped the
shutter of his ICA camera. When developed, the ten-by-fifteen-centimetre
negative plate showed a wounded Mayor Gaynor, still standing but with
knees buckling, supported by his aides, and clearly in a state of shock and
trauma, with blood on his face, beard and hands. Seeing the image, the
World's city editor, Charles Chapin (who was later sentenced to Sing Sing
for the murder of his wife) was heard to exclaim, "What a wonderful
thing. Look, blood all over him—and exclusive too." Chapin ran the
photo across four columns of page one. After striking the mayor,
Gallagher continued firing, and one shot hit New York's commissioner

of street cleaning, William Edwards, who weighed 135 kilos, as Edwards tackled the assailant and held him pinned to the deck. Given the dramatic nature of the events, as well as the high hopes Gaynor's allies shared for his political future, the story was, in the words of the Toronto *Globe*, "an event of more than civic or even national importance" but one of truly international significance, as the statement itself seems to prove. The press followed closely the condition of the mayor, who recovered in a couple of months but was left with a rasping voice and a permanent cough, as doctors decided to leave the bullet lodged in his larynx rather than risk removing it.

After the shooting, the mayor, until then a radical reformer, suffered in a series of scandals, much to the delight of his enemies, such as William Randolph Hearst, proprietor of the New York *Journal*, whom Gaynor had defeated in the mayoral election of 1909. Gaynor wrote and spoke vividly about the attempt on his life, leaving one of the few accounts of what being attacked by an assassin feels like. But he revealed little of his thoughts about Gallagher, saying cryptically, "I am content. My great hope is that the event will help to make me a better man and more patient and just."

The morning after the attack, the *New York Times* described Gallagher as someone "who does not look like a man who would attempt assassination. His appearance is that of a man of sullen temperament. If you met him walking down the street you would never think that he was a sulky churl [but rather] a happy-go-lucky Irishman who has kissed the Blarney stone and is ready for a joke and a slap on the back with all comers." The mayor refused to bring charges against Gallagher, who was sentenced instead for wounding Edwards and given a twelve-year prison term. Later a commission declared him insane, and he was transferred to the New Jersey state asylum, where he died of paresis. The exact nature of his paralysis, however, is unknown; some have speculated that the root cause was syphilis.

Six days after being nominated for re-election (as an independent), Gaynor died at sea aboard the liner *Baltic* en route to Liverpool. Some said that his funeral procession in New York exceeded even that of Abraham Lincoln there in 1865 in terms of the solemnity of the occasion and the number of mourners.

RESOURCES: *Park Row* by Allen Churchill (New York, 1958); *Great Moments in News Photography from the Historical Files of the National Press Photographers' Association* by John Faber (New York, 1960). Biographies of Gaynor have appeared at generational intervals since 1931; the most recent is *The Mayor Who Mastered New York* by Lately Thomas (New York, 1969).

GALLINARI, Prospero (b. 1950), killed Aldo Moro (1916–1978), the former prime minister of Italy, in one of the most notorious and long-lived assassination dramas of the day. On March 16, 1978, Moro was being driven through Rome on his way to parliament. Because of recent terrorist activities, he was accompanied by a large security contingent. The motorcade was stopped by a lorry blocking the street. The vehicle had been placed in Moro's path by members of the Brigate Rosse (Red Brigades). Eleven terrorists (ten men and one woman), wearing stolen Alitalia uniforms, opened fire with automatic weapons. Five of Moro's bodyguards were killed in the ambush and Moro was then abducted.

In the days that followed, hundreds of messages, mostly false, were issued by members or supporters of the Red Brigades. Eventually the authorities were able to distinguish authentic communiqués. They learned that the kidnappers were demanding the release of fourteen Red Brigades members, including the group's founder, Renato Curcio, who were being tried en masse in Turin. Rather than give in to the demands, the Italian government mobilized fifteen thousand police and six thousand troops to find the Brigades members and retrieve Moro. For nearly two months, Moro was held by the terrorists, who forced him to write letters to members of the Italian government begging them to give in. The Red Brigades also released photographs of the prime minister and announced that he would be tried in their "People's Court" on charges of "acting against the interests of the people and of aiding the imperialists of America and West Germany." Letters written under duress by Moro were sent regularly to government officials with copies to major newspapers in Rome and Genoa. On April 15, the Red Brigades announced that Moro had been found guilty and sentenced to death. One letter, which turned out to be false, claimed that Moro had been executed and his body dumped in a frozen lake near Rome. Investigators called in military divers before the deception was revealed. On April 20, a photograph of Moro was released by the terrorists that showed him holding a copy of a newspaper dated one day earlier. With the photograph came the warning that the Red Brigades would kill Moro in two days unless their demands were met.

On May 9, 1978, Moro's bullet-riddled body was found in the boot of an abandoned automobile parked symbolically halfway between the headquarters of the Communist Party and the headquarters of the Christian Democratic Party. After members of the Red Brigades had been investigated and interrogated for five years, informants finally revealed the names of guilty parties. In 1983, thirty-two members of the Red Brigades were arrested for the murder. The authorities soon determined that two members of the brigade had been instrumental in the death: Laura Braghetti, who was seen as Moro's jailer, and Prospero Gallinari, who had fired the bullets that killed him. In court, Braghetti spat on Antonio Savasta, one of the key informers, shouting, "You bastard, you would even sell your own mother." By contrast, Gallinari seemed to be in good humour throughout his trial; calm and polite, he even joked with his fellow prisoners, all of whom were kept in cages. The thirty-two defendants were sentenced to life imprisonment. Later, the Red Brigades would issue a statement that the "phase of revolutionary struggle which began in the early 1970s on a broad wave of radical student and working class movements . . . is substantially finished." The text urged supporters to "seek new means of revolution."

RESOURCE: *The Aldo Moro Murder Case* by Richard Drake (Cambridge, Massachusetts, 1995).

GARRETT, Patrick Floyd (1850–1908), the assassin of Billy the Kid (1859?–1881), his former friend, was a southerner born and bred who in his late teens went west, where he became a cowhand and buffalo hunter. In 1880, he was elected sheriff of Lincoln County, New Mexico Territory (NMT), which was then experiencing what history calls the Lincoln County War (1879–1881), in which well-capitalized ranchers and merchants fought groups of smaller ones for control of the local economy. In accepting the office, Pat Garrett, once aligned with the latter, tacitly transferred his allegiance to the former. As their agent, he was assigned, or assigned himself, the task of tracking down the desperado Henry McCarty a.k.a. Henry Atrim a.k.a. William Bonney a.k.a. Billy the Kid. On the night of July 14, 1881, Garrett lay in wait for his prey in a darkened bedroom at Peter Maxwell's ranch, about forty kilometres from Fort Sumner, NMT, and shot him twice without asking him to surrender, indeed without speaking at all. The following year, a friend of Garrett's,

Ash Upson, was the ghost-writer for a book bearing Garrett's name, *The Authentic Life of Billy the Kid*. Thereafter, Garrett laboured as, by turns, a peace officer, rancher, customs collector and generally unsuccessful businessman, in various parts of the Southwest. On February 29, 1908, he was shot to death near Las Cruces, NMT. Some believe that his killer was Wayne Brazel, a rancher who confessed to the crime but was acquitted, or else Carl Adamson, who was in contention with Brazel for the purchase of property owned by Garrett. Others believe that Garrett was shot by John Miller, a professional killer, who was lynched in an unrelated matter in 1909. Several accounts suggest that Garrett was shot in the back of the head while urinating by the side of the trail.

RESOURCES: *Pat Garrett* by Leon C. Metz (Norman, Oklahoma, 1974); *Pat Garrett's Last Days* by Colin Rickards (Santa Fe, 1987); *Billy the Kid: A Short and Violent Life* by Robert M. Utley (Lincoln, Nebraska, 1989).

GERARD, Balthazar (1564–1584), assassinated the Dutch ruler Prince William of Orange (1533–1584), also known as William the Silent. Gerard was a Catholic zealot, William a Protestant one. Another factor in the killing was that in 1566 William had turned over his lands to Spain and left the country, in the hope that the Spanish would restore order and end the internal strife between Calvinists and Catholics. Spain's solution was to establish a tribunal known as the Council of Blood. Under the tribunal more than eight thousand Dutch Protestants were executed, while Spanish taxes slowly strangled the economy. William returned in 1569 and was the leader of Dutch resistance to Spanish occupation, although he refused to allow himself to be crowned king. In 1581, Philip II of Spain placed a bounty of twenty-five thousand crowns on William's head. The reward led to numerous assassination plots over the next three years. These included a poisoning attempt, another with explosives and yet another with a pistol (William was wounded in the head). Gerard had approached Spanish authorities and requested an advance on the reward to finance his own attempt. The Spanish refused but assured him that he would be paid on completion of the assignment. Gerard then appeared at William's court at Delft, claiming to be a Calvinist who had escaped persecution in Spanish-occupied territory and asking for monetary relief. The prince was apparently touched by Gerard's story and gave him the funds that Gerard used to buy pistols.

On July 10, 1584, Gerard returned to William's court, supposedly to petition the prince for a passport. After speaking to William, Gerard pretended to leave, but actually hid in a corridor outside the prince's dining room. When William left the dining room later that day, Gerard fired two of his pistols at close range. William staggered but did not fall, and was quickly taken away, only to die shortly afterwards. Gerard fled the scene but was apprehended within minutes as he was attempting to scale a garden wall.

Gerard was executed in a manner typical for one guilty of regicide. He was tortured on the rack and his right arm was burned off with a red-hot iron. His flesh was then torn from his body with red-hot pincers. His abdomen was cut open and his bowels torn out. Next, his legs and his remaining arm were cut off. Amazingly, he is reported to have still been alive after all of this. And so finally his heart was cut out and thrown in his face. According to eyewitness reports, Gerard never cried out in pain. Philip II paid the reward to Gerard's parents, after raising the funds by ransoming William's son. Although Gerard was a criminal to Dutch Protestants, he was a hero to Dutch Catholics. His head was preserved by sympathizers and for the next fifty years there was an unsuccessful movement to have Balthazar Gerard declared a saint.

RESOURCE: *William the Silent, Prince of Orange, 1533–1584, and the Revolt of the Netherlands* by Ruth Putnam (New York, 1911).

GERSDORFF, Rudolf-Christoph Freiherr von (1905–1980), attempted to assassinate Adolf Hitler (1889–1945), the German chancellor, on March 21, 1943. Gersdorff was allied with Major General Henning von Tresckow in a group of conspirators within the German military intent on the removal of Hitler. After the failure of the conspirators' attempt to bomb Hitler's plane on March 13, 1943, a new opportunity presented itself. Within the Third Reich, March 21 was set aside as Heroes' Memorial Day, and Hitler was scheduled to speak at the Unter den Linden Armoury in Berlin. Following the speech, he would meet with wounded veterans and then view an exhibit of captured war materiel from the Russian Front. Gersdorff, depressed and despondent since the death of his wife the previous year, agreed that he was ideally suited to be used as a human bomb, killing both Hitler and himself. At the time, he was a colonel attached to the Army Group Centre in Russia and was scheduled to be on hand to answer any questions Hitler might have about the display.

The British-made bombs from the March 13 attempt, which had failed to explode due to defective detonators, were retrieved, repaired and given to Gersdorff to hide in the pockets of his greatcoat. A problem persisted with the bombs' timing mechanisms, which were triggered by acid that ate through a wire to the detonator. Even the thinnest piece of usable wire still meant that ten minutes would elapse between activation and explosion. Precise timing was crucial, but any attempt to gain specific information about when Hitler planned to appear or how long his speech might run would have aroused suspicion. Gersdorff was forced to wait until Hitler was just about to view the exhibit to activate his bombs. Hitler gave a short speech, spoke briefly to some of the wounded veterans and then approached Gersdorff, who saluted with his right hand while his left activated the bombs. As ill luck would have it, Hitler seemed not even to look at the display but hurried out of the hall. Even when Hermann Goering tried to engage him in conversation on one of Hitler's favourite topics (opposition to Hitler from the Russian Orthodox Church), Hitler brushed him off abruptly. He left the hall no more than two minutes after Gersdorff had activated the bombs. Gersdorff hastily went to a lavatory where he deactivated them. Later, with his brother, he hid them in Breslau, and returned to the front.

There are many explanations for Hitler's rapid departure. He himself believed that he was protected by fate in such situations. Others might say he suffered from paranoia. Some have speculated that Gersdorff might have acted nervously, making Hitler suspicious. Although he never attempted to assassinate Hitler again, Gersdorff is one of the few who conspired to assassinate Hitler who was not picked up after the failed bombing in July 1944.

RESOURCE: *Widerstand, Staatsstreich, Attentat 1933–1945: Der Kampf der Opposition gegen Hitler* by Peter Hoffmann (Munich, 1970).

GNASSINGBE, Eyadema (b. 1937), assassinated Sylvanus Olympio

(1902–1963), the president of Togo. On January 13, 1963, Olympio was arrested by a group of disgruntled ex-members of the military led by a former master sergeant, Etienne Gnassingbe (who later changed his first name to Eyadema, which means "courage"). The rebels claimed Olympio was on his way to the US embassy to seek asylum when he was apprehended. After allegedly refusing a chance to resign, Olympio struggled against his captors and attempted to flee, only to be gunned down in the street. Gnassingbe always has claimed to be the person who fired the fatal shot or shots.

Gnassingbe was born in what is now northern Togo, a region that long has felt oppressed by the more prosperous south. After only six years' schooling, he joined the French colonial forces and saw action in Indo-China and Algeria before being sent back to Togo when that country became independent in 1960.

Under Olympio, Togo gradually became a dictatorship. Before opposition parties were banned outright in 1962, political opponents were often framed and jailed or exiled. Olympio also provoked the wrath of the country's Roman Catholics by clashing with Togo's archbishop. In addition, he imposed heavy taxes on growers of cocoa and coffee, two of Togo's largest exports. But the issue that eventually led to Olympia's assassination was his refusal to increase the size of the Togo army, which had only four hundred men. When returning veterans of the French colonial forces such as Gnassingbe found that there was no room for them in Togo's military, they began to plot.

Following Olympio's assassination, Eyadema's career began a spectacular rise. Becoming a lieutenant immediately after the shooting, he rose to become a lieutenant colonel by 1965. In 1966, when the military again overthrew the government of Togo, Gnassingbe was chosen to become the new president. He is thus one of the few twentieth-century assassins to become a ruler. His regime has been a difficult one. A rise in the international price of phosphates, another principal export, created an impression of wealth and prosperity. When the price of the commodity fell, Togo found itself mired in debt. Major government works projects were abandoned. Despite widespread opposition to his government, however, Gnassingbe has kept himself in power by satisfying the military.

RESOURCE: *Sylvanus Olympio: Un destin tragique* by Atsutse Kokuvi Agbobli (Abidjan, Ivory Coast, 1992).

GODSE, Nathuram (1910–49), assassinated Mohandas Karamchand Gandhi (1869-1948), the Indian spiritual leader and the father of India's independence. On January 30, 1948, just after 5:00 p.m., M.K. Gandhi emerged from his quarters at Birla House in New Delhi to hold a prayer meeting in the garden with several hundred people who were to pray for Hindu-Muslim unity. Gandhi, who was being supported by two of his grandnieces as he was weakened by a recent fast, was approached by Godse. Dressed in a bulky khaki tunic, Godse had his hands held in a traditional Hindu greeting. As Gandhi moved closer, Godse bowed slightly, then pulled a Beretta automatic pistol from the tunic and shot the Mahatma once in the abdomen and twice in the chest. Gandhi is supposed to have said *"Hai Rama! Hai Rama!"* ("My God! My God!") as he fell to the ground; he is also reputed to have looked up at his attacker and made a sign of forgiveness. Gandhi was rushed back to the house, where he died within the hour. Godse, who had already decided not to try to flee, stood silently waiting to be arrested, but was not approached at first because he was still armed. At last a member of the Indian air force grabbed him by the wrist, and Godse released his weapon. Police quickly surrounded Godse to prevent the crowd from lynching him.

Godse was born to a Hindu family that had already lost three sons in infancy. In order to trick or appease the spirits that had been depriving the family of sons, Godse was treated like a girl and his nose was pierced in the female fashion. Although he was born with the name of Ramchandra, he was soon renamed Nathuram—literally "Ram who wears a nose ring." The deception appears to have worked, as Nathuram was followed by three younger brothers, including Gopal, who would later join his big brother in the conspiracy against Gandhi.

In childhood, Nathuram was reputed to have special powers. He would stare at the family goddess and fall into a trance, then recite scriptures or Sanskrit hymns that he had never heard before. The family would then ask him questions; his answers were considered to be from the goddess herself. But this practise ended when Godse was in his teens.

Godse's father was a minor postal official whose job required him to move from place to place quite frequently. In 1929, when Nathuram was nineteen, the family relocated to Ratnagiri on the west coast, a community notable only for the fact that the British had exiled Vinayak Damodar Savarkar there. Savarkar was a firebrand who called for violent revolt against the Raj. Godse soon fell under the spell of this revolutionary Hindu who, in addition to his call for independence, favoured elimination of the caste system and oppression of the lower classes and espoused the re-conversion of Hindus who had embraced Christianity or Islam. Godse was a high school early-leaver who was working as a carpenter, but soon became Savarkar's secretary and learned to read and speak

English. He also joined Savarkar's political party, the Hindu Mahasabha, which called for Indian independence as a whole and Hindu nation. While the party was not intolerant of other religions, it did call for an end to special status for India's Muslims. Godse was arrested in 1938 for participating in a protest march in Hyderabad, where Hindus were being discriminated against. He served a year in prison for his actions.

In 1944, Godse became founding editor of the newspaper the *Marathi Daily Agrani* (literally, the *Forerunner*). Also working at the paper, as production manager, was Narayan Apte. These two men were later joined by Godse's younger brother Gopal, Mandan Lal Pahwa, Vishnu Karkare, Digambar Badge and Shankar Kistayya in a conspiracy to eliminate Gandhi. They were bitterly opposed to the partition of the country into mainly Hindu India and mainly Muslim Pakistan. They felt that Gandhi's policy of appeasing Muslim interests was destroying India. It is quite likely that Godse's old mentor Savarkar was either also a member of the group or at least aware of the plot against Gandhi.

As terrorists, the conspirators were inept. Their first attempt to kill Gandhi was on January 20, 1948. The group had purchased pistols and grenades as well as two slabs of gun cotton. The plan was to ignite one of the slabs of gun cotton to create a diversion, then shoot Gandhi during the ensuing panic. At the last minute, the group hastily decided to disguise themselves, but their disguises were comical at best. They also decided to use assumed names, but because they had picked the aliases so hurriedly, none of the conspirators could remember his comrades' choices. The gun cotton did not produce an explosion loud enough to cause any disturbance, and the pistols were defective and did not fire. So the only result of the plot was the arrest of Pahwa, though it was at that point that police learned of a conspiracy against Gandhi. The remaining members of the group examined their failure and concluded that they were incapable of an elaborate assassination plan. Godse therefore decided to act on his own.

Gandhi's funeral procession was viewed by well over one million people. He was cremated and his ashes were spread over fifty different rivers. All in all, more than ten million witnessed some part of Gandhi's funeral. Godse as well as the other conspirators were tried for the assassination, and Godse read a ninety-two-page handwritten statement taking full responsibility for the act. He blamed Gandhi for the partition of India as well as the perceived emasculation of Hinduism, citing Hindu legends of violence for the greater good to justify his actions. On

February 10, 1949, the court acquitted Vinayak Savarkar, sentenced four of the conspirators to life and found Godse and Narayan Apte guilty of the murder and sentenced them to be hanged. On November 14, 1949, Godse and Apte were led to the gallows shouting "India united." Godse thanked his jailers for treating him well. When the trapdoor opened, Apte's neck was broken and he died instantly. Godse dangled for nearly fifteen minutes before being strangled by the noose.

RESOURCES: *The Murder of the Mahatma* by G.D. Khosla, the judge in the Godse case (London, 1963); *The Men Who Killed Gandhi* by Manohan Malgonkar (Madras, 1978); *Gandhi's Murder & After* by Gopal Godse (Delhi, 1989).

GOLDMAN, Emma (1869–1940), was perhaps the most famous or notorious anarchist of her day, and while strictly speaking not herself a would-be assassin, she did conspire with her much less well-known colleague Alexander Berkman (1870–1936) to commit one of the signal such acts in American history, the attempt on the life of Henry Clay Frick (1849–1919), the Pittsburgh steel magnate and art collector. Frick was chair (1889–1900) of the Carnegie Steel Co. In a development of national significance, unionized workers at the firm's Homestead, Pennsylvania, mill went on strike in 1892 to protest Frick's refusal to negotiate a collective agreement. Frick hired three hundred Pinkerton strikebreakers to keep the plant open and evicted the workers from their company-owned homes. On July 6, in what now seems the inevitable clash, three Pinkertons and ten workers were killed; the state militia was called out to restore order.

Goldman and Berkman, who were running a series of small businesses in New York (the latest was an ice cream parlour) to support their feminist and anarchist activities, decided that Frick must be killed to avenge the steelworkers' deaths. Such an *Attentat* or terrorist act, they hoped, would cause labour to rise up against employers. Berkman, known as Sasha, insisted that Goldman not go with him to Pennsylvania but remain behind to explain his deed to the world. He first thought of killing Frick with a bomb but discarded the notion in favour of shooting him. To get money for a pistol, Goldman tried to engage in prostitution but her first john, sensing that she was not really a member of the profession, merely gave her some cash and asked nothing in return; the remainder of the money she borrowed from a family member.

At about 1:55 p.m. on July 23, Berkman, who was registered at a local hotel as "Rakhmetov," barged into Frick's office, posing as the head of a rival firm of strikebreakers. He fired three shots at Frick, two of which found their mark; Frick fell wounded to the floor, where Berkman tried to finish him off with two blows from a knife, only to be stopped, not by Pinkertons, but rather by genuine workers, who beat the assailant unconscious. This is symbolically important, because the attempt on Frick did not swing labour to the anarchist cause or even move it measurably to the left. Police confiscated a capsule of dynamite Berkman kept in his mouth before he could use it to commit suicide.

The case became a sensation and did much to further the already dangerous stereotype of the anarchist assassin. In New York, police persecuted Goldman to such an extent that she was forced to assume the name "E.G. Smith" and work in a bordello—not as a prostitute but as a seamstress, her original trade, both in present-day Lithuania, where she was born, and later in America following her immigration in 1885. From that point on, this tireless champion of individual liberties, already ridiculed as "Red Emma," would come to be called "the most dangerous woman in America." For his part, the sincere and otherwise harmless Berkman was sentenced to twenty-two years in prison, of which he served fourteen. After his release in 1906, he published his moving autobiography, *Prison Memoirs of an Anarchist*.

During the First World War, Goldman and Berkman agitated for free speech and against conscription. Each was sentenced to two years' imprisonment. In the post-war "red scare" they were among those deported to Russia even though they were American citizens: an important episode in the early career of J. Edgar Hoover, the future FBI director. (When Frick died, Berkman is said to have quipped that the capitalist had been "deported by God.") Goldman saw the new Soviet system as even more repressive than Western capitalism and in the early 1920s published two brave books outlining her findings. Both radicals were destined to further exile, Berkman largely in France, where he committed suicide, and Goldman in Canada.

RESOURCES: *Living My Life* by Emma Goldman (New York, 1931, two vols.); *Rebel in Paradise: A Biography of Emma Goldman* by Richard Drinnon (Boston, 1961); *Nowhere at Home: Letters from Exile of Emma Goldman and Alexander Berkman*, ed. Richard and Anna Maria Drinnon (New York, 1975); *The Battle for Homestead 1880–1892: Politics, Culture,* *and Steel* by Paul Krause (Pittsburgh, 1992); *The River Ran Red: Homestead 1892*, ed. David Demarest and Fannia Weingartner (Pittsburgh, 1992); *Henry Clay Frick: The Gospel of Greed* by Samuel A. Schreiner, Jr. (New York, 1995); *Triumphant Capitalism: Henry Clay Frick and the Industrial Transformation of America* by Kenneth Warren (Pittsburgh, 1996).

GORGULOV, Paul (1895–1932), assassinated Paul Doumer (1857–1932), the president of France, on May 6, 1932, while Doumer was attending a book sale held as a benefit for French veterans of the First World War. As Doumer passed through the hall, chatting with the various authors who were there that day, he was approached by Gorgulov, who fired five rounds from a revolver, two of which struck the president, one in the face, the other in the shoulder. A third bullet hit Claude Farrère, the sponsor of the benefit. Doumer was quickly taken to hospital, where surgeons removed the bullets and pronounced that the president was expected to make a complete recovery. Doumer died that evening.

Gorgulov, who was quickly surrounded by security officers at the scene of the shooting, was a refugee from Ukraine and a medical doctor trained in Prague. Since 1930 he had been in France, which at the time of the assassination was undergoing elections for the constituent assembly. The fact that a conservative president had been killed by a Russian soon led to rumours that Doumer had been shot by communists and that the GPU, precursor to the KGB, was doubtless involved. The Soviet Union denied such claims and accused France's White Russian refugee community of the murder.

In fact, Gorgulov was actually neither Red nor White but Green: that is, a member of the Ukrainian nationalist faction that attempted to establish an independent Ukraine during the Russian Civil War. The Greens were known for their fascism and anti-Semitism, and they conducted numerous campaigns against Ukrainian Jews. They were also ineffectual against the Red Army. Gorgulov claimed to be the president of the Russian Fascist Party. He had written a pamphlet entitled *The Green Programme for Russian Salvation*. He explained that a recent treaty between France and the Soviet Union convinced him that the French government and therefore President Doumer were in league with the Bolsheviks, "like the United States." When he heard that Doumer was to make a personal appearance at the book sale, he saw his chance to send a message to the government. While waiting for Doumer to arrive, Gorgulov purchased three books and inscribed them "Paul Gorgulov, chief of the Russian Fascists, who has just killed the President of the French Republic."

Once in custody, Gorgulov expressed admiration for Adolf Hitler and Benito Mussolini. He further declared that he had hoped his act would compel France to declare war against the Bolsheviks. Nonetheless, Gorgulov was pronounced sane and declared fit to stand trial. After a short proceeding, he received the death sentence. In his final moments, Gorgulov pleaded with his executioners: "Please make sure my children are not brought up as Bolsheviks or Communists." In the elections held two days after the shooting, the left wing made substantial gains and formed a coalition government.

RESOURCE: *Paul Doumer, le président assassiné* by Jacques Chauvin (Paris, 1994).

GRYNSZPAN, Herschel Feibel (1921–194?), whose assassination of a Nazi diplomat in Paris led to the brutal pogroms known as Kristallnacht, was born in Hanover. His action was spurred by the decision of the Polish government in October 1938 to declare invalid the passports of all Polish citizens living abroad. The policy affected seventeen thousand Polish Jews living in Germany, whom the Nazi government ordered expelled immediately. The Jews were placed in sealed cattle cars and were released into the no man's land between Germany and Poland, refused entry by either nation. They had no shelter or food, and suffered terribly until the Polish authorities finally relented and allowed them into Poland.

Grynszpan, seventeen at the time and living illegally in France, learned of these abuses in letters from his parents. On November 17, 1938, he purchased a pistol and went to the German embassy, asking to see the ambassador, claiming to have important documents that he wished to turn over to the German government. He was referred to the third secretary, Ernst vom Rath (1909–1938). Once alone with him in vom Rath's office, Grynszpan fired his weapon five times, hitting vom Rath twice. Vom Rath died November 9. The death was Germany's excuse for launching, that same day, their Crystal Night, in which thirty thousand Jews were sent to concentration camps and at least two hundred synagogues burned or otherwise destroyed and store windows broken (hence the name Kristallnacht). Also, the German Jewish community was fined one billion marks.

Grynszpan was arrested by French authorities and was in prison awaiting trial when the Nazis invaded France. In July 1940 he was extradited to Germany, where the Nazis planned to use him as the centrepiece of a show trial to prove the existence of a worldwide Jewish plot against Germany. But the trial, scheduled to begin May 11, 1942, never took place. Rumours suggested that Grynszpan had been advised by French lawyers to claim that he and vom Rath had engaged in a homosexual affair. If true, it would appear that Nazi authorities cancelled the trial in order to avoid the embarrassment of testimony about a homosexual union between a German and a Jew. Grynszpan was never heard from again. He was probably executed secretly or exterminated in one of the Nazi death camps.

RESOURCE: *Political Assassinations by Jews: A Rhetorical Device for Justice* by Nachman Ben-Yehuda (Albany, New York, 1993).

GUAJARDO, Jesús (1880–1920), a colonel in the Mexican cavalry fighting in support of President Venustiano Carranza's central government, assassinated Emiliano Zapata (1879?–1919), the principal insurgent in the southern part of the country during the Mexican Revolution of 1910–1919. In March 1919, Zapata wrote to Guajardo, commander of the fifteenth cavalry regiment, asking him to defect to Zapata's rebel army, which had occupied Mexico City on three occasions. Guajardo was in jail at the time, having been found drinking in a bar instead of hunting for Zapata's forces in the hills as ordered. Zapata reasoned that Guajardo, known as the ablest horseman and one of the top commanders in the federal forces, would be an ideal acquisition. The letter, however, was intercepted by the person who had ordered the arrest of Guajardo, General Pablo Gonzáles, commander of the government forces in Morelos. Gonzáles confronted Guajardo and informed him that Zapata's letter was enough evidence to have Guajardo shot for treason. Guajardo offered to play along with Zapata, gain his confidence, then arrange his assassination. He hastily composed an answer to Zapata, telling him that he was planning to defect with three hundred of his soldiers as well as arms and ammunition. Zapata seemed to throw his usual caution to the winds on receiving this response, as his army, composed of indigenous people such as himself, had become depleted in its guerilla campaign. Fresh men and particularly weapons were exactly what he needed.

On April 7, Zapata made a series of attacks to divert the Mexican authorities while Guajardo and his men pretended to mutiny in Cauautla. Guajardo's men reached the town of Joncatepec on April 9 and seized it in Zapata's name. As a sign of good faith, fifty former Zapatistas who had deserted to the regular forces and provided information on Zapata's forces were executed. Later that day, Guajardo and Zapata met for the first time. The rebel leader embraced "Citizen Guajardo," who had arrived with over six hundred troops and one mounted machine gun, as well as rifles and ammunition. Guajardo and Zapata agreed to meet again the next morning at Chinameca, a small town where Guajardo claimed to have secreted his main store of munitions.

On April 10, Zapata and a group of bodyguards entered the town and encountered Guajardo's men lined up in ranks, in honour-guard fashion. As Zapata rode in front of the troops, three bugle blasts, the traditional signal to present arms, sounded. After the final flourish, Guajardo's men raised their rifles in unison and fired on Zapata, killing him instantly. Zapata's supporters fled in panic; nine of them were gunned down but the rest managed to escape. Guajardo ordered his men to stop firing and to retrieve Zapata's body, as he needed the corpse as proof that Zapata was dead. Gaujardo had the body taken to the local police station where it was photographed. Later, motion picture cameras were sent for to record Zapata being lowered into his grave. Guajardo was rewarded by the Carranza government with fifty thousand pesos and a promotion to brigadier general. But his fortunes declined in 1920 when Carranza was assassinated by forces loyal to Alvero Obregón, who soon seized power. Obregón had every reason to prosecute the assassin of Emiliano Zapata, whose stature had grown in death. Guajardo therefore was arrested and after a brief court martial executed by firing squad.

RESOURCES: *Zapata and the Mexican Revolution* by John Womack, Jr. (New York, 1969); *Villa and Zapata: A Biography of the Mexican Revolution* by Frank McLynn (London, 1999).

GUITEAU, Charles J. (1841–1882), a crank office-seeker and would-be lawyer, became the most infamous assassin of his day when, in July 1881, he fatally wounded US president James A. Garfield (1831–1881), who lingered on until the autumn, throwing the country into a political crisis. In 1880, the Republican Party was split into two powerful factions: the Half-Breeds led by Senator James G. Blaine and the Stalwarts led by Senator Roscoe Conkling. The Stalwarts were strong supporters of the patronage system; one favourite issue for them was control of the custom houses at American ports, which were not only a major source of government revenue from tariffs on foreign goods but were also a source of spoils for themselves. The period 1877–1881 was a low point for the Stalwarts, as their opponent, Republican president Rutherford B. Hayes, had proven to be honest and intelligent. When Hayes decided not to seek a second term, however, the Stalwarts worked for the nomination of a candidate who had a been boon to their ambitions in the past: Ulysses S. Grant. For their part, the Half-Breeds nominated Blaine. After thirty-four ballots, the nominating convention was clearly deadlocked. Eventually, sixteen delegates cast their votes for a dark-horse candidate, Senator James A. Garfield of Ohio. The majority then switched their votes to him as a compromise, and Garfield, nominally a Half-Breed but without backing from either faction, was nominated. To reunite the party, Garfield chose Chester A. Arthur, a Stalwart, as his running mate. In the ensuing election, Garfield defeated the Democratic Party nominee, Winfield Hancock, by the barest of margins in the popular vote; the Republicans would have been defeated if a few thousand votes in New York State had gone the other way.

One man who felt that his work for the Republicans was key to winning New York was Charles Guiteau. Born in Freeport, Illinois, the son of an unsuccessful businessman and a mother who died when her son was only nine, Guiteau was a child who could not keep still and suffered many beatings from his authoritarian father. As a young man, he received an inheritance from his grandfather and tried to use the money to study at the University of Michigan, but he failed the entrance examination and later refused to take preparatory classes. At his father's urgings, he then joined the Oneida Community, a famous utopian commune rooted in radical Christianity, socialism and free love. He was an enthusiastic convert, but did not endear himself to the other members; on the matter of free love, the women of the community refused to sleep with the short and unattractive Guiteau, whom they referred to as "Charles Gitout." Eventually, Guiteau left Oneida and sued the group, claiming payment for the work he had done for them. As Guiteau had signed an agreement before entering Oneida that waived payment for labour, this suit came to nothing. Guiteau therefore decided to become a lawyer himself, and he clerked briefly at a law office in Chicago but was fired for incompetence. His experience, brief though it was, along with his ability to memorize short legal passages, allowed him to pass the simple oral examination that was the only requirement for admittance to the Illinois bar at that time. In his one and only case as a criminal lawyer, Guiteau gave a rambling summation, stopped halfway through and simply sat down. He soon decided that criminal law was not his forte and found that he could do much better at collecting overdue debts, following debtors and harassing them until they paid. Unfortunately, he began to embezzle some of the money collected on others' behalf and soon he had no clients at all.

The practice of defrauding his clients was part of Guiteau's general irresponsibility in financial matters. Guiteau rarely if ever paid a bill, was constantly being evicted from apartments and offices and frequently had his possessions seized by landlords. Other lawyers foolish enough to take Guiteau on as a partner soon realized that, no matter what agreement they had made concerning splitting expenses, they would never be paid. Guiteau's wife (because he believed she came from a wealthy family, he married a librarian he met at the YMCA) sometimes had to beg former landlords to return some of her clothing simply so she could continue working. Guiteau seemed concerned only with well-tailored clothes for himself, which usually he never finished paying for, and prostitutes. He contracted syphilis from one encounter, but refused to see a doctor as he found the whole affair humiliating. Eventually Guiteau's wife divorced him. As they needed to prove adultery in order to obtain the divorce, Guiteau allowed his wife to catch him with a prostitute.

His reputation destroyed in Chicago, Guiteau began following the evangelist Dwight Moody, eventually becoming an usher in the Moody organization. In time he was even allowed to preach, though the quality of his evangelizing was so poor that Moody fired him. Nevertheless, Guiteau began advertising himself as an evangelist who had been trained by Moody, and he travelled throughout the northeastern states delivering sermons to small audiences. A review of one of his performances in the *Daily Journal* of Newark, New Jersey, concluded: "Although the impudent scoundrel had talked only 15 minutes, he suddenly perorated brilliantly by thanking the audience for their attention and bidding them good-night. Before the astounded [audience of] 50 had recovered from their amazement, or the half-dozen bill collectors who were waiting for an interview with the lecturer had comprehended the situation, the latter had fled from the building and escaped."

In summer 1880, Guiteau found himself in New York at the height of the election season. Realizing that the easiest way to secure a well-paying position where he would have to do little work was through a political patronage appointment, he began campaigning for the Stalwarts. He wrote a speech endorsing Grant. When Grant lost the nomination to Garfield, Guiteau crossed out Grant's name and replaced it with Garfield's and had five hundred copies printed for distribution among Republican leaders, one of whom he hoped would deliver it. Although the Republicans were polite (it was an election year), Guiteau's contribution was not accepted and Guiteau had to give the speech himself. At a Harlem social club, before a crowd of six, Guiteau began, but as attrition spread through the audience, his voice dropped to a low murmur until he stopped speaking altogether and left the hall. Nevertheless, when Garfield won New York, Guiteau was convinced that his speech had been the factor that swung the state to the Republicans.

Having met Garfield several times during the campaign, he began sending the new president letters indicating that he would be willing to accept a diplomatic post in either Paris or Vienna. Garfield never responded. Other Republicans were more blunt. Guiteau began pestering Blaine, who became Garfield's secretary of state, until Blaine finally told him, "Never speak to me again on the Paris consulship as long as you live." Even so, Guiteau wrote to Garfield saying that Blaine favoured him for the Paris position. He also wrote Blaine saying that Garfield had recommended him for it. Guiteau spent many days in the corridors of the Executive Mansion hoping for an appointment to see the president. The White House was filled with office-seekers and crackpots, and White House staff tended to see Guiteau as the latter rather than the former. In time, Guiteau concluded that he was being discriminated against because of his support of the Stalwarts. Vice-President Arthur was a Stalwart and so Guiteau thought he might be an ally. Therefore he came to the conclusion that only by shooting Garfield could he ever secure a government position. Guiteau purchased a revolver and began stalking the president, who tended to travel without bodyguards. In addition, when Guiteau did not know where Garfield was, he would ask White House security about the president's whereabouts and the guards would tell him.

On July 2, 1881, James A. Garfield entered a railway station in Washington to embark on a short vacation and enrol his sons in school.

The only other government official with him was Blaine. Guiteau emerged from the ladies' waiting area where he had been hiding and, raising his pistol, fired twice. The first bullet merely grazed the president's arm but the second entered his back approximately ten centimetres from the spine, fractured a rib and came to rest just below the pancreas. Garfield fell to the ground but did not lose consciousness. He tried to calm his hysterical sons while the station master sent for police. A bystander apprehended Guiteau, who was promptly imprisoned. Garfield was taken to the White House to recuperate and Guiteau was held without charge while the authorities waited to see if he would be booked for attempted murder or murder.

Medicine in the 1880s was undergoing a debate on the question of whether maintaining antiseptic conditions for a patient was important. The head physician for the president, Dr D.W. Bliss, was not a believer in the need for antiseptic conditions. Because the medical team could not locate the bullet, the wound was constantly probed and searched by unwashed fingers and unsterilized instruments. The doctors released overly optimistic daily reports on the president's prospects for recovery. In time, Garfield suffered septicemia and his condition steadily worsened. The extreme heat of the Washington summer made Garfield even more uncomfortable, and a primitive air-conditioning unit was developed by which air was blown through a hastily constructed ice house and from there into the president's bedroom. Eventually Garfield insisted that he be moved from Washington; he was taken to Elberon, New Jersey, where he died September 19. Guiteau was charged with murder.

No lawyer was willing to defend him save his brother-in-law, George Scoville, who considered arguing that although his client had shot Garfield, the president's death was due to medical malpractice. In the end, however, Scoville used the obvious defence: insanity. He subpoenaed several high-ranking Republicans to testify about their dealings with Guiteau. Even the new president, Chester A. Arthur, gave a written deposition. In all, Guiteau had met with and was known by at least four past or future US presidents: Grant, Garfield, Arthur and Benjamin Harrison. All of them seemed to indicate that Guiteau was insane. Both the prosecution and the defence called leading alienists to testify as to Guiteau's mental condition. One defence witness pointed out that the flat shape of the top of Guiteau's skull was indicative of insanity, but an expert witness for the prosecution attributed the appearance of flatness to Guiteau's hairstyle. Yet another clinical witness testified that Guiteau was sane because the insane were all in poor physical health whereas Guiteau's health was sound.

Guiteau spent much of the trial harassing his lawyer and the witnesses. The judge threatened to remove him if he did not stop, but understood that expulsion would confirm the allegations that Guiteau was insane and so left the defendant free to interrupt the proceedings at will. The jury returned a verdict of guilty and Guiteau was sentenced to death. Guiteau was convinced that President Arthur would pardon him for his service to the Stalwarts, when in fact Guiteau's declaration of being "Most stalwart of the Stalwarts" had damaged the faction's image. Indeed, Senator Conkling was forced to resign his seat due to Guiteau's allegations that Conkling was an ally of his. Eventually, Congress passed the Pendleton Act, which called for government jobs to be assigned according to ability rather than political service.

Guiteau believed that he would be free to embark on a lecture tour about his crime. He remained so confident that samples of his handwriting (he sold autographs, only to complain that he wasn't receiving all the proceeds) show a strong, steady hand, free of stress or tremor, within a few days of his hanging on June 30, 1882. Guiteau was taken to the gallows, where, before a large group of spectators, he began reading a poem that he declared would be an ideal song when set to music. A song, purportedly written by Guiteau, was recorded and released in 1924 and may be found in Josh Dunson and Ethel Raim's *Anthology of American Folk Music* (New York, 1973). It concludes: "And now I mount the scaffold to bid you all adieu./ The hangman now is waiting, it's a quarter after two./ The black cap is over my face, no longer can I see,/ But when I'm dead and buried you'll all remember me." In fact, this is not a song written by Guiteau, who instead delivered a rambling poem, of which an excerpt is: "I am going to the Lordy, I am so glad,/ I am going to the Lordy, I am so glad./ I am going to the Lordy,/ Glory Hallelujah! Glory Hallelujah!/ I am going to the Lordy." As was the case throughout his life, Guiteau could not finish the poem, and he dropped the paper on the scaffold. His final words were, "Glory, ready, go."

Garfield was the penultimate American president to have taken part in the Civil War (McKinley was the last). The archly cynical journalist Ambrose Bierce served under General Garfield at Shiloh and Chickamauga. In 1881, as Garfield spent the summer in his unsuccessful effort to fight off the effects of Guiteau's bullet and the meddlesome fingers of too many attending physicians, the country was gripped in the kind of national vigil more commonly associated with the age of television than the age of the telegraph. Bierce, being Bierce, made a joke of the matter: "Things have come to a pretty pass when a man can't keep his name out of the newspapers without shooting the chief magistrate of our beloved country," he told his readers. But in fact Bierce was as moved as anyone, and his mind was naturally cast back to the war, now a generation in the past; Garfield's assassination is what started him to turn his hand to Civil War stories, his most lasting legacy as a writer.

RESOURCES: *The Trial of the Assassin Guiteau: Psychiatry and the Law* by Charles E. Rosenberg (Baltimore, 1989); *The Murder of James A. Garfield: The President's Last Days and the Trial and Execution of His Assassin* by James C. Clark (Jefferson, North Carolina, 1993). Guiteau's papers are in the special collections library at Georgetown University.

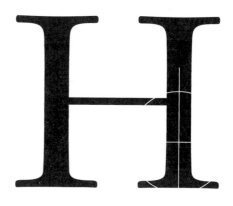

HAGAN, Thomas (a.k.a. Talmadge Hayer) (b. 1943), assassinated Malcolm X (1925–1965) on February 21, 1965, shortly after the charismatic Black Muslim leader took the podium at the Audubon Ballroom in Harlem in New York City. The facility had been hired for the day by the Organization for Afro-American Unity, a group founded by Malcolm X (who was born Malcolm Little). Malcolm opened the meeting with the standard greeting *"As-Salaam Alaikum"* ("peace be with you"), to which the audience responded *"Wa-Alaikum-Salaam"* ("and peace be with you"). At that instant, a man shouted, "Get your hand out of my pocket." The strange utterance was a pre-arranged signal for four other members of the audience to begin a commotion. The speaker said from the stage, "Hold it. Let's cool it brothers." Those were his last words. One of the men immediately withdrew a Luger pistol and, approaching to within about 2.5 metres of the stage, shot Malcolm in the chest while another conspirator threw a smoke grenade from the back of the room and yet another shot the speaker again, using a sawed-off shotgun. As Malcolm fell to the floor, Thomas Hagan used his pistol to fire round after round into Malcolm's body; he was still firing as the other assailants fled. The noise, panic and confusion froze Malcolm's bodyguards, but as the assassins were running away, one of the security personnel, Reuben X Francis, returned fire, hitting Hagan in the thigh. As the others escaped, Hagan fell to the floor, where he was severely beaten by Malcolm's supporters until police took him away. Malcolm was rushed to a nearby hospital and pronounced dead within fifteen minutes of arrival.

Little is known of the assassins of Malcolm X. The only one arrested at the scene originally gave his name as "Tommy" but later changed his answer to "Talmadge Hayer." But a check of his fingerprints revealed he had been arrested previously as "Thomas Hagan". In any case, he denied being a Black Muslim, though eyewitness reports and photographic evidence clearly established that Hagan was a member of a Muslim mosque in New Jersey (and a member of its karate team). Hagan also was discovered to be married with two children.

Police later also arrested Norman 3X Butler and Thomas 15X Johnson, associates of the Prophet Elijah Muhammad (1897–1975), the leader of the Nation of Islam, a rival sect, of whom Malcolm X had once been a follower. In fact, as a Nation of Islam member, Malcolm quickly became a popular figure, leading to personality clashes with Elijah Muhammad (also known as the Last Messenger of God), who believed that Malcolm was more concerned with his own career than with service to the group. Malcolm, for his part, noticed that Elijah Muhammad did not adhere to the requirements for being a good Muslim, particularly the prohibitions against marital infidelity. In 1964, Malcolm left the Nation of Islam and formed the Organization for Afro-American Unity, causing a severe split in Black Muslim ranks. The Nation of Islam began denouncing the former leader, claiming that he was a hypocrite and was destroying African-American unity. From condemnation, the attacks soon moved to veiled threats against Malcolm's life.

Hagan claimed that he was recruited for the conspiracy by two men and that he never learned the names of his fellow conspirators. The plotters first considered killing Malcolm at his home, but realized that security there was too tight. When they attended a meeting at the Audubon Ballroom, they discovered that although there were many security guards present, no one was searched for weapons. Hagan has also said that neither Butler nor Johnson was part of the conspiracy. At the trial of the three men, Hagan changed his story on several occasions. He claimed to be an innocent bystander who found in the toilet the weapons that were later discovered on his person. Later he denied his involvement in the Nation of Islam and even his proper name. By the time Hagan declared under oath that neither Butler nor Johnson was involved, the jury had no reason to believe him. Butler's lawyer also pointed out that Butler had visited a hospital on the day of the shooting to receive treatment for thrombophlebitis, a condition that would have made it impossible for him to run from the scene. In addition, both Butler and Johnson were well-known devotees of Elijah Muhammad. Because of the threats from the Nation of Islam, not to mention a fire-bombing of Malcolm's house several days before the shooting, security for the meeting had been tight. No prominent member of the Nation of Islam could have slipped into the meeting without being noticed. Nevertheless, Hagan, Butler and Johnson were all found guilty of the murder of Malcolm X and each received twenty years' imprisonment. While in prison, all three men legally changed their names: Hagan to Mujabid Abdul Halim, Butler to Muhammad Abdul Aziz and Johnson to Khalil Islam. Hagan stopped denying that Hagan was his original name and that he was not a Black Muslim, but he continued to maintain the innocence of the other two.

In 1985, all three were paroled from prison. Hagan began working at a homeless shelter in Manhattan. He has said that he will continue to seek *tawbah* (repentance) for his deed. For obvious reasons, the man now known as Mujabid Abdul Halim prefers to keep as low a profile as possible. A minor stir was created when Muhammad Abdul Aziz (the former Norman 3X Butler) was named as the Nation of Islam's new captain for New York City and the East Coast region. An article in the *Village Voice* entitled "Malcolm X's Killer Appointed to Run Malcolm's Mosque" led to a media frenzy, culminating in Aziz taking a polygraph test to prove his innocence. A similar commotion was created in 1995 when an article in the *New York Post* declared that Louis Farrakhan, the Nation of Islam leader, was responsible for the conspiracy. Farrakhan sued the newspaper successfully. In spite of this seeming vindication, Malcolm X's daughter, Qubilah Bahiyah Shabazz, was arrested that same year for attempting to procure a hitman to kill Farrakhan.

The exact details of who ordered the assassination of Malcolm X will probably never be known, with some Black Muslims believing that the FBI lay at the back of the scheme. Long after his arrest and trial, Thomas Hagan finally gave up the names of people he alleged were his co-conspirators, identifying Benjamin X Thomas, Leon X Davis, William X Bradley and William X Kinley, all from Nation of Islam Mosque Number 25 in Newark, New Jersey. No attempt has been made to prosecute any of them.

RESOURCES: *The Death and Life of Malcolm X* by Peter Goldman (New York, 1973); *The Messenger: The Rise and Fall of Elijah Muhammad* by Karl Evanzz (New York, 1999).

HAMUD, Hamud Mohamed (1946–1972), assassinated Sheik Abeid Amani Karume (1905–1972), vice-president of Tanzania and chairman of the ruling Revolutionary Council, on April 7, 1972, when four gunmen stormed the headquarters of the Afro-Shirazi Party where Karume was playing cards with some associates. While three of the gunmen subdued guards at the door, the fourth, Hamud, entered the building and opened fire with a machine gun. Karume was sprayed with bullets and died instantly. As Karume's bodyguards returned fire, Hamud was shot in the brain and also died on the scene.

Sheik Abeid Amani Karume was a near-illiterate who became a union organizer in Zanzibar. Using his labour connections, he grew prominent in the Afro-Shirazi Party, a nationalist Marxist organization that replaced the pro-British government shortly after independence in December 1963. At once the country's social and economic pecking order, of whites followed by Asians followed by Arabs followed by Blacks, was turned upside down. In retaliation for generations of discrimination, the newly empowered Blacks, led by Karume, began widespread looting, raping and killing among the non-Black minority. Also under Karume, Zanzibar merged with Tanganyika to become Tanzania. Although Tanzania's president was the Tanganyikan Julius Nyerere (1922–1999), the real power was still held by Karume as vice-president. Under Karume, European holdings in the new republic were quickly nationalized, while the People's Army continued the official persecution of Asians, Europeans and Arabs.

Hamud Mohamed Hamud was a lieutenant in the Tanzanian army. His father, Mohamed Hamud, had also been an assassin who, shortly before independence, fatally stabbed a member of the legislative council. His death sentence had been commuted to life imprisonment by the sultan. Shortly after the revolution, however, Mohamed Hamud was rearrested, beaten, tortured and then forced to dig his own grave before being shot. Yet the exact motives for Karume's assassination will never be known as none of the assassins survived the event. After the shooting, and Hamud's death, the other conspirators tried to escape, pursued by virtually the entire People's Army. One of the assassins killed himself when he was surrounded; the other two died in a shootout with troops less than twenty-five kilometres from the scene.

RESOURCE: *Tanzanie, Tanganyika, Zanzibar* by Bernard Passot (Paris, 1985).

HARRELSON, Charles Voyde (b. 1938), is an American assassin and killer-for-hire who once admitted his involvement in the murder of President John F. Kennedy but later recanted. In 1968, Harrelson, a Texan described at various times as a professional gambler and a "wanderer," was convicted of contract killing. Later, in 1973, he was convicted of killing a grain dealer for a $2,000 fee. In 1982, he and another career criminal, a narcotics smuggler named Jamiel ("Jimmy") Chagra, were found guilty of conspiring to kill a federal district judge, James G. Wood, Jr., who was gunned down by rifle fire outside his San Antonio home on May 29, 1979. Wood, the first federal judge to be murdered in more than a century, had been scheduled to preside over a drug case involving Chagra. Harrelson, who was already in prison when they were indicted following a large-scale FBI investigation that involved more than seventy agents and cost over $4.7 million, claimed to have been in Dallas on the day of the Wood killing, for which the prosecution said he was to be paid $250,000. Many conspiracy theorists believe that Harrelson was one of the mysterious so-called hoboes rounded up by Dallas police in the railway yard adjoining Dealey Plaza immediately following the Kennedy killing but released without being charged—indeed, apparently without any records of the arrest. In a prison interview, Harrelson agreed with a British documentary filmmaker that one of the men in the notorious photographs of the arrests did indeed bear a striking resemblance to him. In 1988, Harrelson began to seek a new trial in the Judge Wood case, claiming that he had not been represented adequately; the process was still underway in 2000. Harrelson's son, the actor Woody Harrelson, is said to have researched his role in Oliver Stone's 1994 film *Natural Born Killers* by visiting his father in federal prison, where he remains.

HARVEY, William (1915–1976), conspired repeatedly, and sometimes comically, to assassinate the Cuban president Fidel Castro (b. 1927). In the early 1960s, the Central Intelligence Agency (CIA) in the United States, under pressure from the Kennedy administration, which inherited the initiative from the Eisenhower White House, was plotting the overthrow of Castro's communist regime. The project, code-named Operation Mongoose, looked at several different possibilities for Castro's removal. When an American invasion of Cuba was halted at the Bay of Pigs, the CIA's thoughts turned from invasion to assassination. The head of Operation Mongoose was an atypical CIA agent, William Harvey, a large and imposing figure, loud, abusive and a heavy drinker. He was also so obese that he had special permission to fly first class because he was too big to fit into an economy-class seat. Harvey was also a gun enthusiast, arriving at work each day with a different pistol. In debate, he was known for withdrawing his handgun du jour, unsnapping the safety and levelling the weapon at people with whom he felt he was losing an argument.

Although Operation Mongoose never mounted a serious attempt to assassinate Castro, many different schemes were discussed, each more outlandish than the last. The CIA recruited the Mafia to assist them in the undertaking. The Mafia responded eagerly, as Castro's revolution in 1958 had led shortly thereafter to their expulsion from the island, with its lucrative gambling industry. As a go-between, the CIA used the eccentric multi-millionaire Howard Hughes, whose connections to organized crime came through his holdings in Las Vegas. (This after the mafia's reputed financial genius, Meyer Lansky, had already announced a $1-million bounty on Castro.)

Eventually, Harvey met with Santos Trafficante, Florida's Mafia boss, and began discussing plans. The CIA's first suggestion, sending a mob hitman to Cuba, was rejected immediately. Trafficante explained that unlike political assassins, organized crime's professional killers did not engage in missions where they would surely be caught.

In February 1961, the CIA provided Trafficante with botulism pills to be put in Castro's food. Trafficante accepted them but later informed Harvey that Castro had stopped eating at restaurants and that it was impossible to poison his food at home. Undeterred, the CIA later supplied Trafficante with poisons, sniper rifles and explosives. What it did not know was that Trafficante had no intention of actually trying to kill Castro. Although he was powerful in Florida, the adopted home of most Cuban refugees, Trafficante had no personal stake in the "liberation" of Cuba. Unlike Lansky, he had never been involved heavily in Cuban gambling, and realizing the risks of attempting to kill the Cuban leader, he decided to take any and all of the weapons that the CIA offered and put them to use domestically. With each new weapon, Trafficante offered a fresh excuse why it could not be used. Many believe it more than probable that the CIA's weaponry was employed in the assassination of Mafia informants and rival bosses.

As time passed, the CIA's plans to eliminate Castro exceeded the boundaries of reality. It had been experimenting with the idea that a Cuban civilian could be hypnotized to assassinate Castro and retain no memory of having done so. Then the agency began to speculate on how to poison a box of Castro's favourite cigars or to lace cigars with explosives. The plan was abandoned, because a) if Castro received the cigars as a gift while in the United States, where he was scheduled to address the United Nations, the assassins would be revealed, and b) Castro had a habit of passing out cigars to guests. Knowing that Castro was an enthusiastic scuba diver, the CIA then began speculating on killing Castro underwater; plans for a bomb disguised to look like a conch shell were discussed but never acted on. The agency thought it had its opportunity when an American lawyer was allowed to enter Cuba to negotiate the release of men captured after the disastrous Bay of Pigs landing. The lawyer was to present Castro with a wetsuit, and the agency's labs made one that was infected with tuberculosis bacilli. But the fact that Castro's death would be traced back to the United States made the idea no more practicable than poisoned cigars.

The CIA had been working with a new mind-altering substance that it felt would discredit Castro if he could be dosed with it: lysergic acid diethylamide (LSD). The agency speculated that if it could spray LSD into a radio studio before Castro delivered a nationwide address, the Cuban people would rise up and overthrow their stoned leader. Logistical difficulties prevented the plan from being carried out. Similar reasons kept the CIA from spraying Castro's shoes with thallium salts, a powerful depilatory that would cause the leader to lose his hair, eyebrows and his trademark beard—with a corresponding loss of machismo and mass appeal. Perhaps the most absurd plan for the elimination of Castro was based on spreading rumours in Cuba that the country had been chosen to be the site of the return of Jesus Christ but only after Castro was killed; the CIA was prepared to re-enforce the gossip by sending a submarine to the Cuban coast on the appropriate night and to fire star shells into the sky, creating a bright light that the devout, they hoped, would take as a sign of the Second Coming. This plan, nicknamed "Elimination by Illumination," was also abandoned.

In addition to its misplaced trust in the Mafia, the agency never quite grasped that at that stage the people of Cuba were not particularly eager to remove Castro, so fresh were the memories of brutality and corruption under his American-supported predecessor, Fulgencio Batista. Dissidents who could have been part of an insurgency had fled to the United States. Also, the CIA's network of operatives in Cuba was heavily compromised by Cuban double agents. The final downfall of Operation Mongoose came when the attorney general, Robert Kennedy, younger brother of President John Kennedy, learned that the CIA was using the Mafia's assistance. Neither Kennedy objected to planning

Castro's assassination, but Robert Kennedy was furious at the collaboration of the public and private sectors, as he had been actively attacking the power of Mafia leaders. He was shocked that some of the Mafiosi he was prosecuting were receiving government funds as part of Operation Mongoose. He angrily informed Harvey that the government of the United States of America did not enter into partnerships with organized crime bosses. Obviously, Kennedy had forgotten that Washington and the Mafia worked hand-in-glove during the Second World War against the Axis powers. President Kennedy ordered Mongoose shut down. The end came in 1962, just as the CIA was beginning to realize that its Mafia contacts were not acting in good faith.

The following year, William Harvey was transferred to the CIA's Rome station, where his abusive manner escalated to the point that a number of European operatives wrote blistering reports to Washington about his conduct. Harvey was soon recalled to the United States, where he was given the less demanding role of heading a study of audio security for CIA stations. On his last day in Rome, the CIA threw a farewell party for Harvey. After the event, Harvey walked to the American Embassy on the Via Veneto and urinated against the wall of the building. Shortly after returning to the United States, he retired from the agency due to poor health.

During the early 1960s, the CIA was plotting the assassination of several leaders around the world. Although the exact involvement of the CIA in the assassinations of Patrice Lumumba of the Congo and Rafael Trujillo of the Dominican Republic (both 1961), and of Abdul Kassem of Iraq and Ngo Dinh Diem of South Vietnam (both 1963), is at best difficult to trace, the failed conspiracy against Castro involved a source of information harder to suppress: the Mafia. Many Mafiosi arrested throughout the 1960s and 1970s were willing to speak of their CIA involvement. This led to new deaths such as that of Sam Giancana of Chicago, a veteran of the Mongoose misadventures, who was murdered in 1975, just before he was due to speak before a Senate committee investigating US government assassination plots. Johnny Roselli, who had brought Trafficante into the plot, was killed a year later.

RESOURCES: *Who's Who in CIA*, anonymous (Berlin, 1968); *The Man Who Kept The Secrets: Richard Helms and the CIA* by Thomas Powers (New York, 1979).

HAYASHI Yukichi (1891–?), a Japanese community leader in Shanghai before and during the Second World War, shot and wounded W.J. ("Tony") Keswick in January 1941. Keswick was a British spy and the taipan of the famous British trading firm Jardine, Matheson, his family's business. The incident took place in the Chinese city's days as the major treaty port, in which Japanese, Americans, Russians, British and assorted European nationalities lived and worked immune from Chinese laws and taxes. Between their invasion of Manchuria and their military take-over of Shanghai and Hong Kong ten years later, the Japanese community in Shanghai grew considerably—though more slowly than its influence in local affairs. A poor showing by Japan in the 1936 municipal council election caused Hayashi, a wealthy one-time brothel owner, to write in his own blood that he took personal responsibility for his country's humiliation in the matter. The council election of 1940, the last one to be held before the Japanese military takeover, had similarly unflattering results. The following month, at a meeting of the Japanese Ratepayers' Association, of which he was about to be replaced as chair by Keswick, Hayashi spent a half hour denouncing voters from the stage. Later, back in the audience, he rose and fired at Keswick, wounding him slightly along with a Japanese councillor and a Japanese municipal official. The audience then rose up in Hayashi's support, hurling furniture and other objects at the platform. Hayashi stood calmly with his hands in his pockets waiting to be arrested but was carried away on the shoulders of the enthusiastic crowd. He was, however, arrested by Japanese consular police and released under bond awaiting trial, which was held in Nagasaki.

He was found guilty and sentenced to two years' hard labour (suspended for five years); in time, the sentence was reduced to one year's suspension, and Hayashi returned to Shanghai in August 1941, four months before its occupation by the Japanese, which took place within hours of the Japanese attack on Pearl Harbor. Assassinations were so common in Shanghai in the 1930s and 1940s that people commented that the local version of the biblical injunction "an eye for an eye" was "a judge for a judge and an editor for an editor." Keswick died in 1990.

RESOURCE: *Secret War in Shanghai: An Untold Story of Espionage, Intrigue, and Treason* by Bernard Wasserstein (New York, 1999).

HEPBURN, James, fourth Earl of Bothwell (1535?–1578), assassinated

Henry Stewart, Lord Darnley, consort of Mary Queen of Scots, on February 10, 1567, while Darnley (b. 1546?) was recuperating at Kirk o'Field in Edinburgh from an illness that was most likely syphilis. He was there at the command of his wife, Mary Queen of Scots (1542–1587), who had been staying with him but who had left that evening for an engagement, ordering Darnley to remain at home. That night Kirk o'Field was destroyed in an enormous explosion. Darnley was found dead outside of the house. The official cause of death was given as strangulation. Although the exact details of how Darnley escaped before the explosion, and of who strangled him, were never known, the person widely thought responsible was the Earl of Bothwell.

Mary and her husband (her second; she had married a Frenchman but knew that in order to secure the Scots throne she would have to marry a Scot) had never got along. Darnley was technically king of Scotland, but Mary was the true ruler; Darnley had no power or authority on his own. What's more, Darnley was jealous of those whom Mary favoured for advice instead of relying on his own—particularly David Rizzio, an Italian musician on whom Mary became more and more dependant for counsel. On March 9, 1566, a group of armed men seized Rizzio while he was dining with Mary and killed him in the presence of the queen, who was six months pregnant. Darnley was known to have been behind the murder and further suspected of hoping that the shock of the event would cause Mary to miscarry. But she did not miscarry, and her son James (later James VI of Scotland and James I of England) was born three months later.

The desire to kill Darnley was Mary's, but the deed itself was carried out by her favourite, Bothwell, who was also most likely her lover. The assassination created a scandal so great that Mary and Bothwell were forced to flee Scotland. On April 24, Mary was "kidnapped" by Bothwell. On May 7, Bothwell divorced his wife. On May 15, Mary married Bothwell. The official story was that Bothwell had kidnapped Mary, raped her and informed her that the only way she could clear her reputation (rape victims at the time were judged as adulterers) was to marry him. Even Mary's closest supporters did not believe that she had gone unwillingly with Bothwell. Evidence of Mary's complicity in the Darnley assassination was provided by a series of documents known as the Casket Letters, which, although certainly forgeries, sealed her fate. With no support in Scotland, Mary fled to England, where she was protected by her cousin Elizabeth I. On February 8, 1587, Mary was executed for her participation in the Babington Plot to kill Elizabeth. Bothwell had decided to avoid England and instead travelled to Norway, where be became involved in another scandal with a married woman and was imprisoned until his death. His embalmed body was displayed in a church at Faarevejle in what is now Denmark.

RESOURCE: *Darnley: A Life of Henry Stuart, Lord Darnley Consort of Mary Queen of Scots* by Caroline Bingham (London, 1995).

HEROLD, David E. ("Davy") (a.k.a. Mr. Harris, a.k.a. Boyd) (1842?–1865), a failed drugstore clerk described by contemporaries as intellectually handicapped, was one of the conspirators hanged in the matter of President Abraham Lincoln's assassination in Washington in 1865. He was the only male among seven children of a widow who made her home within the federal navy yard near the capital. John Wilkes Booth recruited him at a livery stable. His assignments were two: to accompany Lewis Powell to the home of the secretary of state, William H. Seward, as an accomplice to Seward's murder, and then to ride with the party of conspirators to the Confederate lines after the assassinations of Lincoln, Seward and the vice-president.

On the evening of April 14, 1865, Booth killed Lincoln and Powell wounded Seward, but a third man, George Atzerodt, lost his nerve before he could make an attempt on Andrew Johnson, the vice-president. Only Booth and Herold met at the rendezvous point and rode south, stopping at the home of Dr. Samuel Mudd, who set the leg fracture Booth suffered at some point during the getaway. Although the search for the conspirators began in confusion, hindered by rivalry between the army and the secret service, once organized, it became the largest manhunt in US history up to that time, with fifteen hundred detectives and ten thousand troops scouring the towns and countryside south of Washington. The reward posted for Herold was $25,000, only half the price on Booth's head (the first time in American history that photographs of the accused were used on reward posters). On April 24, the two fugitives, pretending to be brothers and Confederate veterans, induced genuine Confederate veterans to ferry them across the Rappahannock River, but Herold was unable to resist bragging about their real identities. The soldiers shied at the revelation but before parting company directed

Herold and Booth to the farm of a Southern sympathizer, Richard Garrett, where they would be welcome. Herold did not repeat his indiscretion, but in time Garrett became suspicious anyway. Finally the two were asked to move on but permitted to stay one more night if they spent it in a tobacco barn rather than the house. Meanwhile, Union cavalry threatened one of the Confederate officers from the ferry into revealing the fugitives' location, and at about 2:00 a.m. on April 26, a squad of twenty-six federal troops arrived at the Garrett farmstead and surrounded Booth and Herold in the barn. The troopers were under the command of a lieutenant and a sergeant, Boston Corbett; the latter suffered from auditory delusions, believing that God was speaking to him directly. The federals set the barn alight to force out the conspirators. Herold crawled out of the burning outbuilding to surrender, telling the soldier ordered to guard him, "I always liked Mr. Lincoln's jokes." Booth refused to surrender. Before he could be captured, Booth was killed by Corbett, acting contrary to orders.

Herold was tried along with seven other conspirators and was among the four who were hanged on July 7, 1865. At the trial, a Washington physician was called to testify on Herold's behalf but could say only that "I consider him a very light, trivial, unreliable boy; so much so that I would never let him put up [that is, fill] a prescription of mine if I could prevent it, feeling confident that he would tamper with it if he thought he could play a joke on anybody. In mind I consider him about 11 years of age."

RESOURCES: *Myths after Lincoln* by Lloyd Lewis (New York 1929; reprinted as *The Assassination of Lincoln: History and Myth* [Lincoln, Nebraska, 1994]); *The Lincoln Murder Conspiracies* by William Hanchett (Urbana, Illinois, 1983).

HERRERO, Rodolfo (1885?–1964), assassinated Venustiano Carranza (1860–1920), the president of Mexico, on May 21, 1920, when Carranza and a handful of supporters with five million pesos in gold and silver were spending the night in the village of Tlaxcalantongo. At this time, a rebellion, coinciding with the general elections, had forced the president from Mexico City. The entourage had been travelling by train to Veracruz, but railway workers aligned with the rebels sabotaged the lines and the group was forced to proceed by foot. At Tlaxcalantongo,

Carranza met General Rodolfo Herrero, who had been charged with protecting the presidential party. After settling in for the night in a small hut, the president and his men were woken by the sound of gunfire and shouts of "Death to Carranza, Long live Obregón" (Carranza's opponent in the election). Soldiers began to fire on the hut. Carranza, hit in the thigh, reached for his rifle, but was shot again before he could rise to defend himself. In all, Carranza was shot four times in the attack and died within minutes.

Herrero was a former rebel chieftain, active since 1912. He had commanded an armed force in the Puebla region for several years before joining the regular Mexican forces. Some years earlier, a family feud with the governor of the south-central state of Puebla led to the execution of Herrero's father, an act later blamed on Carranza, who had not been innocent of such doings. One factor in his overthrow was his perceived involvement with the assassination of Emiliano Zapata, though a bigger consideration was most likely his attempt to appoint a political non-entity, Ignacio Bonilla, to succeed him as president. Two of Mexico's leading generals, Pablo Gonzaléz and Alvaro Obregón, who felt that they should be next in line, split with Carranza over the issue and began the rebellion that would force Carranza from the capital. After Carranza's death, Obregón seized power and deleted constitutional provisions that excluded anyone who had ever participated in a revolt against the government from assuming office.

There is considerable although not conclusive evidence that Obregón ordered Herrero to kill Carranza. Obregón, nevertheless, called an immediate investigation into Carranza's death. Herrero testified that Carranza had actually committed suicide. He also attempted to bribe the doctors performing Carranza's autopsy to confirm his story. The doctors, however, refused Herrero's enticement and pointed out that the positioning of the four rifle bullets eliminated suicide as a possible cause of death. The enquiry dismissed the case against Herrero for lack of evidence. Shortly thereafter, Herrero was stripped of rank for being "blinded by Carranza's example," a veiled reference to Carranza's assassination of Zapata. Obregón was not officially implicated in the Carranza assassination.

Carranza was buried with no official honours, but his funeral drew an enormous crowd of mourners; an estimated eighty thousand people sang the national hymn as his body was lowered into a grave in a peasants' cemetery. In 1942, with Carranza's enemies either dead or politically inactive, Carranza's body was exhumed and reburied with full official honours in the crypt of the Monument to the Revolution. Carranza's four sons, who had fled for their lives in the wake of the assassination (some of Carranza's relatives who were not quick enough to realize their peril were shot by government forces) began political careers of their own. Alvaro Obregón went on to serve one term as president before he too was assassinated.

RESOURCE: *Venustiano Carranza's Nationalist Struggle* by Douglas W. Richmond (Lincoln, Nebraska, 1983).

HINCKLEY, John W., Jr. (b. 1955), opened fire on US president Ronald Reagan (b. 1911) on March 30, 1981, apparently in a misguided attempt to impress the Hollywood actress Jodie Foster (b. 1962), with whom he is said to have been obsessed. Hinckley was the child of a wealthy family; his father, John W. (Jack) Hinckley, Sr., owned an oil company, but relations between the two were strained. The young Hinckley, however, was devoted to his mother Jo Ann (until 1981, nicknamed "Jodie"). Hinckley was a failed university student who relied on his parents for support while fantasizing about a career in music emulating his role model, John Lennon. After Lennon's assassination in 1980 at the hands of Mark David Chapman, Hinckley travelled to New York to join other mourners in front of Lennon's apartment building.

In 1976, Hinckley saw Martin Scorsese's *Taxi Driver*, a film about an assassin loosely based on Arthur Bremer and in which Jodie Foster plays an underage prostitute. Hinckley watched the movie at least fifteen times; it would provide inspiration for his later actions. He began to purchase guns and practise with them. He also made many attempts to meet and speak with Foster, conversing with her on the phone at least twice before she began refusing his calls. Hinckley then stalked her on the campus at Yale University, where she was then a student; residents at the women's dormitory where Foster lived nicknamed him "Mr. Toxic Shock."

By 1979, Hinckley's reading centred on books about assassins, serial killers and mass murderers; one of Hinckley's final term papers at Texas Tech was plagiarized from the mass murderer Charles Starkweather. Before attempting to kill Reagan, Hinckley considered opening fire on the Yale campus, shooting Senator Edward Kennedy and shooting up the Senate chamber at random. In 1980, the same year he had his first sexual experience (with an underage prostitute), Hinckley began to follow President Jimmy Carter. By early autumn 1980, polling numbers indicated that Carter would lose the presidential election to Ronald Reagan. Hinckley then decided to stop tracking Carter and wait until the new president was elected.

Hinckley's attempt on Reagan took place after Reagan had been in office slightly more than two months. The site was one of the entrances to the Washington Hilton hotel at 1919 Connecticut Ave. NW, where Reagan had just addressed a gathering of union leaders. Hinckley fired six shots. The first hit the presidential press secretary James Brady in the head, causing serious brain damage (and leading, in time, to passage of the Brady Bill, which placed new restrictions on the sale of handguns). The second shot hit a Washington police officer, Tom Delehanty, in the neck, while the next was a clean miss, striking a building across the street. The fourth bullet wounded a secret service agent, Tom McCarthy, in the stomach and the fifth made contact with the bulletproof window of the presidential limousine. Hinckley's final shot entered Reagan's body below the left armpit, struck the seventh rib and glanced off the bone, puncturing one lung and lodging near the heart. Reagan was rushed to hospital where emergency surgery saved his life.

At Hinckley's trial, several psychiatrists testified about the defendant's mental state and a CAT scan of Hinckley's brain was entered into evidence by the defence; *Taxi Driver* was screened for the jury. Hinckley was found innocent by reason of insanity and was committed to the St. Elizabeths psychiatric hospital, whose other famous inmates have included Ezra Pound. In 1998, Hinckley sought conditional release, claiming that he was no longer a threat to anyone. An earlier attempt had ended in failure when it was learned that he had been collecting photographs of Jodie Foster and corresponding with the serial killer Ted Bundy. The 1998 application was also rejected, after it was discovered that Hinckley had developed an obsession over a hospital pharmacist, Jeanette Wick. The song "Hinckley Had a Vision" was a hit for various punk bands.

RESOURCES: *Breaking Points* by Jack and Jo Ann Hinckley with Elizabeth Sherrill (Grand Rapids, Michigan, 1985); *On Being Mad, Or Merely Angry: John W. Hinckley Jr. and Other Dangerous People* by James W. Clarke (Princeton, New Jersey, 1990).

HÖDEL, Max (1857–1878), one of Europe's least successful assassins, attempted to kill Wilhelm I (1796–1888), the German kaiser, on May 11, 1878. As was his daily custom, Wilhelm was travelling by carriage from the palace in Berlin along the Unter den Linden; large crowds were assembled along both sides, hoping for a glimpse of him. Hödel was among them, fighting to gain a good vantage point. But the spot he had selected was soon blocked by a water wagon operated by Mrs. Julius Hauch, who was selling water to the spectators. As the carriage passed the water wagon, Hödel shoved Frau Hauch out of his line of fire and then aimed a revolver at Wilhelm. Incensed at being pushed, the woman shoved back at the precise moment Hödel discharged his weapon, causing his shot to go wild to the extent that the kaiser probably didn't realize that he was being attacked. Hödel then struck the water-seller on the side of the head with his revolver and brushed his way to the front of the crowd, firing again. Again he missed. He crossed the street to fire yet again, this time at a spectator (whom he missed) trying to apprehend him. Hödel then fell to his knees and, steadying his aim by gripping the pistol with both hands, fired at Wilhelm a third time, missing once more. By then, Wilhelm realized that somebody was trying to shoot him, and he ordered the carriage to halt, instructing his driver, who was soon joined by others, to capture the assassin. Fleeing the scene, Hödel ran into an alley and fired at his pursuers, missing them. Hödel was grabbed by a man named Kohler but fought him off (Kohler died eight days later from internal injuries received in the struggle). The kaiser's driver stepped forward from the surging crowd and attempted to beat Hödel to death on the spot. Only the intervention of Carl Krüger, a labourer, saved the assailant from this premature end. In the initial confusion, police arrested both Hödel and Krüger, though the latter was soon released.

Hödel was an illegitimate child born to a teenager in Mackern. At thirteen, he was publicly flogged in nearby Leipzig on a charge of theft and later placed in the Zeitz Reformatory, where he was pronounced a kleptomaniac. In time, he was released and apprenticed to a tinsmith, whose trade he mastered. In 1877, by now a journeyman, Hödel began attending meetings of the German Social Democratic Party and later worked for it diligently until assigned to sell subscriptions to the party periodical, *Die Fackel*. Early in 1878, a notice appeared in *Die Fackel* that he was no longer associated with the publication or the party. Rumours, which Hödel substantiated to a great degree, held that he was expelled from the party on the grounds of being an anarchist, though some believe that he was caught embezzling subscription money.

Hödel left Leipzig and arrived in Berlin on April 26, renting inexpensive rooms and purchasing a revolver that cost eight marks. The week before Hödel attempted to assassinate Wilhelm, he posed for a portrait photographer, informing him that soon there would be international demand for the image as the subject of it would be dead within the week. At his trial, Hödel first claimed that he was not trying to kill Wilhelm but rather to commit suicide in his presence so as to bring the plight of the German workingman to the kaiser's attention. A large group of eyewitnesses, however, spoke of Hödel's attempts to get a clear shot and of the way he aimed so carefully to fire at the leader a third time. Faced with this evidence, Hödel confessed and was found guilty.

Although most experts believed that Hödel would serve a long prison term, as the kaiser had not been harmed, the penalty for attempting to kill the kaiser was the same as for succeeding: death by beheading. On August 16, after eating two steaks and drinking a bottle of wine, Hödel was led to the prison courtyard and beheaded by an axe. His head bounced twice on the ground before coming to rest, and his eyes opened and closed twice.

RESOURCE: *Anarchism in Germany—Volume 1: The Early Movement* by Andrew R. Carlson (Metuchen, New Jersey, 1972).

HORSLEY, Albert E. (a.k.a. Harry Orchard, a.k.a. Thomas Hogan) (1866–1954), assassinated Frank R. Steunenberg (1861–1905), a former governor of Idaho, on December 30, 1905, as Steunenberg was returning to his home in Caldwell, Idaho. As the retired politician opened the gate, he tripped a wire, causing his mailbox, which contained a bomb whose main component was more than four kilos of dynamite, to explode. Steunenberg was blown more than three metres into his front yard and died within the hour. Authorities proceeded to close off all means of egress from the town. No man, woman or child was allowed to leave Caldwell until the assassin was found. Every drifter or other stranger was questioned intensely. In time, the investigation led to Thomas Hogan, who had been in and out of Caldwell several times during the past few months. Hogan declared that he was in town to buy sheep, but a search of his hotel room found traces of explosives.

Hogan was revealed as Harry Orchard, a self-confessed union terrorist, born Albert E. Horsley in Northumberland County, Canada West, the second child of a family of eight. He began work at a very young age and after an unremarkable career in a dairy, making cheese, he emigrated, at age thirty, to the United States. After a succession of menial jobs, Horsley became a miner. Shortly thereafter, he joined the Western Federation of Miners (WFW), an anarcho-syndicalist group affiliated with the Industrial Workers of the World (IWW), popularly called the Wobblies.

The story of the attempt to bring organized labour into the mining industry in western North America is one of deadly violence on both sides—police, military and Pinkerton strikebreakers on the one hand, terrorists and assassins on the other. Horsley claimed to be a union terrorist and, once in custody, confessed to involvement in several previous bombings. What's more, he claimed that he had been hired to kill Governor Steunenberg in revenge for Steunenberg's persecution of the WFW. Horsley insisted that the order came from William Dudley ("Big Bill") Haywood (1869–1928), a founder of the IWW in 1905 and one of the leading unionists of the period. Horsley confessed to virtually every unsolved union bombing on record, but parts of his written confession were discovered later to be in the hand of a famous Pinkerton operative named James McParland, the man who had infiltrated the Molly Maguires in the anthracite coal fields of Pennsylvania. The leading Canadian historian of the radical labour movement of the time depicts Horsley as a "hapless [...] half-wit hired by McParland to frame Haywood" and give "false testimony in an attempt to railroad union leaders," receiving a reduced sentence in return. Seeking evidence they claimed linked Haywood to the assassination, the Pinkertons began following him in Denver. But the investigators were inept; Haywood knew he was being shadowed and quickly figured out why. One of the operatives was photographed and his likeness was featured prominently in Haywood's *Miner's Magazine*, a copy of which Haywood sent to McParland.

Because American laws of state-to-state extradition applied only to those who crossed a state boundary after commission of a crime, and Haywood had been nowhere near Idaho when the assassination took place, the Wobbly could remain legally safe in Colorado. So the Pinkerton men kidnapped him, threw him in a railway boxcar, nailed shut the doors and instructed the locomotive engineer to travel to Idaho without stopping. Once arrested in Idaho, Haywood retained America's most celebrated criminal lawyer, Clarence Darrow, whose first action was to attempt to have the case dismissed on the grounds that his client had been kidnapped. The US Supreme Court, which already had shown itself to be unsympathetic to labour, ruled that by what means the suspect arrived in Idaho was immaterial but that once there he was liable for prosecution. Two other labour leaders, Charles H. Moyers and George A. Pettibone, were also indicted.

The trial, conducted in Boise, Idaho, in 1907, was one of the most sensational in American history up to that time. The small city swarmed with press, miners and Pinkerton agents with enough arms to go to war with their adversaries if need be. The actress Ethel Barrymore and the baseball star Walter Johnson made celebrity appearances. The defence was aided at the outset when a key prosecution witness, Steve Adams, a paid informant of the Pinkertons who had claimed to be an accomplice, recanted his confession on the grounds that it had been extracted from him under threat. Without Adams's testimony and after McParland's handwriting had been detected in Horsley's written confession, the prosecution was left with only Horsley's oral testimony, and Darrow cross-examined Horsley until the jury concluded that the witness's word was worthless. The jury found Haywood not guilty of conspiring to murder Steunenberg. Later, Darrow also secured the acquittal of Pettibone, and the case against Moyers was dropped.

In the end, only Horsley was convicted in the assassination of Governor Steunenberg and only intervention by Pinkertons saved him from the death penalty. Agent McParland spent the rest of his life (he died in 1914) attempting to have Horsley pardoned for the co-operation he had shown during the investigation. Although Horsley was never paroled, his stay in prison was not uncomfortable. Prison officials gave him a private room with electricity. Outside money paid for machinery and the prison provided free labour for Horsley to begin a shoe-manufacturing business, whose profits he was allowed to keep. Horsley refused to speak about the case for the rest of his life. When he died at eighty-eight, he left an estate valued at approximately $10,000. Haywood, whose WFM split with the IWW over the question of violence, was indicted for sedition during the First World War. While free on bail, he fled to the Soviet Union, where his remains were buried with the highest honours in the Kremlin wall near those of other national heroes.

RESOURCES: *Big Bill Haywood and the Radical Union Movement* by Joseph Robert Conlin (Syracuse, New York, 1969); *Big Bill Haywood* by Melvyn

Dubofsky (New York, 1987); *Big Trouble: A Murder in a Small Western Town Sets off a Struggle for the Soul of America* by J. Anthony Lucas (New York, 1997); *Roughneck: The Life and Times of Big Bill Haywood* by Peter Carlson (New York, 1983); *Rebel Life: The Life and Times of Robert Gosden— Revolutionary, Mystic, Labour Spy* by Mark Leier (Vancouver, 1999).

HU Han-min (1879–1936) led the conspiracy to assassinate Liao Chung-k'ai (1878–1925), a contender for the leadership of the Kuomintang (KMT, or Nationalist Party) in China. With the death of its leader, Dr. Sun Yat-sen, in 1925, the party was in disarray. Sun had managed to pacify both the left and right wings of the KMT, a difficult task indeed as the right despised communism and the left still included many avowed communists. On August 20, 1925, in Canton, Hu, a hired gunman, opened fire on Liao Chung-k'ai, the leader of the leftist faction, and Chen Chi-lin, the senior officer of the KMT's propaganda bureau officer. Liao was shot several times and died on the scene; Chen managed to live three days. Hu was never identified as the trigger man, but rumours of his involvement began to circulate. Hu, who was strongly anti-Communist, had been a republican since 1905 and was the former editor of the republican newspaper *Min Pao* (*People's Journal*).

Helping Sun to organize uprisings in southwestern China, Hu was instrumental in the capture of Kwangtung during the 1911 revolution. In 1914, he joined the KMT and was soon known as Sun's right-hand man. He headed the conservative faction of the KMT that looked on in distress as communists swelled the party's ranks. The government at the time relied on advice from Mikhail Borodin, a representative from the Soviet Union. Borodin rose to a position of great prominence in the KMT government, thus angering the right further. With Sun's death, Hu decided to seize control and drive the communists out.

Hu was implicated in the shooting of Liao when his (Hu's) cousin, Hu Yisheng, was arrested for his role in the assassination. KMT officials faced a serious problem. Attempting to arrest and try Hu for Liao's death would split the party and likely destroy it, as Hu had the support of the entire right wing. Yet to keep a known killer in the government would seriously damage, at best, the party's credibility. The compromise was to send Hu abroad until his actions were less distinct in common memory. Accordingly, he was made ambassador to the Soviet Union, where meetings with Joseph Stalin only strengthened his anti-communism.

In January 1926, Hu's supporters managed to have him elected to the KMT's central executive committee, and he returned to China to assume the post. But he was no sooner back than he began to denounce the KMT-Chinese Communist Party alliance. The following year, communists were purged from the KMT, leading to the struggle that would continue until 1949, when the communists defeated the KMT in the Chinese Civil War and the KMT left the mainland for Formosa (Taiwan). Hu's disputes within the KMT did not end after the communist expulsion. In 1931, Hu split with the KMT's leader, Chiang Kai-shek, over questions concerning China's provisional constitution. Chiang had Hu placed under house arrest. Hu was set free after the Japanese invaded Manchuria in 1931. He then travelled to Hong Kong where he published the *Three People's Principles Monthly*, a magazine devoted to condemning the KMT for not opposing the Japanese strongly enough. In December 1935, Hu was elected to the KMT's central executive once again but he died in 1936 before he could assume office.

RESOURCE: *Hu Han-min hsien-sheng nien-pu* by Chiang Yung-Ching (Taipei, 1978).

HUERTA, Victoriano (1845–1916), ordered the assassination of Francisco I. Madero (1873–1913), the president of Mexico, who was under house arrest at the time, following a coup. Madero and his vice-president, Pino Suarez, were led to a car, which they were told would take them to the railway station, where a train would carry them into exile. The pair became suspicious when the automobile drove past the station and proceeded to the Calle Lecumberri penitentiary. Major Francisco Cardenas, one of the military men who were escorting them, shot Madero in the head with a pistol, killing him instantly, and then killed Suarez. The car's driver was then taken into custody and made to sign a statement without being allowed to read it. While the driver was being taken away, he saw soldiers shooting at the automobile that had held Madero, putting hundreds of bullet holes into the body of the car but being careful not to strike the engine or the fuel tank. The statement the driver signed stated that Madero loyalists had attacked the car in an attempt to free the former leaders. The official verdict was that Madero and Suarez were shot while attempting to escape.

Huerta, the mastermind behind Madero's assassination, was a commander of government forces in Mexico City, a career soldier who had graduated from the Military College of Mexico, where he excelled in mathematics and astronomy. In the 1910 revolution, he fought with the Zapatistas in Morelos. When the dictator Porfirio Diaz resigned, Huerta escorted him into exile.

The new government under Madero faced strife from the first day in office. Madero was popular with the Mexican people. He had run against Diaz in 1910, when, even though he was incarcerated and the election was rigged, he did quite well. But he could not tame the other leaders of Mexico's revolution. Emiliano Zapata, for one, refused to disarm or disband his private army until he and his men were given the lands they were promised. In addition, Madero was considered a threat to many leaders, including Huerta, who wished to seize power for themselves. Two generals who were plotting Madero's downfall, Felix Diaz and Bernardo Reyes, were imprisoned for their attacks on the government, but they continued to plot Madero's ouster from their prison cells, assisted by Huerta.

The enemy that proved Madero's undoing was the United States, in the person of its ambassador, Henry Lane Wilson (1857–1932). Madero was eager that Mexico should regain control of its oil industry from American companies, and he met frequently with Wilson, who assured him that if Madero was willing to allow American business to exploit Mexico's natural resources, Wilson could assure him that America would recognise his government immediately and send aid to suppress rebellion.

In February 1913, Madero was forced to release Diaz and Reyes, who immediately formed an army and attacked the National Palace. Huerta, who was supposed to be defending the palace but was really aligned with the insurgents, ordered Mexico City to be shelled. The shelling had no effect on the rebels, but loss of life and property damage were so high that the period is referred to as Mexico's "Ten Tragic Days." Eventually Huerta demanded Madero's resignation. Madero's wife pleaded with Wilson for American support or at least a guarantee that Madero would not be hurt. Wilson refused. But when Huerta asked Wilson whether Madero should be imprisoned or exiled, Wilson responded, "Do what is best for the peace of the country." Huerta interpreted the remark as condoning Madero's assassination. With Madero out of the way, Huerta seized control of the country, and within a month of taking office was opposed by Governor Venustiano Carranza who, along with the revolutionary leaders Alvaro Obregón, Pancho Villa and

Pablo Gonzalez, formed the so-called Constitutionalist Army and launched an offensive against the Huerta regime. Zapata, although not allied with the Constitutionalists, fought Huerta's forces independently.

Wilson, meanwhile, was trying to convince Washington to recognise Huerta as president and send military aid, but the American elections of 1912 had removed the Republican Party from office. The new American chief executive, Woodrow Wilson, had no interest in propping up Huerta, nor did the administration have any patience for Henry Lane Wilson, a lifelong Republican, whose position was a reward for service to his party. In July 1913, Henry Lane Wilson was recalled to the United States. Shortly after he arrived, his government announced that he had offered his resignation and that it had been accepted. The former diplomat returned to his native Indiana, where he lived out his life.

In 1914, an incident involving the USS *Dolphin* led to US Marines landing in Veracruz, an event that cost Huerta much of his already dwindling support. Huerta fled Mexico and lived for a time in London before moving to Barcelona. In 1915, he was arrested by US agents in Newman, New Mexico, and detained for a short period at Fort Bliss in El Paso, Texas, before being released on the grounds of poor health. Victoriano Huerta died of cirrhosis of the liver in El Paso.

RESOURCE: *Francisco I. Madero* by Stanley R. Ross (New York, 1955).

ISLAMBOULI, Khaled el (1957–1982), assassinated Anwar Sadat (1918–1981), the Egyptian president, to protest against Sadat's peace accord with Israel. On October 6, 1981, Sadat was reviewing a military parade in Nasr City as part of Egypt's celebrations of the anniversary of the beginning of the Yom Kippur War. Sadat was supposed to be wearing a 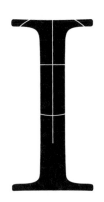 bullet-proof vest, but he had removed it when he found that it spoiled the line of his bespoke uniform from London. About an hour into the parade, a unit of Soviet-built Zil-151 flatbed trucks carrying field artillery passed by. Suddenly one of the vehicles pulled away from the unit and stopped in front of the reviewing stand. Khaled el-Islambouli emerged from the truck, took a grenade from his pocket and tossed it into the crowd. The device failed to explode, as did a second one. By then the three-man truck crew emerged firing AK-47 assault rifles. Islambouli threw a third grenade, which did explode, and then produced a submachine gun and also fired on the stands. In all, hundreds of rounds were discharged into the crowd of Egyptian political figures, foreign dignitaries and diplomats. Sadat was shot several times and was pronounced dead on arrival at hospital, though doctors worked two hours trying to revive him; ten others also died and more than a dozen were injured. Not until the assassins had exhausted their ammunition did Sadat's bodyguards return the conspirators' fire. One of the four assassins was killed outright; the others, including Islambouli, were captured after being wounded.

Khaled el-Islambouli was brought up in a conservative, fundamentalist, ultra-nationalist home. He always had desired a career as a military pilot. When he failed the examinations he switched to the artillery, and graduated from military school with honours and was commissioned a lieutenant.

For several years, Sadat had been pursuing peace with Israel. In 1979, he signed the Israeli-Egyptian peace treaty with Israel's prime minister, Menachem Begin. Abroad, the two men were hailed, and they shared the 1979 Nobel Prize for Peace. At home, Sadat's efforts sparked intense opposition. Islambouli had read a self-published religious text entitled *The Absent Prayer*, which stated that if the leadership of a Muslim nation was hypocritical, then removing the leaders by any means possible was a morally justifiable act. Islambouli contacted the book's author, Abdel-Salam Farag, and formed the nucleus of an *anqud* or cell of which he made himself military leader, with Farag as the spiritual head. Realizing that the book would draw unwanted attention, they burned all but fifty or sixty copies.

Farag had many disciples whom he brought into the conspiracy, including other military men who would figure in the actual assassination, which the conspirators believed would cause a fundamentalist uprising that would sweep the pro-Western government from power. In addition to securing arms for the attack (the army had ordered all weapons used in the parade to be unloaded and their firing pins removed), Islambouli used his authority to ensure that the three men in the truck with him that day would all be members of the *anqud*. One of those chosen for the attack was Abbas Mohammed, renowned as the top marksman in the Egyptian army. After the assassination, police swept down on the *anqud*, arresting more than eight hundred people. After intensive questioning, twenty-four were tried for conspiracy. The four survivors from the attack—Islambouli, Mohammed and Abdul Salam, along with Farag and Ataya Reheil—were executed.

RESOURCES: *Autumn of Fury: The Assassination of Sadat* by Mohamed Heikal (London, 1983); *Egypt from Nasser to Mubarak: A Flawed Revolution* by Anthony McDermott (New York, 1988).

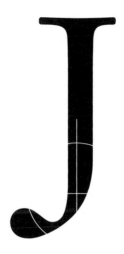

JACKSON, Arthur (b. 1935), attempted to assassinate the American film and television actress Theresa Saldana (b. 1955) in Hollywood on March 15, 1982. He waited for her to enter a car outside her home, asking, "Are you Theresa Saldana?" As Saldana turned to answer, Jackson produced a knife that he had bought for five dollars and stabbed her in the chest repeatedly. Saldana attempted to fight off her attacker, but managed only to severely cut her hand when she tried to grab the knife. Jackson continued to stab Saldana until the blade bent against her breastbone. A passerby pulled Jackson off his victim and immobilized him until police arrived; after surgery and twenty-three units of blood, Saldana recovered.

Jackson was a Scot with a long history of mental illness, which was first noted officially when, at seventeen, he asked his family physician to castrate him and open up his head so that the dirt on his brain could be removed. He was voluntarily committed to Kingseat Mental Hospital in Newmacher where he was treated with both insulin coma and shock therapy. These produced no sign of progress, but as a voluntary patient Jackson was entitled to sign himself out of the institution, which he did after less than five months.

Jackson was fascinated by the United States, his chief source of information coming from the movies he saw in Aberdeen. His first celebrity obsession was with Joseph Cretzer, an American bank robber who was shot to death in a prison riot at Alcatraz. After seeing the 1940 film *The House across the Bay*, which was shown with newsreel footage of the riot in which Cretzer was killed, Jackson became convinced that he and Cretzer were twinned souls. Moreover he believed that Cretzer's soul was imprisoned in limbo and became determined to free it.

Jackson's mother decided that after leaving the mental hospital her son should stay with relatives in Canada. In January 1955, Jackson took advantage of its proximity to move to the US, where he obtained a job (for a short time) in New York City. Because his immigration status in the United States was that of a resident alien, he was a candidate for military service, and was drafted into the US Army. His stay in the army was short and ended for predictable reasons. He believed that obeying orders was a sign of weakness and refused even the simplest commands. After two courts martial, Jackson was examined by army psychologists who concluded that he was insane; he was granted a Section 8 discharge.

After his stay in the army, Jackson began an in-depth study of Cretzer, locating old newspaper articles explaining exactly where, when and how Cretzer was shot. In 1961, Jackson wrote a long and rambling letter to President John F. Kennedy containing veiled threats on the president's life. After a check of his background by the US Secret Service, Jackson was deported to Scotland. Back in Aberdeen, he continued his study of American motion pictures and Joseph Cretzer. He occasionally travelled to London. In 1966, Jackson returned to America, this time entering the country illegally and visiting San Francisco and Alcatraz (the prison had been closed since 1963). After sneaking into an office building to use a typewriter to produce an identification card with Cretzer's name and statistics, Jackson was arrested and again deported to Scotland. He then consulted with numerous doctors for strange procedures such as removing blood vessels from his eyelids (as he felt they were disfiguring his soul) and removing a mole that he felt was sapping his strength. He also consulted with a lawyer to sue a neighbour he claimed was "possessed with a demon compulsion to cause distractions."

Jackson had been living, off and on, with his mother. She, too, was schizophrenic. In 1980, she died, leaving him completely alone in the world, as Jackson had no friends or family with whom he was on speaking terms. Although not close in the traditional sense (neither Jackson nor his mother expressed normal emotions, nor did they ever touch each other), Jackson was devastated by her death.

A few months later, Jackson saw the film *Defiance* starring Jan-Michael Vincent and, in her first starring role, Theresa Saldana. For a series of strange reasons (such as the fact that the movie had a character named Montana, which was the state where Cretzer was born), Jackson believed that clues provided in the film would lead to the liberation of Cretzer's soul. Jackson became enamoured of Saldana, and in his mind it seemed natural that his love should lead to her murder. Jackson concluded that by killing Saldana he would be allowed to be executed in the exact same place and manner that Cretzer had been shot in 1946.

Jackson flew to America. In spite of his two previous deportations, he had no difficulty entering the country. After arriving in New York, he called the number for Saldana's apartment that he had found in a New York telephone directory he had consulted in Aberdeen. When he was told that Saldana was living in Los Angeles, he purchased a bus pass and travelled cross-country. On arriving in California, he began making calls to studios and agents trying to find Saldana's address. These inquiries alerted Saldana's associates that an insane man was looking for her. Saldana herself began receiving calls. Then Jackson hired a private investigator to find Saldana's address, which the investigator did from her motor vehicle registration.

Jackson was charged with attempted murder, but because his trial came shortly after those of Dan White and John Hinckley, both assassins who were found to be insane, the courts were in no mood to grant a plea of insanity. So Jackson, despite his obvious mental instability, was tried as mentally competent and sentenced to sixteen years in prison.

In California, a prison term could be cut short by time served and good behaviour, and Jackson was eligible for parole in 1989. But while he was imprisoned, authorities made a startling discovery about Arthur Jackson: that in the 1960s, during his trips to London, he had been engaging in armed robberies and, in a 1967 bank holdup, had shot and killed Anthony Robin Fletcher, a bystander who tried to apprehend him, believing that Jackson's gun was a starter's pistol. Under normal circumstances Jackson would have been paroled, deported to Britain and tried for Fletcher's murder. Saldana, however, believed that it was possible that Jackson might be acquitted of the murder, now over twenty years old, make his way back to the United States once more and again try to kill her. Indeed, Jackson sent her letters while in prison telling her that he would use a gun next time to ensure that their souls could be together in paradise. Saldana used these letters to argue successfully that releasing Jackson would constitute a threat to her life. In 1991, Jackson was sentenced to an additional sixteen years in prison for threatening Saldana. If Jackson is ever released in California, he will be deported to the United Kingdom to be tried for the murder of Fletcher. Saldana, however, is determined to see that Jackson is incarcerated in California for the rest of his life.

RESOURCE: *Obsessed: The Stalking of Theresa Saldana* by Ronald Markham and Ron LeBreque (New York, 1994).

KALUGIN, Oleg Danilovich

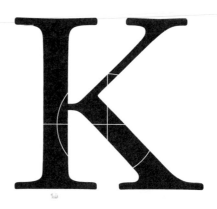

(b. 1934), arranged the means to assassinate Georgi Markov (1929–1978), the Bulgarian author and broadcaster, in one of the most celebrated and innovative political assassinations of the Cold War era. On September 7, 1978, Markov, who had defected to London from Soviet-dominated Bulgaria, was walking from his car to the headquarters of the BBC World Service, where he worked as a broadcaster. As he crossed Westminster Bridge, he felt a sharp pain in his right thigh and turned to see a man standing at a bus stop with an umbrella in his hand. The man said "I'm sorry" in English with a heavy eastern European accent and then promptly hailed a taxi and drove off. Markov entered the BBC and delivered his nightly broadcast. At home several hours later, he became ill. His leg stiffened and he was racked by fever and nausea. Markov went to hospital and told doctors (and later others) that he suspected he had been poisoned by the man with the umbrella. He died four days later, at which point British intelligence became interested in the case. An examination of Markov's body eventually revealed an almost invisible platinum-iridium pellet that secreted ricin, the toxin which is derived from castor oil seed and of which even a minuscule amount is fatal; no antidote is known.

Although the actual assassination of Markov was undertaken by the Bulgarian secret service, the means were provided by the KGB in Moscow. Bulgaria's president, Tudor Zhivikov, had ordered the killing expressly. Once a friend of Zhivikov's, Markov had infuriated him by writing and producing a play highly critical of the Bulgarian government in general and Zhivikov in particular, as well as by his anti-Bulgarian commentary on the BBC and Radio Free Europe. But the Bulgarians needed a way to kill Markov without arousing suspicion. They sought the help of the KGB, which assigned Kalugin to the case.

Kalugin was a second-generation KGB operative, his father having become an agent in the early years of Stalin's rule. He was also a devoted communist, even though he knew better than any civilian the excesses of the Stalinist period. Fluent in English, he had posed as a student in America in the late 1950s and was a correspondent for Radio Moscow in the 1960s. Kalugin worked in America until 1970 when he returned to the Soviet Union as head of the KGB's counter-espionage department, in which capacity he received the Markov file from the KGB chief (and future Soviet premier), Yuri Andropov.

KGB men were not enthused about the project. High-visibility assassinations were not the kind of killings that the KGB practised in the West. Yet the request to "physically remove" Markov had come from Zhivikov himself and the Soviet Union felt a strong obligation to an ally. The result was that the KGB would plan what they hoped would be an undetectable assassination but leave implementation to the Bulgarians. Orders were sent to the Operational and Technical Directorate, which conducted experiments on non-traceable poisons. Their work was not always perfect. One agent had rubbed a jelly onto the Soviet dissident Alexandr Solzhenitsyn that was supposed to give him a heart attack but only made him ill. The laboratories, however, were constantly experimenting. The Soviets gave the Bulgarians a choice: a jelly that poisons on contact with the skin, a poison that had to be consumed or a poison pellet that would be fired into the victim. The Bulgarians chose the last alternative. The Soviets then created a pellet smaller than the head of a pin and an umbrella that fired it silently at close range. The Bulgarians experimented with the umbrella by firing it at a horse and then at a prisoner sentenced to death. The pellets had to be redesigned after testing, as the prisoner's pellet failed to kill him.

Finally, in summer 1978, Kalugin dispatched the final version of the umbrella gun and new pellets. Although the method was supposed to be undetectable, the secret was soon revealed. Vladimir Kostov, a Bulgarian defector living in Paris, already had had a stinging encounter with a foreign man with an umbrella, but for unknown reasons the poison had failed to do its job and the pellet was removed from his leg intact for examination by first French and later British intelligence.

Although he had been a KGB operative for over twenty years, Kalugin participated in only this one assassination, or "wet job," to use the KGB term. Kalugin later became deputy head of the KGB in Leningrad, from which position he revealed, in 1990, the Soviet participation in Markov's death. At the same time he became involved in the radical faction of the democracy movement, leading to his arrest after the short-lived military coup in 1991. Kalugin was cleared of all charges in

Russia and unsuccessfully stood for office in the elections of 1992. In 1993, while in England to give an interview to the BBC, Kalugin was arrested for his part in the Markov assassination, but as he had not participated directly, the charges were dropped. Kalugin has stated that the new Bulgarian government knows the identities of those responsible for the Markov assassination but refuses to prosecute or name the killers. Kalugin is retired and lives in Moscow.

RESOURCE: *Spymaster* by Oleg Kalugin (London, 1994).

KAPLAN, Fanny (1887–1918), was the mysterious member of the Socialist Revolutionary Party who most observers believe shot V.I. Lenin (1870–1924) in the chest outside a Moscow factory on the night of August 30, 1918. Lenin suffered two bullet wounds in the incident; from that point forward his health declined, culminating in his death, probably from a stroke, on January 21, 1924, aged 53.

Kaplan was born in Volinski and at sixteen became an anarchist. In Kiev in 1906, Kaplan, who was called Dora by her colleagues, was wounded when a bomb exploded prematurely. She was sentenced to death but the sentence was commuted to imprisonment because of her age (nineteen). While incarcerated, she changed her views "and became a Socialist Revolutionary [SR]"—specifically, a follower of the SR moderate Victor Chernov. She also lost her sight. Surgery restored her vision in 1917 but she was kept in a series of prison hospitals.

When in the first few months after the October Revolution the Bolsheviks suppressed dissent by dissolving the constituent assembly, the Socialist Revolutionaries became dangerously alienated. A weak and eccentric figure, prone to nervous collapse, Kaplan on her release tried to enlist as an SR terrorist but was refused. Thereupon she and a few other disaffected members decided to pursue terrorist acts themselves, and soon merged with Grigori Semionov, head of the Civil-Wartime Socialist Revolutionary Party (one of whose commandos, a man named Serheyev, assassinated a figure named Volodarski, one of the new Soviet's leaders in Petrograd). When Semionov defected to the Bolsheviks, he was replaced by Lidia Konopliova, with whom Kaplan had been associated. This cell first thought of poisoning Lenin or injecting him with a deadly organism, hoping thereby to demoralize the Red Army. Instead they opted for assassination with a pistol (either a revolver or a Browning automatic—testimony differs).

The attempt took place from a distance of two or three metres at about 10:00 p.m. outside a factory Lenin had been visiting. He was between the factory steps and his automobile, surrounded by a crowd, when, according to key witnesses, Kaplan fired at least three shots, one of which passed unmolested through Lenin's coat. Kaplan was apprehended a short distance from the scene, standing under a tree, holding an umbrella, conspicuously remaining still while all about her fled in panic. Kaplan was interrogated on six occasions and stuck to her contention that she was the assassin and had acted alone. At about 4:00 p.m. on September 3, 1918, the commandant of the Kremlin, Pavel Malkov, led Kaplan through a blind alley within the Kremlin to a yard where armoured cars raced their motors to mask the sound of the execution. She was shot from behind and her body destroyed.

RESOURCES: *Sud nad terrorom* by N.D. Kostin (Moscow, 1990). Opposing experts debate the still controversial case in the *Soviet Weekly* of October 25, 1990.

KERN, Erwin (1897–1922), became the drive-by assassin of Walter Rathenau (1867–1922), the German foreign minister, on June 24, 1922, when Rathenau was en route from his Berlin home to his office. Rathenau rode in an open automobile despite warnings from German security of the danger from extremists. As the car proceeded down the Königsallee, another automobile pulled up alongside and its driver, Kern, fired an automatic pistol at Rathenau, whose chauffeur stopped and radioed for help. A grenade was also thrown into the Rathenau car before the attackers drove off. Rathenau suffered a fractured spine and a broken jaw from the grenade explosion and also had five bullet wounds; he was taken home, where he died a few hours later.

The original plan for killing Rathenau came from Hans Stuberauch. The son of a German general and a committed monarchist and anti-Semite, Stuberauch believed that Rathenau (who was Jewish) was either involved with, or had knowledge of, the worldwide Jewish conspiracy outlined in the *Protocols of the Learned Elders of Zion*. A casual remark in Rathenau's book *Zur Kritic der Zeit*, referring to the notion that the European economy was controlled by three hundred men, seemed to prove to anti-Semites that there was indeed a Jewish conspiracy to control the economy and that Rathenau was part of it. Stuberauch also believed that Germany's defeat in the Great War could be ascribed to Jewish betrayal.

Eventually, Stuberauch became aquainted with Kern, a member of the Organisation Consul, a terrorist group that had participated in the aborted 1920 putsch led by Wolfgang Kapp. Kern approved of the assassination idea but realized that, at seventeen, Stuberauch was too unstable and young to handle the assignment. Utilizing his contacts among Germany's radical right, Kern assembled a small band of terrorists to carry out the task.

Rathenau had enraged the far right by signing the Treaty of Rapallo with the new Soviet Union. After the assassination, members of the far-right Nationalist faction faced enormous hostility from others in the Reichstag and the general public. Several members carefully distanced themselves from Kern's actions even though they either knew about them in advance as individuals or had even approved. A decisive act such as killing Rathenau, they hoped, would start a right-wing coup. But with the general public furious with the assassins, the rightists were forced to lie low.

After a massive manhunt, Kern and an associate were surrounded in a tower of Saaleck Castle in Turringia. Rather than give himself up, Kern first shot his associate dead and then shot himself through the head. The other conspirators were turned over to the authorities by friends and family who wished no part in aiding the assassins. Eventually, thirteen rightists were found guilty of participating in the assassination. The sentences for the remaining conspirators ranged from two months, in the case of a youth who had been found tearing down wanted posters, to fifteen years, in the case of Ernst Techow, one of the men in the attack car. Public support for the Weimar government in the wake of the assassination helped to shore up the shaky and generally unpopular political system imposed on Germany by the Allied Powers after the First World War. Eventually the Nazis would seize power and destroy the Weimar government.

RESOURCE: *Der Rathenaumord: Gegen Rekonstruktion einer Verschwörung die Republik Weimar* by Martin Sabrow (Munich, 1994).

KIM Jae Kyu (1926–1980) was the assassin of South Korea's president Park Chung Hee on October 26, 1979. On that date, President Park (1917–1979, in power since 1963) arrived at the compound of the

THE BOOK OF ASSASSINS

Korean Central Intelligence Agency (KCIA) for a private dinner with Kim, head of the KCIA and a long-time friend; the president's four bodyguards were excluded from the dining room. The subject that evening was to be the totalitarian turn Park's government had taken in recent months. For example, Park had caused widespread unrest by banning labour unions and forcibly removing the leader of the opposition, resulting in the resignations of all sixty-nine elected members of the New Democratic Party. Kim had been sending reports and memoranda to Park for some time requesting that the president soften his policies and pacify his opponents. At the dinner, Kim confronted Park's chief of the presidential security force, Cha Chi Choi (b. 1934), who had prevented Kim's reports from reaching the president. Cha's reaction to the allegations was to insult and belittle Kim. As the meal proceeded, Kim left the table to get a handgun and to instruct his agents to shoot Park's four bodyguards as soon as they heard shooting from the dining room. Later, he excused himself again, to confirm that his men had their instructions and were ready to act. When Kim returned to the dining room for the second time, his argument with Park and Cha intensified. Kim demanded Cha's resignation. Cha accused Kim of incompetence. Kim produced his pistol, shooting first Cha, then Park. Kim's agents proceeded to kill Park's four bodyguards.

Kim and the agents responsible for the other shootings were taken into custody. Government sources originally declared that the principal shootings were accidents, the result of the argument between Kim and Cha. In light of the fact that six people had died in two separate rooms, the government soon changed its story and charged Kim with murder. On December 20, 1979, Kim and four of his agents were sentenced to be executed.

RESOURCE: *Kankoku o shinkansaseta juichinichi-kan* by Kap-che Cho (Tokyo, 1987).

KOCAN, Peter (b. 1947), attempted to assassinate Arthur Calwell (1896–1973), leader of the Australian Labour Party, on June 21, 1966, as Calwell was concluding a speech at the Mosman Town Hall in Sydney. The gathering had been raucous. In the run-up to an election, Calwell had created considerable controversy by declaring himself opposed to the use of Australian conscript soldiers in the war in Vietnam. After the meeting, Calwell went to his car. He usually drove with the windows open, a habit he learned in boyhood when the family car was prone to send exhaust into the passenger compartment. That night, however, he either forgot to lower the windows, or decided not to (the evening was cold) or had not yet had the time. Whatever the case, the car windows saved his life. As he was about to drive off, Kocan appeared next to the car and fired a sawed-off .22-calibre rifle, but the bullet was deflected by the glass, though Calwell was struck in the face by glass shards and bullet fragments. Although his face was horribly scarred, Calwell suffered only superficial wounds. Kocan ran off, but he was chased down and apprehended.

Kocan's birth name was Peter Douglas, but his father died before he was born and his mother remarried. The assailant was schizophrenic, a condition that made it difficult for him to make friends or hold a job. Working as a field hand or occasional factory labourer, he became drawn to extreme right-wing politics. He attended meetings of the Young Rhodesian League. He also wrote to the Sydney headquarters of the Australian Nazi Party to declare his admiration for Adolf Hitler, particularly the fact that Hitler "killed himself at the right time." Kocan's hatred of communists and communist sympathizers put him at odds with the Labour Party.

When Calwell denounced the war in Vietnam, Kocan decided that he must be killed. As is the case with many such insane assassins, Kocan was seeking publicity. He told police that he had to shoot somebody important to prove he was "different from all the nobodies." He informed them that he had hoped to shoot the US vice-president, Hubert H. Humphrey, who had visited Australia recently, but that American security proved too stringent. When Kocan read that Calwell would be speaking at Mosman Hall, he saw his chance of assassinating a public figure. When he was asked why he shot Calwell, Kocan responded, "Because I disagree with his politics." Significantly, when asked whether he would have shot the Conservative leader, Prime Minister Henry Holt, he said that he would. But when he was asked if he would have shot the premier of New South Wales, Robert Askin, Kocan said no, because Askin "wasn't important enough." Kocan was sentenced to life imprisonment but on December 30, 1966, he was transferred to the Morisset asylum for the criminally insane. In 1968, he wrote to Calwell apologizing for the assassination attempt. Calwell forgave him and told Kocan if he could give any aid to him and his mother that he would.

RESOURCE: *Be Just and Fear Not* by A.A. Calwell (Hawthorn, Victoria, 1972).

KŌNUMA Tadashi (b. 1911) assassinated Inoue Junnosuke (1869–1932), a former governor of the Bank of Japan who had the ill luck to be Japan's finance minister during the Great Depression of the 1930s, when he returned the country to the gold standard and pursued a tight-money policy whose deflationary effects intensified the economic slowdown. His undoing, however, was his refusal to increase the military budget, a decision that made him seem pacifistic, a dangerous way to be perceived in the Japan of the time. His actions caused the ultra-rightist, nationalistic and pro-military Ketsumeidan (Blood Brotherhood or League of Blood) to plot to have him killed, a job that fell to Kōnuma Tadashi, a former baker's assistant and carpenter's apprentice who was more than eager to perform an act in the name of the emperor. Presented with a Browning automatic pistol that had belonged to a decorated air force officer shot down in China, he travelled to the Komagome Elementary School in Tokyo where Inoue was scheduled to give a speech concerning the impending elections. At 10:02 a.m. on February 9, 1932, the finance minister alighted from his car and received a welcoming committee that was waiting on the pavement. Kōnuma emerged from the crowd and fired three times, striking the minister's right lung and spine. Inoue died within seconds. Kōnuma was arrested and tried for the murder. Although sentenced to life imprisonment, he was freed in 1940 when elements sympathetic to the aims of the Blood Brotherhood had taken control of the government.

Inoue was replaced as finance minister by Takahashi Korekiyo, who took Japan off the gold standard, increased government spending through deficit financing and, most important for his own survival, increased military expenditures. Although Kōnuma became notorious as an assassin, he enjoyed a great deal of support among Japan's right wing as a man of action whose loyalty to the nation was above his respect for the law.

On February 26, 1965, in a ceremony honouring the attempted coup of 1936, Kōnuma shared a stage with fellow assassins Sagoya Tomeo, who shot Prime Minister Hamaguchi Osachi in 1930, and Mikami Taku, who killed Prime Minister Inukai Tsuyoshi in 1932.

RESOURCE: *Japan's Imperial Conspiracy* by David Bergamini (New York, 1971).

KUBIS, Jan (1913–1942), along with Joseph Gabcik (1912–1942), assassinated Reinhard Heydrich (1904–1942), a high-ranking Nazi official and a personal favourite of Adolf Hitler. Tall, with blond hair and blue eyes, Heydrich was a rarity among Nazi leaders: the epitome of the Nordic Aryan superman. A former naval officer, he had risen from political chief of the Munich police to be deputy leader of the SS under Heinrich Himmler. In 1941, Heydrich was made *Reichsprotektor* of Bohemia and Moravia in conquered Czechoslovakia. Within three weeks of assuming the post, he had ordered over three hundred executions. Any real or apprehended revolt was suppressed bloodily, earning him the nickname "Hangman Heydrich." He was also instrumental in planning the Holocaust.

By early 1942, the Czechoslovakian government-in-exile decided that Heydrich must be eliminated. Intelligence indicated that Heydrich drove daily in an open car along the Dresden-Prague road. The conspirators waited near a hairpin curve in the road where Heydrich's car would be forced to slow down. They then opened fire while Kubis threw a grenade, which detonated at the back of the car, blowing it apart. Heydrich emerged from the wreckage firing his pistol, but quickly fell. He had been skewered by several steel springs from the upholstery when the car exploded. He died eight days later. The assassins fled and were given sanctuary by the priests of Karl Borromaeus Church in Lidice. But their whereabouts were revealed to the SS and everyone in the church was killed. Retribution did not end there. When the Nazi propaganda minister Joseph Goebbels heard of the assassination, he executed 152 Jews in Berlin and dispatched another three thousand Jews to the death camps. In Czechoslovakia, the Nazis made an example of the village of Lidice. Every male in Lidice over sixteen was executed. While some women were also killed outright, most of the women and children were sent to the camps. The village itself was burned to the ground and then bulldozed. In all, 1,331 Czechs from Lidice were killed and the townsite itself was completely obliterated.

RESOURCES: *The Assassination of Heydrich* by Jan G. Weiner (New York, 1969); *Assassin! From Abraham Lincoln to Rajiv Gandhi* by Paul Garbutt (Shepperton, UK, 1992).

LAWRENCE, Richard (1800–1861), the first person to attempt to murder a US president, was a British-born house painter who approached Andrew Jackson under the Capitol dome on the morning of January 31, 1835, and fired a pistol from only two metres away. The pistol misfired. Lawrence then withdrew a second weapon, which also misfired. Jackson had begun to cane his assailant to the floor when some of his supporters, including Congressman David Crockett, leapt on the attacker and subdued him. Lawrence first claimed that Jackson had killed his father. When this claim was proved false, Lawrence responded that he was the rightful heir to the British throne. He was judged insane and sent to prison. By his second term, Jackson had received more than five hundred written threats on his life and he seemed to place no special importance on Lawrence's action, except that he rigorously disputed the defendant's alleged insanity and argued instead that Lawrence had been in the employ of a political enemy, Senator George Poindexter of Mississippi, who "would have attempted it long ago, if he had had the courage." When reloaded later, both of Lawrence's pistols worked perfectly.

RESOURCES: *Andrew Jackson* by Robert Remini (New York, 1966); *Old Hickory: A Life of Andrew Jackson* by Burke Davis (New York, 1977).

LEKERT, Girsh (d. 1902), a cobbler, was executed for shooting and wounding Viktor von Val', the Russian governor general of Vilnius, a city that, with only brief respites as part of Poland and capital of Lithuania, was ruled by Russia from 1795 and thereafter by the USSR. Until its Jewish population was virtually eliminated by the Nazis in the Second World War, Vilnius was a traditional centre of Jewish learning (and Jewish agitation). No coincidence, then, that it should have been the birthplace, in 1897, of the All-Jewish Workers' Union, or Bund (German and Yiddish for union), whose territory encompassed Lithuania, Poland

and Russia and was a major force for social change. Although the Bund had renounced terrorism, it by and large applauded the actions of Lekert, which came in May 1902 after von Val' ordered the flogging of twenty-eight people (twenty-two Jews, six Polish Catholics) for taking part in a May Day demonstration. Because the floggings had demoralized the Bund, Lekert was celebrated as a martyr following his execution at the hands of a military tribunal. He was viewed as a great champion of Jewish honour and dignity. For years the anniversary of his death was commemorated as a holiday.

RESOURCE: *Russia under the Last Tsar: Opposition and Subversion, 1894–1917*, ed. Anna Giefman (Oxford, 1999).

LIBENYI, Janos (1830–1853), a Hungarian nationalist, attempted to assassinate Franz-Joseph (1830-1916), head of the Austro-Hungarian Empire, on February 18, 1853, as the emperor, accompanied by his aide, Count Maximilian O'Donnell, walked along the ramparts of Vienna. As they strolled, the two heard the shouts of a woman who had seen Libenyi approaching the emperor from behind carrying a knife. Franz-Joseph turned and bent over to try to make out the woman's words, at which point Libenyi stabbed at where the emperor's back had been only a second earlier, striking him near the collar bone instead. Heavy gold braid on the emperor's uniform deflected the blade somewhat, but the knife struck his neck nonetheless, causing no serious injury but only profuse bleeding, from which the emperor would need several weeks' convalescence. O'Donnell struggled with the attacker as passersby joined in and disarmed and immobilized the assassin until the authorities could take him away. Franz-Joseph returned to the Hofburg under his own power. He stated that his wound made him a casualty much like the soldiers who had died suppressing a revolt in Milan earlier in the week. As for Libenyi, he was a member of the Guild of Tailors and an admirer of the Hungarian nationalist Lajos Kossuth, who had been exiled for his views and had refused to accept a pardon that was conditional on swearing loyalty to Franz-Joseph. As he was led away by police, Libenyi was heard to shout, "Long live Kossuth!" He claimed to have acted on his own. Authorities were sceptical, but after a week of torture he failed to change his story. He was hanged at Simmering, Vienna's ancient execution place. Franz-Joseph was not a popular ruler. The Austro-Hungarian empire was breaking up because of strong nationalist sentiments in what would later be Hungary, Italy and Czechoslovakia. The attempt on his life, however, gained Franz-Joseph a great deal of sympathy and temporarily raised his popularity. To commemorate his survival, the Votivkirche (memorial church) was built on the spot where Libenyi committed his crime. Within a few months, however, Franz-Joseph was as unpopular as ever. An illicit song about the assassination made the rounds of Vienna during the 1850s. One of the stanzas went: *"Auf der Simmeringer Had'/ Hat's an Schneider verwaht,/ 's g' schiecht eahm scho' recht,/ Warum sticht er so schlecht?"* That is: "On Simmering Heath/ the storm blew away a tailor./ Serves him right,/ why did he stab so clumsily?"

RESOURCE: *Franz-Joseph, Emperor of Austria* by Eugene Bagger (New York, 1928).

LÓPEZ , Rigoberto (1930–1956), was the assassin of Anastasio Somoza (1896–1956), the much-feared president of Nicaragua. On September 21, 1956, Somoza was in León to attend a convention of his Partido Liberal Nacionalista (Nationalist Liberal Party). The meeting coincided with the anniversary of Nicaragua's victory over William Walker, the nineteenth-century American filibuster who usurped the Nicaraguan presidency. After the day's political work, Somoza was relaxing at the Casa del Obrero, a workers' club, when López approached the table and fired four shots from a snub-nosed .38-calibre revolver at a distance of about 4.5 metres. Colonel Camilo González Cervantes, Somoza's aide, grabbed the assassin by the hair and disarmed him. Somoza's body-guards, who later were alleged to have been drunk at the time, began to fire at the assassin, who died within seconds. Estimates of the number of times López was shot range between thirty-five and seventy. Once the guards had emptied their weapons into the body, they kicked it and spat on it, then dumped it on the pavement, where it remained the next morning—before disappearing, never to resurface. Somoza was still alive. The bullets had struck his right thigh, right shoulder, right forearm and the base of the spine. The US ambassador, Thomas Whelan, realizing that Somoza was the most politically compliant leader of Nicaragua that America could hope for, arranged for two top US surgeons to be flown to Panama and for Somoza to meet them there. Somoza managed to tell Whelan, in English, "I'm a goner." Somoza was correct. Despite extensive surgery and the finest medical care available in the Canal Zone, Somoza died seven days later.

López was a native of León but had not lived there for several years. A freelance journalist, he had been forced to flee Nicaragua and took refuge among the Nicaraguan refugee community in San Salvador, where he and his friends talked constantly of liberating Nicaragua and returning home. López insisted that if Somoza were killed a spontaneous uprising would bring down the Nicaraguan government. His friends countered that Somoza's death would do no more than replace one dictator with another. Eventually López decided that he was through talking about change and that he would act alone. He purchased a revolver and also, in an unusual show of insight for an assassin, a life insurance policy, naming his mother as beneficiary. López then re-entered Nicaragua posing as a salesman, following Somoza, awaiting the opportunity to strike. The club, where the president and his security would be accessible and unsuspecting, seemed the perfect choice. In a letter to his mother before leaving San Salvador, López wrote: "I hope you take this calmly and realize that what I have done is a duty that any Nicaraguan who loves his fatherland should have carried out long ago."

Within eight hours of Somoza's death, a new dictator emerged: his son Luis (1922–1967), who was convinced that his father's assassination was part of a communist conspiracy, for which twenty-one Nicaraguans were arrested and tortured. After a brief trial, sixteen were found guilty and sentenced to prison terms ranging from nine to fifteen years. Four years later, three of them were shot "while attempting to escape." The Somoza family continued to rule Nicaragua until 1980, first under Luis, later under Somoza's other son, Anastasio (1925–1980). After the elder Somoza's death in 1956, the Somoza-backed newspaper *Novedades* ran a contest offering a cash prize for the best poem eulogizing the slain leader. The winning entry was a flowery one entitled "Renowned Paladin and Cavalier Glory of America," submitted anonymously. When it was published, readers realized that the initial letters from the first fourteen lines spelled out the name Rigoberto López.

RESOURCE: *Dictators Never Die: A Portrait of Nicaragua and the Somoza Dynasty* by Eduardo Crawley (New York, 1979).

LUCHENI, Luigi (1873–1910), assassinated Elisabeth (1837–1898), the Austro-Hungarian empress, on September 10, 1898, confronting her in Geneva, where she was about to board a lake steamer to Montreux. Lucheni stabbed her through the heart (he had been studying an anatomy book to perfect his aim) with a stiletto he had made himself from a sharpened file and a handle whittled from a piece of firewood. The empress's fall was broken by her hair, which she wore in a large bun that cushioned her skull. Lucheni started to run off but was apprehended before he had travelled more than a few metres. At the moment of his capture, he was the only one present aware of what had actually happened. His knife thrust was so fast that eyewitnesses swore he had knocked Elisabeth down with his hand. Even Elisabeth was unaware that she had been stabbed in the heart. The wound was so small that there was no sign of blood until her clothes were removed; although she felt a pain in her chest, this was first attributed to fear and shock. After assuring everyone that she was all right, she continued on her journey but collapsed once aboard the vessel, which returned to Geneva immediately. Doctors were summoned, but Elisabeth was dead before the day was out.

Lucheni was the son of a single mother who had abandoned him as an infant. His early life was a series of foster homes and orphanages. Intelligent and industrious, he went to work on the railway between Parma and Spezia when he was just nine. Later he was drafted into the Austrian army and assigned to the Cavalleggeri Monferrato Regiment. He excelled as a soldier, receiving many commendations and a promotion to lance corporal, though later he was demoted for procuring civilian clothing for a sergeant who was being punished. Nevertheless, Lucheni was singled out for praise by the unit's commander, Prince Raniero de Vera d'Aragona, who later took him on as his batman. A dispute over wages led to Lucheni's resignation in 1897.

Shortly after leaving service, Lucheni began to read anarchist literature. Poor all his life, he was intrigued by the idea of destroying the concepts of wealth and privilege. His travels took him to Switzerland, where he was employed as a labourer on the new post office building in Lausanne, but he was injured on the job. While he was being treated in hospital, the authorities learned of a book of anarchist songs among his effects, along with a drawing of a bludgeon with the caption "For Umberto," a reference to Umberto I of Italy. But the suspicions were not followed up, as Lucheni was deemed incapable of violence. In fact, Lucheni had already decided to kill a member of the nobility even if he hadn't yet selected one. Umberto was the first choice, but a lack of funds made travelling to Italy impossible.

Empress Elisabeth was visiting Geneva, but she wished to travel incognito. A source at the hotel where she was staying, however, revealed the empress's presence to local newspapers. When Lucheni read that the empress was close, he knew that he had found his target. After his arrest, Lucheni claimed that, when apprehended, he was running to the police station to surrender. Lucheni seemed to revel in the attention his action created. He was genuinely delighted when police informed him that his attack had been successful, disappointed when told that there was no death penalty in Switzerland, as his dreams of assassination had always ended with his execution. When asked why he had killed Elisabeth, he replied: "As part of the war on the rich and great. A Lucheni kills an empress, but would never kill a washerwoman." Lucheni wrote a long statement to a liberal Italian newspaper he thought would be sympathetic, but the editor responded with a blistering editorial against the use of violence and Lucheni in particular. Undeterred, Lucheni wrote to many other papers and to individuals, signing his letters "Luigi Lucheni, anarchist, and one of the most dangerous of them." Prison authorities, realizing that Lucheni was revelling in his notoriety, refused to give him his mail. Thus he never saw the supportive letters from European anarchists nor the death threats, including a remarkable one containing sixteen thousand signatures of Viennese women, "the women and girls of Vienna [who] sign to avenge the fearful crime which you have committed against our beloved Empress." The petitioners went on: "Do you know, ravenous beast, what you deserve? Listen monster. We should like to lay you out on a table—yes, kind-hearted though we are, we could look on in pleasure while both your arms and feet were cut off. In order to sweeten your sufferings, we would wash your wounds in vinegar and rub them with salt. If you survived it and recovered, they could do something of that sort again. Or we could make another proposal to you: Let the same instrument be driven into your heart as you plunged it into our beloved Empress—but slowly! Won't you try the experiment? Accursed be the whole of your remaining life, miserable cruel monster. May what you eat do you no good. May your body be a source of nothing but pain to you, and may your eyes go blind. And you shall live in eternal darkness. Such is the most ardent wish of the women and girls of Vienna for such an infamous wretch as you."

At his trial before a jury of forty men, Lucheni made no excuses and refused to seek leniency. The closest Lucheni came to an explanation was that poverty made him desire to kill someone wealthy. His lawyer offered the feeble argument that if Elisabeth were still alive, she would have been among those who would request mercy for Lucheni. With the death penalty not an option, Lucheni was sentenced to life imprisonment with no chance for parole. On October 16, 1910, he was sent to solitary confinement for an altercation with a guard. While there he hanged himself with his belt.

It should be noted that Elisabeth was chronically depressed. Her mood was described as "perpetual melancholia." She had never recovered from the suicide of her son, Prince Rudolf, and often spoke of dying— "alone, far from my loved ones, and for death to take me unawares."

RESOURCES: *Elisabeth: Empress of Austria* by Count Egan Corti (New Haven, 1936); *The Lonely Empress* by Joan Haslip (Cleveland, 1965); *Death by Fame: A Life of Elisabeth of Austria* by Andrew Sinclair (New York, 1999).

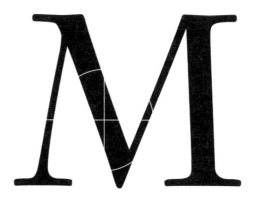

MacNAGHTEN, Daniel

(1816–1865), assassinated Edward Drummond (1792–1843), secretary to British prime minister Sir Robert Peel (1788–1850), on January 20, 1843, as Drummond was leaving Sir Robert's residence in Downing Street in the company of the Earl of Haddington. MacNaghten, who had been following the three men, produced a pistol from his coat and shot Drummond in the back. A passing "Peeler" or bobby (both nicknames derived from Sir Robert, who had founded the forerunner of the Metropolitan Police) apprehended MacNaghten while he was attempting to pull a second pistol. Drummond was taken to his home, where a surgeon removed a ball near his stomach. Although the wound itself was not serious, the surgery proved fatal: Drummond died five days later from its complications. In custody, MacNaghten revealed nothing more than his name. In his pocket, police found a bank deposit slip for the considerable sum of £750, causing them to suspect that he had been paid for the shooting. After his hearing on January 21, MacNaghten was more forthcoming. Shooting Drummond was a case of mistaken identity, he confessed, as he had thought he was shooting Sir Robert Peel. A skilled tradesman from Glasgow, MacNaghten through diligence acquired his own woodworking business, but later became delusional. Following an incident in which he was not allowed to vote in a general election, he came to believe that he was bedevilled by the Tories, to whom he also attributed his frequent headaches. He seldom slept, because he felt that when he was at rest the Tories would come to persecute him. His mental illness worsened with time. When he attempted to seek help from police, they did nothing, leading him to conclude that they were in league with his persecutors. On numerous occasions he complained that spies were following him, but he could produce no evidence. Eventually he sold his business (the source of the large bank deposit) and travelled to France. But the same demons that pursued him in Britain also tormented him there.

At McNaghten's trial, a number of witnesses testified that they believed that he was insane and should be put in restraints. The prosecution attempted to argue that many people with the same delusions had been found fit to stand trial and that the defendant's condition should not be a factor in the case. But the defence provided expert witnesses in psychology, including the director of Bethlehem Royal Hospital, also known as Bedlam, who stated that recent advances in the study of the mind had changed the definition of insanity. The jury agreed with defence arguments that MacNaghten was not responsible for his actions and found him innocent by reason of insanity. MacNaghten was committed to Bedlam, where he spent the rest of his life. The verdict angered both the prime minister and Queen Victoria, who had also been the targets of assassins, and the House of Lords appointed a commission of judges to determine the exact definition of insanity in criminal cases. This action resulted in the set of guidelines known as the MacNaghten Rules, which stated in part that "it must be clearly proved that at the time of committing the act, the party accused was labouring under such a defect of reason, from disease of mind, as to not know the nature and quality of the act he was doing; or if he did know it, that he did not know what he was doing was wrong." The MacNaghten Rules were the basis for determining criminal insanity in Britain until 1957.

RESOURCES: *The Political Life of Sir Robert Peel: An Analytical Biography* by Thomas Doubleday (London, 1856); *Sir Robert Peel: A Historical Sketch* by Henry Lytton Earle Bulwer (London, 1874).

MACRINUS, Marcus Opellius (*c.* 165–218 CE), the prefect of the Praetorian Guard, an elite corps of Roman soldiers with sole responsibility for guarding the emperor, organized the assassination of the emperor Caracalla (Marcus Aurelius Antoninus) (188–217 CE). Macrinus was born to a poor family in Caesarea but trained in law and finance, expertise that allowed him to rise in the military, where he gained the trust of Caracalla, who made him prefect. Caracalla was noted for his cruelty. Since assuming the throne after assassinating his brother Geta, he had killed many rivals and senators. He considered himself a martial emperor, usually wearing the uniform of a common soldier as he conducted massive campaigns against Macedonia and Egypt in imitation of those of his idol, Alexander. The wars were extremely expensive and led to the debasement of Roman coinage. Although Caracalla earned a great deal of animosity in the senate and among the populace on various grounds, his downfall was due to his inattention to affairs of state while he was in the field with his army. Caracalla was so uninterested in events in Rome that he ordered Macrinus to read and deal with all correspondence from Rome while he himself directed the troops.

One day Macrinus received a dispatch from Rome that discussed Caracalla's plans to have Macrinus arrested and executed. Realizing that the only way to save himself was to kill the emperor, Macrinus organized a small group of soldiers to perform the deed. On April 8, Julius Martialis, who held a grudge against Caracalla after being passed over for a promotion that he believed he deserved, stabbed the emperor with a dagger. Martialis was hunted down and killed. Macrinus replaced Caracalla as emperor. Although he had organized the assassination, Macrinus went to great lengths to distance himself from the event, understanding that Caracalla was popular among the Roman troops and to be known as Caracalla's assassin would put his own life in jeopardy. Macrinus immediately proclaimed Caracalla a god, thus earning him the army's support.

The third century CE was notable for military men who rose up and took the throne, only to be killed shortly thereafter. Macrinus was not an exception. After the Roman invasion of Macedonia bogged down, Macrinus signed a peace agreement that the troops found humiliating. Meanwhile, Caracalla's family organized a revolt in Syria. Elagabalus, the high priest of the Sun God at Emesa, was sponsored as a rival to the throne. In 218 CE, soldiers loyal to Elagabalus defeated Macrinus's army. Macrinus fled to Antioch, but was soon captured and executed.

RESOURCE: *The Decline and Fall of the Roman Empire* by Edward Gibbon (London, 1776–1788).

MAGEE, Patrick (b. 1951), a member of the Irish Republican Army, attempted to assassinate Margaret Thatcher (b. 1925), the British prime minister, during the Conservative Party conference at Brighton on October 12, 1984, when the PM and most of her ministers were gathered at the Grand Hotel for the annual event. Late that evening, Thatcher was sitting in her suite reading a document that an MP had insisted she review before it was presented to other party members. Suddenly, a bomb exploded. As another party member reported: "The whole thing went down like a pack of cards." Sections of the hotel were sent flying hundreds of metres, its windows were blown out and the six floors above cascaded into Thatcher's suite, completely demolishing the lavatory—where, Thatcher said, she probably would have been, preparing for bed, had she not been handed the paper late in the evening. As it was, five people, including one Conservative MP, Sir Anthony Berry, died in the blast.

Security for the convention had been tight, but the bomb had been placed long before the gathering began. Magee had checked into the hotel under the name Roy Walsh twenty-four days earlier. Working quietly, he tore down one wall in the toilet of room 629, planted a bomb loaded with forty-five kilos of gelignite set to go off during the conference, then seamlessly repaired the wall. Police, realizing that the bomber had to have checked into the hotel within the previous month, investigated over eight hundred people from fifty countries. Only one of the possible suspects could not be found: the fictional Roy Walsh. A palm print lifted from a registration card he had signed revealed that Walsh was in fact Patrick Magee, whose prints were on record from a previous arrest in Norwich. He was soon arrested. Dubbed "the Brighton Bomber," he was sentenced to eight life sentences with no chance of parole for thirty-five years. While in prison, Magee began studying for his Ph.D., but was destined not to complete his studies. In January 1999, after serving only fourteen years, he was released as part of the Good Friday accord on Northern Ireland.

RESOURCE: *Northern Ireland: The Thatcher Years* by Frank Gaffikin (London, 1990).

MARCIA (d. 193 CE), the concubine of the Roman emperor Commodus (161–192 CE) following the banishment of his wife, Crispina, in 182, later organized Commodus's assassination. She was an intelligent woman whose counsel Commodus often took, but then he displayed little interest in the daily complexities of ruling the Roman Empire, being content mostly to keep Rome's enemies at bay by paying tribute while, at home, killing anyone he suspected of plotting against him, including most of his own family. Commodus also possessed a streak of vanity, renaming the city Commodianus and the Roman legions the Commodian legions. He loved the arena and staged huge events at which races, gladiatorial contests and the wholesale slaughter of exotic animals could last for days or weeks. He thought himself a gladiator and dispatched many gladiators personally; he scandalized the senate by appearing there in gladiatorial garb. Eventually he became mentally unstable. He came to believe that he was the reincarnation of Hercules and took to wearing a lion skin and carrying a club. At about the same time, Marcia was losing favour with him. Realizing that she could be executed, as many of his former favourites had been, she began plotting his death in a conspiracy with Eclectus, the court chamberlain, and Laetus, the prefect of the Praetorian Guard. On January 31, 192, she poured Commodus a cup of poisoned wine, which he drank, with results that were merely sickening rather than fatal. Knowing that the emperor must die before he could recover and kill her, she ordered a wrestler named Narcissus, whom the emperor kept on hand to practise his wrestling technique, to strangle him in his bed chamber. The conspirators chose Pertinax as the new emperor. Unfortunately for them, Pertinax was killed by the Praetorian Guard after ruling for only a few months. After this, the guard decided to auction rule of the Roman Empire to the highest bidder. Didius Julianus won and then, in a bid to solidify his hold, ordered the execution of the conspirators. Didius Julianus lost the empire, and his head, shortly thereafter, when he tried to avoid paying the Praetorian Guard the price he had promised.

RESOURCE: *The Decline and Fall of the Roman Empire* by Edward Gibbon (London, 1776–1788).

MARCOS, Ferdinand (1917–1989), later the president of the Philippines, assassinated Julio Nalundasan (1890?–1935), the newly elected congressman for the second district of Ilocos Norte, on September 20, 1935, thus giving notice of the ruthlessness that would grow as his career proceeded. Nalundasan was shot in the back with a .22-calibre target pistol as he stood on his front porch, brushing his teeth. The bullet passed through his heart and lungs. Nalundasan screamed, *"Jesus Maria y José! Me pegaron una tira!"* ("Jesus, Mary and Joseph! I've been shot!") and died on the spot.

Nalundasan's political career had been gained at the expense of Mariano Marcos (1900–1945), the incumbent for the second district, who had been defeated in a three-candidate race in 1931. Although Nalundasan had finished a poor third in the election, Mariano Marcos, Ferdinand's father, blamed him for splitting the vote. A career politician, Mariano

Marcos spent four years in near-poverty as a minor civil servant while awaiting the next election. When he faced Nalundasan again, in a two-candidate race, Nalundasan defeated him soundly. On election night, Nalundasan supporters staged an impromptu parade, using an open automobile to display two coffins, one for Bishop Labayan Gregorio Aglipay, leader of the Republican Party to which Marcos belonged, the other for Mariano Marcos, to signify the death of his political career as well.

Although not particularly close to his father, the young Ferdinand Marcos, a law student at the University of the Philippines, was outraged by the insult to his family. He also had a personal reason for hating Nalundasan, for with his father's drop in income, Ferdinand had had to earn his own tuition. The junior Marcos was a member of the university shooting team. He later claimed to be the best shot in the Philippines, though in fact he was not even the most expert marksman on the squad. After the authorities had apprehended, questioned and released someone completely unconnected with the shooting, attention turned to the murder weapon, which was determined to have been taken from the locker of the U of P shooting club. Marcos was arrested for the murder of Nalundasan in 1938, a full three years after the assassination, and another year passed before the case went to trial. Marcos had applied for bail so that he could finish his law studies, and his lawyer staged one delaying tactic after another until Marcos graduated. By then the case had attracted national attention and young Ferdinand Marcos had become a celebrity. The case against Marcos hinged on the testimony of Calixto Aguinaldo, who claimed to have been with the Marcos family when the idea of killing Nalundasan was proposed. He also claimed to have accompanied Ferdinand to Nalundasan's home the night of the shooting.

On December 1, 1939, Marcos was convicted of murder and sentenced to from ten to seventeen years' imprisonment. He was offered a pardon by President Manuel Quezon but turned it down. Instead he launched an appeal in an attempt to clear his name. Marcos found an important ally in Justice José B. Laurel, who at eighteen murdered a man but had been acquitted. Gossips suggested that Laurel was Marcos's natural father. In any case, the jurist presided over the appeal himself. Marcos meanwhile used his contacts to outfit his cell with a law library, so that he could study for his bar examination, as well as a ping-pong table, for relaxation. Marcos passed his test with a mark of ninety-eight per cent, the highest in the history of the bar. Convinced that he had cheated, the examiners then gave him an oral examination, on which he scored over ninety-two per cent. When asked if it was true that he could recite the constitution from memory, backwards, Marcos demonstrated that he could. During the second trial Marcos handled his own defence. After submitting a brief of more than eight hundred pages, Marcos appeared in court dressed in white from head to foot to symbolise his innocence. His brilliant cross-examination of Calixto Aguinaldo, plus the presence of the sympathetic judge, led to an acquittal.

In a short time, war broke out between the Philippines and Japan. Marcos, an officer in the militia, was given command of his own unit. His war record has been the subject of much embellishment. Marcos later claimed that he was the most decorated Allied soldier, passing over the fact that most of the medals were given to him in 1962, shortly after he became president. One act that Marcos did perform during the war, however, was to shoot Calixto Aguinaldo, whom he claimed he had discovered looting a bank. Publicly, Marcos would always deny any connection to the Nalundasan murder in public but in private he could be more candid. When asked by a cousin of his wife, Imelda, if he had shot Nalundasan, Marcos replied, "That's kid stuff." During debates, Marcos had a habit of pointing his finger at opponents as though mimicking a pistol. At one point in his congressional career, he was reprimanded for threatening members of the opposition this way. Although Nalundasan's name was not mentioned, the implication was apparent to all. During an official visit to the United States in 1965, Marcos presented Lyndon B. Johnson with the head of a wild water buffalo that he claimed to have shot personally. State Department officials, who had the responsibility of dealing with this somewhat gruesome gift, nicknamed it Nalundasan.

Just as Marcos's career began with one assassination, so it ended with another. On August 21, 1983, Benigno Aquino, Jr., a long-time opponent, arrived at Manila airport after a lengthy exile. As he emerged from the plane, he was shot in the back of the head. The act was seen as having been sponsored by Marcos. Soon afterwards Marcos called an election, in which he defeated Corazon Aquino, the victim's widow. The results were rigged so blatantly that Marcos won his home district with a hundred per cent of the vote after more ballots had been cast than there were registered voters to mark them. This was taken as the final act of corruption, and Marcos was forced to resign and flee the country. He died in Hawaii in 1989.

RESOURCE: *The Marcos Dynasty* by Sterling Seagrave (New York, 1988).

MATHEWS, Robert Jay (1953–1984), was leader of a group of American neo-Nazis that, in a celebrated case, assassinated Alan Berg (1934–1984), a popular and controversial radio talk-show host, on June 18, 1984, as Berg arrived at his home in Denver. As he left his car, Berg picked up a can of dog food he had bought for his Airedale, Fred, and lit the last cigarette of the hundred he smoked every day. Thereupon he was shot thirteen times with a .45-calibre MAC-10 machine pistol that had been converted from semi-automatic to fully automatic fire. He died instantly.

Mathews, the organizer of the ambush, was head of a group called the Order, also referred to by the name Silent Brothers or its German translation, *Brüder Schweigen*. How Mathews came to Nazism is a mystery. Unlike many other neo-Nazis, he was the product of a slightly liberal middle-class environment, but was involved with far-right organizations from an early age. At eleven, he joined the John Birch Society. During his teens, his fascination with the extreme right would be accompanied by an obsession with firearms. At sixteen, he became a Mormon, because he approved of the Mormons' conservative lifestyle and short haircuts. He was active in a Mormon-led tax revolt despite the fact that he had never yet paid income tax, writing several letters to the Internal Revenue Service informing it that income tax was unconstitutional and that its organization was secretly controlled by the Kremlin. By 1972, Mathews was also active in the Sons of Liberty, a paramilitary group. By twenty, he was well-known to both the IRS and the FBI. In 1973, when he was working as a miner in Arizona, he filed an income tax return declaring that he had ten dependants. The IRS was unconvinced; Mathews was arrested for tax fraud and sentenced to six months' probation. By summer 1974, Mathews told his family that he would no longer work for far-right organizations. He left Arizona for Metaline Falls, Washington, a small community with an all-white population. Over the next few years Mathews cleared twenty-one hectares of land he had purchased partly with a loan from his father and was raising a family (having married a woman he met through a magazine advertisement). By 1978, however, he was again involved with the far right. After reading *Which Way Western Man*, a racist book published by William Pierce's National Alliance, he became a convert to the Pierce organization.

He then read *The Turner Diaries*, a novel promoting racial warfare, whose protagonist, Earl Turner, overthrows the US government by destroying the economy through counterfeit currency, armed robbery, lynching and assassination. In the end, Turner himself dies in a nuclear suicide bombing of the Pentagon. *The Turner Diaries* inspired Mathews to found the Order, for which he recruited like-minded racists such as David Lane, Bruce Pierce (no relation to William Pierce), Randy Duey, Gary Yarborough, Richard Scutari and Andrew Barnhill. Although few in number, the Silent Brothers had the self-assigned mission of over-throwing the federal government and provoking racial genocide. At first, their efforts were comically inadequate. They began to counterfeit banknotes, but the bills were so poorly printed that they failed to pass even the most cursory inspection. By 1983, the group was committing armed robberies, starting with a pornographic video store (where they got away with $369) and progressing to a Seattle bank ($25,952), a Spokane bank ($3,600) and two armoured cars in Seattle ($43,345 and $500,000 respectively). The robbery campaign culminated in an armoured car holdup just outside Ukiah, California, in which the bandits, with the help of a Brinks employee, netted $3.6 million.

With the relative failure of their counterfeiting operation and the over-whelming success of their armed robberies, the Order began to discuss the next step in their emulation of *The Turner Diaries*: assassination. Their first intended target was the Baron Rothschild, the financier. They even went so far as to build an explosive device to be delivered by a suicide bomber, but no one in the Order, despite a vow to die for the cause, felt he should perish in a suicide attack. In fact, the Order's first target was a fellow racist, Walter West, because he was seen as a possible security risk. West was taken to a remote spot in Idaho, beaten with a hammer and shot in the head; his body, which the killers said they had buried in a shallow grave, has never been recovered. With West out of the way, the group turned to more conventional enemies. Mathews collected information on four other possible victims: the television producer Norman Lear; Morris Dees, a civil rights lawyer and founder of the successful Southern Poverty Law Center; William Wayne Justice, an improbably named Texas judge who had ordered the integration of a housing project; and Berg, a Jewish former criminal lawyer in Chicago (he had defended Lenny Bruce and Jackie Mason on obscenity charges), now a radio talk-show host in Denver, where he had built a career out of arguing, belittling and degrading guests and callers. Particular targets of Berg's were spokesmen for neo-Nazi groups. Mathews sent Jean Craig, the mother of his mistress Zillah Craig, to Denver to follow Berg and to report on his habits.

In June 1984, Mathews, along with Bruce Pierce, David Lane and Richard Scutari, travelled to Denver to kill Berg. With Mathews and

Scutari acting as lookouts and David Lane as getaway-car driver, Bruce Pierce hid near Berg's driveway. Although the MAC-10 had a thirty-round clip, the gun jammed less than halfway through. The four conspirators escaped. By this time, tracking down members of the Order had become a priority of the FBI, with several hundred agents assigned to the case. The big break came with the arrest of Tom Martinez, a Mathews supporter who had been caught passing the Order's counterfeit money. In exchange for being put into the witness relocation program to escape reprisals from his fellow neo-Nazis, Martinez gave the FBI the names of Berg's assassins. On October 18, Gary Yarborough narrowly escaped arrest after a shoot-out with the authorities in Idaho. Inside his home, the FBI found a shrine to Adolf Hitler and a large cache of weapons including the MAC-10 machine pistol that had killed Berg. Using some of the proceeds from their robberies, the Order rented cottages on Whidbey Island in Puget Sound, less than an hour from the Canadian border. In November, Martinez, now working with the FBI, contacted Mathews and demanded a meeting. Mathews and Yarborough met him in Portland, Oregon. Martinez was secretly accompanied by a large number of FBI agents. When Mathews spotted twenty FBI agents who had surrounded the motel at which the neo-Nazis were staying, a firefight ensued. Yarborough was arrested but Mathews escaped with a wounded hand after being hit by a stray bullet and made his way back to Whidbey Island. The authorities, however, learned about the "compound" from Yarborough.

On December 7, 1984, a day still remembered by neo-Nazis as "Martyr's Day," dozens of agents descended on the island. The other neo-Nazis surrendered, but Mathews barricaded himself in his cottage and was determined to finish the matter. The next day, with no end to the standoff in sight, the FBI fired three M-79 starburst flares into the wooden cottage. As the building burst into flames, Mathews continued to shoot at the FBI while stores of ammunition began exploding around him. At their peak, the flames from the cottage rose more than sixty metres in the air. Mathews died in the fire; the remaining members of the Order were tried in Seattle under the Racketeer-Influenced and Corrupt Organizations Act. In 1987, David Lane and Bruce Pierce were each sentenced to 150 years in prison for Berg's murder.

RESOURCES: *Talked to Death: The Life and Murder of Alan Berg* by Stephen Singular (New York, 1987); *Web of Hate: Inside Canada's Far-Right*

Network by Warren Kinsella (Toronto, 1994). The former was the basis for Oliver Stone's 1988 feature film *Talk Radio*.

McCALL, John ("Jack") (a.k.a. Bill Sutherland) (1850?–1877), the archetypal western misfit who shot and killed James Butler ("Wild Bill") Hickok (b. 1837) while the legendary frontier peace officer, army scout, buffalo hunter and "pistoleer" played poker at Nuttall & Mann's No. 10 saloon in Deadwood, Dakota Territory (DT), on August 2, 1876. A native of Kentucky, McCall, like Hickok, had been in Deadwood only a short time, attracted by the gold rush taking place there. Hickok, eschewing his usual practice, for he was a man with many enemies, was not sitting with his back to a wall. Such negligence made it a simple matter for McCall to approach Hickok from behind and kill him with a single pistol shot to the back of the head. Hickok died instantly, the bullet striking the base of the brain, slightly right of centre, and exiting through the right cheek, lodging in the wrist of a fellow poker player named William R. Massie, a former Mississippi riverboat captain. McCall then tried to shoot some of the bystanders, who overpowered him, but his revolver misfired repeatedly and he was quickly taken into custody. McCall was put on trial the following day by an unofficial miners' court, as Deadwood, being located illegally on aboriginal land, had no recognized judicial system since the community had no right even to exist. The trial, held in a theatre, was covered by a Chicago newspaper reporter who described the defendant as being cross-eyed, snub-nosed and full of bravado and with "a thick crop of chestnut hair [and a] small, sandy mustache." The surviving poker players and the two bartenders on duty at the time of the incident all testified that McCall had taken Hickok unawares, shouting, "Damn you, take that!" Despite garbled suggestions that McCall was avenging the death of a family member, no motive was ever established satisfactorily. Evidence did reveal, however, that Hickok had bested McCall at poker only a few days before the assassination but that Hickok had treated him kindly, offering him fatherly advice and giving him money for breakfast.

Surprisingly, McCall was found not guilty. But as the proceedings had no standing in jurisprudence, friends of the deceased petitioned for the case to be retried in the nearest proper court, at Yankton, DT (now South Dakota). Thus McCall was rearrested on August 29 and taken to Yankton, where he nearly succeeded in escaping from jail before his trial could begin on December 1. McCall now told the jury (and also, in a private interview in his cell, Hickok's elder brother) that he had been hired to do the killing by a gambler named John Varnes, but this seems to have been a fact that McCall recalled at the eleventh hour, in the shadow of the noose; he was found guilty on January 3, 1877, and sentenced to death. After several pleas for commutation failed, McCall was hanged at Yankton on March 1, 1877. The suggestion that Hickok, at the moment of death, was holding "aces and eights, the dead man's hand," has no basis in the contemporary accounts but is an invention of later romanticizers, as is the suggestion that McCall and Hickok had been rivals in love.

RESOURCES: *Alias Jack McCall: A Pardon or Death?* (Kansas City, Kansas, 1967) and *Wild Bill Hickok: The Man & His Times* (Lawrence, Kansas, 1996), both by Joseph G. Rosa.

McLEAN, Roderick (d. 1921), the man who on March 2, 1882, made the last of seven attempts on the life of Queen Victoria (reigned 1837–1901), was an aspiring poet who had sent the queen a poem dedicated to her. The poem was returned unread with a letter informing McLean that the queen did not receive unsolicited poetry. Incensed at his rejection, McLean fired at Victoria with a revolver (the first usage of a revolver in a British assassination attempt) as her carriage was leaving Windsor Station. At first, Victoria did not realize that she had been shot at, assuming the noise she heard was nothing more than an engine letting off steam. Two boys from Eton rushed McLean and beat him with their umbrellas until police arrived. Victoria later praised the boys' heroism in front of their entire school. Being somewhat behind the times in matters of weaponry, she was also intrigued by the use of a revolver—a weapon that could be fired repeatedly with no need for priming—though such pistols had been in use for two generations (Samuel Colt's patents having been granted in 1835–1836).

McLean, it was discovered, had shown signs of insanity ever since an accidental head injury in 1866. In fact, he had been released from an asylum only a few months before his dramatic episode. He was therefore ruled insane and was committed to Broadmoor Asylum where he lived his remaining years. Victoria experienced such a rush of loyalty and support from her subjects following McLean's action that she was heard to remark that it was "worth being shot at—to see how much one is loved."

RESOURCE: *Queen Victoria, A Portrait* by Giles St. Aubyn (London, 1991).

McMAHON, Thomas (b. 1948), an Irish Republican Army terrorist, assassinated Lord Louis Mountbatten (1900–1979), the last viceroy of India and a cousin of Elizabeth II, on August 27, 1979, as Mountbatten and members of his family were aboard their yacht *Shadow V* in Donegal Bay off the northwest coast of Ireland. McMahon's weapon was a bomb that blew the fishing-boat-like vessel out of the water. The incident took place near Mountbatten's summer residence at Cassiebawn Castle, less than twenty kilometres south of the Northern Ireland border. The bomb detonated shortly after Mountbatten and his family had put out for a day of setting lobster pots. In addition to the earl, the explosion killed the earl's grandson Nicholas Knatchbull and a local lad, Paul Maxwell. The Dowager Lady Brabourne, the mother-in-law of Mountbatten's daughter, died a few days later. Mountbatten's daughter, Lady Brabourne, and his grandson Timothy Knatchbull survived the incident.

The bombing was part of a widespread attack by the IRA's Provisional Wing ("the Provos"). On the same day, other bombings in Northern Ireland killed eighteen British soldiers and one British tourist. McMahon, who was considered a bomb expert, probably received his training in Libya, a known supplier of arms and instruction to the IRA. The device, which he built, was smuggled onboard by himself or an accomplice, and was detonated by radio from a vantage point about three kilometres away (the effective range of the radio signal). McMahon, however, was not the person who triggered the bomb. Three hours before the explosion, he and an associate were arrested on suspicion of being members of the IRA, and McMahon was in custody when the vessel was blown apart. After the explosion, however, authorities took a special interest in their prisoner. Forensic experts examining McMahon's clothing found traces of nitroglycerine and flakes of green paint that matched that on the hull of the *Shadow V*. Investigators later deduced that the attacks by the Provos were an effort to best the actions of a rival IRA faction, the Irish National Liberation Army, which had been responsible for the assassination of a British Tory MP, Airey Neave, five months earlier. The killing of Mountbatten, the Allied commander of the Southeast Asia theatre in the Second World War, had more to do with infighting within the IRA than with the cause of uniting Ireland. McMahon was found guilty of murder and sentenced to life in prison, where he began to distance himself from the IRA. In 1996, he became part of the day-release program at Mountjoy Gaol in Dublin. On August 7, 1998, he was freed as part of the Good Friday Peace Agreement.

RESOURCE: *Mort d'un amiral: L'IRA contre Mountbatten* by Roland Marx (Paris, 1985).

MEDINA, Fernando Abal (1947–1970), was the assassin of Pedro Eugenio Aramburu (1903–1970), former president of Argentina. On May 29, 1970, two men in army uniforms appeared at the Aramburu home, announcing that they had been sent to provide extra security. Aramburu's wife let them in and then left to go shopping. While she was gone, the pair kidnapped Aramburu and led him at gunpoint to a car with two confederates inside and drove off. Several terrorist groups claimed credit for the kidnapping, though the abduction was obviously the work of the Juan José Valle-Montomeros Command, also called the Montomeros or Valle Command, a group loyal to the former president Juan Perón, who had been removed from power after a coup in 1955. The command took its name from a Perónist general executed by the government that replaced Perón after his ouster. Aramburu had been a member of the general staff during the coup. Communiqués from the kidnappers announced that Aramburu would be tried for executing twenty-seven Perónist rebels after the failed Perónist counter-coup in 1956. On June 1, a message from the abductors declared that Aramburu had been found guilty and would be executed. The message also declared no negotiations for his release would be entertained. Sources are in conflict about whether Aramburu was killed on June 2 or June 4. On July 16, his body was found in the boot of a car about 480 kilometres from Buenos Aires. He had been shot twice in the chest.

The mastermind of the kidnapping and assassination, Medina was a Marxist-Perónist of middle-class background and deep Catholic faith, who is reputed to have received terrorist training in Cuba. On July 1, 1970, several Montomeros were killed or wounded in a gun battle with police following an attempted bank robbery in La Caera, a suburban town near Cordoba; the survivors provided the authorities with Medina's name as the person responsible for Aramburu's death. On September 8, police announced that Medina had been killed in a shoot-out with officers, as had another suspect, Carlos Gustavo Ramus. In the meantime, Aramburu's death already had led to the fall of the Argentinean government; a military coup on June 8 removed President Juan Carlos Ongania, and Perón, from his exile in Spain, called for nationwide revolution and announced that he would return to Argentina "at any moment I can be useful for something." Perón would return to Argentina the following year and serve as president again until his death in 1974.

Although already dead, Aramburu was kidnapped by Perónists for a second time. On October 17, 1974, a group of Montomeros took Aramburu's body from the cemetery and declared that they would return it only after the remains of Perón's first wife, Eva, were repatriated to Argentina from Spain. Eva Perón's body arrived home a month later, and Aramburu's body was returned, as promised.

RESOURCE: *Aramburu: La verdad sobre su muerte* by Aldo Luis Molinari (Buenos Aires, 1993).

MENDOZA, Benjamin (b. 1935), attempted to kill Pope Paul VI (1897–1978) on November 28, 1970. The incident took place in Manila, which the holy father was visiting as part of a tour of the Middle East and Asia, an undertaking through which he had been suffering from fatigue, the result of age, the length of the trip and, in the few days before the attack, a flu virus. While at the airport, accompanied by Philippines president Ferdinand Marcos and his wife Imelda, the pope was approached by a man dressed as a priest and carrying a cross. As the man drew near, he withdrew a thirty-centimetre knife and attempted to stab the pope in the neck. Mendoza was quickly grabbed by the bishop of Singapore, Anthony Galvin, a former rugby player from Yorkshire, who held him until police took him away. The pope appeared untouched, according to reports from the scene, and forgave his assailant.

Mendoza was an artist from Bolivia. Ligoa Duncan, the owner of a Madison Avenue gallery in New York, called him "a fine artist; I just can't understand what happened to him." She also mentioned that he was much influenced by Salvador Dali and admired Dali's ability to generate publicity. Louis Ruocco, another gallery owner, described Mendoza as: "More of a convoluted personality than crazy. He knew exactly what he was doing. He was a very cunning fellow." The press began referring to him as "the mad painter." Mendoza was an aboriginal American who blamed the Catholic Church for the oppression of his people. He claimed that he wanted to kill the pope in order to spare them further "hypocrisy and superstition." First he considered a symbolic attack, but as time passed his thoughts turned to murder. He wanted to use a gun, but the problems of obtaining a firearms permit and taking a pistol through customs were more than he could surmount. Instead he carried the knife in a wooden box with a large crucifix on top and obtained priestly raiment as a disguise.

After a psychiatric hearing declared him fit to stand trial, Mendoza was charged with attempted murder, illegal possession of a weapon and causing a public scandal. After a short trial, during which he publicly burned a Bible, Mendoza was found guilty of attempted murder and sentenced to just over two years' imprisonment. Pope Paul continued his tour as scheduled. Not until the pontiff returned to Rome did the Vatican doctor announce that Mendoza had succeeded in striking that day in Manila, although the wounds were little more than scratches. The pope had chosen to say nothing about them.

RESOURCE: *Keepers of the Keys: John XXIII, Paul VI, and John-Paul II—Three Men Who Changed the Church* by Wilton Wynn (New York, 1988).

MERCADER, Jamie Ramón (a.k.a. Jacques Mornard, a.k.a. Jacson Mornard, a.k.a. Frank Jacson) (1914–1978), the man who killed Leon Trotsky (1879–1940), co-founder with Lenin of the Soviet state and the father of the Red Army, was one of the cleverest and most professional of assassins. A second-generation communist, he was born in Spain but moved with his mother and siblings to France as a child, following his parents' separation. While in France, his mother became involved, politically and perhaps intimately, with several French communists. The young Mercader eventually joined Republican forces in Spain, rising to the rank of lieutenant. It was in Spain that the GPU (precursor of the KGB) recruited him to assassinate Trotsky, who had settled in Mexico after internal exile in Soviet Central Asia (1927–1929), and then, following his expulsion by Joseph Stalin, to periods in Turkey (1929–1933), France (1933–1934) and Norway (1934–1936). During these years, Trotsky survived several assassination attempts by the GPU, and his last home in Mexico City (he had first lived with the painters Diego Rivera and Frida Kahlo) was surrounded by a re-enforced concrete wall and patrolled round the clock by armed guards. In his study Trotsky kept a loaded revolver and had an alarm button on his desk.

On August 20, 1940, Trotsky admitted to the study a man he knew as "Jacson Mornard." More a casual acquaintance than a friend, Mornard/Mercader, posing as a journalist, had asked Trotsky's help with an article he was writing on Napoleon. As Trotsky read the draft, Mercader sat on the edge of his desk, blocking Trotsky's access to the alarm and the revolver. With Trotsky's attention thus diverted, Mercader produced an Alpinist's ice hammer (not a common ice pick, as legend insists) and drove it into Trotsky's skull. He attempted to strike his target a second time, but Trotsky, a tough old man, fought him off and staggered out of the room for help. With Mercader subdued by guards, Trotsky was taken to hospital where he died the next day.

Under the name Monard, Mercader was put on trial. At first he said he had acted in self-defence. Later he claimed the killing was a *crime passionnel*, as he had fallen in love with Trotsky's wife. Still later he claimed that he had been a Trotskyite who had become disenchanted with his hero after meeting him. In the end, he was sentenced to twenty years in prison, but even after two decades the truth failed to emerge: that Mornard was in fact Mercader and was in the employ of the GPU as part of an elaborate plot to assassinate Trotsky, whom Stalin believed he had made a mistake in merely exiling. Trotsky, so long as he lived, would be a rallying point for anti-Stalinist agitation. Indeed, so great was Stalin's obsession that the GPU's dossiers on Trotsky filled three floors of its headquarters. The GPU had already infiltrated Trotsky's entourage, including his personal guard, but all their attempts to kill Trotsky had failed. In order to finish the job, a special man was needed. Years later it became known that Mercader was being handled by Pavel Sudoplatov (1907–1996), the Soviet intelligence genius who, on Stalin's orders, assassinated the exiled Ukrainian dissident Yevhen Konovalets with a poisoned box of chocolates.

Mercader had many talents. He was outgoing and gregarious, handsome and charming. He spoke perfect French and Spanish, and his English was good enough to let him pass as an American. In a reversal of the usual gender roles, Mercader seduced a woman as part of his plans. That woman was Sylvia Ageloff, the sister of Trotsky's personal secretary as well as a close personal friend of the Trotskys. Mercader told Ageloff that he was a journalist working for an organization called the Argus Company. According to Mercader, the Argus Company never met with the writers, accepted everything that the writers submitted and never informed the writers which publications were printing the articles. As far-fetched as this sounds, Ageloff never questioned this unusual business, and she began receiving three thousand francs each month for writing articles on psychology.

Angeloff introduced Mercader to Trotsky. Trotsky was cordial, although not entirely comfortable with this so-called journalist. He confided to his wife that the young visitor's work was amateurish. Nevertheless Trotsky agreed to help him. Mercader's plan was to kill Trotsky instantly with a blow to the head, then leave the study and announce that Trotsky wished to be left alone, then make his escape. The GPU hoped that Mercader would be killed immediately after assassinating Trotsky, thus tying up all loose ends of the affair. The fact that Trotsky escaped Mercader and told his guards not to kill him dashed the expectations of both Mercader and the GPU.

The fact that Mexico did not have capital punishment meant that Mercader would receive a long prison sentence. Thus in 1943, he began serving his twenty years. While in prison, he was studied by a series of psychiatrists and other specialists. The prisoner claimed that he was Belgian and had been born in Teheran. While the Mexican authorities were sceptical of anything Mercader said, they could never crack his story. He claimed to be an adept horseman and hunter. He claimed he was, as he had told Trotsky, a journalist. He also claimed to be an expert mountaineer. His knowledge of all of these subjects was tested, and, with the exception of his claim to know mountaineering, all were proven false. Mercader insisted that his examinations be conducted in French, even though Spanish was his first language. In brief, Mercader did whatever he could, short of telling the truth, to make the authorities continue to test him. Either he was pleased with himself for keeping the deception going, or was simply bored and lonely, relishing the opportunity to speak to educated men and keep himself occupied. The psychiatrists' reports on the prisoner were faulty. Mercader had a photographic memory and was almost impossible to trip up. But they did conclude that he was overly devoted to his mother and had a strong resentment of his father and noted that he was left-handed (traits found no more commonly in assassins than in the general population, later studies have shown). They concluded that he was a latent homosexual, which rankled the macho "Belgian." By passing him a note written in Russian saying that his mother was about to be executed, they discovered that he could read the language. Mercader had strong reason to fear for her life as well as his own, for Caridad Mercader was taken to the Soviet Union as an insurance policy to ensure Mercader's silence. Mercader knew that the GPU (later the NKVD) had no loyalty towards its operatives. One of the infiltrators of Trotsky's private circle, Robert Sheldon Harte, had been abducted shortly after the assassination. His body was later discovered in a shallow grave covered in quicklime. On at least two occasions plans were developed to break Mercader out of prison. Once Mercader revealed such a scheme to prison authorities to increase his security. Mercader knew he was safer in prison than he was in the custody of the NKVD. What's more, his stay in prison was a fairly comfortable existence. Mercader enjoyed a steady flow of cash while in custody. His cell was well-appointed with a gramophone and a large collection of records. His meals were delivered from an expensive restaurant, and he even managed to keep a mistress. After the assassination, Sylvia Ageloff was arrested as an accomplice. Mercader, although he had simply used Ageloff as a pawn, had become somewhat attached to her over the two years they had been together and steadfastly maintained that she was innocent. That, plus the obvious hatred Ageloff felt towards the man who had used her, was enough to acquit her.

In 1960, after serving seventeen years of his sentence, Mercader was released. He was met by two officials from the Czechoslovakian embassy. The three men flew to Cuba and from there went to Czechoslovakia. Mercader disappeared for a few years, then was found in Czechoslovakia working as an electrical repairman (a trade he had learned in prison). He later retired to Cuba, where he died in 1978. For their service to the Soviet Union, Mercader and his mother both received the Order of Lenin. In the Mexico City suburb of Coyoacan, Trotsky's home at 45 avenida Viena is a tourist site. One of Trotsky's bodyguards, known as "Jake," was found in the early 1970s running a grocery in suburban Minneapolis. A local conservative group's discovery of his true identity led to a boycott of the shop.

RESOURCES: *The Mind of an Assassin* by Don Levin (New York, 1959); *The Life and Death of Leon Trotsky* by Victor Serge and Natalia Trotsky (New York, 1973). Mercader has also entered the popular culture, as in Bernard Wolfe's thriller *The Great Prince Died* (New York, 1959) and Joseph Losey's film *The Assassination of Trotsky* (1972).

MERINO, Martin (1790–1852), attempted to assassinate Isabella II of Spain (1830–1904, reigned 1833–1868). On February 2, 1852, Isabella encountered Merino, a priest, in the corridor of the palace in Madrid. As Merino approached and knelt before her, the queen thought he was going to present her with a petition; she reached out her hand. Instead Merino produced a dagger and stabbed her in the chest. Although the wound was serious, Isabella recovered. Merino was a republican and was suffering from a bilious disease that may have affected his sanity. He was apprehended immediately. When pressed to explain his actions, he offered three words: "She deserved it." Isabella was subject to criticism not only for her rule but also for her scandalous private life. Merino's attack was rumoured to be part of a widespread conspiracy against the monarchy, but intensive questioning failed to provide any evidence of this. Other gossip held that Isabella wished to pardon the ageing maddened priest. While such was possible, given Isabella's capacity for mercy in certain circumstances, there is little hard evidence. Martin Merino was defrocked and, after a brief trial, sentenced to death. He was paraded through the streets of the capital facing backwards on a donkey with his hands tied behind his back. At the conclusion of his ride, he was hanged. Isabella, never a popular ruler, was the recipient of a wave of sympathy after the attack, but the support would prove short-lived. In 1868, she was forced to abdicate in favour of her French brother-in-law, the Duke of Montpensier. After taking the throne, Montpensier challenged Isabella's cousin Enrique, the Duke of Seville, who had called him "a puffed-up French pastrycook." After three attempts by each of the duellists, Montpensier finally shot and killed Enrique. Rule passed to Amadeo of Spain, but two years later Amadeo abdicated in favour of a republic. In 1874, Isabella's son Alfonso ascended to the throne as Alfonso XII.

RESOURCE: *Asi Cayo Isabel II: Siglo de pasión política* by Rafael Oliva Bertrand (Barcelona, 1955).

MERLO, Enrique Haroldo Gorrian (code name "Ramón") (b. 1942),

leader of the team that assassinated Anastasio Somoza (1925–1980), former dictator of Nicaragua. On September 17, 1980, Somoza set out in a white Mercedes-Benz from his home in Asunción, Paraguay, where he had lived in exile since being deported from the United States. As Somoza and his chauffeur drove down the avenida España, they encountered a blue pickup, which pulled in front of them, forcing them to stop. Guerrillas then raked Somoza's car with machine-gun fire. A few seconds after shooting began, one of the attackers fired a bazooka, tearing off the top of the automobile, killing those inside.

The chauffeur's body was blown across the street, decapitated and legless; Somoza's was reduced to pieces.

"Ramón," the leader of the attack, was a high officer of the Argentinean People's Revolutionary Army or ERP (Ejército Revolucionario del Pueblo), a large, disciplined and surprisingly well-funded revolutionary force. He and a number of other ERP members, including the infamous Captain Santiago (real name: Hugo Iruzun), had come to Nicaragua in 1979 to assist the Sandinista rebels to overthrow the Somoza regime, whereupon they found themselves at loose ends: being a revolutionary army, they had no real function in Nicaragua once the fighting stopped. One night in Managua they discussed the fate of Somoza, blaming him for the disciplined camps of ex-Nicaraguan National Guard members (also known as Contras) who raided farming communities periodically. Ramón believed that if Somoza were dead the Contras would lose their funding and be dissolved (in fact, the Contras were funded from the United States by the CIA). The rebels agreed that their next operation should be Somoza's assassination. Numbering about a dozen, they made their way to Colombia separately in order to plan and train for the attack. Santiago, a well-known military instructor, led the others in calisthenics and weapons drill, while Ramón taught them disguise, forgery and other espionage arts. The rebels had a well-stocked library with such titles as *Day of the Jackal*, *The Spy Who Came in from the Cold*, *The Red Orchestra* and *The House on Garibaldi Street*. Ramón contracted with a weapons dealer in Costa Rica to purchase several automatic rifles, hand-guns and a bazooka with two Chinese-made rockets. He realized that Somoza's car would be bullet-proofed (although some of the assassins' bullets pierced it anyway). When he decided that the time was right and the men and women who were his co-conspirators were ready, he easily arranged for the arms to be smuggled into Paraguay in crates marked "Automobile Parts"; the labelling was designed to mislead the hired smugglers rather than the authorities, because the border was quite porous, especially with regard to consumer goods and machinery. With false documentation the conspirators travelled to Asunción, where they began to search for Somoza, who had been staying out of sight. Interviews with a number of cab drivers eventually revealed that Somoza was living at 436 avenida General Genes, the same street where Paraguay's leader, Alfredo Stroessner, resided. The assassins purchased a magazine kiosk just down the street from Somoza's home from which to observe his movements. As they got to know their quarry, they reasoned that the attack should take place as close to Somoza's home as possible. They rented a mansion nearby, using forged letters and documents indicating that one of the conspirators was scouting a short-term rental for the singing star Julio Iglesias, who supposedly would be shooting a movie in the country. In the circumstances, the conspirators asked the landlady to be discreet; she agreed on the condition that she would get to meet the famous tenant.

On September 17, all was in readiness. Ramón led a team of four shooters while Santiago fired the bazooka. The original plan called for firing the bazooka at the very beginning, but the first shell was a dud. Weapons experts advise that one should wait thirty seconds before releasing a dud bazooka shell so that the weapon can cool. Santiago waited less than ten seconds before reloading and burned himself in the process. After the assassination, the Paraguayan authorities sealed the border and started an intense manhunt.

Somoza had made few friends in Paraguay. His bellicose manner and alcoholism did not endear him to the conservative Paraguayans, particularly President Stroessner. Yet the idea of a foreign group assassinating a resident was intolerable. In a case of mistaken identity, eyewitnesses led Paraguayan authorities to waste considerable time hunting for international terrorists who were not in the country. Most of the conspirators, equipped with well-forged papers, passed police checkpoints and made their way back to Argentina. Only one key figure was captured: Hugo Iruzun, alias Captain Santiago, whose hideout was surrounded on September 18. Later reports indicated that police found Santiago eating cereal and reading Karl Marx. After a ninety-minute gun battle, Santiago was dead from two wounds to the chest. Merlo is still at large.

RESOURCE: *Death of Somoza: The First-Person Story of the Guerrillas Who Assassinated the Nicaraguan Dictator* by Claribel Alegria and Darwin Flakoll (Willimantic, Connecticut, 1996).

MIKAMI Taku (b. 1906) assassinated Inukai Tsuyoshi (1855–1932), the Japanese prime minister who took office in 1931, determined to end the crisis caused by Japan's occupation of Manchuria. Inukai was noted for his uncompromising stances as well as his desire for friendly relations with China, and intended to negotiate a settlement with the Chinese government that would legitimize Chinese sovereignty over the region while still allowing a measure of local autonomy. Such a challenge to the authority of the Japanese army abroad was dangerous. The 1930s in Japan are notable for the rise of extreme rightism, nationalism and militarism, forces that people opposed at their own risk. Mikami Taku, a native of Saga Prefecture in Kyushu, an area with a long history of radical dissent, led a group of young officers that was especially angered by Inukai's actions. Mikami had been taught the politics of Japanese ultra-nationalism by his grandmother, who sent a wire to his commanding officer stating that Mikami's mother had just died, thus securing him the leave he needed to carry out the assassination, which was scheduled to take place on May 15, 1932.

Several teams of young officers planned to bomb or otherwise attack key political figures and installations, believing that their actions would trigger a spontaneous uprising that would restore absolute rule by the emperor. Mikami's group was given the assignment of killing Inukai. On the appointed day, Mikami and his men, in two taxicabs, drove to the prime minister's residence and asked a receptionist if they could see Inukai. When informed that Inukai did not receive visitors on Sundays, they politely asked a uniformed police officer on duty to take them to Inukai's private apartments. The policeman engaged the soldiers in conversation while another officer, in plain clothes, attempted to leave the lobby to summon help. His departure was noticed and the young militants shot and wounded him. Leaving one member behind to watch the receptionist and two policemen, the rebels searched the house. They captured and threatened several servants, but none of them would assist the assassins. Finally, after hearing noises behind a door, the assassins broke into Inukai's apartment. Inukai's bodyguard was waiting just inside, but the soldiers managed to shoot him before he could draw his revolver. Rushing over the body of the security man (who died ten days later), the assassins confronted Inukai in his dining room. Inukai demanded that the soldiers remove their boots before entering his quarters. Refusing the request, they informed Inukai that they were there to kill him and asked if he had anything to say before he died. Mikami and another officer took Inukai to a side room while the remaining assassins held pistols on Inukai's daughter, maid and personal physician. Inukai tried to talk sense to his attackers until Mikami shouted "*Mondo muyo*" ("No use discussion") and Mikami's companion shot the prime minister in the face. The bullet tore Inukai's nose, passed through the roof of his mouth and out his right cheek. As Inukai slumped forward, Mikami shot him again, in the temple. Their work done, the young soldiers made their way back through the residence. On the way out they encountered another police officer whom they shot twice before emerging from the building and re-entering the waiting taxis.

Inukai was still alive when they left. The prime minister told his staff that he wanted the attackers to return so that he could talk to them. Inukai was bleeding badly, but was coherent and in control of his faculties. His physician decided that transporting him to hospital would not be worth the risk, so Inukai was put to bed and given blood from his son (no blood tests had been conducted, but luckily Inukai's son's blood was a match). Inukai called an emergency cabinet meeting at his bedside. Despite isolated attacks and a great deal of gunplay outside important civic buildings, the spontaneous uprising that was crucial to the plan failed to materialize. At 9:30 p.m., Inukai began throwing up blood. He was given a sedative, which caused him to lapse into a coma. By 2:30 a.m., he was dead. The officers who had killed him travelled to the home of the war minister to tell of what they had done, hoping that the minister would call out the army to make the coup a success. But the minister was wisely absent at the time and the plotters were received by the vice-chief of staff, who had them arrested.

The courts martial that followed what became known as the May 15th Incident were a sensation throughout Japan. A petition seeking clemency for the assassins contained more than 350,000 signatures. The court officers also received over one hundred thousand individual letters in support of the young officers. Nine men from the town of Niigata chopped off their little fingers and sent them to the war ministry in a jar of alcohol as a sign of their own agreement. In the end, all the defendants were found guilty but only light sentences meted out. Those who participated but had not shot anyone were sentenced to four years in prison, only to be released early, owing to good behaviour, as part of the New Year celebrations in 1935. Mikami was sentenced to fifteen years' imprisonment but was released in a general amnesty in 1940. At the end of the war, Mikami was officially purged—forbidden to hold any official position—by the American occupation forces. Once the occupation ended, however, he stood for office as a far rightist. Although he received ninety thousand votes, he failed to win a seat in the upper house of the Diet. In 1961, he was arrested again for conspiracy. Mikami had decided that the Japanese government must be overthrown and contacted several members of the Self-Defence Forces about staging a military coup. He was quickly reported to police. Mikami stated that he had meant no harm but only wanted action on three issues: bribery, taxes and unemployment. What has come to be called the Three Nothings incident was not taken especially seriously. Mikami was sentenced to three years' imprisonment. Shortly after his release in 1964, he appeared on a podium with two fellow assassins from the 1930s, Sagoya Tomeo and Kōnuma Tadashi.

RESOURCE: *Japan's Imperial Conspiracy* by David Bergamini (New York, 1971).

MIRO, Ruben (1911–1970), a lawyer from a well-established family active in politics, assassinated José Antonio ("Chichi") Remón (1909–1955), the president of Panama, on January 2, 1955, at a Panama City racetrack where Remón, an avid sportsman, had gone to watch some of his own horses compete. At 8:00 p.m., at least two men armed with machine guns strafed the presidential party while it sat on the illuminated terrace of the clubhouse. The gunfire killed one bodyguard instantly and seriously wounded Remón and several other persons, including his personal secretary, Olmedo Fabrega. Shot several times, Remón died in hospital less than an hour later. Police soon had several suspects, one of whom died in custody; they were all followers of the former president, Arnulfo Arias, and they had nothing whatever to do with the plot against Remón.

By January 6, detectives found one of the gunmen, Miro. He was known to be brilliant though somewhat disturbed and to have amassed large gambling debts that virtually bankrupted his family. When confronted with evidence showing that he had purchased the weapons used in the attack, Miro confessed but made a shocking pronouncement: that he was hired to carry out the assassination by José Ramón Guizado, the former vice-president and present leader of Panama, who was immediately removed from office and placed under house arrest. Guizado was tried by the National Assembly, found guilty and sentenced to six years and eight months in prison. In his appeal, he claimed that although he had been aware that Miro was plotting against the president, he did not regard the scheme a serious threat to the president's life.

In 1957, after a change in government, both Ruben Miro and José Ramón Guizado were acquitted, in closed proceedings, on all charges. Guizado retired with all the rights and privileges of a former president but Miro did not fare so well. He set up a revolutionary organization that was quickly smashed by the authorities. Miro returned to the practise of the law. On January 1, 1970, almost fifteen years to the day after he had killed Remón, Miro was himself slain by machine-gun fire on a deserted road near Chepo, less than sixty-five kilometres from the racetrack where Remón died. Miro named José Edgardo Tejada and Luis Carlos Hernandez as his accomplices.

RESOURCE: *The Remón Era: An Analysis of a Decade of Events in Panama, 1947–1957* by Larry LaRae Pippin (Stanford, California, 1964).

MIURA Gorō (1846–1926), a Japanese general, ordered the assassination of Min Bi, consort to King Kojong of Korea. On October 8, 1895, Japanese soldiers entered the Korean royal palace, overwhelming the guards on duty and stabbing to death the Min Queen, as she was usually referred to. This action, while furthering the Japanese conquest of the peninsula, was arranged personally by Miura; acting without orders, he had assembled a special team for the purpose. Min, unlike most consorts, had been highly influential throughout Korea, having worked to secure high-ranking positions for members of her family. Her hostility towards the Japanese made it difficult for Japan to dominate Korea's government and economy. Miura realized that the conquest of Korea would succeed only when she was out of the way. After the killing, Miura was recalled to Japan, where he was tried and found guilty of conspiring to assassinate the Min Queen. Sources vary on the subject of his punishment, some claiming that he served less than a year in prison, others stating that he served no time at all. The assassination created an international stir. When Kojong feared that he would be killed next, Russia offered him asylum in its legation in Seoul. In the long run, killing the Min Queen accomplished its purpose: in June 1896, Japan and Russia signed an agreement allowing Japan to station troops in Korea, though the Japanese occupation would not be completed until after the Russo-Japanese War of 1904–1905. Korean nationalists were outraged by the assassination, and "Righteous Armies" sprang up to fight against Japanese rule. Miura's military career was not harmed by his involvement in the murder, and in 1897 be became active in politics, campaigning against an increase in land taxes as part of the Kensei Honto Party. In 1910, he was appointed to the privy council and became a powerful backroom politician. A centrist, he tried to straddle the line between the nationalist and liberal factions.

RESOURCE: *Imperialism, Resistance, and Reform in Late Nineteenth-Century Korea* by Vipan Chandra (Berkeley, California, 1988).

MOORE, Sara Jane ("Sally") (b. 1930), attempted to assassinate US president Gerald Ford (b. 1913) on September 24, 1975, less than three weeks after Lynette ("Squeaky") Fromme's attempt on the same figure. Moore was born to a comfortable middle-class family in Charleston, West Virginia (where as a teenager she patronized a food store where Charles Manson's mother was a cashier). A certified public accountant, Moore married five times and was the mother of four. She left her fifth husband in 1973 and began working for the People in Need Program, an organization set up by Randolph Hearst as part of the ransom for his daughter Patricia, who had been kidnapped by the Symbionese Liberation Army (SLA). Because of the ties between People in Need and the SLA, Moore was approached by the FBI to become an informant. After the FBI appealed to her sense of patriotism, she agreed to inform on her associates, but when she confessed to a close friend within the movement that she was spying on him, she was cut off from the radicals who were her only friends. Furthermore, two of her contacts were killed shortly afterwards, and she was warned that she would be the next to die. Desperate to re-establish her credentials within the movement, Moore purchased a .44-calibre revolver and began taking target practice. When Ford was scheduled to appear in San Francisco, Moore called the city police and tried to tell them that she had been assigned by the Secret Service to test its presidential security system. Not believing her story, the police contacted the Secret Service, who confiscated her weapon. They did not, however, take her into custody, on the grounds that they had determined that she was incapable of actually attempting an assassination. On September 22, 1975, Moore purchased a .38-calibre Smith & Wesson revolver and stood in the crowd awaiting the president's appearance. When Ford arrived, Moore fired a single shot that missed Ford by several metres and hit a bystander in the groin. She was apprehended immediately. One of Moore's first statements after the shooting was, "I'm not a Squeaky Fromme." After pleading guilty to attempted assassination, Moore began serving a life sentence, and has been in prison ever since. In 1983, as an inmate of the Dublin Federal Prison Camp in northern California, she led a successful campaign to provide kosher food for Jewish inmates.

RESOURCE: *Squeaky: The Life and Times of Lynette Alice Fromme* by Jess Bravin (New York, 1997).

MORRAL, Matteo (1880–1906), attempted to assassinate Alfonso XIII of Spain (1896–1941) on May 31, 1906, the day the king married Princess Victoria, daughter of Prince Henry of Battenberg and granddaughter of Queen Victoria. After a lavish ceremony, the royal couple rode in an open carriage through the streets of Madrid to receive the cheers and best wishes of crowds lining their path. A large floral bouquet was thrown in front of the coach in the calle Major. The flowers, landing on the right-hand side of the vehicle, hid a bomb, which exploded as the royal couple leaned out the left side, a fact that probably saved their lives. In all, thirty-one soldiers and bystanders were killed in the blast; the carriage horses were either killed outright or so badly wounded that they had to be put down. The queen fainted but Alfonso revived her, signalled that they were both all right and escorted his bride to another carriage. The queen smiled and waved as she walked between vehicles, and the king ordered the driver to take them back to the palace slowly, so as to demonstrate their lack of fear. The assassin escaped without detection.

Matteo Morral was born to a wealthy family in Sabadell, an industrial centre in Catalonia. Described as taciturn, morose and ill-balanced, he had frequent arguments with his father over politics. An excellent scholar, Morral received advanced education in Spain and Germany before entering the Escuela Moderna, which was founded and run by the anarchist Francisco Ferrar. Morral eventually managed the school's library and ran its publishing program, which produced mostly books by Ferrar. While at the Escula Moderna, Morral became infatuated with Soledad Villafranca, a teacher. The relationship of Morral, Villafranca and Ferrar has been the source of a great deal of speculation, with interpretations ranging from *ménage à trois* to love triangle. For her part, Villafranca maintained that she never had any interest in Morral but was infatuated with Ferrar. Some sources go so far as to describe Morral as a syphilitic deviant. In any case, the breakdown of the relationship between Morral and Villafranca led to Morral's despondency and his plan to kill Alfonso. He travelled to Madrid and rented an apartment with a balcony that would overlook the route of the wedding party.

The source of the powerful and sophisticated bomb remains unknown; Morral had no experience or training with explosives, and investigation of Ferrar proved that he too was incapable of creating such a device. After the bombing, Morral walked to the offices of José Nakens, the editor of the republican newspaper *El Motin*. Although not an anarchist, Nakens was a friend of Ferrar and had shown sympathy for the anarchist Michael Angiollilo, who had assassinated Premier Antonio Cànovas del Castillo in 1897. Morral told Nakens what he had done and asked him to help him escape. Nakens was shocked and demanded he leave, but Morral refused, telling Nakens he had nowhere to go. As they talked, Morral kept one hand in his pocket, which, as Nakens feared, contained a pistol. Nakens took Morral to a friend's to spend the night and get him new clothes. En route, the two heard passersby speak about the assassination attempt. One person said to Morral: "If I knew the assassin I would drag the coward's heart out." Morral replied, "I would do the same if I knew him." Morral left the capital by train the next day, but he was apprehended by a station guard at Torrejon de Ardoz, about twenty-two kilometres away, on June 2, whereupon he panicked and shot his captor before turning the weapon on himself.

Authorities arrested Ferrar and Nakens for their participation in the assassination and escape. Nakens claimed that he had acted out of fear for his life; he was sentenced to nine years in prison, but because of his age (he was over sixty) and his standing in the community, he was soon released. Ferrar was accused of being the mastermind of the operation. A cheque for a thousand pesetas (about £40) made out to Nakens by Ferrar was taken as evidence that Ferrar had bribed Nakens into helping Morral. In fact, the money proved to be a royalty advance that Ferrar had sent Nakens for a book Ferrar was hoping to publish. Ferrar was even accused of manufacturing the bomb. In spite of the prosecution's zeal, none of the charges was proved and he was released.

RESOURCES: *The Life, Trial, and Death of Francisco Ferrer* by William Archer (New York, 1911); *Every Inch a King: Alphonso XIII, A Study of Monarchy* by HRH Princess Pilar of Bavaria and Major Desmond Chapman-Huston (New York, 1932).

NAKAOKA Konichi (b. 1902), a railway employee, assassinated Japanese Prime Minister Hara Takashi (1856–1921), a moderate liberal in a difficult position. A former journalist and home minister on several occasions in previous governments, Hara became prime minister in 1918 and immediately had to deal with conflicts between liberals who favoured universal male suffrage and rightists who favoured autocratic rule by the emperor. Although Hara had an absolute majority in the lower house, he would not use his influence to bring about the liberal position, because he feared reprisal by the rightists. Nevertheless, Hara was assassinated by a rightist. Nakaoka Konichi, a young man prone to depression, had been telling his fellow workers that he was going to commit hara-kiri. His words sounded empty. He responded. "You wait and see. I will cut hara." His listeners did not realize that he was referring not to his belly but to Prime Minister Hara. On November 4, 1921, Nakaoka caught up with his victim at a Tokyo railway station and stabbed him; Hara died on the station floor, and Nakaoka was immediately apprehended. Nakaoka was determined to be of unsound mind, though fit to stand trial. He was found guilty, but due to his mental condition he was given a light sentence of twelve years' imprisonment. He was released from Sendai Penitentiary in 1934 as part of a mass amnesty declared after the birth of Crown Prince Akihito. Japan, by then in the grip of the right-wing ultranationalists, greeted the assassin of a liberal prime minister as a hero, and he was met on his release by a large group of well-wishers. Wealthy rightists looked after his material needs for the rest of his life. Nakaoka, however, did not appreciate his notoriety and chose to emigrate to Manchuko, territory that recently had been seized from China and needed Japanese settlers. After the Second World War, Manchuko, now once again known as Manchuria, was returned to China, and Nakaoka went home to Japan, declaring that he would never leave the country. Shortly afterwards, he deliberately vanished.

RESOURCE: *Japan's Imperial Conspiracy* by David Bergamini (New York, 1971).

NAMBA Daisuke (1899–1924) attempted to assassinate Japan's prince regent Hirohito (1901–1989) on December 27, 1923, as Hirohito proceeded by carriage to the Diet in Tokyo for the official opening of a new session. When the carriage stopped at the Toranomon intersection, Namba emerged from the crowd lining the street and approached carrying a walking stick. When within range, he removed the end of the stick, revealing a concealed pistol, and fired at the prince through his carriage. The bullet missed Hirohito's face by a few centimetres. Namba was apprehended at the scene while the prince continued on his way. Namba Daisuke came from a wealthy family in Yamaguchi Prefecture. In his youth, he was a loyal supporter of the imperial system and even mentioned joining the army. At about nineteen, however, he began to study the works of such foreign radicals as Karl Marx; by 1919, he was a confirmed activist who had participated in Japan's universal male suffrage movement. In 1921, an article by Kawakami Hajime, a leading Japanese Marxist and noted authority on Marxist thought, convinced him that only the self-sacrifice of dedicated communists could bring about revolution. In 1923, Tokyo was severely damaged by earthquake, blame for which was fixed on Koreans and anarchists, two groups whose persecution increased from already high levels. Lynchings of fellow leftists and Koreans convinced Namba that assassination of the prince was a reasonable response to the sufferings of his fellow radicals. Soon after his arrest, Namba was pronounced insane, though documents released later showed that officials knew this to be untrue but felt they had to pacify an agitated populace. After a closed trial, Namba was sentenced to death on November 13, 1924, and executed two days later. Although Japan endured numerous assassinations in the period 1921–1940, this was perhaps the only one committed by a leftist. Yet it led to further repression of the left, culminating in the Peace Preservation Law of 1925, which allowed authorities to arrest suspected communists and hold them without trial.

RESOURCE: *Thought Control in Prewar Japan* by Richard H. Mitchell (Ithaca, New York, 1976).

NELBÖCK, Johann (1903–?), assassinated Moritz Schlick (1882–1936), one of the most influential philosophers of the first half of the twentieth century, in Vienna on June 22, 1936. As Schlick ascended a flight of steps outside the University of Vienna, Nelböck, one of his former students, approached him, revolver in hand, and fired four times, two of the bullets piercing the heart. Schlick, a physicist turned philosopher, clung to life for less than an hour. Schlick is considered the leader of the Vienna Circle, a group out of whose meetings logical positivism evolved, although he was atypical of the members, being a conservative surrounded largely by socialistic thinkers. For example, he had supported the near-fascistic regime of Chancellor Englebert Dollfuss as a bulwark against German imperialism, though in general he believed that the work of the Circle was hindered by politics. After becoming chair of the philosophy department, Schlick continued to teach graduate students, which is how he came into contact with Nelböck, who completed his Ph.D. under him. At some point during their relationship, however, Schlick began to receive threats from Nelböck, who, although he had in fact been awarded his Ph.D., felt that Schlick had rejected his dissertation, which was entitled *Die Bedeutung der Logik in Empirismus und Positivismus (The Significance of Logic in Empiricism and Positivism)*. Nelböck also suffered from the delusion that Schlick was trying to steal his girlfriend. After making serious threats against Schlick's life, Nelböck was sent for examination at an asylum and diagnosed as a paranoid schizophrenic. Doctors noted that Nelböck's insanity seemed to be triggered by only one subject: Moritz Schlick. After being held for observation, Nelböck was released, whereupon he resumed his threats. At one time, Schlick had hired a bodyguard but now he chose to ignore his attacker's ravings. Nelböck was arrested at the scene of the assassination, found fit to stand trial, confessed to the murder and sentenced to ten years' imprisonment. The light sentence seems to have been in consideration of his emotional instability, combined with the fact that the Vienna Circle had fallen into official disrepute due to its leftist inclinations. In 1938, when Vienna was absorbed into Nazi Germany, Nelböck was released from prison to join a German penal battalion. In 1941, he applied to the Nazis for a full pardon, claiming that he killed Schlick because Schlick was Jewish (which in fact he was not). Possibly confusing Schlick with another member of the Vienna Circle—Otto Neurath, who was both a Jew and a socialist—the Nazis granted the request, and all Nelböck's rights were restored. After the war, finding himself under Soviet occupation, Nelböck declared himself a communist and took a minor administrative job for the USSR. The Vienna Circle continued to meet after Schlick's death, but by 1938 most members had fled Austria. Ironically, this dispersal helped to make logical positivism known throughout the world, particularly in Britain, the Scandinavian nations and especially the United States, where Schlick once had taught and where one of the Circle's supporters, Ludwig Wittgenstein, already was highly influential.

RESOURCE: *Rationality and Science: A Memorial Volume for Moritz Schlick in Celebration of the Centennial of His Birth*, ed. Eugene T. Gadol (New York, 1982).

NICHOLSON, Margaret (1750?–1828), in most respects an unremarkable Englishwoman, was granted an audience with King George III (1738–1820) on August 2, 1786, in order to present him with a petition. As the monarch glanced down at the paper, Nicholson produced an old ivory-handled knife and attempted to stab him, first with a wild swing that missed the mark entirely, then with a thrust that was deflected by the king's coat; the material actually bent the blade. At that point Nicholson was seized; George, who had personal experience with such matters, realized that Nicholson was mad and requested that the guards treat her with care. Nicholson had been a servant most of her life. In her last position, in 1783, she had an affair with a valet that not only cost her her job but also left her unable to find another position. She turned to needlework to eke out an existence. At about the same time she began to see herself as the rightful ruler of England. In July 1786, she sent a letter to the Privy Council, condemning George III as a pretender and usurper. The Privy Council ignored her petition. After the stabbing attempt, a search of her quarters revealed writings concerning her belief that she was the rightful ruler, including several unsent letters to powerful people requesting support for her claim. On August 8, 1786, she was brought before the Privy Council where two physicians recommended committal. She was sent to Bethlehem Royal Hospital where she was judged sane enough to work. She spent the rest of her days there, doing much the same sort of labour she had performed for wealthy families.

RESOURCE: *Royal Murders: Hatred, Revenge, and the Seizing of Power* by Dulcie M. Ashdown (Stroud, Gloucestershire, 1998).

NIKOLAEV, Leonid Vasilevich (1904–1934), assassinated the Leningrad political leader Sergei M. Kirov (1886–1934) on December 1, 1934. A Politburo member and Stalin's heir apparent, Kirov entered the Smolny preparing to report on the Moscow plenary session of the Central Committee of the Communist Party, from which he had returned recently. At the entrance to the building, Kirov's bodyguard was detained by the NKVD so that he entered the building alone. Once inside, he might have noticed the absence of security guards who usually flanked the stairways and entrances. Kirov was walking along the third-floor corridor when Nikolaev, who had been hiding in a lavatory, shot him in the back of the head. Kirov died within seconds. Nikolaev was supposed to shoot himself as well but apparently fainted instead; he was arrested as he lay on the floor.

A poor specimen physically and mentally, Nikolaev had a clubfoot and as a child was beaten so unmercifully by his father that the pummellings were said to have caused the epileptic seizures from which he suffered the rest of his life. He joined the Communist Party in 1920, during the Russian Civil War. He belonged to a group within the party charged with responsibility for seizing grain from the peasants. After the Civil War, he demanded an official post and was eventually given a position with the Leningrad Workers' and Peasants' Inspection (the RKI), though he was soon demoted for incompetence. When the RKI mobilized unnecessary members for heavy labour, Nikolaev was transferred to a work crew. He refused his posting on health grounds and was dismissed from the party. Only by a direct appeal to Moscow was he reinstated (though he was never offered a new position). Unemployment heightened his resentment of the Soviet bureaucracy.

During the late 1920s and early 1930s, Stalin was consolidating his power and despatching his rivals. Kirov, considered his natural successor, had to be eliminated. The NKVD had been observing Nikolaev for some time and concluded that he was an excellent choice as a potential assassin. An NKVD agent struck up a friendship with him and pointed out to him that Kirov, being the chief bureaucrat in Leningrad, would be an ideal target for his frustrations. Nikolaev needed little prodding. He had studied assassins from the past, particularly Charlotte Corday. The NKVD detained Kirov's bodyguard (who died immediately after the assassination in a suspicious traffic accident) and removed security from the building. From that point on, however, Nikolaev acted alone.

After his arrest, Nikolaev was instructed to implicate followers of Zinoviev (another rival of Stalin's) in a conspiracy. He refused. Even a direct appeal from Stalin, who had arrived in Leningrad to handle the investigation personally, failed, for by that time Nikolaev realized that he had been duped by the NKVD. So it was then that Nikolaev was tried in secret, because he knew too much; he was executed before the month was out. By comparison, the trials of Nikolaev's alleged co-conspirators were far from secret. Hundreds of party members were interrogated (a process that involved more brainwashing and torture than actual interrogation); all confessed. They were then given show trials. The trials lasted two years and implicated actual, suspected or even potential rivals to Stalin's power. By the time the show trials ended in 1936, thousands of Soviet citizens had been executed or sent to work camps in Siberia.

RESOURCES: *The Rise and Fall of Stalin* by Robert Payne (New York, 1965); *Stalin and the Kirov Murder* by Robert Conquest (New York, 1989). Certain revisionist authorities, from Adam Ulam in the 1970s to Oleg Khlevniuk in the 1990s, have attempted to distance Stalin from the crime. But the most recent analyst, Amy Knight in *Who Killed Kirov? The Kremlin's Greatest Mystery* (New York, 1999), indicts Stalin after drawing on recently released archives in the former Soviet Union.

NJOROGE, Nahashon Isaac Njenga (1937–1969), assassinated

Thomas Mboya (1930–1969), Kenyan economic affairs minister and the right-hand man of President Jomo Kenyatta (1888–1978). On July 5, 1969, Mboya entered a chemist's shop to buy some lotion for a rash. As he was leaving, Njoroge, who had been stalking him, began firing a .38-calibre Smith & Wesson revolver. Mboya was hit twice, one bullet severing his aorta. He was pronounced dead on arrival at hospital. The assassin fled the scene, provoking an extensive manhunt. The trail soon led police to Njoroge and the murder weapon. Njoroge admitted the gun was his but claimed to have lent it to an unnamed friend on the day of the attack. Njoroge also said, "Why do you pick on me? Why not the big man?" But he refused to name any "big man" in a plot to assassinate Mboya. Kenya was suffering from clashes between the Luo and Kikuyu tribes, a situation made worse by the fact that Mboya was a Luo and Njoroge was a Kikuyu. Njoroge was a political activist with military experience but had been eking out a living as a mechanic. In protesting his innocence, Njoroge claimed to have known Mboya for several years and said that he regarded him as a friend. Njoroge was found guilty of the murder and executed, in secret, in November. The Soviet press quickly condemned the Western powers as the architects of the assassination, but the fact that Mboya was the sort of conservative anti-communist leader that the West usually attempted to prop up leads one to dispute the charges. In fact, some believe since Njoroge had received military training in Bulgaria that the USSR was more likely to be behind the shooting. Then, too, Mboya's killing was doubtless an extension of tribal struggles, though Mboya did not identify himself with the Luo, believing that Kenya needed to place itself above such rivalries.

RESOURCE: *Tom Mboya* by David Goldsworthy (Nairobi, 1982).

NOBILING, Karl (1848–1878), attempted to kill Kaiser Wilhelm I of Germany (1797–1888) on June 2, 1878, as the kaiser took his daily carriage ride along Unter den Linden in Berlin, a regimen Wilhelm refused to alter although less than a month earlier he had been the target of an assassination attempt by Max Hödel along the same route. Wilhelm seems to have agreed with most of the authorities in believing Hödel was insane and that the possibility of someone else trying to kill him was slight. Yet as Wilhelm passed a rooming house at No. 18, Dr. Karl Nobiling, who had taken rooms at this address as part of his plot, aimed a double-barrelled shotgun out a third-floor window and fired. The first blast had little effect, although some of the pellets may have struck the kaiser in one arm. The second blast, however, hit the eighty-one-year-old emperor in the shoulder, face, back and arms, causing him to slump backwards in his seat, convincing spectators that he had been killed. But Wilhelm survived the attack, because June 2 was a Sunday and he was therefore wearing his steel helmet rather than the cloth military cap he favoured during the week. This stroke of fortune deflected much of the load of shot that otherwise would have pierced his brain. The carriage was quickly driven back to the palace, where surgeons examined the victim, discovering more than thirty pieces of shot in Wilhelm's body; they removed all but a few of these, the extraction of which they considered too risky. Despite shock and severe loss of blood, the hardy ruler survived.

Police, spectators and the military charged 18 Unter den Linden and ran to Nobiling's perch. Realizing there was no escape, Nobiling shot himself in the head with a revolver, but the wound was not fatal. A military officer took him into custody and protected him from the wrath of the crowd. While transporting him to prison in Berlin's notorious Green Carriage (the German equivalent of a Black Maria: a police van used for mass arrests), the driver, anxious to get Nobiling into custody while he was still alive, ran into a low arch over the street. The driver broke his neck and died instantly.

Nobiling was the son of a career officer in the Prussian army and both of his brothers had followed the same path. The assassin was an intellectual who received the finest private education and excelled at his studies, particularly in agriculture and political science. He completed his doctorate in agriculture in 1876 with a dissertation entitled *Beiträge zur Geschichte der Landwirtschaft des Saalkreises der Provinz Sachsen (Contributions to the History of Agriculture in the Saal District, Province of Saxony)*. During his student days, Nobiling became a supporter (but not necessarily a member) of the Social Democratic Party and spoke at student gatherings against class privilege and the monarchy. He confessed to friends that he attended meetings in order to be heard but that his real wish was to found a new, more left-wing party. He moved to Dresden after graduation but began to travel extensively. In the months leading up to the attempt on Wilhelm, he visited London, Paris, Brussels, Zurich, Vienna, Prague, Cologne and St. Petersburg. British authorities claimed after the shooting that they had warned their German counterparts to be on guard against a further attempt on Wilhelm based on remarks that an informant had heard from Nobiling, an assertion that the Germans denied. During this period, Nobiling supported himself writing magazine articles on agriculture. In January 1878, he rented the room from which he was to attempt the assassination. Berlin police sought to connect Nobiling and Hödel as proof of a widespread conspiracy. Although many witnesses claimed to have seen the two together, most such testimony turned out to be bogus or attributable to mistaken identity. What is known for certain is that Nobiling was highly critical of Hödel's poor planning and marksmanship. Whereas Hödel had missed three times from close range with a pistol, Nobiling, for all his lack of interest in the military, was an excellent shot; although his attempt was from a far greater distance and with a much less effective weapon, he did not miss his target.

In the aftermath of the shooting, Berlin police arrested 563 persons on dubious—at times, absurd—charges. Yet of those arrested, only forty-two were acquitted. In one case, a drunken man was sentenced to two and a half years in prison for saying "Wilhelm is dead, he lives no more." A worker in no way connected with the assassination was handed out four years' imprisonment for saying, "Hödel is a dumbbell, but Nobiling planned his attempt well." Five of the accused committed suicide before trial.

Chancellor Otto von Bismarck, on hearing news of a second attempt on the kaiser's life, immediately dissolved the Reichstag and called new elections, knowing that, with anti-socialist sentiment running high, the Social Democrats, so long a thorn in his side, would lose much of their power. After the Hödel incident, Bismarck had attempted to pass a law banning socialists altogether but the measure had been defeated soundly. The second attempt on the kaiser, by a gifted product of the upper-middle class who was clearly not insane, shocked the German public. When the new government was formed, anti-socialist legislation passed quickly and easily. The bill banned organizations that exhibited socialist, communist or anarchist leanings as well as their newspapers, magazines and books. All political meetings had to be approved by the police, and any person judged to be a bad influence could be expelled from his or her community if resident there less than six months. Bismarck was somewhat disappointed with the new legislation, having hoped to prevent socialists from standing for office and to fire civil servants without a pension if they were thought to be socialistic.

Although the Social Democratic Party survived—in fact, became the most populous party in the Reichstag by 1914—real power was split between the kaiser and the chancellor. As to Nobiling, the wounds he suffered in his suicide attempt led to his death in September 1878 before he could be tried. Bismarck noted in his memoirs that the kaiser was showing his age before Nobiling's attack, especially mental confusion and geriatric depression, but that after the shooting he seemed to be more alert and vigorous than he had been in years. Indeed, several months after the incident, Wilhelm himself was heard to say that "Nobiling knew better than the doctors what I wanted: a good letting of blood."

RESOURCE: *Anarchism in Germany, Volume 1: The Early Movement* by Andrew R. Carlson (Metuchen, New Jersey, 1972).

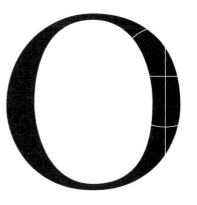

O'FARRELL, Henry James (1833–1868), attempted to assassinate Prince Alfred, the duke of Edinburgh and duke of Saxe-Cobourg and Gotha (1844–1900), the second son of Queen Victoria, during a royal visit to Australia on March 12, 1868. Having just left a fundraising picnic lunch for the Sailors' Home in Sydney, Alfred was being taken to see a group of aborigines perform a ceremonial dance when O'Farrell shot him from behind with a pistol. The prince exclaimed, "Good God, I am shot: my back is broken." In fact, the ball entered between the sixth and seventh ribs but did not hit any vital organs; the prince was probably saved by his heavy jacket and double-thick braces, which slowed the projectile. O'Farrell tried to fire a second time; a spectator grabbed his hand. Shooting wildly now, O'Farrell hit a bystander in the foot before being disarmed. Onlookers tried to kill O'Farrell with their bare hands, and a rope was thrown over a nearby tree to dispense immediate justice, but O'Farrell was hustled onto a ship by police, who also saved him from being killed by sailors on board.

A native Dubliner, O'Farrell, the youngest of eleven children, emigrated to Australia with his family as a boy. The family prospered there and young Henry studied the law, though he abandoned the field later to enter a seminary. Acquaintances recalled at this period a shy, quiet but industrious youth and a good scholar. Shortly after his twentieth birthday, O'Farrell suffered a nervous collapse, and the seminary deemed his "proclivities…inappropriate to the calling," after which he tried his hand at mining and sheep farming. At this time, associates characterized him as a quick-witted, intelligent businessman. By the mid-1860s, however, O'Farrell suffered a relapse following a series of financial setbacks. What money remained he lost by speculating in mining shares. By this time, he was drinking heavily. He also suffered from epilepsy. At this low point in his life, O'Farrell became a self-professed Fenian. In January 1868, he wrote to two Dublin newspapers announcing his intention to kill Prince

Alfred. The editors did nothing, assuming that the threats were hollow or that, the post being so slow, the deed already had taken place.

O'Farrell took a room overlooking the spot where the prince would arrive in Sydney, but did not fire from this nest, fearing that he would strike innocent people. On February 5, he hired formal clothes and tried to gain admittance to a ball in the prince's honour; he was turned away because he did not have an invitation. Finally, when the picnic was scheduled during the week of St. Patrick's Day, O'Farrell had his chance. Alfred was never in mortal danger from his wound. The bullet was relatively easy to remove; in fact, the prince underwent the surgery while he sat in a chair without the benefit of anesthesia, attended by two recently arrived nurses specially trained by Florence Nightingale. Within ten days, the prince resumed his official duties.

Despite O'Farrell's history of mental disturbances, he was found fit to stand trial. When arrested, he declared that he was acting on orders from Ireland; later he admitted to acting alone, but the authorities refused to believe that he was not a genuine Fenian. In spite of pleas for mercy from Prince Alfred, O'Farrell was hanged at Darlinghurst gaol on April 21 before an audience of one hundred distinguished observers.

RESOURCES: *Narrative of the Visit of His Royal Highness the Duke of Edinburgh to the Colony of Victoria, Australia* by John George Knight (Melbourne, 1868); *The Fenians in Australia, 1865–1880* by Keith Amos (Kensington, NSW, 1988).

ŌISHI Yoshio (1659–1703) was the leader of the Forty-seven Rōnin (leaderless samurai) who assassinated Lord Kira Yoshinaka. (1641–1703), an official of the Tokugawa shogunate. On January 31, 1703, Ōishi Yoshio and his band of forty-five rōnin (one of the group was left behind due to his advanced age and poor health) attacked the heavily guarded residence of Kira Yoshinaka. from both the front and rear entrances. They managed to kill or force off Kira's troops without incurring a single casualty. They found Kira hiding in a storeroom and dragged him out into the courtyard, where he was offered the chance to commit seppuku (ritualistic suicide). When Kira refused, Ōishi drew the sword that had belonged to his former master, Asano Naganori, and cut Kira's head off. The forty-six men then took the head to the grave of Asano, announcing that Asano's honour had been redeemed.

Asano Naganori had been summoned to the imperial palace in Edo to take up a position at court. Not knowledgeable in matters of courtly protocol and etiquette, he was supposed to rely on Kira Yoshinaka, the head of palace protocol, for advice and guidance. But Kira insisted on substantial bribes for this assistance. Asano refused to pay. Kira began to humiliate him publicly, hoping to provoke a reaction. Eventually, Asano attacked Kira with his sword, wounding him slightly. By drawing his sword within the imperial palace, Asano breached protocol, a violation that demanded his immediate death. Asano committed seppuku. By law, all of Asano's lands and titles were forfeited as a result of his dishonour. His family was impoverished and his several hundred personal samurai were declared rōnin. Ōishi Yoshio recruited forty-six of the rōnin to avenge their master. Realizing that Kira would be expecting an attack, the rōnin appeared to be shiftless and indolent for two years, so as to lure Kira into a false sense of security; some became street merchants, others beggars; Ōishi turned to gambling and alcohol. When the rōnin became convinced that Kira was not expecting them, they regrouped and attacked. After the ceremony at their master's grave, they presented themselves at court to proclaim their deed and turn themselves in. The shogun faced a serious dilemma. On the one hand, what the rōnin had done was a criminal act punishable by execution. On the other hand, by avenging their master, they had shown the admired qualities of bushido, the samurai warrior code. The public supported the rōnins' actions. Indeed, during the long period when they affected disinterest in revenge, the rōnin were insulted and despised for not avenging Asano's death. To punish such heroes would be unpopular and would bring bushido into disrepute. As a compromise, the shogun offered the rōnin a choice: commit seppuku and be buried as honourable men or refuse and be executed as criminals. The forty-six men who had actually participated in the raid chose the former; they were split into four groups, each with a lord assigned to supervise the proceedings; the bodies were buried next to Asano's.

Within the year, a play had been produced about the incident but was closed by authorities. In 1706, however, Japan's greatest dramatist, Chikamatsu Monzaemon, produced a puppet play based on the events, though the most famous dramatic work inspired by the Forty-seven Rōnin was *The Treasury of Loyal Retainers* (*Kanadehon Chushingura*), written in 1748. The names were fictionalized, but people who saw the play referred to the leading characters as Asano, Ōishi and Kira. Since the eighteenth century, the story has been the inspiration for many novels, plays and, more recently, motion pictures. The theme of loyalty superseding the rule of law has been the justification offered by almost all of Japan's assassins and has contributed importantly to the way assassination is perceived in Japan.

RESOURCE: *Ōishi Kuranosuke no Nazo* by Takano Kiyoshi (Tokyo, 1993).

O'LAUGHLIN, Michael (1835?–1868), was the only member of the assassination conspiracy against US president Abraham Lincoln to die of natural causes soon after the affair. He and Samuel Arnold, another of the alleged conspirators, were childhood friends of each other and of John Wilkes Booth. In September 1864, in Baltimore, Booth recruited them in the first of two foiled plots to kidnap Lincoln. Booth later travelled to New York to purchase weapons and ammunition; he entrusted them to O'Laughlin for safekeeping. By that time, O'Laughlin, described in contemporary accounts as both witty and hard-drinking, was a deserter from the Confederate forces, and earned his living in a Baltimore livery stable and feed barn. The original kidnapping plan centred on snatching Lincoln from Ford's Theater in Washington and holding him for ransom; Booth assigned O'Laughlin and Arnold the task of turning off the gaslights in the hall so that the deed could be carried out in a few moments of darkness. This plan, and a subsequent one to kidnap Lincoln from his carriage, came to nothing, whereupon O'Laughlin and Arnold, who roomed together, left Washington for Baltimore on March 20, 1865.

At least some of O'Laughlin's subsequent dealings with Booth had to do with getting Booth to repay $500 that O'Laughlin had lent him. Few doubted, however, that O'Laughlin was a minor conspirator in the subsequent death plot—that, in the words of the specifications of the military commission that judged him, he was among those who "did combine, confederate, and conspire together at Washington City, within the Military Department of Washington, and within the intrenced [*sic*] fortifications and military line of the United States, [and proceeded] unlawfully, maliciously, and traitorously to kill and murder Abraham Lincoln" on April 14, 1865.

O'Laughlin and Arnold were arrested at Baltimore and Fortress Monroe, Virginia, respectively, on April 17. The relative speed with which they were taken into custody is probably attributable not to the federal government's prior knowledge of the kidnapping and murder plots, as some conspiracy students have maintained, but rather to quick thinking by James McPhail, the provost marshal of Baltimore. McPhail, who had known O'Laughlin's family for thirty years and was aware of O'Laughlin and Arnold's connections to Booth, wired the authorities in Washington of his suspicions and tracked down the pair himself. At the trial, two defence witnesses, one a former Union officer, testified that they spent the entire evening of the murder in the company of O'Laughlin and Arnold, who thus could not have been near the scene of the crime. Four of the eight persons charged were hanged; the other four received prison sentences—in the cases of O'Laughlin, Arnold and Dr. Samuel Mudd (the rural physician who set Booth's broken leg), life terms. The sentences were to be served in Albany, New York, but the venue was quickly changed to Fort Jefferson in the Dry Tortugas, off Florida, one of the most isolated of American forts and one of the most unhealthy. A yellow fever epidemic at the prison claimed O'Laughlin in 1868. By stepping in to staunch the epidemic once the medical staff themselves had succumbed to the disease, Dr. Mudd won his freedom.

RESOURCES: *A True History of the Assassination of Abraham Lincoln and of the Conspiracy of 1865* by Louis J. Weichmann, ed. Floyd E. Risvold (New York, 1975); *The Lincoln Murder Conspiracies* by William Hanchett (Urbana, Illinois, 1983); *Memoirs of a Lincoln Conspirator* by Samuel Bland Arnold, ed. Michael W. Kaufman (Bowie, Maryland, 1995).

ORLOV, Aleksei Grigorevich (1737–1808), assassinated Peter III (1728–1762) of Russia. On July 5, 1762, Orlov entered the room of the former czar, who had abdicated after only a few months in favour of his wife, Catherine the Great, and was under house arrest in Ropsha. The two men began drinking and continued throughout the evening. When Orlov assumed that Peter was too drunk to defend himself, he strangled him with a cord. The next day he sent a letter to Catherine declaring that Peter had died in a brawl with his guards.

Orlov was the brother of Grigorii Orlov (1734–1783), a long-time lover of Catherine (1729–1796). Catherine was originally Princess Sophia of Anhalt-Zerbst but was baptized Catherine in the Orthodox Church. As a young girl, she had been transported to Russia at the command of the Empress Elizabeth to marry Peter. Elizabeth realized that

Peter, who would one day be czar, was weak-minded and immature, and that marrying him to a strong, intelligent woman such as Catherine would improve him. The marriage, however, proved to be a sham. Peter was possibly sterile and likely impotent as well (though he enjoyed cavorting with prostitutes). Catherine, who realized that the most important part of her position was to produce an heir, had to find a substitute means of doing so. During their marriage, Catherine produced three children, probably by Grigorii Orlov. They were accepted as legitimate heirs in spite of Peter's declaration that he had "no idea how my wife becomes pregnant."

Peter, who was also of German heritage, had angered the military by ending Russia's war with Prussia and instead embarking on a campaign against Denmark. He had also alienated himself from much of the aristocracy, so that he had no allies when Catherine and Grigorii Orlov moved against him. But even as an exile in Ropsha, a former czar was still a potential threat.

Grigorii and Catherine agreed that his brother should deal with the problem, after which Catherine was to reward the Orlovs for their service. Aleksei was promoted from sergeant in the guards to second major of the Preobrazhenskii Guards Regiment and major general in the army; he was also awarded the order of Aleksandr Nevskii and estates with several hundred serfs. Aleksei was also made a count (along with his other brothers) and given two hundred thousand rubles.

In 1769, Aleksei became commander of naval operations in the Mediterranean. Despite having no naval experience, he was responsible for a remarkable victory against the Turks in which all but one of thirteen Turkish ships-of-the-line were destroyed. The Turks suffered nine thousand casualties to only thirty Russian casualties. After this, Aleksei was additionally decorated and rewarded. Grigorii also benefitted from the deposition of Peter III. He too was awarded the order of Aleksandr Nevskii and promoted to major general; he also became a gentleman of the chamber and adjutant general and was presented with a diamond-encrusted sword. But he was not permitted to marry Catherine, as she realized that marrying Orlov would endanger her hold on the throne and possibly force her to abdicate. By 1774, Catherine had replaced Orlov as her lover with Potemkin. Nevertheless, Orlov was pensioned off with 250,000 rubles, ten thousand male serfs and the title prince of the Holy Roman Empire. Catherine was succeeded by her son Paul I. Like his nominal father, he too would be assassinated.

RESOURCES: *Peter III, Emperor of Russia; the Story of a Crisis and a Crime* by Nisbet R. Bain (Westminster, 1902); *Reform and Regicide: The Reign of Peter III of Russia* by Carol S. Leonard (Bloomington, Indiana, 1993).

ORSINI, Felice (a.k.a. Francisco Pinelli, a.k.a. Tito Celsi, a.k.a. Georges Hernagh, a.k.a. Thomas Allsop) (1819–1858), an Italian revolutionary and nationalist, attempted to assassinate Louis Napoleon (Napoleon III) (1808–1873), emperor of France, at the Paris opera in 1858. Orsini's father was Andrea Orsini, a member of the Carbonari, a largely upper-middle-class nationalist group; he was also one of only about five hundred survivors of the twenty-four thousand Italians who invaded Russia with Bonaparte's army. For all his family's radicalism, Felice Orsini was reared in an atmosphere of privilege. As a young man, he was sent to live with his uncle, a wealthy hemp merchant. As a teenager, he entered a Jesuit seminary, but less from piety than from a desire to hide out following the accidental shooting of a servant. The Jesuits expelled him after learning that he had joined Young Italy, the radical republican nationalist group formed by Giuseppe Mazzini. He then continued his studies at secular schools, eventually earning a law degree, even though his main passion was military science, including strategy, ordnance and fortification: interests, curiously, that were not accompanied by a desire to join the army.

In 1844, he was arrested for his involvement in Young Italy and was sentenced to life imprisonment, but was released in 1846 when a new pope, Pius IX, declared an amnesty for all political prisoners. Orsini then travelled to Tuscany but was expelled for campaigning for press freedom. In 1848, he joined the Civic Guard, a revolutionary group fighting Austrian rule in Milan, and quickly rose through the ranks, becoming a captain by the time the rebellion was quashed a few months later. That autumn, the pope fled Rome following the assassination of Count Rossi, and the Roman Republic was established, whereupon Orsini returned to the former papal states and was elected a representative from his home province of Forli.

By spring 1849, however, the republic had been invaded by Austria and France. The president of the French republic, Louis Napoleon (who later become emperor after a coup), was sympathetic to the cause of Italian nationalism. Indeed, in his youth Napoleon had been a member of the Carbonari. He realized, however, that in order to cement his position as president, thus advancing his agenda for becoming emperor like his famous uncle Napoleon Bonaparte, he had to satisfy Catholic opinion by coming to the pope's aid—an action that inevitably would earn him the wrath of Italian nationalists, who accordingly made him a favourite target of assassination attempts.

With the fall of the republic, Orsini appealed to the British government for a diplomatic pass to escape arrest and execution; the request was granted, and he made his way to Nice, where his uncle set him up in the hemp trade. Through his mentor Mazzini, Orsini continued to work towards revolution in Italy, publishing in 1852 a book on Italian military topography. The subject was especially important to Mazzini, who was constantly attempting to raise a revolutionary army to overturn the many governments that made up what is now Italy. One such attempt, the following year, was led by Orsini, whose force of twenty-nine men, carrying only fourteen muskets among them, was captured near Sarzana in Piedmont. After a short prison stay, he was exiled to England, where he was reunited with Mazzini, who found him a position with a society of Italian expatriates and sympathizers.

Handsome, intelligent, articulate (even in English, despite his thick Italian accent), and possessing excellent revolutionary credentials, Orsini made an ideal spokesman and was often used to appeal to British MPs to support Italian nationalism. On February 24, 1854, he was guest of honour at a banquet at the American consulate that celebrated Washington's birthday by honouring modern revolutionaries. Despite his success in England, however, Orsini missed Italy and his family (even though his wife had left him and taken their daughters with her). Posing as one Tito Celsi, a hemp dealer from Ravenna, he obtained a passport to return to Italy, where, with a group of Mazzini's supporters, he set out for Massa with a boatload of arms. The vessel was captured, but Orsini escaped and made his way to Geneva. With the names Celsi and Orsini both known to the authorities, he posed as a Swiss mercenary and joined the pope's Swiss Guard, a position from which he felt he could work towards revolution. In autumn 1854, Mazzini asked him to go to Milan and join a revolutionary army there; he obeyed the request. A Milanese informant, however, revealed the plans for an uprising to the Austrians, who were threatening Italy at the time. Using a new alias, Georges Hernagh, Swiss watchmaker, Orsini fled to Vienna, but police there discovered his identity, for Orsini, posing as a German-speaking Swiss, in fact could not speak German.

He was sent back to Italy and held, pending trial, in the Castle San Giorgio at Mantua, a prison which was considered escape proof. Orsini was questioned at length with the understanding that once the Austrians had gained all the information from him they could, they would try him, find him guilty and shoot him. Orsini seduced the wife of one of the guards and with her help began plotting a mass escape. Saws were smuggled into the prison, along with specie (to bribe guards) and opium (to incapacitate those who refused money). Unfortunately, the guards Orsini co-opted were dismissed and the prisoner placed in solitary confinement (with his saws and money). So he began sawing through the bars on his window. Guards were supposed to check the bars daily for signs of tampering, but as Orsini was considered a gentleman and a scholar and not the type to attempt to flee, his window was not scrutinized. Using sheets and towels, Orsini made a rope almost fifty metres long to descend to the ground. On March 30, 1856, he escaped, and his uncle paid to have him smuggled out of the country into England. The episode made Orsini an internationally renowned figure and a darling of English society.

Mazzini, on meeting him again, urged him to return to Italy to raise yet another army, but by this time Mazzini had fallen out of favour with most other Italian nationalists, who considered his military campaigns laughable and tragic. After all, his poorly conceived plans had been no danger to Austrian ambitions in Italy; indeed, his failures had led to many mass executions. Orsini and Mazzini split over this issue.

While in England, Orsini wrote, in English, *The Austrian Dungeons in Italy*, which sold more than fifty-five thousand copies in the first year. He embarked on a lecture tour throughout Britain to comment on some of the political issues that the publishers had edited out of the work. In 1857, he followed, again in English, with *The Memoirs and Adventures of Felice Orsini*, another sensational publishing success. Both books, and Orsini himself, were attacked by Mazzini's dwindling band of supporters, most of whom were English sympathizers rather than other Italian nationalists. Orsini decided to form a rival group to Mazzini's. Realizing that it would be best to focus on a spectacular event, he began to plan an act that Mazzini had been advocating for years but had never been able to attempt: Napoleon III's assassination. As Tito Celsi, Orsini had seen, in Belgium, a new type of grenade, which exploded on contact instead of by means of a fuse. He modified the design and the charge until he had designed a bomb that, for its size, was more powerful than any other such device. An English associate (a foreigner was thought less likely to attract suspicion) commissioned the construction of six of the devices from a machinist who was told that it was a new type of gas fixture. Orsini obtained a passport under the name Thomas Allsop to make his way back to the continent. He left England with £450 and a kilo of fulminate of mercury, an extremely dangerous explosive that destablized if not kept damp. The grenades were tested in England and exceeded the conspirators' expectations. Orsini then took them into France, carefully paying the applicable duties on gas fixtures, and assembled his co-conspirators: Guiseppe Pieri, Carlo di Rudio and Antonio Gomez. They awaited the perfect opportunity.

On January 13, 1858, Orsini learned that Napoleon III was scheduled to attend the opera house in the rue Lepelletier the following evening. The program, whose theme was royal murders, included selections from Rossini's "William Tell" and Auber's "Muta di Portici," a recitation of Alfieri's "Mary Stuart" and a ballet depicting the assassination of Gustav III of Sweden. Orsini and his men took up their positions outside the opera house and waited for Napoleon to arrive. Police spotted Pieri, a wanted man in France, and took him into the police station, where he was discovered to be carrying a bomb, a revolver, a dagger and a great deal of English and French currency. However suspicious they were, the authorities did not act quickly enough to stop the assassination, as Napoleon's coach was approaching the opera house even as Pieri was being searched. Gomez threw his bomb, which went wide of its target and exploded in the centre of Napoleon's military escort. Orsini and Rudio then threw theirs. One exploded directly beneath the carriage, knocking it on its side. In all, ten people were killed, three blinded and more than 140 wounded, but Napoleon suffered only a cut on his nose and decided to attend the performance, where the audience gave him a standing ovation for his bravery under fire. During the entertainment, officials showed him pieces of the bombs. The empress, whose gown was covered in blood (not her own), put one of them into her handbag as a souvenir.

The three conspirators escaped from the scene. Orsini, who had been struck on the forehead by fragments of one of the grenades, wandered up the street, discarding weapons and other evidence along the way, and stopped at a pharmacy to have his wounds treated. Rudio, who had been sharing rooms with Pieri, was the first of the conspirators apprehended by police, who found Gomez in a tavern shortly afterwards. Orsini, when cornered, tried to pass himself off as an Englishman from Kent. When the police asked him how far Kent was from London, he answered about thirty kilometres. Realizing that an Englishman would have expressed the distance in miles, officers took him into custody, and his true identity was soon revealed.

With the conspirators rounded up, Napoleon III decided to aid Italian nationalism, a cause he always had favoured. In any event, much of the territory that would make up a unified Italy would come at the expense of his enemy, Austria. Orsini's trial was thus a platform from which the defendant could tell the world of his motives. Rather than censor the proceedings and prevent the defendant from speaking of his goal—both standard procedure in political cases—Napoleon allowed the French press to cover the trial in detail. Napoleon went so far as to commission a letter from Orsini, which was promptly released to the foreign press. Jules Favre, considered the ablest lawyer in France, was retained to defend the assassins. Orsini claimed to have no animosity towards France but only towards Austria. He freely admitted his involvement in the assassination attempt. Although all the conspirators were found guilty, Napoleon wished to pardon them. The public, however, was determined to see them punished, less for the attempt on Napoleon than for the civilian deaths and injuries. Orsini, Pieri and Rudio were sentenced to death and Gomez to life imprisonment.

The trial had made Orsini a figure of even greater renown. He was a hero in Italy, admired throughout much of the rest of the world, and even enjoyed a reasonable degree of support in France. Napoleon, who was grateful to Orsini for the pretext to challenge Austrian rule in Italy, tried desperately to find a way to commute his sentence in a way that would not damage his own popularity. Alas, he found none. Two days before his execution, Orsini wrote Napoleon asking for mercy not for himself but rather for his accomplices. He denounced assassination as a means of bringing about political change and thanked the emperor for his assistance as regards the dream of Italian unity. This letter, too, Napoleon made public. On March 13, 1858, Orsini, Pieri and Rudio were assembled in the prison courtyard to be executed by guillotine. At the last moment, Rudio was pardoned by Napoleon but for Orsini and Pieri there was no reprieve. Orsini shouted his final words as loudly as he could: "*Viva l'Italia! Viva la Francia!*" A moment later, his head lay in the basket.

Orsini's failure to assassinate the emperor was his greatest success. Napoleon had given him a bigger audience than he ever could have achieved otherwise. Although he paid with his life, his deed advanced the cause of Italian independence more than killing Napoleon could have done. Napoleon continued to release Orsini's writings even after the executions. His advisers worried that official endorsement of Orsini's beliefs was tantamount to a declaration of war against Austria. In 1859, Napoleon III crossed the Alps with an army of two hundred thousand to fight against the Austrians. Although this attempt failed, the eventual outcome was obvious: in 1860, the rulers of Piedmont united with the papal states against Austria, which in 1866 gave up its territorial claims. The unification of Italy was complete.

RESOURCES: *The Bombs of Orsini* by Michael St. John Packe (London, 1957); *Napoleon III, A Life* by Fenton Bresler (London, 1999).

OSWALD, Lee Harvey (a.k.a. A. J. Hidell, a.k.a. O.H. Lee) (1939–1963), the supposed assassin of US president John F. Kennedy, or one of them, is among the most compellingly unknowable figures in American history since Thomas Jefferson, if admittedly in a rather different way. Continuing public fascination with him may be traced partly to the fact that evidence tampering in the case makes the crime impossible to figure out, partly to the fact that Oswald was a far more complex individual than the stereotype presented to the public in the aftermath of the tragedy and partly to the fact that public perceptions of him have changed over the years.

On December 13, 1963, three weeks after the assassination, the singer Bob Dylan was given an award in New York in recognition of his work in the civil rights movement. In his acceptance remarks, Dylan said he had "to admit that the man who shot President Kennedy, Lee Oswald... I don't know [...] what he thought he was doing, but I got to admit that I [...] saw some of myself in him. I got to stand up and say I saw things that he felt in me...." The audience of civil libertarians was aghast that anyone would take free speech to such an extreme, and the remarks almost ruined Dylan's career. Looked at from the vantage point of the following century, however, they don't seem alarming in the least. Both young men were essentially self-educated working-class intellectuals with strong emotional ties to the outsider tradition that is forever at war with middle-class institutions and values. Oswald was a serious student of politics and can be considered the only American assassin to have composed a proper manifesto outlining what he considered were necessary changes to the system of democratic government.

If he was a lot like Dylan, Oswald was also a lot like John F. Kennedy. Not only were both Oswald and Kennedy fixated with politics and its workings, but both were intrigued by espionage (Kennedy helped to create the American vogue for Ian Fleming's James Bond novels) without having conspicuous talent for surviving life in the clandestine world—quite the opposite, in fact. Dealey Plaza in Dallas, where Kennedy was shot, was to Oswald what the Bay of Pigs in Cuba was to Kennedy: a mesmerizing fiasco into which one stumbled, from which one could not extricate oneself. Both were reared by adults with links to organized crime: Kennedy by his father, a multi-millionaire former bootlegger (among many other things), Oswald by his uncle, a small-time New Orleans bookie. And both were charismatic. This is not usually a word associated with Oswald, but one can't overlook that his singular personality impressed itself on people. In 1957, when he was an eighteen-year-old private in the Marine Corps stationed at El Toro Marine Air Station at Santa Ana, California, Oswald so intrigued an apprentice writer named Kerry Thornley that Thornley wrote a novel using him as the basis of his main character. In a sense, Oswald was Kennedy without the wealth and privilege.

Oswald was born in New Orleans, traditional base of American plotters and filibusters, where just after his third birthday his mother placed him in an orphanage for more than a year. He attended elementary school in Fort Worth, Texas, until he and his mother moved to New York, where Oswald was arrested for truancy (the autodidact's crime) and sent for psychological evaluation. The following year, 1954, mother and son returned to New Orleans, where in 1955 Oswald dropped out of high school and joined a Civil Air Patrol unit led by David Ferrie, a defrocked priest who flew missions for both the CIA and organized crime and who most students of the conspiracy believe to have been involved in the plot to kill Kennedy. In 1956, the Oswalds returned to Fort Worth, where Oswald quit another high school in order to enlist in the marines. He was stationed at various places—San Diego, Biloxi, El Toro—before being posted to Atsugi Naval Air Station in Japan, the place from which America's super-secret U-2 surveillance aircraft undertook missions. Oswald was a radar operator. Later, in May 1960, when, in what was seen as a mutually belligerent incident, a U-2 crashed in the Soviet Union and the pilot was captured, President Dwight Eisenhower first denied the existence of such aircraft. As for Oswald, despite accidentally shooting himself in the foot and two courts martial for minor offences, he was promoted to private first class. In September 1959, he was granted a hardship discharge. The following month he materialized in Moscow, requesting Soviet citizenship. When the request was refused, he attempted suicide. An internal Soviet document, one of a batch given to US president Bill Clinton by Russian president Boris Yeltsin in 1999, described Oswald as being "of sound mind but very strong willed, and if his request for permission to remain in the USSR were turned down again he might repeat his suicide attempt." So he was allowed to remain in the country, but was given a job and an apartment in Minsk in present-day Belarus, well away from the seats of power. Because of his defection, his marine discharge was changed from "honorable" to "dishonorable." One of the most inventive theories of what took place in Dealey Plaza holds that Oswald was not aiming primarily at Kennedy but at the president's limousine mate, Texas Governor John Connally, who as navy secretary at the time had been responsible for the Marine Corps when Oswald's status was revised downward. In June 1960, J. Edgar Hoover, director of the FBI, circulated a memo warning agents that an imposter might be using Oswald's identity.

Oswald formed a romantic relationship with first one Russian woman, Ella Prokhorchyk, and later with another, Marina Prusakova, who would become his wife. When Prusakova first met him in Minsk in March 1961, she assumed that he was a native speaker of Russian, albeit one with a curious accent, suggesting that he came from a far distant part of the USSR. They married in April 1961 and had the first of their two children in April 1962, but Oswald was not granted Soviet citizenship. By June 1962, the Oswalds began a slow journey to United States; they settled in Dallas, where Oswald was interviewed by the FBI—routinely, most believe, but some insist he was recruited. There is indeed evidence that Oswald became a low-level FBI informant in Dallas, but then the enduring conundrum of Oswald is that there is evidence of a sort for both sides of every proposition, not all of it forensically unassailable. In the Second World War, Royal Air Force pilots would drop *glitter* (strips of aluminum foil) like confetti in order to jam the Nazi radar; the story of Lee Oswald is bright with such deceptive glitter. The most genuinely scholarly of Oswald researchers, Peter Dale Scott, late of the University of California at Berkeley and the person who unearthed the two National Security Agency action memos proving that Kennedy tried to dismantle the CIA following the disastrous Bay of Pigs invasion of April 1961, believes that Oswald was lured into the multipartite conspiracy of public and private interests by the FBI, which asked him to help investigate the illegal trade in small arms. Jack Ruby, the Dallas gangster who knew

Oswald and who, many believe, was in Dealey Plaza at or near the time of the assassination, was in the gun trade, among others. Early in 1963, Oswald bought a .38-calibre Smith & Wesson revolver and a Mannlicher-Carcano rifle in separate mail-order transactions, using his Hidell alias. The former was the standard handgun of criminals and police: in fact, similar to the weapon with which Ruby would kill him before the year was out. The shoulder weapon, an obsolete Italian design used in the invasion of Ethiopia, the Spanish revolution and the Second World War, always had had a poor reputation for reliability, even for workability, so much so that the Nazi alpinist Heinrich Harrer, as he recounted in his book *Seven Years in Tibet*, refused to take one when he had the chance after escaping from a British prisoner of war camp in India, feeling that no rifle at all was better than a Mannlicher-Carcano.

At this time, Mr. and Mrs. Oswald were living in a second-storey flat at 214 Neeley Street in Dallas, in the backyard of which Marina is said to have taken the photographs of Oswald holding his two weapons, images that did much to fix his guilt in the minds of the 1960s public. Oswald contended that the photos were fakes. Certainly a number of the doc-uments in Oswald's hand are forgeries, perhaps a majority of them, including some created by the KGB to suggest the involvement of American intelligence agencies in the conspiracy, though little outside help can have been required to implicate them.

Leaving his family behind in Texas, Oswald spent the period April to September 1963 in New Orleans. During this time, the FBI was apparently out of contact with him, much to the later displeasure of Hoover. Oswald spent that spring and summer building up a public profile as a pro-Cuban activist but all the while associating with the anti-Castro underground movement as well as people with fresh ties to both the FBI and the CIA, such as David Ferrie; a local private investigator named Guy Banister, former special agent in charge of the FBI Chicago field office; and Clay Shaw, a New Orleans entrepreneur and former CIA contract agent, who Jim Garrison, the New Orleans prosecutor, unsuccessfully brought to trial for his part in the conspiracy after all the other persons known as probable conspirators had died or been killed. At one point during this final New Orleans interlude, Oswald was interviewed on radio and television after being arrested in a scuffle with Cuban exiles who found him distributing pro-Cuban leaflets in the Vieux Carré. After September, other men using Oswald's name were reported in Texas and Louisiana, in a path running parallel to a well-known gunrunners' route.

Meanwhile, the genuine Oswald visited Mexico City, supposedly to try to obtain a visitor's visa from the Cuban embassy there.

Oswald returned to Texas but not to his family. Instead, in October, the month he turned twenty-four, he took an $8-a-week room in a rooming house at 1026 North Beckley Avenue, Dallas. It would be his address for the last twenty-two days of his life. He rented the room using the name O.H. Lee, and began work as a minimum-wage warehouseman at the Texas School Book Depository, facing Dealey Plaza, in the West End, along the route that the motorcade was to take. Then as now, this part of Dallas owed its existence to the courts and to the city, county and state bureaucracies. Today, only the sixth floor of the Depository is open to the public as a museum; the other half-dozen storeys are used to house old Dallas County records. The district where the Kennedy assassination took place dates to before the Second World War. The Triple Underpass under which the motorcade was about to pass when shots rang out was built in 1934, Dealey Plaza (named after the former owner of the *Dallas Morning News*) in 1936, the Depository in 1937, the surprisingly steep hillock now called the Grassy Knoll and its surrounding pergolas (a Franklin Roosevelt make-work project) in 1938.

Approaching Dealey Plaza on November 22, 1963, the motorcade slowed to perhaps as little as sixteen kilometres an hour, the result of a last-minute change in the route that has never been explained, except by the postulation that it permitted triangulated crossfire from the Depository, the DalTex Building nearby (both to the president's rear) and the Grassy Knoll (up ahead). Numerous people present on the scene, including journalists and police, believed they saw or heard gunfire from the Knoll. Mrs. Kennedy climbed out on the trunk of the limousine to retrieve a part of her husband's brain tissue, unthinkingly making herself an excellent target, so that the nearest Secret Service agent, Clint Hill, hopped onto the car from the rear and sheltered her as the driver sped away to Parkland Hospital, where the president was declared dead.

All debate on the assassination boils down to whether Kennedy was fired at from the front, as the amateur 8-mm motion picture shot by Abraham Zapruder, a Dallas clothing manufacturer on his lunch hour, tends to suggest, despite mysterious attempts to doctor certain frames of the film, or whether he was shot at only from behind. On this question hinges the matter of conspiracy and the puzzle as to who the shooters might have been. Facts are scarce; rumours and third-hand information abundant. Bill Bonanno, the former Mafia chieftain, claims he was told by Johnny Roselli, a gangster later murdered, that he, Roselli, fired the fatal head shot from a storm drain and hid the rifle in upstate New York. That Oswald was present in the Depository when the Kennedy motorcade passed below, no one doubts. But every chain of every piece of evidence connecting Oswald with the shooting has been broken, whether it be the rifle, his fingerprints or even the late president's brain. The last of these disappeared from the National Archives, some believe at the request of Robert Kennedy, the president's brother, to prevent it becoming an object of morbid curiosity: the same reasoning used to explain why the bronze coffin in which the president's body was returned from Dallas to Washington was dumped into the Atlantic Ocean in 1965. Yet throughout the entire case the indifference to commercialization is almost as obvious as the desire to obscure the evidentiary trail. For example, the new president, Lyndon Johnson, almost immediately ordered the limousine in which Kennedy was riding to be scrubbed clean of evidence and repaired; but now, when its value to prosecutors has passed, the car is on display at the Henry Ford Museum in Dearborn, Michigan. Some blood-stained pieces of the seat-cover fabric are in private collections, as are the wristwatch, sunglasses, money clip and wallet Kennedy was carrying when he was killed. Most troubling of all was the Zapruder film, which clearly showed the fatal shot to Kennedy's brain. The film was bought by *Time* and *Life* magazines and was not available for study during the crucial years immediately following the assassination; it became property of the government only much later, and Zapruder's survivors were finally compensated for it in 1999. Virtually every piece of physical evidence has been rendered worthless by the legal standards for determining guilt. This is true of evidence that tends to support the accusation against Oswald as well as that which would support his innocence.

The assassination took place at 12:30 p.m. local time. In the pandemonium, Oswald left the Book Depository in an apparently leisurely fashion and returned by bus and taxi to the room on North Beckley for the last time and picked up his revolver. The landlady, whose children now own the property, saw a Dallas police car pause outside and heard it honk, as though signalling, before moving on. Oswald waited anxiously for a while, then set off in an agitated state. Some speculate that this is when he realized that he had been set up as, in his own memorable phrase, "just a patsy." Before he got far—the intersection of 10th Street and Patton Avenue—he was stopped by a young Dallas police officer, Jefferson Davis Tippit, who had been assigned to this precinct only that day, because of personnel changes connected with the presidential visit. A few people believe that Tippit was part of a rightist paramilitary force within the department. Some even believe that he was sent to kill Oswald. The theory is that though Oswald didn't kill anyone, he certainly knew there was a conspiracy that extended beyond the borders of Texas and Louisiana. Under the laws then in effect, the killing of the president would have been under state jurisdiction, the same as any other murder investigation, unless it could be proved that an interstate conspiracy existed, in which case the affair became a federal matter—and harder to contain. But if Tippit was himself an assassin, he left Patrol Car No. 10 without drawing his service revolver, and was found dead in the street with three gunshot wounds. Four witnesses saw parts of this fatal confrontation. One identified Oswald, another described a large man (Oswald was small and slight), and two others described a pair of assailants, one of whom might or might not have resembled Oswald. Shell casings from two different pistols were found at the scene, some from a .38 revolver like Oswald's, others from an automatic. Exact matching was not attempted. Displays at the JFK Assassination Center in Dallas posit that Tippit's killer was one Roscoe Whitehorse, who some go so far as to contend had been one of the Kennedy assassins only an hour earlier and whose wife worked for Jack Ruby at the Carousel Club, a downtown strip joint. Plotting Oswald's path on a city map makes for easy speculation that Oswald's destination when he left the rooming house may have been 233 South Ewing, and specifically Apartment 207, the residence of Ruby, for Oswald seems to have been heading there in a straight line, using short cuts. This is a motel-type building by which a freeway now passes, giving it a far greater air of seediness than it must have had even when it was occupied by so pathetic a figure as Ruby. (What an odd pair they must have made: the 1930s-era gangster and the existential punk, the modernist and the beatnik, in league together some-how.) By about 1:35 p.m., Oswald was walking west on Jefferson. He likely knew the conspirators, official and otherwise, were after him. When another patrol car passed, he nipped into the front alcove of a shoe store, pretending to window shop. A few doors along, at 231 Jefferson, he sneaked into the Texas Theater, where a Van Heflin war movie was playing. Some have speculated that this is where he was to meet his controller in the event of trouble. Instead he met more police, pouring in through the back door. There was a brief struggle during which Oswald tried to fire his revolver before being arrested by one of the officers, Nick McDonald. Illegal possession and the acts of aggression committed in the theatre are the only serious crimes of which Oswald can be accused with absolute certainty.

Simply on the basis of its pink stucco façade, a combination of Spanish colonial and art deco, or the outrageously 1950s neon sign, the Texas Theater, which has been closed since 1991, should be a protected landmark. But repeated attempts by citizens have been blocked by city hall. The cinema now sits vacant in a neighbourhood that, like many of the older sections of central Dallas with which Oswald is associated, collapses around it. But then Dallas has been cool to the memories of Oswald *and* Kennedy. The museum at the Depository, called the Sixth Floor, opened only in 1989 and then as a local rather than a state or federal initiative, and Dallas remains perhaps the only large city in the United States without a street, school, library or park named after Kennedy.

Dallas police were quick to tell the world that Oswald had a Communist Party membership card on his person when arrested; in fact, as became known only much later, he had two draft cards (one as Oswald, another as Aleck James Hidell), a Marine discharge card in the name of Hidell and a document known as a DD 1171—a defence department "Uniformed Services Identification and Privilege Card," a piece of ID commonly issued either to active military personnel in need of outside medical care or to civilian employees of the military working overseas. Curiously, police at one point put another prisoner in Oswald's cell. The prisoner, John Elrod, revealed thirty years later that Oswald told him that he was involved in (Elrod's words) "some sort of a gun deal" with Jack Ruby and others. Oswald was interrogated by Dallas police (without a lawyer to represent his interests) but revealed nothing, and was publicly denounced as the assassin of Kennedy before being charged on November 23. Late the following morning, while handcuffed to detective Jim Laevelle (familiar to history for the white Stetson he wore), Oswald was gunned down by Jack Ruby. Oswald, who was clearly quite bright, once stated that his ambition was to write fiction: "stories of American life." Instead he wrote the fiction of his own life. Was he a spook and, if so, whose? Was it possible that he could be connected to government, organized crime, the anti- and the pro-Castro forces all at the same time, with the Russians possibly thrown in? Or was he an intelligence wannabe scorned by intelligence professionals because, instead of someone who had gone to Yale, he was a person whom the system had failed and so joined the marines at seventeen in an effort to get an education? We shall never know. He left a myth as some people leave ghosts. Continued assertions about Oswald "doubles" finally led to exhumation of the body in 1981. Observers, including the undertaker who embalmed Oswald, found a) that the grave had been disturbed and b) that Oswald's head (as matched to Marine Corps dental records) had been severed from the body—the identity of the latter not being checked.

Soon after the assassination, a psychic and astrologer named Jeanne Dixon became famous retroactively for having predicted the assassination as early as 1956. (She also predicted that the Third World War would begin in 1958 and that the USSR would win the moon race.) In 1998, the novelist Gore Vidal, who shared a common step-parent with Mrs. Jacqueline Kennedy and was part of the Kennedy circle, told an interviewer in *Wired* magazine, "Actually we always thought JFK would be shot—by an angry husband."

How did the people in power respond to the Kennedy assassination? To head off other inquiries and calm an agitated public, President Lyndon Johnson created the Warren Commission, chaired by the respected former Supreme Court chief justice but including Allen Dulles, whom Kennedy had fired as director of central intelligence after the failed Bay of Pigs invasion of Cuba. In a heroic feat of publishing if not necessarily of investigation, the commission released a twenty-six-volume report only ten months later, one which, by performing various contortions, managed to convince the public that Oswald was the sole shooter and that he acted on his own initiative, not as part of a conspiracy. Subsequent investigatory committees and changing public opinion have chipped away at these conclusions. Institutions always have been more eager to accept the lone-assassin theory than have individuals. Institutions as different as the American Medical Association and the liberal *Washington Post* have been vociferous counter-critics of those who challenge the convoluted yet simplistic findings of the Warren Commission. The *Post* went so far as to fire its film reviewer in 1991 for writing a favourable review of Oliver Stone's film *JFK*, which revived public interest in the case by reflecting the assertions of two authors, Jim Garrison and Jim Marrs, that Kennedy was killed by teams of professional assassins as part of a vast plot involving Johnson and Richard Nixon (who, by coincidence, happened to be in Dallas on the day of the shooting).

Yet Johnson feared for his own life at the time. As vice-president, he was riding in a car two vehicles behind the president's and, on hearing shots, thought that he had been caught in a general ambush. A Secret

Service agent named Rufus W. Youngblood threw Johnson to the floor of the car and shielded him with his own body; Youngblood retired as deputy director of the Secret Service in 1971. In tapes made public in 1997, Johnson is heard conversing with J. Edgar Hoover the day following the assassination, asking how many shots were fired. "Three," Hoover replied. "Any of them fired at me?" Johnson asked. Hoover answered: "No.... All three at the president [who] was hit by the first and the third. The second shot hit the governor." This claim contradicts the heart of the Warren Commission findings, which is that three bullets were fired by Oswald, one missing, one striking the president, the third striking both the president and the governor.

Internal FBI documents released in 1998 show that Hoover was furious that the FBI had not put Oswald on its "security index" of people considered a threat to the lives of public officials. In his later years, Johnson made clear that he thought a conspiracy lay behind the killing, but did not elaborate. As for Nixon, he referred to the assassination only as a part of the larger entity he called "the Cuban thing." For his part, Fidel Castro always has denied any Cuban connection to the events in Dallas, but many believe that he was indeed pulling some of the strings, in retaliation for the combined CIA-Mafia plan to assassinate him and various other affronts extending back to the Eisenhower administration. As for the KGB, whatever the view of the officers in Minsk, the ones in Moscow came to believe that President Johnson was indeed implicated in the plot. Drs. James J. Humes and J. Thornton Boswell, the two doctors who led the second autopsy on Kennedy's body once it was returned from Dallas— the autopsy, many claim, in which the wounds were altered—always insisted, as did all but one of those at the initial autopsy, that Kennedy was killed by two bullets fired from the rear, as the Warren Commission maintained. Mrs. Marina Prusakova Oswald Porter, who first supported the official findings of her husband's guilt and maintained the position for many years while living in Minnesota, far from the scene of the crime, later recanted and returned to the Dallas area, where she became a vigorous champion of Oswald's innocence. In the meantime, she had co-operated with Priscilla Johnson McMillan in the writing of *Marina and Me* (New York, 1977), which virtually indicted Oswald.

RESOURCES: The vast literature on the subject of Oswald and the Kennedy assassination includes many unusual works propounding unusual theories. One book, for example, claims that Kennedy was accidentally shot by a

Secret Service agent. No doubt a work will appear claiming that Kennedy was killed by a drunken driver. Such is the power of denial and the desire for closure, conflicting emotions that are the most significant features of the works by all concerned. An important book in the anti-Oswald camp, a reaction to the many more lenient ones that appeared in the aftermath of Stone's film, is *Case Closed: Lee Harvey Oswald and the Assassination of JFK* (New York, 1993) by Gerald Posner, who meticulously demolishes all the conspiracy theories most zealously. Another is *Oswald's Tale: An American Mystery* by the novelist Norman Mailer (New York, 1995), based in part on old KGB files on Oswald in Minsk, which Mailer's business partner purchased, augmented by heavy reliance on Priscilla Johnson McMillan. Mailer argues that the Warren Commission was correct in its findings but adds a new twist by suggesting that Oswald committed murder while still in the Marines. *Rush to Judgement* by Mark Lane (New York, 1966) was the first important book to speculate and theorize about a conspiracy to kill Kennedy. Lane has remained one of the most important, tireless and prolific researchers on the subject, his work only slightly marred by revelations in the 1990s that the KGB had secretly, and without his knowledge, subsidized some of his research. *Legend: The Secret World of Lee Harvey Oswald* by Edward Jay Epstein (New York, 1978) is thus far the most comprehensive attempt at a biography of Oswald; the difference between journalism and literature is well illustrated by the fact that Don DeLillo relies on *Legend* for most of his facts about Oswald's external life but creates a far more three-dimensional character in his novel *Libra* (New York, 1988); Epstein can be supplemented by *The Search for Lee Harvey Oswald: A Comprehensive Photographic Record* by Robert J. Groden (New York, 1995). Other important works arguing conspiracy include *Conspiracy: Who Killed President Kennedy* by Anthony Summers (New York, 1980, rev. 1989); *The Plot to Kill the President* by G. Robert Blakey and Richard N. Billings (New York, 1981); *Contract on America: The Mafia Murder of President John F. Kennedy* by David E. Scheim (New York, 1988); *On the Trail of the Assassins* by Jim Garrison (New York, 1988); *Crossfire: The Plot That Killed Kennedy* by Jim Marrs (New York, 1988); and *Deep Politics and the Death of JFK* by Peter Dale Scott (Berkeley, 1993). *The Secret Team* by Fletcher Prouty (New York, 1973) draws on the author's experience as liaison officer between the Pentagon and the CIA and head of clandestine operations in the Joint Chiefs of Staff office during the Kennedy years to take on the subject of just who the supposed professional assassins were and how they operated; Prouty is the inspiration for the character Mr. X in Stone's film *JFK*. Recent scientifically rooted books of interest are *Assassination Science: Experts Speak Out on the Death of JFK*, ed. James H. Fetzer (Peru, Illinois, 1997), in which scholars in fields as different as philosophy and brain surgery suggest that evidence was altered to eliminate traces of a second gunman or additional gunmen, and *Silencing the Lone Assassin: The Murders of JFK and Lee Harvey Oswald* by John Canal (St. Paul, 2000), whose approach is technologically based. Also of interest are *The Sword and the Shield* (New York, 1999) by Christopher Andrew and Vasily Mitrokhin, a KGB defector who claims that the Soviets forged links between Oswald and the CIA, and two CD-ROMs, *Book of Facts: JFK Assassination* (Macmillan Digital USA) and *Executive Action Encyclopedia of the JFK Assassination* by Donald Freed and Mark Lane (Zane Publishing).

OTHO, Marcus Salvius (32–69 CE), organized the assassination of the Roman emperor Servius Sulpicius Galba (3 BCE–69 CE). Otho was born to a common family that rose in status during his childhood because of its service to the emperors Augustus and Claudius. Later, Otho became close to Nero and joined the mad emperor at the orgies for which he was noted; but the two men had a falling out over Otho's wife, Poppaea, whom Nero desired. Nero appointed Otho to be governor of Hispania Lusitania while keeping Poppaea in Rome as his mistress. Shortly afterwards, in a fit of rage, Nero kicked her to death. Otho, who mourned his wife for the rest of his days, joined the revolt against Nero led by Servius Sulpicius Galba. The revolt succeeded, and Galba, helped in great part by troops loyal to Otho, marched to Rome as the new emperor. But Galba made enemies quickly, such as when he refused promised payment to the Praetorian Guard for their assistance in dispatching Nero. What's more, he had senators murdered at will. Perhaps his gravest mistake was naming Piso Licinianus rather than Otho as his heir. Otho became so furious that he began plotting Galba's death. On January 15, 69, a group of soldiers and members of the Praetorian Guard attacked and killed the emperor and his heir, cutting off their heads and placing them on spikes to be paraded round the Castra Praetoria. Otho succeeded Galba as emperor, but was immediately embroiled in a civil war, as Vitellius, governor of Germania, led a revolt against him. On April 16, 69, after losing a key battle to the rebels, Otho killed himself and was succeeded by Vitellius. In all, Rome had four different emperors in a one-year period. Only Vitellius died of natural causes.

RESOURCE: *The Decline and Fall of the Roman Empire* by Edward Gibbon (London, 1776–1788).

OUFKIR, General Muhammad (1920?–1972), attempted to assassinate King Hassan II of Morocco (b. 1929) on August 16, 1972, as Hassan was flying back to Morocco from France. The royal aircraft was strafed and badly damaged by five Moroccan air force jets. A radio plea from a mechanic on Hassan's plane beseeched the attackers to stop for the sake of the innocents on board, as the monarch was already dead. The attackers ceased fire and flew off. In fact, the voice on the radio was Hassan's own. When the plane landed at Rabat airport, the quick-thinking Hassan disembarked to participate in welcoming ceremonies. As soon as he was visible, however, eight air force jets began strafing the runways. Eight persons died in the second attack and at least forty-seven others were wounded. Hassan, however, dived for cover and was unharmed. Later, a third air attack was made, on the guest house attached to the royal palace. Hassan was not there and so again escaped harm. The planes were attached to the Kenita air base, which had been taken over by forces loyal to the defence minister, Muhammad Oufkir, who had risen through the French army while Morocco was still a French possession. He had served in Indo-China and was later involved in the negotiations for Moroccan independence. After independence, Oufkir suppressed the Rif uprising of 1958–1959. His policy of exterminating entire villages gave him a reputation for ruthlessness and cruelty. In 1965, he was entrusted with ending riots in Casablanca, a task he carried out in his usual bloodthirsty manner. Oufkir was convicted in France of the kidnapping and presumed murder in Paris of the Moroccan leader Mehdi Ben Barka, a case that strained French-Moroccan relations throughout the 1960s. Hassan had survived a coup and assassination attempt in 1971. Oufkir was with him at that time and was considered a Hassan loyalist. Captured airmen from the 1972 attack quickly revealed that Oufkir was indeed responsible; he had, they said, cited palace corruption and the danger of a left-wing coup as his reasons. Within a week, Oufkir was dead, his body riddled with bullets. The official cause of death was suicide.

RESOURCE: *Hassan II: Le défi* by Albin Michel (Paris, 1976).

OXFORD, Edward (b. 1822), was the first of seven men who attempted to assassinate Queen Victoria (reigned 1837–1901). In London on June 10, 1840, Victoria, three months pregnant at the time, was riding with her husband, Prince Albert, up Constitution Hill when they approached Oxford, who was standing no more than six paces from the open carriage. In the words of Albert, Oxford "stood there in a theatrical position, a pistol in each hand... suddenly he stooped, put a pistol on his arm, aimed at us and fired. The bullet must have gone over our heads, judging by the hole made where it hit the garden wall." Oxford, who was immediately seized, was rumoured to have been given the pistols by Ernest Augustus, king of Hanover, the Queen's uncle, who would have assumed the throne if Victoria had died without an heir. Such allegations were groundless. After examination, the eighteen-year-old Oxford was found insane. He spent the next twenty-seven years in Broadmoor Asylum. He was released in 1867, but was forced to leave Britain.

RESOURCE: *Victoria: The Young Queen* by Monica Charlot (Oxford, 1991).

PAHLEN, Peter Aleksieevich (Count Pahlen of St. Petersburg) (1745–1826) led the group of thirty nobles who on the night of March 23/24, 1801, entered the bedchamber the Russian czar, Paul I, son of Catherine the Great, and ordered him 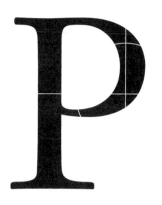 to abdicate. When the czar refused and put up a struggle, he was struck with a chair, beaten and finally strangled to death with a scarf. Thus ended the four-year reign of an eccentric and autocratic monarch whose handling of the nobility and the gentry was as vicious as his handling of the peasantry. He treated generals as his personal slaves, rescinded certain privileges of the aristocracy and refused ordinary subjects the right to travel abroad. The only person he truly trusted was Pahlen—curiously so, since Pahlen was in some sympathy with the gentry. The extent of both the czar's individualism and his trust in the count is shown by the following item, which was gazetted in the official newspaper on December 30, 1800: "His Majesty, the Emperor, perceiving that the European powers cannot come to an accommodation, and wishing to put an end to a war which has raged fourteen years, has conceived the idea of appointing a place to which he will invite the other potentates to engage together with himself in single combat . . . for which purpose they shall bring with them, to act as their esquires, umpires and heralds, their most enlightened ministers and able generals. . . . He will bring on his part Count Pahlen. . . . "

The situation reached a crisis point in mid-March 1801 when Paul issued a warrant for the imprisonment or banishment of the czarina and their two sons. Pahlen realized that he alone was in a position to assassinate Paul and ensure the succession of the elder son, Alexandr. The plan enjoyed at least the tacit support of the upper classes, as they believed that Alexandr was a comparative liberal (indeed, perhaps too overtly so, having had a French revolutionary named Laharpe as his tutor). At all events, they felt they would be (and, in general, indeed were) better off under Alexandr, who was himself at least aware of the conspiracy, as he insisted that his father not be harmed. Alexandr first announced that his father had died of a stroke. But soon after his coronation, he refused to prosecute the assassins, who were advised simply to quit the court and retire, which they did.

RESOURCES: *A History of the Nineteenth Century Year by Year* by Edwin Emerson, Jr. (New York, 1900); *Paul the First of Russia, The Son of Catherine the Great* by K. Waliszewski (London, 1913).

PARCHE, Günter (b. 1954), attempted to assassinate Monica Seles (b. 1974), professional tennis star from Yugoslavia, on April 30, 1993, when Seles, then the top-ranked female player in the world, was competing in the Hamburg Open. Seles was not at her best that day as she was recovering from the flu. She was competing against Magdalena Maleeva of Bulgaria and was ahead 4-3 in the second set after taking the first set 6-4. At this point there was a rest break for the players, and Seles was sitting on a bench. As she leaned forward for a towel, Parche leapt onto the playing area, withdrew a serrated boning knife from a plastic shopping bag and stabbed Seles in the upper back, between the shoulder blades. He was grabbed by security as he was attempting to stab her a second time. Seles was rushed to hospital, where an MRI revealed that the blade had missed her spine by millimetres. Over the next few days, as the tournament continued, Seles was visited by several fellow tennis players, including the German star Steffi Graf.

Parche's motive, investigators learned, revolved round Graf, with whom he had developed an obsession; the walls of his room were covered in Graf posters that he had produced himself from blow-ups of magazine photos. He made it a point to send Graf small amounts of money on her birthday. He had also purchased a video camera (an expensive and difficult item to obtain in his native East Germany) to record Graf's games. Relatives later told authorities that Parche would be moved to tears whenever Graf won, and that when she lost, he would be plunged into a suicidal despair.

In 1990, Seles defeated Graf at the Lufthansa Cup in Berlin. Parche was devastated that Graf had been beaten in her home country. Yet Parche's interest in Graf was not patriotic but rather sexual. He described her as "a unique woman. Her eyes sparkle like diamonds. She is an absolute dream woman. I really want to emphasize that; it comes straight from the heart." As for Seles, Parche was less complimentary: "She is not pretty. Women shouldn't be thin as a bone." After Graf's loss in Berlin, friends and associates at the factory where Parche worked teased him about his idol's loss. Parche quit his job and travelled to the west (the two Germanys having been reunified). He became obsessed with removing Seles from competition. By March 1991, Seles had dethroned Graf as the world's number-one female tennis player; Parche prayed daily that she would break her arm. He planned to attack her during the French Open, but his passport was not in order and he was not allowed to enter France. He had to wait until Seles returned to Germany to make his attempt.

A psychological assessment of Parche after the attack on Seles declared that he was pathologically depraved. His obsession with Graf "reflected an unreal idealization, probably unconscious sexual elements and a fanaticism, which went as far as self-sacrifice." Parche said that he realized that he would probably serve fifteen years for his actions but that the attack had been worthwhile. He was charged with aggravated assault and declared fit to stand trial. His defence centred on his limited intelligence and emotional immaturity and emphasized that his intent was not to kill Seles but to wound her only enough to keep her from competing. The prosecution, however, alleged that Parche was trying to murder Seles and that, in addition to his obsession with Graf, he was also a racist who hated Serbs (Seles, although of Hungarian descent, was born in what is now Serbia). In the end, the court found for the defence. It also ruled that the defendant was no longer a menace to society and would not attack again. Parche was sentenced to two years' imprisonment, with the sentence suspended. After another night in jail (at his own request) he was set free.

The decision was condemned by professional tennis players the world over. The prosecution appealed the case, and at the second trial Seles was asked to testify. Although her physical wound had healed, she was still feeling psychological ill effects from the attack. In German courts, a victim testifies from the prosecution desk with his or her back to the defendant. Seles, for obvious reasons, could not abide the idea of turning her back on her attacker again; she did not testify. The second trial ended in the same verdict and sentence as the first. Two more years passed before Seles returned to competitive tennis, at the Canadian Open in Toronto.

RESOURCE: *Monica: From Fear to Victory* by Monica Seles and Nancy Ann Richardson (New York, 1996).

PASSANNANTE, Giovanni (1849–1910), attempted to murder Umberto I of Italy (1844–1900), on November 17, 1878, when the monarch was visiting Naples on a tour of his new kingdom. The procession, financed by a special tax, was especially lavish. As Umberto and Queen Margarita rode in an open coach, Passannante approached with a red handkerchief over his left hand, jumped onto the running board and discarded the covering to reveal a dagger. The queen's screams alerted Prime Minister Benedetto Cairoli, who was riding with the royal couple and moved forward to shield the king. Passannante's weapon first caught Cairoli in the thigh, but the wound was not serious; a second glancing blow struck Umberto, but caused no more than a scratch. Umberto began to pummel Passannante with his still-sheathed sword while the queen beat the attacker repeatedly with a bouquet of flowers with which she had been presented earlier in the day. Eventually, police surrounded the carriage and took Passannante away.

He was born near Salvia into a family that eked out a meagre existence in farming. An earthquake destroyed the farm in 1857, and Passannante, aged eight, became a beggar. By the time he was thirteen, he had found work as a cook for a wealthy family, but his right hand was severely scalded by boiling water, making him dependent on his left. He was an intelligent lad but too poor to attend school; a priest taught him to read, and he would be a voracious reader for the rest of his life, including, in time, books on radical politics. He became an anarchist. In 1870, he was arrested for putting up posters calling on the people to rise up and overthrow the rich. He was dismissed from his job and sent to prison for several months. This experience made him all the more eager to devote his life to anarchism. After leaving prison, Passannante opened a trattoria with a partner, who absconded with the money, leaving the business bankrupt. Passannante moved to Naples, where he continued to work, off and on, as a cook. People who knew him from this time regarded him as a hard-working man with a generous spirit. When Passannante heard that Umberto was coming to Naples, he traded his jacket for a knife with a blade ten centimetres long. Passannante later claimed that his intention was simply to wound the king, as a lesson to others. He pointed out that if he had wished to kill Umberto, he surely would have used a bigger knife or poisoned the blade. The authorities took in hundreds of possible suspects: so many, in fact, that Umberto ordered them to stop arresting people unless they had evidence against them. But the authorities continued to torture Passannante to make him reveal the names of his fellow conspirators.

By the end of the century, an anarchist attacking a member of the nobility would become a commonplace event, but in 1878 the Passannante affair seemed a new development in European politics and the trial was a sensation all over the world. Umberto was not a popular king, and as the proceedings went on, the quiet and polite Passannante gained a great deal of sympathy among Italians. At first he refused counsel but was assigned a lawyer considered one of the best in Naples. Unfortunately for Passannante, however, his lawyer was a monarchist, as were the prosecutor, both judges and all nine members of the jury. Passannante was heard to remark: "If you want to kill me, kill me. Don't make up lies about me." But the trial, which lasted two days, brought witnesses whose testimony was clearly false. The prosecutor, who had written an award-winning book against the death penalty, demanded that Passannante be executed. The defence said only that there was no penalty for attempted regicide, that if the jury believed that Passannante's intention was merely to wound, then the death penalty was inappropriate for what normally would be considered assault. After ten minutes' deliberation, the judges sentenced Passannante to death.

Umberto, under pressure from the international press and from Passannante supporters at home, and at the moment enjoying a rise in popularity for surviving the assassination attempt, commuted the sentence to life imprisonment, though Passannante said that he would prefer to be killed. He was kept in solitary confinement, in a cell with no light, tethered to a wall with a chain only one metre long. Within a short time, he went insane. When he died, his skull and brain were taken by scientists who wished to study the characteristics of the "assassin-type." In a private letter to Kaiser Wilhelm of Germany, Umberto wrote: "These things are among the little risks of our profession." Umberto's only public statement on the attack came when he was hosting a dinner party. As the meal was being served, Umberto said: "Let us be seated and let's not keep the cooks waiting; you have seen, ladies and gentlemen, what they are capable of."

RESOURCE: *Giovanni Passannante: La vita, l'attentato, il processo, la condanna a morte, la grazia 'regale' e gli anni di galera del cuoco lucano che nel 1878 ruppe l'incantesimo monarchico* by Giuseppe Galzerano (Scalo, 1997).

PATE, Robert (d. 1895), the fifth of seven would-be assassins of Queen Victoria (reigned 1837–1901), was the only one to do her physical harm.

On May 27, 1850, Pate, a retired officer of hussars, mounted the queen's open carriage while she was riding with three of her children. As she passed Cambridge House, 24 Piccadilly, Pate struck the queen about the face and head with his walking stick. Victoria lost consciousness for a moment, but within a few seconds was able to tell her attendants that she was all right. Victoria had been given a parasol lined with chain mail to protect her, but she refused to carry it. On this occasion, however, her sturdy bonnet absorbed most of the blows. Pate was sentenced to seven years' transportation to Tasmania, after which he returned to England. Victoria was more shocked and outraged by this attempt than by any other. To her, while the idea of assassinating a monarch was understandable, the idea of physically assaulting a woman was unthinkable—especially with children present. Victoria escaped with no more than a few bruises and a swollen and blackened eye. She decided that this temporary disfigurement should not prevent her from appearing in public as her absence might encourage other assassins. Accordingly, on the evening of the attack she appeared at the Royal Opera House. The performance was interrupted by the playing of "God Save the Queen" and a five-minute ovation from the audience.

RESOURCE: *Royal Murders: Hatred, Revenge, and the Seizing of Power* by Dulcie M. Ashdown (Stroud, Gloucestershire, 1998).

PATLER, John (b. 1938), the slayer of George Lincoln Rockwell, America's most infamous neo-Nazi, began as one of Rockwell's most ardent supporters. Rockwell (1918–1967), the so-called Führer of the American Nazi Party (ANP), was a publicity-seeker, eager to get his name and face on television and into the newspapers in order to attract like-minded people to his cause. Among his exploits were his picketing the premiere of the movie *Exodus* and his speaking tours of college campuses where he was certain to draw student protests. A more devious tactic was his alignment of the ANP with the Black Muslim movement on the grounds that both favoured segregation of the races. Rockwell even spoke at a Muslim conference in Chicago in 1962, telling an audience of five thousand African-Americans that Malcolm X was heroic and Elijah Muhammad was the "Adolf Hitler of the black man" (intending the latter as a compliment). The FBI declared Rockwell more of a nuisance than a menace, as his followers never numbered more than a few dozen.

At Rockwell's headquarters, a house in Arlington, Virginia, nick-named Hatemonger's Hill, he usually had between twenty and thirty like-minded individuals living with him, but the cast was forever changing, often because of personality clashes. Among the longer-term residents was Patler, who claimed to have grown up in an Italian section of New York where conflicts with African-Americans and Puerto Ricans engendered his racist beliefs. After an undistinguished career in the marines, Patler left his wife and children (one of whom was reportedly named Horst Wessel after the German Nazi martyr) so that he could better serve Rockwell. A printer by trade, he was editor of the official party organ, *The Stormtrooper*. But in March 1967 he was expelled from the party and forced to leave the compound, apparently because he had caused discord between dark-haired, dark-eyed Nazis and blond-haired, blue-eyed ones (Patler himself was among the former). Thereupon, Patler formed his own group, the American National Party, with its own magazine, *Kill*, which called for the assassination of all who got in the way of white supremacy.

On August 25, 1967, Rockwell was leaving a local coin laundry in the Washington, DC, area when he was shot by Patler from a hiding place on the roof of the plaza where the laundromat was located. Rockwell was hit twice, once in the chest and once in the head. He died at the scene. Patler fled but was picked up by police forty-five minutes later at a bus stop slightly more than a kilometre away. Without Rockwell, the American Nazi Party fell apart due to conflicts with its new leader, Matt Koehl, whom some suspected of involvement in the assassination. Pronounced fit to stand trail, Patler was convicted of Rockwell's murder and given a twenty-year sentence on December 17, 1967. Described as a model prisoner, he was paroled on August 22, 1975. His present whereabouts are unknown.

RESOURCE: *America in Hitler's Shadow: The Anatomy of Nazism* by Leland Bell (Port Washington, New York, 1973).

PEROVSKAIA, Sophia (1854–1881), was commander of the Narodnaya Volya ("Will of the People") terrorists who assassinated Czar Alexandr II (1818–1881) in St. Petersburg. On March 1, 1881, Alexandr left the safety of the Winter Palace to view a military parade. He had been in seclusion in the palace due to recent attempts on his life by Narodnaya

Volya. On this occasion, a full-scale attempt would be mounted by bomb-throwing terrorists to finish the czar once and for all. When Perovskaia observed that Alexandr was taking an unexpected route, she quickly redeployed the bombers to positions along the Nevsky Prospekt. The first bomb was thrown by a nineteen-year-old student named Rysakiv. It exploded behind the czar's carriage. Although two guards and one observer were killed, and the carriage was severely damaged, Alexandr was unhurt. Indeed he emerged from the wreckage to observe the damage, in spite of his guards' urging that he quickly move to another vehicle. At that moment, another member of the cell, Ignaty Grinevitsky, ran towards the czar. He was carrying a nitroglycerin bomb, which he detonated at Alexandr's feet. The blast killed Grinevitsky instantly. Another twenty men were killed or wounded. Alexandr's legs were torn off and one of his eyes was blown from its socket. He requested to be moved to the palace to die. He expired in a matter of hours.

Sophia Perovskaia was born to an aristocratic family. Her father, Lev Nikolaevich Perovskaia, had been governor of St. Petersburg. His authoritarian and abusive manner endowed his daughter with a distrust of men in general and a loathing of official authority. After 1866, Lev Perovskaia lost his position and was unemployed and heavily in debt. Sophia, up until then, had been educated by nurses and governessess. Afterwards, she attempted to make up for her lack of formal education by voracious reading. In 1869, Perovskaia enrolled in the Alarchin courses, a series of lectures for women with little formal education. The courses eventually led to her joining with other women in discussion groups from which men were excluded. The courses and discussion groups created a rise in political consciousness among the women of St. Petersburg. Perovskaia realized that as long as education was available only to the well-born, political change was impossible. She left St. Petersburg in 1872 to assist a village teacher in Samara. From there she trained as a medic and travelled from village to village treating the peasants and raising their political awareness, distributing anti-czarist pamphlets along with smallpox vaccinations. When she returned to the capital, she joined a group of like-minded comrades who were creating informal schools for workers where they could discuss politics with the proletariat. She also worked with prisoners in the Peter and Paul Fortress after bribing a guard to allow her entry. In 1874, Perovskaia was arrested for her illegal activities but was cleared of all charges and allowed to go free. After attempting to orchestrate a breakout at a prison near Kharkov, she was arrested again. This time she escaped and began living the life of an underground fugitive.

In 1878, she returned to St. Petersburg, where an assassination attempt by Vera Zasulich had created a division in the populist organization Land and Liberty. In spite of initial misgivings, Perovskaia supported the radical wing, Narodnaya Volya, which became committed to killing Alexandr. Although Alexandr was considered a liberal (he had freed the serfs in 1861), his reforms were too little too late. In November 1879, Perovskaia assisted the terrorists in digging a tunnel under a set of railway tracks to blow up the czar's train. The attempt was a failure, destroying one of two trains in the imperial entourage but not the one carrying the czar. Perovskaia was personally devastated by this event. A lifelong populist, she had come to accept the idea of political violence as long as only the intended target was hurt. The idea of killing innocent people depressed her. Nevertheless, she was to be one of two coordinators of a final and successful attempt, and when the other ringleader, Andrei Zheliabov, was arrested shortly before the plot could get underway, Perovskaia took sole command. When her group finally succeeded in killing the czar, she took no joy in her actions. What had been hoped for had been achieved, but at an enormous cost in innocent lives. She refused to join in celebrations with other members of Narodnaya Volya. She also decided not to attempt to flee the country. The police, meanwhile, were conducting a massive search for the regicides. Aided by informers, they arrested Perovskaia on March 10. At her trial she did not deny her involvement in the assassination and offered little defence. Along with five others, she was found guilty and sentenced to death. On April 3, 1881, they were led to the gallows. As her final act, she hugged each of her comrades before she died—with the exception of Timofei Rysakov, who had co-operated with the authorities.

RESOURCE: *Sof'ia Perovskaia* by Aleksandra Kornilova-Moroz (Moscow, 1931).

PETTERSSON, Christer (b. 1944), the only person yet brought to trial in the assassination of Swedish prime minister Olaf Palme, eventually had his conviction overturned on appeal and was paid three hundred thousand crowns—only to admit later, in November 1999, that he couldn't remember whether he had killed Palme or not. On the evening of February 28, 1986, Palme (b. 1927), a social democrat, and his wife,

Lisbet, left the Grand Cinema in central Stockholm and were headed for the subway on their way home, about 1.6 kilometres distant. Palme had dismissed his bodyguards a short time earlier. As the couple passed an art-supply shop (the exact spot is now marked with a plaque in the pavement), an unidentified man approached them from the rear, killing Palme with an armour-piercing bullet fired from a .357 Magnum and slightly wounding Mrs. Palme with a second shot before vanishing into the night. Police arrested Pettersson, an alcoholic petty thief who once spent time in jail for killing a man with a bayonet, and charged him with the murder after Lisbet Palme picked him out of a police identity parade. He was sentenced to life imprisonment, but the appellate court later acquitted him on the grounds of insufficient evidence; the government had to pay compensation to Pettersson and one other suspect.

Conspiracy theorists implicated their favourite villains—the American CIA (Palme had opposed the Vietnam War), the P-2 Masonic Lodge, the Mossad. One more unusual theory connected the killings to the Kurdistan Workers' Party (PKK), because Palme had refused asylum to several former PKK members, especially Kesire Yildirim, the ex-wife of the rebel leader Abdullah Ocalan; she had lived in Sweden in the early 1980s. This theory was the choice of the chief of police, who was later dismissed from his post for bugging the homes of Kurdish immigrants. In the first ten years after the assassination, a special police unit, at one time employing more than three hundred detectives, followed up some eighteen thousand leads, none of them fruitful. The murder weapon was never found.

In 1996, the prolific self-confessed South African assassin Eugene de Kock accused one of his fellow former members of the apartheid regime of being behind the murder. This view was later echoed by de Kock's predecessor, Dirk Coetzee, who named a second ex-colleague but said that eighty to ninety South African agents were involved in the plot to kill Palme, a vocal opponent of their regime. The operation, both de Kock and Coetzee said, was code-named Operation Long Reach.

On November 11, 1999, Pettersson stunned the nation when he told an interviewer on television: "I don't think I did it, but I could have. If I had pulled out a gun, I did it in a semi-conscious state. I woke up in a police cell and I didn't even know where the police station was." A forensic psychiatrist explained that Pettersson suffers from brain damage of a type that could cause him to forget such an incident. Officially, the case remains open.

RESOURCES: The Palme case has been fictionalized in the Swedish film *The Last Contract* by Kjell Sundrall (1999), based on a Swedish novel published anonymously.

PLANETTA, Otto (1899–1934), was a former army sergeant and a member of the Austrian Nazi Party who assassinated Englebert Dollfuss (1892–1934), chancellor of Austria. On July 25, 1934, a group of approximately 150 Austrian Nazis, under the direction of the German SS, attempted to overthrow the Austrian government in order to install a puppet regime under Anton Rintellen (1873–1946) to facilitate an *Anschluss* (or joining together) of Germany and Austria. Dollfuss, the "Pocket Chancellor," so named because he stood less than 1.5 metres, had been instilling a sense of Austrian nationalism in order to prevent popular opinion swinging in favour of union with Germany. Adolf Hitler, born in Austria but now German chancellor, had been attempting to create the *Anschluss* since his elevation to the chancellery in 1933. Dollfuss had not only been rallying his people to Austrian nationalism but also attempting to sway Benito Mussolini of Italy to the cause of Austrian independence. Germany felt that the elimination of Dollfuss and his government was the key to *Anschluss*.

Austrian Nazis (a group that included six police officers, six police investigators, two superintendents of police and one police inspector) stormed the chancellery and burst into Dollfuss's office. Planetta, dressed in a bogus officer's uniform, shot Dollfuss twice in the neck. Another group of Nazis captured the transmitter of Austrian radio, the Ravag, and announced that the Dollfuss government had resigned and that Rintellen had been named chancellor. Executives of the Ravag, however, had barricaded themselves on the upper floor of the building and sent word to another studio to refute the broadcast. Austrian police used grenades to clear the rebels from the radio station. The chancellery was surrounded by police and soldiers while the Nazis inside attempted to negotiate their way out of a coup attempt now gone horribly wrong. Dollfuss was lying on the floor of his office bleeding to death. His pleas for a doctor were dismissed. He began to ask for a priest, but this request was also ignored. Within three hours of the shooting, Dollfuss was dead.

Reports on the shape of the negotiations between the Nazi rebels and the Austrian authorities are contradictory. Some say that the rebels were offered safe passage to Germany provided that nobody had been hurt. Others contend that the rebels had been offered safe passage without condition simply as a ruse to break the siege. In either case, the Nazis within the chancellery gave themselves up. In the aftermath, Italy, which had ambitions on certain portions of Austrian territory that it felt was owed as a result of the First World War, issued a statement prohibiting Nazi Germany from using this incident as a pretext for invasion of Austria. The Germans denied their role in the attempted coup, claiming they knew nothing of the incident. But the German propaganda ministry had prepared articles and political cartoons to be inserted in Nazi newspapers. Some were inadvertently published in Munich, robbing the Nazi denial of any credibility. The Nazis also had stationed troops along the German-Austrian border to occupy Austria once the coup had succeeded, but these troops were pulled back due to Italian pressure. When the Austrian authorities attempted to arrest Rintellen, he tried to commit suicide by shooting himself in the chest, but the bullet only pierced one of his lungs. Rintellen recovered and was eventually sentenced to twenty years' imprisonment for his role in the coup attempt. Rintellen denied any knowledge of the plot, but police discovered papers he had drawn up naming his new cabinet. Eventually, in 1938, the Nazis released Rintellen when a forged telegram was used as a trick to force *Anschluss* on the Austrians. Planetta and six others were sentenced to death for their roles in the attempted putsch. As the Nazis were led to the gallows, their final words were "Heil Hitler."

RESOURCE: *Assassination in Vienna* by Walter B. Maass (New York, 1972).

POWELL, Lewis Thornton (a.k.a. Lewis Paine, a.k.a. Lewis Payne) (1844-65), was a Confederate States intelligence operative who tried to assassinate William H. Seward (1801–1872), the American secretary of state, in Washington on the evening of April 14, 1865, as part of the conspiracy, led by John Wilkes Booth, to kill Abraham Lincoln and key members of the cabinet. Reared in Florida, the son of a clergyman, Powell enlisted in the infantry in 1861, aged seventeen. Bouts of serious illness delayed his entry into combat, but he recovered to take part in such famous battles as Antietam, Chancellorsville, Fredericksburg and Gettysburg. At the last of these, Powell was captured and held as a prisoner of war. In September 1863, however, he escaped, with the help of a Union uniform and a nurse who had become romantically attached to him. Making his way south, he joined the 43rd Virginia Cavalry under Colonel John Singleton Mosby, a dashing leader of partisan rangers, who controlled much of northern Virginia for a time. There is evidence to suggest that Powell was one of five of Mosby's hand-picked men seconded to the Confederate secret service for a special mission: the kidnapping of Lincoln, who, the South hoped, could be exchanged for Confederate prisoners of war. At some point, as the war was ending in the all-important Virginia theatre of operations, the plan turned to one of assassination instead, undoubtedly without the sanction of the crumbling Confederate government but rather at the instigation of Booth, using some or all of the other potential kidnappers. Their meeting place was a boarding house run by Mary E. Surratt, mother of John Surratt, another of the conspirators. Powell stayed there for three nights in March 1865. On March 14, Powell was betrayed and was arrested as a spy under the name Lewis Payne (for he was a person of numerous names, identities, ranks and cover stories), only to be released almost immediately on agreeing to take the oath of allegiance to the Union, which he did as Lewis Paine. According to testimony given by Powell and by George T. Atzerodt at their subsequent trial, neither man knew his intended target until given his assignment by Booth at 8:00 p.m. on April 14 at the Herndon House, a hotel at 9th and F streets, where Powell was staying. Atzerodt was to kill the vice-president, Andrew Johnson (a task he failed to carry out), while Powell dispatched Seward who, as secretary of state, was third in line of succession to the presidency.

Seward was bed-ridden from an accident, and Powell gained entrance to his house on Lafayette Park, opposite the White House, by posing as a messenger from Seward's doctor, bearing medicine. Pushing past a servant and beating Seward's son with a pistol, Powell repeatedly stabbed the secretary with a silver-mounted Bowie knife bearing the inscription "The Hunter's Companion—Real Life Defender." Seward's life was saved by the cervical collar he wore at the time. Powell then attacked several others on his way out. He was arrested on April 17 as Lewis Payne, the name under which he was tried by a military commission and the one under which he was hanged, along with three others, including Atzerodt and Mrs. Surratt, on July 7. The bodies were buried in unmarked graves beneath the stone floor of the Old Arsenal Prison, where the executions took place, but President Johnson, in the final days of his term, ordered the corpses exhumed and returned to their respective families. The Union officer appointed to defend Powell at his trial based his strategy on the assertion that his client was a naïve pawn in the plot, scarcely literate and of limited mental acuity. The tactic not only failed but was also patently false: Powell was a clever, articulate and resourceful solider who believed that he was acting in the best interest of his country.

RESOURCES: *The Lincoln Murder Conspiracies* by William Hanchett (Urbana, Illinois, 1983); *Alias "Paine": Lewis Thornton Powell, the Mystery Man of the Lincoln Conspiracy* by Betty J. Ownsbey (Jefferson, North Carolina, 1993).

PRINCIP, Gavrilo (1894–1918), became the indirect cause of the First World War when he assassinated Archduke Franz-Ferdinand (1863–1914) of the Austro-Hungarian Empire as well as Ferdinand's wife, the Countess Sophie (1868–1914). A Bosnian-Serbian nationalist, Princip, along with his friends Trifko Grabez (1894–1916) and Nedeljko Cabrinovic (1895–1916), were members in Belgrade of the terrorist organization Young Bosnia. When they learned that Franz-Ferdinand, heir-apparent to the throne, was to visit Sarajevo, they began plotting his assassination. Their plans were uncovered by Colonel Dragutin Dimitrijevic of Serbian military intelligence, who was also a leader of the Serbian terrorist organization, the Black Hand. Dimitrijevic summoned the young terrorists and inducted them into the Black Hand. After having them swear an oath of fidelity, he supplied them with pistols, bombs and cyanide. The cyanide was to be used to avoid being captured alive. The young assassins were then transported from Belgrade to Sarajevo, where they awaited the arrival of the archduke with at least four other assassins from the Black Hand.

On June 28, 1914, Franz-Ferdinand arrived to review Austro-Hungarian troops in the city. Austro-Hungarian authorities had learned that there would be an attempt on the archduke's life, but they decided that the visit should be allowed to continue. They further decided not to use troops to guard the royal visitor as Franz-Ferdinand was no favourite of Emperor Franz-Joseph, who felt that the archduke had married beneath his station. As the Graf und Stift phaeton, the first automobile produced in Austria, drove through the streets lined with spectators and at least 120 police officers, most of the assassins lost their nerve or otherwise suffered a change of heart. Cabrinovic, however, armed his bomb and threw it at the archduke's vehicle. The device exploded beneath a car full of Austrian soldiers that was following Ferdinand's. When Princip, who was farther up the street, heard the explosion, he assumed that the archduke had already been killed and left the parade route to buy a cup of coffee. Arriving safely at the scheduled stop at the city hall, Franz-Ferdinand, furious that there had been an assassination attempt, cut his speech and visit short. He then insisted on being driven to hospital to visit an officer who had been wounded in the bombing. As the driver began backing the automobile out to turn towards the hospital, Princip appeared, having hurried to the scene after learning that the bombing had been a failure. From point-blank range, Princip shot Franz-Ferdinand through the neck, severing his jugular vein. He attempted to fire again when his arm was jogged by a bystander, and his second shot inadvertently hit Sophie. The couple died within minutes. Both Princip and Cabrinovic had taken the poison that Dimitrijevic had supplied, but the doses were too small to do more than make them ill. They were arrested on the scene and stood trial, along with more than twenty others.

Most of the accused were acquitted. Princip and Cabrinovic, however, were clearly culpable, although Princip refused to plead guilty as he believed that killing Franz-Ferdinand was a just act. By law, the assassins could not be executed, as they were juveniles. They were therefore sentenced to twenty years' imprisonment each. While in jail, both Princip and Cabrinovic contracted tuberculosis and died within a few years.

The assassination had far-reaching political consequences. Austria-Hungary made unreasonable demands on Serbia, as a result of the murders, and when Serbia refused to comply the Austro-Hungarians invaded. The European powers were joined by a series of military alliances that quickly drew them into the conflict as well. Russia immediately declared war on Austria-Hungary. Germany, allied with Austria-Hungary, declared war on Russia. Britain and France, allied with Russia, declared war on Germany. From that point on, the conflict became global. Before the war ended, in 1918, ten million people had been killed and twenty million wounded. Historians believe, however, that any such disruption as the death of Franz-Ferdinand could have led to a world war, given the tensions in European politics at the time.

RESOURCE: *The Archduke and the Assassin* by Lavender Cassels (London, 1984).

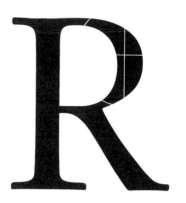

RAMÌREZ, Illich (a.k.a. Carlos, a.k.a. Carlos the Jackal, a.k.a. Cenon Clark, a.k.a. Glenn H. Gebhard, a.k.a. Andres Martinez Torres, a.k.a. Ahmed Ali Fawaz, a.k.a. Michel Khouri, a.k.a. Michel Assaf, a.k.a. Nagi Abubaker Ahmed, a.k.a. Abdurabo Ali Mohamed, a.k.a. Abdallah Barakhat) (b. 1950), attempted to assassinate Joseph Edward Seiff (1905–1982), chief executive of the British retailer Marks and Spencer and president of Joint Israel Appeal, at his London home, on December 30, 1973. Seiff's butler answered the door to a young man waving a pistol in his face and demanding to be taken to Seiff. The butler escorted the young man to the master bedroom. Seeing a man with a gun, Seiff's wife, Lois, called police. When Seiff, who was in the lavatory at the time, heard the butler calling to him, he pushed open the door. The gunman thrust his arm into the doorway and fired once, hitting Seiff in the face. The pistol then jammed, and the gunman heard the sound of sirens. By the time police arrived, however, the assailant had fled. Seiff lay on the floor. The bullet had entered his face just above the upper lip, but had been deflected by his teeth and had lodged in his jaw. Surgery was performed that evening and Seiff recovered. The gunman was Illich Ramìrez, a member of the Popular Front for the Liberation of Palestine on one of his first missions, having only recently been given the code name "Carlos."

Ramìrez was born in Venezuela, where his father, a wealthy lawyer, was a communist—which explains Illich's non-Hispanic given name as well as those of his brothers, Vladimir and Lenin. Ramìrez was a brilliant if erratic scholar who went to Moscow to study at Patrice Lumumba University, a facility run for foreign communists. Although he showed flashes of brilliance there, he was not considered a serious student, but spent the generous allowance cheques his father sent him on drink and women. Eventually he became a convert to the cause of Palestinian liberation and was expelled from Lumumba University for taking part in a protest organized by Arab students. There has been considerable speculation that the expulsion was actually a cover story and that Ramìrez had been headhunted by the KGB, which did indeed often recruit students in such a fashion. Others contend that Ramìrez would have been considered too unstable for such an opportunity. In any event, he left the Soviet Union and joined the Popular Front for the Liberation of Palestine (PFLP), a Palestinian terrorist organization led by Wadi Haddad. His attempt against Seiff had been ordered by Haddad because of Seiff's fund-raising for Israel.

Carlos was known for being cool under fire and had a knack for smuggling weapons and explosives across frontiers, taking suitcases full of weapons into European countries and stashing them with girlfriends who were above suspicion. His activities with the PFLP were mainly terrorist bombings of shops and restaurants. He was especially active in France. On June 27, 1975, in Paris, he was pointed out by an informant to two agents of the Direction de la surveillance du territoire (DST); they were about to arrest him when he escaped by shooting both the agents and the informant. During the subsequent manhunt, a reporter for the *Guardian* in Britain who had just finished reading Frederick Forsyth's 1971 thriller *The Day of the Jackal* became the first person to identify the terrorist as "Carlos the Jackal" (although the real Carlos bore little resemblance to the protagonist of the novel, a book that Carlos himself had not read at the time).

In autumn 1975, Carlos began preparations for a job that would represent the peak of his career: an attempt to kidnap every oil minister of the Organization of Petroleum Exporting Countries (OPEC). On December 21, 1975, while the OPEC ministers were meeting in Vienna, Carlos and five other PFLP members stormed the building where the meetings were taking place and quickly apprehended the dignitaries. A counteroffensive by the Austrian government failed to liberate the hostages, and Carlos warned that the ministers would be shot if another attempt was mounted. Carlos was under orders from Haddad to kill two of the ministers, Sheik Ahmed Zaki Yamani of Saudi Arabia and Jamshid Amouzegar of Iran, no matter what happened. Carlos demanded a plane to transport his team and captives out of Austria. His plan was to fly each minister back to his home country and release him after the government of each nation made an official statement endorsing Palestinian nationalism. In addition, there were demands on the Arab nations for ransom money. Although much of this negotiation was kept confidential, estimates of the total amount of the ransoms range from US$40 million to US$50 million. Austrian officials, fearing a diplomatic disaster if OPEC ministers were killed on Austrian soil, were quick to agree to the first condition. An aircraft was secured and the group was allowed to leave the country. On the journey to the Middle East, Carlos handed out autographs to the hostages. The plan was a success and Carlos wanted the world to know that he was behind it. After further negotiations with the OPEC nations, the hostages were released in Algeria. Neither Yamani nor Amouzegar was harmed.

The kidnapping made Carlos an international celebrity. From this point on, the media would attach his name to every terrorist act that could not be explained. Unsubstantiated reports on his activities became so numerous that he was reported arrested on at least three occasions and pronounced dead at least twice. At one point, three news services reported Carlos's whereabouts on three different continents. The kidnapping, however, also marks Carlos's split with the PFLP. Haddad was furious that Carlos had not killed Yamani and Amouzegar. What's more, the question of what happened to the ransom money has never been answered; Haddad denies ever receiving it, and Carlos denies keeping it for himself.

Carlos became a terrorist-for-hire. After short stays in several Arab countries, including South Yemen, where he instructed other terrorists, Carlos and a group of followers set up operations in East Germany, working with the country's notorious security force, the Stasi. Carlos would sell his services to any nation that would meet his price, one he set very high indeed. An offer made to the Libyan leader Mu'ammer Qaddafi to assassinate US president Ronald Reagan attracted interest but fell flat when Carlos demanded US$100 million and a submarine for the getaway. Nevertheless, Carlos and his small gang of mercenary terrorists did perform actions for Arab and Warsaw Pact nations as well as for organizations not aligned with governments.

In 1982, Carlos had fired a rocket launcher five times at a French nuclear power plant in a mission paid for by a Swiss environmentalist group. The reactor had one-metre-thick concrete walls and damage was minimal. When French police arrested two members of his gang, including his wife, Magdalena Kopp, Carlos sent a letter to the French interior minister threatening to go to war against France if his associates were not released. To punctuate his demands, he planned and carried out several bombings both within France and at French facilities in the Middle East. After that, French officials handled carefully the two captive terrorists who, nonetheless, were, after a swift trial (and a car bombing outside the courthouse), found guilty. They were heavily fined and sentenced to between four and five years' imprisonment each. Within days of the verdict, several French embassies and consulates in the Middle East were bombed. But Carlos's plans to break his confederates out of prison did not materialize. Neither did a scheme to kidnap the incarcerated Nazi war criminal Klaus Barbie from France and then offer him back in a prisoner exchange. Magdalena Kopp was released after three years, having shown herself a model prisoner.

From that point forward, Carlos found safe havens much scarcer. Arab nations in the Middle East were trying to better their relations with the United States, and the Americans insisted that one condition of such improvement was a pledge not to aid terrorists. In addition, the Warsaw Pact nations, which had welcomed Carlos after the OPEC kidnapping, grew tired of this unconventional Marxist and publicity seeker with a taste for high living. With the collapse of European communism in the 1990s, his group was expelled from East Germany, Hungary and Romania, leaving only a rapidly dwindling number of fiercely anti-American Islamic states as potential bases.

In 1993, Carlos was allowed into Sudan and spent a year in Khartoum, where he seemed to abandon terrorism and devote himself instead to the pursuit of pleasure. This proved an outrage to the conservative Islamic Sudanese. When French authorities finally located Carlos in Khartoum, they negotiated with the Sudanese government to permit them to kidnap Carlos and return him to France for trial. On arriving on French soil, Carlos was arrested immediately for the murder of the two DST agents. Despite the irregularity of the manner of his extradition, he was found guilty and sentenced to life imprisonment. In 2000, Ramìrez claimed he was being tortured in prison.

RESOURCE: *Jackal: The Secret Wars of Carlos the Jackal* by John Follain (London, 1998).

RAVAILLAC, François (1579–1610), committed an infamous act of regicide on May 13, 1610, by stabbing to death Henri IV of France while the king's carriage was stalled in Parisian traffic. Henri (b. 1553, reigned from 1589) bled to death in seconds from a severed aorta after Ravaillac's first attempt merely slashed the monarch across the chest. Ravaillac was an unsuccessful barrister who eked out an existence offering religious instruction to children, and his spiritual career gives insight into his mental condition at the time of the assassination. Ravaillac had once been accepted into a religious order, the Feuillants, but was asked to leave after six weeks, because he had experienced visions during his private devotions. The Jesuits later rejected him for the same reason, determining that his visions were in fact mere hallucinations. Ravaillac's motives for killing Henri were as much religious as political. He was furious not only that the king (a Protestant who had embraced Rome as a condition of assuming the throne) had done nothing to halt the spread of Protestantism across France but also that he had proclaimed the Edict of Nantes (1598), which allowed Protestants freedom of religion. What's more, Henri, in his foreign affairs, had allied France with Protestant nobles who opposed the Catholic Hapsburgs.

After the stabbing, Ravaillac made no attempt to flee, and was seized immediately. The authorities were convinced that he had accomplices, or was possibly acting in the service of the Hapsburgs. But after several days of torture, during which most of the bones in Ravaillac's legs were crushed, the assassin still insisted that he had acted alone. At his execution, his right arm (the one used to wield the knife) was plunged into burning sulphur. Pieces of his chest, arms, thighs and calves were pulled from his body by red-hot pincers. Molten lead, boiling oil, heated resin and a mixture of liquid wax and sulphur were poured into the wounds. This procedure was continued for over an hour with the wounds being cauterized to keep him alive. He was eventually tied to four horses and drawn and quartered, after which the sections of his body were torn into small pieces by an angry mob, dragged through the streets and generally defiled. Ravaillac's immediate family members were exiled and the surname was officially banned in France. Henri IV was succeeded by his nine-year-old son, Louis XIII.

RESOURCE: *L'assassinat d'Henri IV 14 Mai 1610—le problème du tyrannicide et l'affermissement de la monarchie absolue* by Roland Mounhier (Paris, 1964).

RAY, James Earl (a.k.a. Eric S. Galt, a.k.a. Ramon Sneyd, a.k.a. Paul Edward Bridgeman) (1928–1998), was the convicted assassin of the charismatic African-American civil rights leader Rev. Martin Luther King, Jr., who was killed by a rifle shot at 6:01 p.m. on April 4, 1968, as he stood on a balcony of the Lorraine Motel in Memphis, Tennessee, a city he was visiting to lend his support to a strike by municipal rubbish collectors. King long had been a target of surveillance and disinformation plots by the FBI and other police and intelligence institutions fearful of his influence and his liberalism, which was mistaken for communist ideology. For his part, Ray was a busy career-long professional thief in his native Midwest who was somehow suddenly transported to a higher and more sophisticated criminal plane. Whether the transmogrification was unassisted is the central question that remains unanswered despite a copious amount of research and many publications. Even the most strident of the anti-Ray writers, Gerald Posner, wonders how "this country boy from a poor white trash background, a petty criminal, [could] suddenly transform himself into an accomplished assassin who not only managed to get his prey, but almost got away with it?" The question is rooted in the class assumptions that afflict so much US assassination research: in this instance, the syllogism is that because Ray, a native of Alton, Illinois, came from humble redneck origins, he was precluded from being smart and clever.

What is known is that Ray was a youngish, good-looking profes-sional thief who had been jailed four times and at the time of the King killing had spent a dozen of the previous sixteen years behind bars. Yet he escaped two of the toughest prisons in the country, one before the King murder and one after. He was strictly a lone wolf and a small-timer, though prolific (he is estimated to have pulled off an average of one or two stick-ups a month). Here, on the question of his being an unaffiliated nickel-and-dime robber and not some cosmopolite and criminal master-mind, is where conspiracy in the King case begins to look plausible.

In April 1967, Ray was on the lam from the Missouri State Penitentiary and early in spring 1968 began stalking King from one public appearance to another, starting in Los Angeles and proceeding to Atlanta, where Ray began using the alias "Eric S. Galt," the name of a defence-industries worker in Toronto, a place which Ray had visited ever so briefly. He also had gone to Montreal, where, he would later claim, he met the person who drew him into a conspiracy under false pretences—the mysterious figure who, depending on the source consulted, was a Latino named Raul or a Québécois named Raoul, a person several inves-tigators claimed to have identified but none has produced.

Only an hour before Ray fired from the bathroom of a rooming house sixty metres away, King and his entourage had been having a pillow fight in the motel, which is now the site of the National Civil Rights Museum. A weapon found at the scene, a Remington .30-06, showed fingerprints that were later matched to Ray's, but the ballistics evidence became muddled, contradictory, inconclusive—and worthless. The assassin fled with seconds to spare and led the authorities on a merry chase in a manhunt that involved thirty-five hundred FBI agents, the largest number ever assembled on a single case. Ray slipped back into Toronto, renting rooms on Ossington Avenue and Dundas Street West as "Ramon Sneyd" and "Paul Edward Bridgeman" respectively. After being at large sixty-five days, he was arrested while travelling through Heathrow in Britain on his way to Portugal (intending, it is thought, to journey to Angola to work as a mercenary). He was travelling under a Canadian passport in the name of "Ramon George Sneyd," in actual fact a Toronto police officer. (The genuine Galt, Sneyd and Bridgeman were innocent Canadians who had been duped when someone made off with their identifies as part of an elaborate escape plan for Ray.)

When returned to the United States, Ray first confessed to the crime. But three days after entering a guilty plea in court, he recanted, saying that his confession had been coerced by his lawyers as a means of avoiding the death penalty. He was sentenced to ninety-nine years. Ray fought long and unsuccessfully to win a new trial, a battle in which he was joined by King's surviving family, among others. Coretta Scott King, the widow, called for establishment of a "truth commission" similar to that set up in South Africa after the end of apartheid. "No one has been brought to trial to answer for the assassination of my husband," she told the press. "This has been a source of immense frustration and pain for me personally and for our family." Their son, Dexter King, pursued his own investigation of the case and shook hands with Ray on television in 1997 while Ray was dying of cancer. The King family, who, critics contend, were manipulated by unscrupulous lawyers, came to believe that President Lyndon Johnson lay behind the conspiracy.

Contrary to press reports following his arrest, Ray had no history of racist behaviour, by the standards of his milieu. His first lawyer in the murder trial characterized him as "an old-fashioned con, respected wherever he has done time." In 1978, a committee of the House of Representatives concluded that Ray killed King but with the assistance of others. In 1993, Lloyd Jowers, who at the time of the murder operated a café on the ground floor of the rooming house from which the shot was fired, claimed that the late Memphis produce merchant Frank Liberto paid him $100,000 to arrange for King's murder but that Ray was not hired for the job. The King family sued Jowers for wrongful death, seeking only a token amount of money to make their point; Jowers lost the case and was ordered to pay $100; he died in 2000, when the US Justice Department tabled a report denying any conspiracy lay behind King's death.

RESOURCES: *The FBI and Martin Luther King, Jr.* by David J. Barrow (New York, 1981; rev. 1999); *Who Killed Martin Luther King, Jr.?: The True Story of the Alleged Assassin* by James Earl Ray and Jesse Jackson (Bethesda, Maryland, 1992; rev. 1996). Gerald Posner's *Killing the Dreamer: James Earl Ray and the Assassination of Martin Luther King, Jr.* (New York, 1998) argues that Ray acted alone in the shooting but was in a low-grade conspiracy with his two brothers, also petty criminals, in order to claim a $50,000 bounty put on King's head by a prominent Southern white supremacist, now dead; but much of his book is consumed with attacking other lawyers and previous writers in the field.

REILLY, Sidney (d. 1925), the British "ace of spies" who failed in an attempt to arrange the assassination of Lenin, was born Sigmund Rosenblum in Odessa of humble origins. As a young man he moved to Brazil and then to England, where he amassed a fortune in business and cultivated the style and élan with which he forever would be associated. At the outbreak of the First World War, when he was living in New York, he joined the Royal Flying Corps, quickly transferring to the Security Intelligence Service (MI6). He spent the next three years in Russia, for which work he was awarded the Military Cross. The assignment that would have had the greatest consequences involved his plot to assassinate Lenin. Back in London after the war, Reilly came under suspicion of being more committed to the cause of the White Russian exiles than that of the War Office. Some even suspected him of links to Soviet counter-intelligence. In 1924, he was lured back into Russia by the Soviets where he was killed by agents of the secret police.

RESOURCES: *Reilly, Ace of Spies* by Robin Bruce Lockhart (London, 1967); *Sidney Reilly: The Story of the World's Great Spy* by Michael Kettle (London, 1983); *Britain's Master Spy: The Adventures of Sidney Reilly—An Autobiography* (London, 1986).

RODRIGUEZ, Roberto Andrade (1850–1938), was not only the assassin of Don Gabriel García Moreno (1821–1875), the president of Ecuador, but also a historian, publisher and prolific writer who, although elected three times, only once chose to accept a political office; he is considered one of the great figures of Ecuadorian history. In Quito, on August 6, 1875, Moreno passed the entranceway of the presidential palace and received the salute of three guards standing by the door—one of whom plunged a sabre into Moreno's back while the other two emptied their pistols into the prone body. Moreno managed to crawl outside but died within minutes. The genuine palace guard then began firing on the attackers, one of whom, Faustino Rayo, was hit and then run through with a bayonet. The others, Manuel Cornejo Cevallos and Rodriguez, escaped.

An extraordinary example of the working-class intelligentsia, Rodriquez was one of fourteen brothers in a poor agricultural family, all of them veterans of Ecuador's Liberal Wars. By eighteen, Rodriguez was living in Quito and studying at a Jesuit school. While there, he began to read the works of Juan Montalvo (1833–1889), which inspired him to become a political activist. The Jesuits did not approve and Rodriguez was expelled, only to enroll in the Central University, where he studied law and was soon at the top of his class. In his spare time, Rodriguez joined in with a group of conspirators formed by Cevallos. When the group read Montalvo's pamphlet *La dictadura perpetua*, it decided to assassinate Moreno, who had won the presidential election by fraud. Lots were drawn to determine who would participate in the attack; Cevallos, Rodriguez and Rayo were selected. After the attack, the conspirators wandered the streets, trying to start the spontaneous uprising they were sure would follow. They shouted, "The country is free, the tyrant is dead." The army, however, was firmly in control. When the conspirators realized that the revolution had failed, their thoughts turned to survival. By September 1875, Rodriguez had fled to Colombia, where he met Montalvo. By 1876, the situation in Ecuador had changed. The new regime headed by President Ignacio de Veintemilla chose not to prosecute the assassins. Rodriguez returned and, in 1877, was elected to the assembly, but he did not take his seat as Veintemilla was persecuting leftists. Although Veintemilla was no friend of the left, he seemed to have a soft spot for the man who had cleared the way for him to seize power.

The cycle for much of the rest of Rodriguez's life would be residence in Ecuador when he felt safe from prosecution alternating with periods of exile when he felt threatened. The same year he was elected to the assembly, for example, he was arrested for his leftist writings, only to be freed quickly through the personal intervention of Veintemilla, who then advised him to leave the country, which he promptly did, working as a teacher in Montalvo's hometown of Ipiales. In 1882, he returned to join a rebel army seeking to overthrow the dictatorship and was named chief of operations. But he was forced to go back to Colombia after government forces defeated the rebels. Early in 1883, he returned to Ecuador again and founded the newspaper *El Sigo*, in which he wrote blistering attacks on the Veintemilla regime. He fled yet again, returning in summer 1883 when a national convention elected him a parliamentary deputy—until conservatives overturned the results and Rodriguez departed once more.

In 1891, while in Peru, Rodriguez was arrested by order of the Ecuadorian government, which sought to extradite him for murder. Using his legal training, Rodriguez was able to avoid extradition. Eventually, however, he was arrested in Colombia for his writings about the government there. After a few months in jail he was released and left the country. His odyssey took him through many other nations. Wherever he went, he continued to write. His 1896 book *Seis de Agosto* told the story of the Moreno assassination in detail. His novel *Pancho Villamar*, which discussed the political situation in Ecuador, received international critical acclaim. In 1927, Rodriguez travelled to Cuba, where he became co-author, with the Cuban historian Roberto Agramonte, of a biography of Moreno. In time, he moved to the United States and became an American citizen. Nonetheless he returned to Ecuador in 1930 to accept an appointment to the senate. His seven-volume history of Ecuador appeared in 1937. Many believe that the attempt to complete the work (by now he was eighty-seven) left him in a state of exhaustion from which he never recovered. He died October 31, 1938.

RESOURCE: *Gabriel García Moreno: Dictator ilustrado del Ecuador* by Julian Bautista Ruiz Rivera (Madrid, 1988).

ROSAMUND (550?–573) planned the assassination of her husband, Alboin (reigned 561–572), the king of the Lombards, on a summer's evening in 572 in what is now northern Italy. As Alboin lay sleeping, Peredeo, a servant known for his strength, entered the king's room with his sword drawn. Alboin always kept his sword at arm's reach while he slept to ward off attackers, but on this occasion Rosamund moved it. Alboin grabbed a small footstool to defend himself, but the powerful swordsman easily ran the king through, killing him instantly. Rosamund was the daughter of Cunimund, king of the Gepids. The Lombards and Gepids had been warring for generations for the spoils of the already fallen Roman Empire. But in 567, Alboin enlisted the Avars, a group of Asiatic Hunnish people, on his side. Alboin offered the Avars all of the Gepid lands and half the booty. By the end of the year, the Gepids had ceased to exist as a separate people, having been assimilated by the Avars and the Lombards.

Alboin's desires towards the Gepids seemed to revolve round Rosamund. He had offered Cunimund peace if he could marry Rosamund but Cunimund refused. After the Gepids' defeat, Alboin married Rosamund and not only had her father killed but also had the top of Cunimund's skull made into a wine vessel, from which he is supposed to have forced Rosamund to drink. This act, legend insists, lay behind her murder plan, for which she enlisted the aid of her lover Helmichis, the king's arms bearer and foster brother. But the two decided that they needed Peredeo to carry out the actual assassination. Peredeo refused to join the conspiracy until one night when Rosamund tricked him into sleeping with her by impersonating his mistress. Once Rosamund revealed her identity and threatened to tell Alboin about the tryst, knowing that Alboin would have Peredeo killed, the duped man agreed to join the conspiracy. Helmichis had hoped to succeed Alboin as king of the Lombards, but the scandal brought on by the assassination was so intense that the conspirators fled for their lives.

Rosamund and Helmichis escaped to Ravenna, where Rosamund caught the fancy of Longinus, the local prefect. Longinus urged Rosamund to kill Helmichis and marry him. She prepared a cup of poisoned wine and presented it to Helmichis. As he drank, Helmichis realized that he was already dying. Holding his dagger to her throat, he made Rosamund drain the contents of the cup, so that the two of them would die together.

RESOURCE: *Rosemunda, la regina barbara* by Lia Pierotti Cei (Milan, 1988).

RUBY, Jack (1911–1967), a Chicago native who spent his entire career in the lower echelons of organized crime, assassinated Lee Oswald (1939–1963), the supposed killer of President John F. Kennedy, in the subterranean garage of the Dallas, Texas, police headquarters at 11:21 a.m. on Sunday, November 24, 1963, in front of scores of police and journalists on the scene and uncounted millions watching live television coverage. He simply walked to police headquarters at Main and Pearl streets—where the original grey-stone building joins the newer brick one, there is a steep ramp (now bearing a sign "Pedestrians Prohibited—Do Not Enter By Ramp")—and sneaked down or was let in by an accomplice. He killed Oswald with a single bullet to the stomach.

Born Jacob Rubenstein, Ruby had family ties to organized crime. He came from a broken home and spent some of his early years in an orphanage. From childhood on, his nickname was "Sparky." He was of the generation that came of age in the 1930s, when Al Capone was no longer a physical presence in Chicago but when the criminal organization he built there still seemed all-pervasive. For the rest of his life, Ruby remained a Depression-era caricature, with slicked-back black hair parted in the centre and a deep appreciation of the industrial urban demimonde. He was a minor figure in gambling and other rackets, and in 1938 became an official of the Scrap Iron and Junk Handlers' Union, a mob-controlled union; he was also named as a suspect in the death of one of its elected officers. By turns a person of rough charm and a pugnacious one with an unpredictable temper, Ruby served as an enlisted man in the Second World War during which time he severely beat a non-commissioned officer for making an anti-Semitic remark; but at war's end was discharged honourably. In 1947, he left Chicago for Dallas, where he adopted the shortened version of his name and was unsuccessful at managing Mafia-owned night clubs and, later, striptease bars. He enjoyed the protection and friendship of Joe Civello and Joe Campisi, considered the number one and number two men in the Dallas Mafia, respectively.

By 1960, Ruby was operating the Carousel Club, a strip joint opposite the Adolphus Hotel in downtown Dallas. The Carousel was a place where local police and criminals intermingled freely. By this time, Ruby was involved in the Mafia's plotting against Fidel Castro. This conspiracy was the result of Castro's closure of the casinos in Havana. At one point, Ruby travelled to Cuba to aid Carlos Marcello, boss of the New Orleans Mafia, whom Castro had imprisoned. By spring 1963, he travelled back and forth between New Orleans and Dallas and was part of the orbit followed by Oswald and other figures involved, or suspected of involvement, in the Kennedy assassination on November 22, an event at which several eyewitnesses have placed Ruby. Numerous witnesses and authorities maintained that Oswald and Ruby were acquainted before their encounter in the police basement two days after Kennedy's death, as a handcuffed Oswald was being transported from the municipal lock-up to the county jail; certainly they had many common acquaintances. Ruby first contended that he slew Oswald to spare Kennedy's widow the ugly necessity of having to testify at Oswald's trial; later, he alluded to shooting Oswald out of fear that anti-Semites somehow would blame the president's death on Jews. Of course, suspicion that Ruby was carrying out a mob hit in order to silence Oswald has never lifted.

On November 17, 1964, Ruby was convicted of first-degree murder in Oswald's death but an appellate court overturned the conviction in 1966 on technical grounds. Before a new trial could be held, Ruby died of cancer, on January 3, 1967, protesting that he knew the full story of the Kennedy assassination but could reveal it only in a controlled environment. He spent the last years of his life in the county jail overlooking Dealey Plaza, where President Kennedy was slain. Following his death, legal questions were raised about ownership of the .38-calibre snub-nosed Colt Cobra revolver, serial number 2744LW, that Ruby had used in the killing. Courts eventually ruled that the weapon properly belonged to Ruby's younger brother. In 1992, the brother commissioned five hundred bullets to be fired from the revolver; these, each with a certificate of authenticity signed by himself, were sold at $495 to aficionados of the Kennedy assassination.

RESOURCES: *Dallas Justice: The Real Story of Jack Ruby* by Mark Lane (New York, 1964); *The Trial of Jack Ruby* by John Kaplan and Jon R. Waltz (New York, 1965); *Moment of Madness: The People vs. Jack Ruby* by Mark Lane (Chicago, 1968); *Who Was Jack Ruby?* by Mark Lane (New York, 1978); *Jack Ruby* by Garry Wills and Ovid Demares (New York, 1968); *Silencing the Lone Assassin* by John Canal (St. Paul, Minnesota, 2000); *The Jack Ruby Trial Revisited: The Diary of Jury Foreman Max Causey* ed. John Mark Dempsey (Denton, Texas, 2000).

SAGOYA Tomeo (b. 1910), a professional petty criminal and a Japanese nationalist, assassinated Prime Minister Hamaguchi Osachi (1870–1931) after Hamaguchi signed a treaty, resulting from a naval conference in London, that established Japan's strength in the Pacific at a level below that of Britain or America. Hamaguchi already had been accused of usurping the power of the emperor as supreme military and naval commander. When he went so far as to call for cutting the navy budget by nearly forty per cent, he became a marked man. In autumn 1930, Sagoya Tomeo, who had become involved with the Aikoku Sha (Patriot's Society), a nationalist group spawned by the Black Dragon Society, was dispatched to Tokyo for the sole purpose of assassinating Hamaguchi if and when ordered to do so. Sagoya spent several weeks stalking Hamaguchi throughout the city. Although Hamaguchi knew he was being followed (the fact had become common knowledge), nothing was done; the chief of police was himself a member of the Black Dragon Society. Meanwhile, as the contentious issue of naval expenditures was debated, Hamaguchi attempted to compromise, suggesting that the navy be given ¥374 million rather than ¥300 million, a figure still far short of the ¥500 million on which the nationalists insisted. Sagoya, who had been awaiting orders, was instructed to kill Hamaguchi. Sagoya spent the night in one of Tokyo's finest brothels, with the bill being paid for by an unknown benefactor. The following day, November 14, 1930, Hamaguchi was about to board a train to join the emperor in watching military manoeuvres. Sagoya caught up with him in the station and shot him once in the stomach, perforating, as was discovered later, his intestines in eight places. Hamaguchi was rushed to surgery, where fifty centimetres of intestines were removed and he was given a transfusion. The bullet had lodged itself deep in the pelvic arch, and removing it was considered too risky to attempt that day. Hamaguchi held on for months until he finally succumbed to either the wound or complications arising from several subsequent surgeries intended to remove the bullet. He died August 26,

1931. Sagoya, arrested on the scene, was freed on his own recognizance while the conspiracy against Hamaguchi was investigated. Three years passed before Sagoya was tried. On November 6, 1933, he was sentenced to death but was soon pardoned by the emperor. Sagoya spent the rest of his life being supported by unknown nationalists and giving speeches to rightist groups. Eventually he became leader of the National Protection Corps, an ultra-nationalist paramilitary group. In 1965, Sagoya appeared on a podium at a rally with fellow assassins Mikami Taku and Kōnuma Tadashi.

RESOURCE: *Japan's Imperial Conspiracy* by David Bergamini (New York, 1971).

SAKAMOTO Ryoma (1836–1867), a famous rōnin (masterless samurai) and one of the most extraordinary figures of 1860s Japan, when the nation was in turmoil, attempted to assassinate Katsu Kaishū (1823–1899), an official of the shogun. The arrival in Japan of the American naval officer Matthew Perry in 1853 was an ultimatum to the previously isolated Japanese to normalize relations with the rest of the world and open themselves to international trade or risk the consequences. Sakamoto Ryoma was in Edo when Perry's flotilla arrived. He participated in military exercises designed, unsuccessfully, to impress the Americans with Japanese military prowess. As Japanese officials began to co-operate with "the foreign barbarians," a pro-shogunate backlash led to internal strife, civil war and assassination. In 1862, Sakamoto, a Tokugawa loyalist and an adept and well-trained swordsman, decided to take up the life of a rōnin. He further determined to assassinate a pro-western official, Katsu Kaishū, who had become Japan's expert on western military technology and commander of the Dutch-built *Kanrin Maru*, the first modern warship in the Japanese navy. Although Sakamoto was impressed with the new military technology, particularly naval, he despised the fact that Katsu seemed only too willing to submit to foreigners.

In December 1862, Sakamoto and a companion arrived at Katsu's castle in Edo and burst into his quarters to inform him that he was about to die. Katsu requested that Sakamoto at least hear him out before killing him. Details of the conversation are lost, but Katsu likely declared that he too was loyal to the emperor and favoured driving out the foreigners but that what Japan needed was western-style technology to be strong in a world that would no longer leave it in peace. He might well have added that the fact that no other Asian nation opposed the West might lead to

Japan's becoming an imperial power in the region. As the discussion progressed, thoughts of killing Katsu left Sakamoto's mind; in the end, Sakamoto was brought round to Katsu's way of thinking and pledged his fidelity. When Sakamoto learned a few days later that another rōnin was coming to assassinate Katsu, he stood guard in order to prevent the killing.

Katsu Kaishū became Sakamoto Ryoma's mentor. Sakamoto recruited other rōnin to join Katsu's academy of modern seamanship in Kobe. He also became commander of the Kaientai, a fleet of mostly merchant ships that kept the residents of pro-Western Choshu Domain (modern Yamaguchi Prefecture) supplied when they were besieged by pro-Tokugawa forces. Sakamoto also began to study political science. He advocated the transferral of power from the Tokugawa shogunate to the emperor, although the emperor, he felt, should not be involved in day-to-day political affairs. A document that surfaced after Sakamoto's death calls for government by consensus. He believed the right course was a bicameral system with an upper house composed of the nobility and a lower house representing the masses. In the last year of his life, Sakamoto began a small trading company that would eventually become the Mitsubishi Corporation. His new beliefs and his prominence came at a price. On November 15, 1867, a group of rōnin recruited by the Tokugawa shogunate burst into Sakamoto's quarters in Kyoto and announced that he was about to die. They then ran him through with their swords. In 1868, the Tokugawa period came to an end and the Meiji Restoration began. Sakamoto is revered today as a pioneer in naval technology and political reform.

RESOURCE: *Ryoma: Life of a Renaissance Samurai* by Romulus Hillsborough (San Francisco, 1999).

SALAS BARRAZA, Jésus (1888–1956), assassinated Francisco ("Pancho") Villa (born Doroteo Arango) (1878–1923), the former revolutionary leader of northern Mexico. Villa was a world-famous romantic rebel. Orphaned as a small boy, he became a servant but killed his master and went on the run. He organized a small group of banditos into a large and well-disciplined army, the Division del Norte, and in 1909 joined the revolt against the dictatorship of President Porfirio Diaz, in whose overthrow he was vital, being a devoted follower of Diaz's rival, Francisco Madero, whom he helped to install in Diaz's place. Villa was a hero to

the peasantry of northern Mexico. He called for land reform, especially the breakup of large estates, and the nationalization of natural resources. When Madero was assassinated in a plot organized by Victoriano Huerta, Villa returned to the field in the civil war that followed Huerta's seizure of power. With the defeat and exile of Huerta, both Villa and his southern opposite number, Emiliano Zapata, attempted to pressure the new president, Venustiano Carranza, to give land to the peasants. Carranza, a conservative who tried to appease wealthy landowners in Mexico and the government and oil interests of the United States, refused such demands. The revolutionary armies began fighting again. Short of supplies and furious with the United States because of its support of Carranza, Villa crossed into American territory, raiding Columbus, New Mexico, on March 8, 1916; nine civilians and eight US soldiers were killed. In retaliation, Washington ordered the invasion of Mexico. Under the command of John ("Black Jack") Pershing, six thousand troops crossed the border into Mexico in pursuit of Villa, who led them on a chase that cost the US government over $100 million and engendered strong anti-American sentiment throughout Mexico. With the overthrow and assassination of Carranza in 1920, Villa negotiated a settlement with the new government. In return for disbanding his army he was granted a rancho at Canutillo, Durango, and his men were given land and a year's pay each.

Three years later, on July 20, 1923, Villa was dead, killed in his automobile as he rode with his driver and five bodyguards from his estate in Canutillo to attend a baptism. As Villa's Dodge touring car, a gift from the Mexican government, passed through the town of Parral, a man standing in the street waved his hat and shouted "Viva Villa." The cheer was a pre-arranged signal for seven gunmen to pepper the vehicle with rifle fire. Hundreds of bullets (which were later proven to be government issue) were spent, and everyone in the car was killed, with Villa himself receiving at least nine wounds. The assassins left the scene of the murder in a somewhat leisurely manner, according to eyewitnesses, stopping several times while leading their horses out of town to talk among themselves and light cigarettes. First reports indicated that Villa was killed by his own men; later ones mentioned the assassins. The commander of the local garrison, however, explained that he could not pursue the killers as he had no horses. President Alvaro Obregón was sceptical of the official version of events in Parral and sent troops to occupy Villa's ranchero, which was held by Villa supporters. A bloody skirmish seemed inevitable, and local residents wired Obregón to withdraw the troops before shooting broke out. The standoff ended when Villa's brother, Hipolito Villa, took control of the property and disbursed the Villistas.

The investigation, such as it was, revealed that the leader of the assassination plot was Jésus Salas Barraza, a representative in Durango's state legislature, who quickly admitted his role, claiming that he had killed Villa "in punishment for his many crimes." He pointed to several cases in which Villa's men had massacred local residents. Why Salas Barraza waited three years after Villa's retirement was left unexplained, as was the question of why he had never spoken out against Villa before shooting him. At first, the Mexican government refused to arrest Salas Barraza, arguing that taking into custody an official of Durango might lead to unrest there. At length, public pressure convinced the authorities to change their minds. Salas Barraza was arrested in August and sentenced to twenty years in prison. Three months later, he was pardoned, with the explanation that being confined in northern Mexico put the prisoner's life in danger from Villa's supporters. Salas Barraza went into seclusion for the rest of his life.

Until recently, accounts of the Villa assassination omitted two elements in the conspiracy: that the orders came from the Obregón government, possibly even from Obregón himself, because the administration knew that as long as Villa lived he would be a rallying point for peasant uprisings, and that the United States was at least a tacit supporter of the assassination, in revenge for the raid on Columbus, the humiliation of Pershing's campaign and the danger to American investment. With the assassination of Obregón in 1928, Villa's reputation was suspended in Mexico while rising around the world. Not until 1976 was his body exhumed from its grave in Parral and reburied at the monument to revolutionary heroes in Mexico City—his body, but not his head. In 1926, grave robbers stole Villa's head. Those responsible, as well as the head itself, were never found.

RESOURCES: *The Life and Times of Pancho Villa* by Friedrich Katz (Stanford, California, 1998); *Villa and Zapata: A Biography of the Mexican Revolution* by Frank McLynn (London, 1999).

SÁNCHEZ, Romeo Vàsquez (1937–1957), a presidential security guard in Guatemala City, assassinated his country's leader, Carlos Castillo

Armas (1915–1957), on July 27, 1957, as Armas and his wife were walking through the palace on their way to the dining room. Sánchez's weapon was his regulation-issue rifle, with which he shot twice, the second bullet severing the president's aorta, causing him to bleed to death within minutes. According to authorities on the scene, Sánchez tried to escape but was thwarted by security officials who blocked the exits. Sánchez fired twice more, both shots going wild. With no hope of escape, he turned the weapon on himself before he could be questioned. Investigators claimed to have discovered communist literature on the assassin's body, but little is known of Sánchez beyond that he was from Mazatenago and was a tailor by trade. He had been taken on as a presidential guard on June 1, 1957, after a background check revealed no political affiliations or criminal record. Indeed, few believed the government's assertions that Sánchez was part of a widespread conspiracy to restore the former president, Jacobo Arbenz, because Arbenz was a broken man living in Mexico since being deposed in a CIA-sponsored coup in 1954 and showed little sign of wishing to return to Guatemala. Authorities quickly rounded up two hundred suspects but were unable to prove a conspiracy.

Many Guatemalans hold that Sánchez was acting for Colonel Francisco Oliva, the defence minister, who quickly stepped in and imposed martial law, or for the Dominican leader Rafael Trujillo, who had supported Armas originally but showed signs of changing his views. After Trujillo's own assassination in 1961, a knowledgeable source in the Dominican Republic called the Armas case "one of those mysteries that Trujillo took with him to his grave."

Armas's military supporters attempted to control the government by offering a puppet candidate, Miguel Ortiz Passarelli, in the presidential elections that took place in October. In opposition was a former general, Miguel Ydigoras Fuentes, who had lived abroad during the Armas regime. The pilot of the plane carrying Fuentes back to Guatemala was informed by the Guatemala air controllers that a lynch mob was awaiting Fuentes. When the pilot attempted to land in El Salvador instead, Fuentes entered the cockpit with a revolver and told the pilot to put down in Guatemala or die. When the plane landed, Fuentes found only a crowd of his supporters. Fuentes won a clear plurality but the government abrogated the results. A frustrated Fuentes appealed to the United States, which persuaded the government to hold a new election and to recognize the winner. This despite the fact that the CIA did not support Fuentes and indeed donated almost $100,000 to his main opponent, José Luis Cruz Salazar. The new election, held in January 1958, gave Fuentes a majority, and he was soon confirmed as president by the Guatemalan congress.

RESOURCE: *Bitter Fruit: The Untold Story of the American Coup in Guatamala* by Stephen T. Schlesinger and Stephen Kinzer (Garden City, New York, 1983).

SAW, U (1900–1948), the former prime minister of Burma, was hanged for masterminding the assassination of Bogyoke [General] Aung San (a.k.a. Bo Teza) (1915–1947), the father of the Burmese independence movement, who, along with seven others, was gunned down in the executive council room of the Secretariat in Rangoon. The shootings, which took place virtually on the eve of Burma's independence from Britain, have perpetuated the instability and repression that have characterized the country ever since.

In August 1940, fifteen months after Britain sent out Sir Reginald Dorman-Smith to be governor general of Burma, Aung San went underground, as one of the legendary Thirty Comrades, and began training in the arts of insurgency for use against the British; another of the Thirty was U Ne Win (b. 1911). A week after their attack on Pearl Harbor, the Japanese entered Thailand and Burma. Both the Thais and the Burmese chose to co-operate with the Japanese—in the latter case, only after severe Japanese bombing raids brought some of the most influential Burmese into line. Aung San saw a Burma dominated by the Japanese as preferable to a Burma dominated by the British, and became a major general commanding the Japanese-backed Burmese Defence Force (later called the Burmese Independence Army, the Burma National Army and Patriotic Burmese Forces), a job for which he was later invested with the Order of the Rising Sun by Emperor Hirohito. With his help, or at least his non-interference, the Japanese continued their conquest of Burma, which they planned to use as a stepping stone to India. By June 1942, Aung San was warning his men "not to interfere in the administration of the country [and] to keep out of party politics." In 1943, Ne Win replaced Aung San as commander, and in August 1944, with the outcome of the war becoming all too clear, Aung San turned against the Japanese. In October, the British take-back of Burma began in earnest, and six months later Aung San helped the British effort by leading a revolt against the Japanese. The following month, the Japanese withdrew from Rangoon for good.

In March 1946, with the war over, Dorman-Smith considered having Aung San arrested for allegedly killing, early in the war, a village headman for being a British sympathizer. This threat may have helped convince Aung San that Burma should reject membership in the Commonwealth when it finally became independent. On June 10, 1947, the Constituent Assembly declared a republic. At about 10:30 p.m. on June 19, a team of gunmen barged into the cabinet room and shot to death Aung San and the others, including an unarmed eighteen-year-old Burmese police officer who had been assigned the post after two armed British soldiers had been withdrawn. The investigation revealed thirteen bullets in the body of Aung San, whose traditional rival, U Saw, was arrested for the murders one month later and tried in a proceeding that lasted 37 days. He was executed on May 8, 1948, at Insein Prison, later notorious as a place of torture by the regime of Ne Win, who led a military coup in 1962, thus establishing the present system of government. Also executed were the actual gunmen, Maung Soe, Thet Hnin, Maung Sein and Yan Gyi Aung; three accomplices and the getaway driver were meted out twenty years' imprisonment each. The remaining defendant, Ba Nyunt, U Saw's henchman, served ten and a half years after turning King's evidence. On January 4, 1948, the Republic of Burma was inaugurated.

Born in Tharrawaddy, U Saw was founder of a newspaper, the *Sun*, that championed his own far-right views and those of his party, the Myochit (Patriots). He was prime minister from September 1940 to January 1942, when he was interned in Uganda for the duration of the war, not returning until January 1947. The others killed in the attack included Aung San's elder brother, U Ba Win, who received eight bullets, and various ethnic, religious and political leaders; for in addition to negotiating independence from Britain, Aung San had negotiated peace between and among most of Burma's various ethnic groups. The set of accords sadly died with him, a fact that has shaped Burmese politics in subsequent years. The room in which the killings took place is now a Buddhist meditation centre. In 1988, Ne Win was superseded but not entirely displaced by a military junta that called for a return to the idea of multiparty elections such as had been held during the last decades of British rule. Despite the junta's preparation, and to its surprise, the voters awarded 392 of the 485 contested seats to the National League for Democracy, a coalition led by Aung San's daughter, Aung San Suu Kyi (b. 1947). The junta abrogated the results and Suu Kyi was placed under house arrest. She remains in a self-imposed internal exile, practising a form of passive resistance based on Gandhian principles. She received the Nobel Prize for Peace in 1991. She lives in Rangoon, across Inya Lake from Ne Win. From time to time, sources appear attempting to implicate the British in Aung San's death, but proof seems to be limited to the fact that U Saw procured the arms used in the killings from a renegade British arms dealer.

RESOURCES: *A Trial in Burma: The Assassination of Aung San* by Maung Maung (The Hague, 1962); *Bogyoke Aung San hne Myanma Arzanimya Lokkyan Hmungyi Atwinyemeya* by Kyin Ho (Fort Lauderdale, Florida, 1992); *Who Killed Aung San?* by Kin Oung (Bangkok, 1993, rev. 1996).

SCHAUMAN, Eugene (d. 1904), the son of a prominent Finnish senator and general public figure, assassinated N.I. Bobrikov, the Russian governor general of Finland, at Helsinki on June 16, 1904. The murder of Bobrikov, who had held office since 1898, followed one of the most controversial in a series of heavy-handed laws affecting what was then a vassal state of czarist Russia: namely, the 1901 legislation that abolished Finland's military and permitted conscription of Finnish youth into the Russian forces. Even though few were actually drafted, this measure, coming as it did after statutes intended to limit use of the Finnish language, was too much to bear for many Finns, who had rejoiced in news of Japanese victories in the Russo-Japanese War. Schauman committed suicide before he could be arrested. A note addressed to the czar was found in one of his pockets; it stated that he had acted alone in order to "convince Your Majesty that great injustice prevails in the Grand Duchy of Finland." Following Bobrikov's death, dominion over Finland was loosened, though this was owed in large measure to the distraction of the 1905–1907 revolution in Russia.

RESOURCE: *Russia under the Last Tzar: Opposition and Subversion, 1894–1917,* ed. Anna Geifman (Oxford, 1999).

SCHRANK, John (1876–1943), a former bartender living on a $25,000 inheritance, shot Theodore Roosevelt (1858–1919) on October 14, 1912, as the former US president was bringing his third-party candidacy (as leader of the Bull Moose Party) to Milwaukee, Wisconsin. Roosevelt was about to enter an automobile, headed for a rally where he was to give a speech, when Schrank produced a handgun and shot Roosevelt at close range. The bullet entered Roosevelt's chest after passing through his spectacles case and all fifty pages of the speech he was to deliver that evening. Schrank was immediately apprehended. Roosevelt was in pain, but he coughed into a handkerchief and did not see blood; this led him to conclude that the wound was superficial. Therefore he decided to proceed with the public appearance, as he believed that as soon as he entered hospital his campaign hopes would be dashed. On the drive to the hall, Roosevelt's aides became concerned as blood began to pool beneath the former president's feet. Roosevelt still refused to cancel the speech. Instead, he used the wound to his political advantage. He began his speech by showing the audience the pierced pages and by declaring, "It takes more than one bullet to kill a Bull Moose." As he continued to speak, a group of doctors tried to get him to cut short his remarks and seek medical attention. Roosevelt would have none of this, and played on the physicians' distress to gain support from the audience. As he continued to speak, Roosevelt opened his coat to show the crowd his bloody shirt. Ben Hecht was covering the speech for the Chicago *Journal* and left this account in his autobiography *A Child of the Century* (New York, 1954): "Surgical bandages wrapped the thick torso under his short cut-away coat. Teddy's voice was fainter and squeakier than I had ever heard it. He held up his hand for silence... and we gave him the auditorium. It looked as if he might topple over, if he kept standing too long." His performance was a triumph. The audience was both shocked and elated by Roosevelt's bravado. Schrank was examined to determine his sanity. His explanation for the shooting was that he had been visited in his sleep by the ghost of President William McKinley, shortly after McKinley's assassination in 1901. According to Schrank, McKinley's ghost had declared that Roosevelt, McKinley's vice-president at the time, had masterminded the killing. Schrank further revealed that McKinley had appeared to him again in 1912 and beseeched him to stop Roosevelt from seeking a third term. After this second visitation, Schrank bought a pistol and began following Roosevelt, awaiting his opportunity.

When physicians finally examined Roosevelt, they concluded that the glasses case and script had saved his life. On determining the bullet's position in Roosevelt's body they decided that the safer course was to leave the slug where it was; Roosevelt carried it in his chest until his death in 1919. Roosevelt was correct in the assumption that his injury would affect his campaign negatively. After the speech, he was forced into hospitalization, as much at his wife's urging as on the advice of his doctors. After a two-week convalescence, Roosevelt was able to give a few short speeches but his campaigning was effectively at an end. The election was won by Woodrow Wilson with 6,293,000 popular votes and 435 electoral votes (including those of Wisconsin). Roosevelt finished second with 4,200,000 popular votes and eighty-eight electoral ones, far outdistancing the incumbent, William Howard Taft, a Republican, who received 3,485,000 votes at the polls but only eight in the electoral college.

Schrank was found to be insane and was committed to an asylum for the remainder of his life. He apparently had no visits from friends or family during his entire time in custody. Those who dealt with him, however, described him as a pleasant individual who seemed perfectly normal and sane with the sole exception of his feelings towards Roosevelt. A story told of Schrank was that he had befriended the men who handled his transfer to the asylum. As they were driving to the institution, a guard remarked that the countryside they were passing through was ideal for hunting and fishing. When the guard turned to Schrank and asked him if he was a hunter, Schrank offered this reply: "I only hunt Bull Moose."

RESOURCE: *Departing Glory: Theodore Roosevelt as Ex-President* by Joseph L. Gardiner (New York, 1973).

SCHWARTZBARD, Shalom (1886–1938), the Zionist assassin of Simon Peteliura (1880–1926), the chief ataman of the short-lived independent Ukrainian Republic (1919–1920), was born in Ukraine and by the turn of the century was a member of a socialist underground organization. The independent Ukraine state was created during the civil war and general confusion in Russia following the Bolshevik Revolution of 1917. Its army was intensely anti-Semitic, taking part in 493 reported pogroms, resulting in the deaths of at least sixteen thousand Jews. When the Soviet Red Army re-annexed the Ukraine, Peteliura fled to Paris, where he lived a comfortable exile in the 1920s. Also in Paris at the same time was Schwartzbard; having fled Russia in 1906 he joined the French Foreign Legion, in which he had a distinguished career and received several commendations. In 1917, Schwartzbard had returned to the Ukraine to fight for the Bolsheviks. After witnessing the Ukrainians' persecution of the Jews, he organized Zionist self-defence groups against the Ukrainian Republican Army; disillusioned with the Russian

Revolution, he returned to Paris in 1920. By 1926, Schwartzbard had discovered Peteliura's whereabouts. On May 25 of that year he accosted Peteliura leaving a restaurant. Schwartzbard shouted to Peteliura that he was taking revenge for the Ukrainian pogroms and shot him five times, killing him instantly. Schwartzbard was arrested on the scene. On October 1, 1927, he was put on trial, during which the defence demonstrated Peteliura's responsibility for the pogroms. On October 27, Schwartzbard was found not guilty and acquitted.

RESOURCE: *Political Assassinations by Jews: A Rhetorical Device for Justice* by Nachman Ben-Yehuda (Albany, New York, 1993).

SFORZA, Caterina (1463–1509), attempted to assassinate Pope Alexander VI (1431–1503) by a then-novel method. In November 1499, Sforza, the countess of Imola and Forli in what is now Italy, faced certain defeat at the hands of an army commanded by Cesare Borgia, the pope's son. A brave woman, she had long been opposed to papal power and had fought at the head of her own troops in battle, a practise not common even among male rulers. She realized that her troops had no hope of defeating Borgia, whose reputation for ruthlessness was so great that she worried about the retribution he would exact on Imola. As Borgia's influence was due to his father, she decided that she must kill the pope. Sforza had long been interested in science, particularly chemistry to preserve her good looks, and in medicine, and she used her knowledge to design an assassination attempt that was far ahead of its time. She prepared a sealed box to transport letters to the pope asking that Cesare not invade Imola. The pleas were wrapped in the bandages of plague victims. Her reasoning was that, as only the pope would handle letters addressed to him, he would be the only one exposed to the disease. But informants at her court warned Borgia, who rode swiftly to Rome, where he found that his father had indeed read the letters but was still in good health. When Alexander heard of the attempt to infect him with plague, he immediately ordered the two messengers who had brought the letters to be quarantined; they were later burned at the stake. On November 24, during a celebration of thanksgiving that his life had been spared, Alexander warned officials that any show of support for Sforza, "the daughter of perdition," would be dealt with harshly. Imola fell before the end of the month; Forli, in December. On January 12, 1500, Caterina Sforza was taken prisoner by

French troops loyal to Borgia and imprisoned in Rome. In 1501, as a result of French intervention, she was freed. When she realized that she could not regain her lands, she retired to Florence where she devoted herself to prayer and good works. At her death in 1509, she left behind a book of her scientific and cosmetic discoveries.

RESOURCE: *Caterina Sforza, A Renaissance Virago* by Ernest Briesach (Chicago, 1967).

SINGH, Beant (1950–1984), assassinated Indian prime minister Indira Gandhi (1917–1984—no relation to Mahatma Gandhi) on October 31, 1984, while Gandhi was crossing the compound between her home and her office to meet with Peter Ustinov for a television interview. Gandhi noticed Singh, who had formerly been a bodyguard in her inner circle and travelled with her abroad several times, and turned to greet him. Singh shot Gandhi three times in the abdomen with his .38-calibre service revolver. A fellow conspirator, Satwant Singh (1963–1984—no relation to Beant, as all Sikh males are named Singh, "tiger"), then opened fire on Gandhi and her bodyguards with a Sten, emptying a 30-round clip. The two men gave themselves up immediately. Beant Singh was reported to have said, "We have done what we wanted to, now you can do what you want to." Singh was born in the Punjab village of Maloya and in 1980 joined the New Delhi Armed Police; in 1982, he was chosen to be a member of the Special Security District, an elite detachment charged with the protection of the prime minister. One reason in particular for his appointment was that he had the same type blood as Gandhi (O negative) and would be available if the PM needed an emergency transfusion. Beant Singh, however, was also a Sikh nationalist. In 1984, Sikh nationalists, under the command of Janail Singh Bhindranwale, had embarked on a terrorist campaign that culminated with the establishment of a Sikh stronghold at the Golden Temple at Amritsar, the holiest of Sikh shrines. An attack on the temple by the Indian army, known as Operation Bluestar, was a fiasco. Underestimating the size and strength of the Sikh forces within the temple, the army fought a three-day battle in which more than a hundred soldiers were killed along with nearly a thousand Sikh militants. The result was widespread rioting in which Sikhs and anti-Sikhs clashed throughout India. Sikh soldiers also mutinied, creating chaos within the Indian armed forces. One of the actions taken was to remove all Sikh security men from Mrs. Gandhi's protective squad. A cabinet minister's Sikh bodyguard had earlier hijacked a plane to protest the Golden Temple massacre. Soon afterwards, however, Indira Gandhi reinstated the Sikh guards, feeling that by showing no fear of Sikhs in her midst she could help heal the country's divisions. Meanwhile, Beant Singh and Satwant Singh, along with at least two other conspirators, were preparing for Gandhi's assassination. On the morning of October 31, 1984, Beant Singh traded shifts with another guard to be close to Mrs. Gandhi. Claiming that he had a stomach complaint and needed to be close to the lavatory, Satwant had switched with yet another guard in order to be by the gate to the compound. By 9:10 a.m., both men were in position and Mrs. Gandhi was in the courtyard. After the shooting, she was rushed to the All-India Institute of Medical Sciences Hospital. She had no signs of life, yet doctors refused to believe she was dead. She was taken to surgery where twelve doctors removed seven bullets from her body, whereupon she was placed on life support and given several units of blood. The official time of her death was given as 1:45 p.m., but it is far more likely that she had died in the courtyard that morning. Beant Singh and Satwant Singh were taken into custody immediately after the shooting. Within minutes, according to commandos who had apprehended them, the two men "attempted to escape." Beant Singh was shot and killed while Satwant Singh was shot eight times but recovered from his wounds. Satwant Singh, along with two other men including Beant Singh's uncle Kehar Singh, were hanged in January 1989.

RESOURCES: *The Great Betrayal: Assassination of Indira Gandhi* by Dilip Bobb (New Delhi, 1985); *Indira Gandhi, A Prime Minister Assassinated* by Harbhajan Singh (New Delhi, 1985).

SIRHAN, Sirhan Bishara (b. 1944), a Jerusalem-born Palestinian, spent nine years as a refugee, with his parents, after being displaced by the creation of the state of Israel in 1947. In 1957, the family immigrated to the United States from Jordan, their entry made possible by the sponsorship of a church in Pasadena, California. Sirhan's father later returned to Jordan alone. In his mid-twenties, Sirhan B. Sirhan applied to become a jockey, but the California racing commission denied him a licence. A few months later, on June 4, 1968, he waited at the Ambassador Hotel in Los Angeles, where Senator Robert Kennedy, forty-two, had established his election-night headquarters as a Democratic candidate for president in the state's primary election, running against Eugene McCarthy. At approximately 1:00 a.m. on June 5, surrounded by entertainment and sports celebrities, Kennedy made a rousing victory speech in the ballroom, ending, "So, my thanks to all of you, and it's on to Chicago [site of the national convention], and let's win there!" Kennedy then took a shortcut through the kitchen, accompanied by his entourage and the establishment's assistant maître d', enroute to the Colonial Room for a formal press conference. At 1:15 a.m., Sirhan emerged from the crowd in the kitchen and shot Kennedy twice from the rear, one bullet entering behind the right ear and lodging in the right hemisphere of the brain, the other entering the right armpit and lodging in the back of the neck. The rounds came from an eight-shot .22-calibre Iver-Johnson Cadet revolver. Before being subdued by the angry crowd (he received a broken finger and sprained ankle in the struggle), Sirhan managed to empty the weapon in a burst of gunfire that also wounded five others, none mortally. Kennedy died in hospital twenty-five and a half hours later. Vice-President Hubert Humphrey dispatched a US Air Force jet to bring Kennedy's body back to Washington, but the gesture was countermanded by President Lyndon Johnson, whose detestation of the Kennedys was as well known as theirs of him. Some witnesses claim that Sirhan shouted "Kennedy, you son of a bitch" as he fired. Notes purportedly kept by Sirhan were later seized by police from 696 East Howard Street in Pasadena, a house he shared with his mother and two brothers. These jottings indicate that Sirhan hoped to murder Kennedy on June 5, fifth anniversary of the outbreak of the Six Day War between Israel and some of its Arab neighbours. One entry reads: "Robert Kennedy must be assassinated.... My determination is becoming an unshakable obsession."

Sirhan was convicted of the murder April 17, 1969, and sentenced to death. Edward Kennedy, the victim's brother, petitioned the authorities for clemency, while Sirhan's lawyers appealed the conviction. Before the appeal could proceed, the state supreme court abolished the death penalty. On June 17, 1972, Sirhan's sentence was commuted to life imprisonment. He has been denied parole at regular intervals and remains a prisoner at the Soledad institution. In January 1970, Ralph Ginzburg's magazine *Avant Garde* polled various celebrities and intellectuals to determine who was "the most hated man in America." Not one of the respondents mentioned Lee Harvey Oswald, but Benjamin Epstein, the director of the Anti-Defamation League, suggested Sirhan, "a man who committed a heinous crime, almost an unnatural act."

RESOURCES: All standard Robert Kennedy biographies (most recently, *Robert Kennedy: His Life* by Evan Thomas [New York, 2000]) discuss Sirhan as a self-directed lone assassin, but in the alternative literature various other theories have persisted. The more important of these speculate that Sirhan was one of two shooters; that he was a virtual robot, manipulated by unknown mind-controllers; and that he was tied to SAVAK, the Iranian secret police under the Pahlavi dynasty. See also *The Killing of Robert F. Kennedy: An Investigation of Motive, Means and Opportunity* by Dan E. Moldea (New York, 1995).

SOLANAS, Valerie (1936–1988), the radical feminist who shot and seriously wounded the artist Andy Warhol in New York City on June 3, 1968, first seemed likely to be infamous for fifteen minutes, but her action brought her document, SCUM *Manifesto*, new generations of readers. SCUM was an acronym for the Society for Cutting Up Men, and the *Manifesto*, first published in 1967 by the author herself, begins: "Life in this society being, at best, an utter bore and no aspect of society being at all relevant to women, there remains to civic-minded, responsible, thrill-seeking females only to overthrow the government, eliminate the money system, institute complete automation, and destroy the male sex." Solanas, born in New Jersey, was molested by her father and beaten by her grandfather. At fifteen, she began living on her own, but graduated from high school and took an undergraduate psychology degree at the University of Maryland and later did some post-graduate work at the University of Minnesota. After her education ended, however, she travelled the country as a prostitute and panhandler before settling in New York in 1966 where she wrote a feminist play, *Up Your Ass*, which she asked Warhol to produce as a film. Warhol later told a reporter that he liked the title but feared the author was an undercover police officer; they apparently reached a verbal agreement for her to turn the play into a screenplay. Solanas then began selling mimeographed copies of her manifesto on the streets, and was approached by Maurice Girodias, the French publisher of erotica, to write a novel based on the work. In May 1967, Solanas demanded that Warhol return the script, only to be told that it had been lost or misplaced. She demanded monetary compensation. Instead, she was given small roles in two of Warhol's films.

Early in 1968 she hatched a plan to assassinate Girodias and waited for him at his hotel for three hours. Tiring, she went instead to Warhol's studio, known as the Factory—calling for Warhol a total of eight times before finding him in at about 4:15 p.m. At that point she discharged three pistol shots while he talked on the phone. The first two shots missed but the third hit Warhol in both lungs, the esophagus, the stomach, the liver and the spleen. She then fired twice at Mario Amaya (1933–1986), a curator at the Art Gallery of Ontario, who happened to be visiting, wounding him with the second shot. She tried to shoot herself in the head but the weapon jammed. Solanas left the studio, only to turn herself in to police at the 13th Precinct at 8:00 p.m., surrendering a .32-calibre automatic and a .22-calibre revolver and explaining her motive by saying that Warhol "had too much control of my life." A judge ordered Solanas detained in the Bellevue psychiatric hospital. The head of the New York chapter of the National Organization of Women called her "the first outstanding champion of women's rights."

On June 28, Solanas was indicted for attempted murder and other charges but in August was declared unfit to stand trial; this decision was later reversed, and in June 1969 she began serving a three-year prison sentence. In the period between her psychiatric detention and her prison time, Solanas threatened Warhol with further possible harm if he didn't give her money and more movie roles and use his influence to get her an appearance on a popular national TV chat show. Warhol rebuffed her demands but refused to testify against her at her trial, an action that is thought to have been a factor in her receiving so light a sentence. In September 1971, she was released from the New York State Prison for Women at Bedford, only to be arrested again in November for making threatening calls to Warhol and others. She then spent a number of years in and out of mental institutions in New York and Florida. In the late 1980s, she surfaced in San Francisco, doing drugs and working as a prostitute. She died poor and alone in a welfare hotel there. Emphysema and pneumonia were the official causes of death.

RESOURCES: SCUM *Manifesto* by Valerie Solanas (Paris, 1968), with essays by Maurice Girodias and Paul Krassner, seems to be a corrupt text and has been superseded by another edition of the same title with a postface by Freddie Baer (San Francisco and Edinburgh, 1996). Much information about Solanas can be gleaned from *The Andy Warhol Diaries*, ed. Pat Hackett (New York, 1989) and *The Life of Andy Warhol* by Victor Brockris (New York, 1989). Solanas's life and ideas have been idealized in Mary Harron's 1996 feature film *I Shot Andy Warhol*.

SOMARAMA, Talduwe (1914–1961), assassinated Solomon West Ridge-way Bandaranaike (1899–1959), Ceylon's prime minister, on September 25, 1959, while Bandaranaike was receiving guests on his verandah in Colombo. After a brief chat with the US ambassador, Bandaranaike turned towards a Buddhist monk who knelt in prayer. As the prime minister pressed his hands together in a worshipful posture, the monk, Talduwe Somarama, rose to his feet and shot Bandaranaike four times with a .45-calibre revolver. Bandaranaike fled into his house, pursued by Somarama, who continued to fire. A sentry shot Somarama in the groin, whereupon the assailant was held down until the authorities arrived to take him away.

In order to avoid hysteria among the guests, Bandaranaike insisted that he was all right. In fact, he had suffered wounds to his liver, stomach, small intestine, transverse colon, large intestine, pancreas, spleen and diaphragm and was rushed into surgery as soon as he was taken to hospital, though he insisted on issuing a statement to the press before he would allow the doctors to operate. When the doctors objected to the length of the statement he was dictating to reporters, Bandaranaike informed the surgeons, "I have always been known for making long political speeches." The surgery lasted five hours. About 2.25 litres of blood were found in the abdominal cavity and more than eleven litres were required in transfusions. The next morning, Bandaranaike was conscious and clear-headed. When his physician told him that he was doing well, Bandaranike responded, "We politicians are a tough lot." During the day he continued to accept visitors and tried to handle government business from his sickbed, but by evening his condition worsened. At 7:40 p.m., he became restless and cyanosed; five minutes later, he was dead.

Talduwe Somarama was an unusual Buddhist. Spurning the traditional diet of simple vegetarianism, he preferred rich foods, particularly pork and eggs. He also smoked cigarettes and was addicted to opium; some reported detecting alcohol on his breath. Also, unlike most Buddhist priests, Somarama was skilled in the handling of firearms. He had been born on a night of a full moon. By tradition, sons born on such nights were automatically sent into the priesthood as it was believed they were doomed to mediocrity in the secular world. Somarama was also trained as an eye doctor in the Ayurvedic system.

He entered into a conspiracy against the prime minister with a fellow priest, Mapitagama Buddharakkhita, whose motives were not religious. A former fundraiser and worker in Bandaranaike's SLEP (Sri Lanka Freedom Party), Buddharakkhita had lost a great deal of money when a shipping

ASSASSINS A TO Z

venture and a scrap-metal business foundered for lack of government contracts and he had been removed by Bandaranaike's order from the board of the Ayurvedic Hospital, the institution with which Somarama was affiliated and where Bandaranaike was a proponent of western medicine over traditional practices. There was also the matter of a series of graphic (but accurate) pamphlets outlining Buddharakkhita's affair with the health minister, Wimala Wijewardene. Bandaranaike, who had Wijewardene in his cabinet to pacify members of Buddharakkhita's faction, not only refused to attempt to ban the pamphlets but rather seemed to be amused by them.

After Somarama began to talk to police, Buddharakkhita, along with a fellow conspirator, H.P. Jaywardena, were charged in connection with Bandaranaike's murder. While the trial was being conducted, parliament met to change legislation outlawing the death penalty that had passed the year before Bandaranaike's death. Because of the wording of the new act, only the actual murderer, Somarama, could be executed. Despite this, both Buddharakkhita and Jaywardena were sentenced to death along with him, though on appeal Buddharakkhita's and Jaywardena's sentences were reduced to life imprisonment. Somarama appealed as well, on the grounds that he had committed the murder before the law was changed, but his appeal was turned down as the government had made the new capital punishment law retroactive. Somarama was executed by hanging in 1961.

RESOURCE: *The Assassination of a Prime Minister* by A.C. Alles (New York, 1986).

SOMOZA, General Anastasio (1896–1956), assassinated César Augusto Sandino (1893–1934), the famous Nicaraguan rebel leader, on February 21, 1934. Sandino had taken to the hills in the 1920s and managed to survive in spite of being outnumbered by government troops as well as the United States Marines, who had invaded the country in 1926. President Juan Bautista Sacasa invited Sandino to Managua under a flag of truce to negotiate peace. The two men dined together. Sandino's forces were encamped in the northern mountains, an area which Sandino demanded should become the semi-autonomous region of Nueva Segovia. The president was agreeable to this, but another guest at the table— Somoza, commander of the Guardia Nacional—opposed such a compromise. After dinner, when Sandino and a group of his supporters left the presidential palace, they were picked up on Somoza's orders and killed.

339

Somoza (nicknamed "Tacho") was the son of wealthy landowners. His expensive education included study at the Instituto Nacional de Oriente and also at a university in the United States where he studied economics, English and baseball. A great admirer of the United States, he worked for influential Americans in Nicaragua during the American occupation of 1926–1933. He married Salvadora Debayle, a member of one of Nicaragua's leading families and the niece of Sacasa, the leader of the Liberal Party. When Sacasa won the US-supervised election of 1932, Somoza was appointed to beef up the Guardia Nacional.

Sacasa was sincere when he invited Sandino to Managua under a flag of truce, but Somoza realized that America's needs would be better suited with Sandino out of the way. Once the American forces withdrew, relations between Somoza and Sacasa began to deteriorate, and the two became completely estranged from each other after Sandino's assassination. In 1936, using the Guardia Nacional as leverage, Somoza overthrew his patron and became president. From 1936 until 1956, he ruled Nicaragua either personally or through puppet presidents as a brutal and tyrannical dictator. On September 21, 1956, he was himself assassinated by Rigoberto Lopez, whereupon Somoza's son Luis became president. Shortly afterwards, Somoza's second son, Anastasio Somoza Jr. ("Tachito"), succeeded to the dictatorship; in 1979, he was forced to flee the country. The rebel army that brought down the Somoza dynasty was known as the Sandinistas in honour of César Sandino.

RESOURCE: *Guardians of the Dynasty: A History of the U.S.-Created Guardia Nacional and the Somoza Family* by Richard Millett (Maryknoll, New York, 1977).

SPANGLER, Edman (sometimes "Edward," familiarly "Ned") (d. 1871), was the most hapless, and the least severely punished, of those convicted of conspiring with John Wilkes Booth to kill Abraham Lincoln, the sixteenth US president, in 1865. Like a number of the others, he had long-established ties to Booth, having once done carpentry work at the Booth family's home in Maryland. Some have theorized that Booth's influence was responsible for getting Spangler his job at Ford's Theater in Washington, where he worked as a carpenter and stagehand. He slept in a livery stable in the alley behind the theatre, the same one in which Booth kept his mare, which Spangler curried for him. Spangler may have been the person who bored a peephole in the door leading to the box used by the presidential party on April 14, 1865. Certainly he had helped to decorate the box with bunting and flags earlier in the day (and hence may have been responsible for stringing the flag in which Booth caught his foot when leaping to the stage). Spangler may also have been given the task by Booth of turning off the theatre's lights at a given signal—in which case, he failed to do so, allowing many of the witnesses to identify Booth, a well-known public figure, as he fled across the stage. What's known for certain is that Spangler's assigned role was to hold open wide the stage door leading to the alley, where Booth quickly mounted his waiting horse, whose reins were held by a youth named John ("Peanuts") Burroughs, who was never charged in connection with the plot. As he performed this service for Booth, Spangler yelled, "Let him by! Let him by!," words which later seemed to prove his complicity. In any event, he was not Booth's first choice for the chore. The assassin earlier had asked an actor friend, Samuel K. Chester, to do the honours, but was refused.

Historians have depicted Spangler as a brooding individual, addicted to spirituous liquors, crab fishing and the Confederate cause. He doesn't seem particularly villainous in long retrospect. Whereas four of his fellow conspirators were hanged and three others given life sentences, Spangler was sent up for only six years, though news of the lenient treatment was withheld from him until virtually the last moment, as from his cell he heard other carpenters like himself building the gallows on which he believed that he too would die. At the dreaded Fort Jefferson, the pestiferous prison fortress about 160 kilometres off the Florida Keys in the Gulf of Mexico, he worked as a handyman and aided his fellow prisoner, Dr. Samuel Mudd, in treating those sick with yellow fever. When the three surviving conspirators at Fort Jefferson were pardoned in 1869, Spangler accompanied Dr. Mudd back to the Mudds' house in Maryland, where he spent the last year and a half of his life. Mudd lived until 1884. After their release, both made sworn statements of their innocence.

RESOURCES: *This One Mad Act: The Unknown Story of John Wilkes Booth and His Family* by Izola Forrester (Boston, 1937); *The Lincoln Murder Conspiracies* by William Hanchett (Urbana, Illinois, 1983).

STAUFFENBERG, Klaus Schenk von (1907–1944), was the most nearly

successful of the numerous people who attempted to assassinate Adolf

Hitler (1889–1945), the chancellor of Germany. On July 20, 1944, Stauffenberg, as chief-of-staff to the commander of the Nazis' reserve army, arrived for a meeting at Hitler's headquarters at Rastenburg in East Prussia. He carried with him a briefcase containing a time bomb. Stauffenberg was an excellent choice to deliver the package. He had lost his left eye, his right hand, two fingers of his left hand and part of one leg as the result of a landmine in Tunisia on April 7, 1943; the guards who normally conducted thorough searches of anyone who came into contact with Hitler let Stauffenberg pass with a minimum of frisking. When the meeting began, Stauffenberg activated the acid fuse, then excused himself to make a phone call, leaving the briefcase underneath an oaken table. A few minutes later, as Hitler was standing over the table reading maps, the bomb exploded. Four of the officers present at the meeting died in the blast. Stauffenberg, convinced that Hitler too had died, left for Berlin and the second phase of the operation, a coup that would ensure that the leadership of Germany would not be left to the Nazis. Hitler, however, had survived, though he was burned and scarred and the explosion had ruptured his eardrums and left him temporarily deaf. The fact that the building was made of wood rather than concrete had allowed much of the explosion to dissipate. Also, an officer at the meeting, Colonel Heinz Brandt, had found the briefcase to be in his way and had moved it to a point where one of the table's heavy legs was actually shielding Hitler from the worst effects of the bomb.

Klaus Schenk von Stauffenberg was born to an aristocratic Prussian family. A devout Catholic, he was described as handsome and brilliant; he was an avid horseman and sports enthusiast who also had an interest in literature and art. He joined the army in 1926 as Hitler was rising to power but, like most Prussian military officers, he was not an admirer of Hitler, whom he described as a baboon. After Kristallnacht, Stauffenberg became convinced that the Nazis were not a joke but a menace. His hatred of the Third Reich continued to grow as he saw persecution of Roman Catholics under Hitler. Nevertheless, as a loyal soldier of Germany, Stauffenberg served with distinction in the Polish and French campaigns. After seeing the effects of Nazi rule in Russia, however, he became convinced that Hitler had to be removed. Another result of his time in Russia was his conversion from liberal monarchism to socialism. After his injury by the mine, Stauffenberg was transferred to Berlin, where he was promoted to lieutenant colonel and made chief-of-staff of the reserves.

By 1944, with the war a lost cause, many German officers had come to embrace the view that Hitler had to be assassinated. To military professionals, the notion of fighting to the last man seemed absurd. Even if somehow the Nazis could have engineered victory, the result would have been a mixed blessing to Prussian officers as Hitler and the Prussian military elite were never on close terms. A rumour, which never disappeared, held that as soon as the war was over Hitler would begin a purge of the Prussian military aristocracy. After the Allied invasion of France, an underground group, including Stauffenberg, began plotting Hitler's murder.

Once the bomb went off, Berlin was plunged into a state of confusion. The reserves were mobilized to occupy the key points in the city and prevent pro-Nazi military units from regaining the government. But many leading officers who knew about the plot refused to commit themselves. They knew that a bomb had exploded, but they did not know if Hitler was dead; they knew only that they would be treated with special harshness if they rose up when Hitler was in fact still alive. The conspirators made a serious mistake of not occupying the propaganda ministry and its radio transmitter at the same time as they took over other key government and military facilities. Joseph Goebbels, a Hitler loyalist to the end, had the radio station broadcast that Hitler was still alive.

When Stauffenberg returned to Berlin he assured his contacts that he had actually seen Hitler's corpse. Stauffenberg's immediate superior, General Friedrich Fromm, was sympathetic to the conspirators but not strongly enough to risk his own neck. When Fromm refused to join the rebellion, Stauffenberg ordered his arrest. Fromm then ordered Stauffenberg's arrest in turn. When Hitler's fate was confirmed absolutely, Fromm's order was the one carried out. Although there were attempts to seize power in Paris, Vienna, Prague and Frankfurt, the rebellion was quickly put down. The attempt on Hitler's life resulted in hundreds of casualties, seven thousand arrests and two thousand executions. In addition, there were secret actions undertaken as retribution. Field Marshall Irwin Rommel, who had passively supported the attempted coup, killed himself. As for Stauffenberg, he was spared the show trial that many of the other collaborators endured. Instead he was immediately court martialled and, along with three fellow conspirators, General Friedrich Olbricht, Lieutenant Fabian Sclabrendorff and General Henning Tresckow, was executed in secret. Fromm would eventually be executed as well. Hitler and the Third Reich lasted another nine months.

RESOURCES: *Der 20 Juli 1944: Annäherung an den geschichtlichen Augenblick* by Herausgegeben von Rudiger von Voss and Gunther Neske (Augsburg, 1984); *20. Juli. Porträts des Widerstands* by Rudolf Lill and Heinrich Oberreuter (Dusseldorf, 1994).

STEINHAGEN, Ruth Anne (b. 1930), attempted to assassinate Eddie Waitkus (1919–1972), a major-league baseball player, in Chicago on June 14, 1949, when she was staying at the Edgewater Beach Hotel, the same hostelry that was playing host to Waitkus and his Philadelphia Phillies teammates. She gave a bellboy five dollars to deliver to Waitkus a note that said, in part, "it is extremely important that I see you.... We're not acquainted...please come soon. I won't take up much of your time, I promise." Shortly before midnight, Eddie Waitkus arrived at Steinhagen's room and sat in an armchair. While saying that she had a surprise for him, Steinhagen walked to a closet and withdrew a rifle and motioned Eddie towards the window, declaring, "For two years you've been bothering me and now you're going to die." She shot him once in the chest, then called the front desk to announce what she had done. Steinhagen's fascination with Waitkus began in 1946 when her brother took her to see the Chicago Cubs at Wrigley Field. She immediately became enamoured of Waitkus, a hard-hitting Cubs first baseman at the time. Over the next several months she began clipping pictures and articles about Waitkus from newspapers, and assembled a shrine to him on her bedroom wall. When she learned that Waitkus was of Lithuanian descent, she began taking Lithuanian lessons. Steinhagen was saddened when Waitkus was traded to Philadelphia, but continued to worship him, much to the distress of her family, who begged her to see a psychiatrist. Although she did visit several therapists, she could not be distracted from her idol. When family arguments about the obsession increased, Steinhagen left home, working as a stenographer/typist and saving her money.

In June 1949, she withdrew her savings and purchased a .22-calibre rifle from a pawnshop. When the Phillies came to town to play the Cubs, Steinhagen checked into their hotel. The night of the shooting she had two whisky sours and a daiquiri to steady herself for her task. Waitkus's wound was serious, the bullet having pierced his right lung and lodged near the spine; he required four surgeries to remove the slug and repair the damage. Nevertheless, he returned to the Phillies in 1950, batting

.284, and appeared in the 1950 World Series as part of the "Whiz Kids" of Philadelphia. Eddie Waitkus was awarded the distinction of being the "comeback player" of 1950, and would continue to play until 1954.

When the police arrested her for attempted murder, Steinhagen declared: "I just had to shoot somebody. Only in that way could I relieve the nervous tension I've been under the last two years. The shooting has relieved that tension." She revelled in the publicity she received, happily posing for press photographers and declaring that if freed she would probably commit another crime just to be reincarcerated. Her only disappointment was that prison authorities would not allow her to read news reports about her deed. She was diagnosed as schizophrenic and pronounced mentally unfit to stand trial. She was committed to the Kankakee State Hospital. In 1952, psychiatrists pronounced Steinhagen cured, whereupon she could have been tried in criminal court if Waitkus had agreed to press charges. Steinhagen became an occupational therapist at the same facility where she was previously a patient. The Steinhagen case was the inspiration for Bernard Malamud's novel *The Natural* (1952).

RESOURCE: *Angels' Halos Haunted: Baseball Tragedies Revisited* by Danny Gallagher (Toronto, 1998).

SULEIMAN, Said Hassan (1959–1999), one of a long line of people to attempt the assassination of Egyptian president Hosni Mubarak (b. 1928, in power since 1981), was shot to death by Mubarak's bodyguards on the afternoon of September 6, 1999, in Port Said. Mubarak was riding in a motorcade through the northern city when he was lightly wounded by Suleiman using a small knife or tool. A police statement later reported that Suleiman, a clothing vendor, was "known for impulsive behaviour and recklessness." Sources were in conflict about whether he was or ever had been a member of a militant Islamic group. The attack came one day before Mubarak spoke at a summit of the Organization of African States. While en route to another such meeting in June 1995, Mubarak's limousine was fired on by Muslim militants in Addis Ababa, the most serious of the documented attempts on his life. Another, in 1994, involved a plot by officers of the Egyptian air force to kill him with explosives. Mubarak was vice-president under Anwar Sadat and became president following Sadat's assassination in 1981, which came as a reprisal for Sadat's having signed a peace treaty with Israel two years earlier.

SURRATT, John Harrison, Jr. (a.k.a. Jack Watson) (1844-1916), was the cleverest, most complex, least severely punished and longest-lived of John Wilkes Booth's fellow conspirators accused in the death of US president Abraham Lincoln in 1865. He was also, like so many of the others, a friend of Booth, but he differed from them in being closer to Booth's own background. Surratt's father was a prosperous businessman in Prince George's County, Maryland, engaging in various enterprises. A town called Surrattsville (now Clinton) sprang up around a tavern he operated there. He was referred to locally as "the Squire." With the death of her husband in 1862, his widow, Mary E. Surratt, who was also the mother of two daughters and an elder son, decided to open a rooming house in Washington, perceiving the need for more such accommodation in a city suddenly swollen by the wartime bureaucracy.

All the Surratts were Confederate sympathizers, and John H. Surratt, Jr. became a paid Confederate courier, carrying documents and money between the Confederate secretary of state and the South's diplomatic and espionage apparatus in Canada. On April 3, 1865, the day that Richmond fell to the Union, he was en route to Montreal but had stopped in Elmira, New York, to study the feasibility of effecting a mass escape of Confederate prisoners of war being held at the latter city, near Buffalo. By then he was already a veteran of Booth's six-month-long comic opera campaign to kidnap Lincoln, further suggesting that this conspiracy, unlike the later one to assassinate, bore the sanction of the Confederate government. Surratt contended that he had broken with Booth over what he saw, correctly enough, as Booth's incompetent leadership.

On the night Lincoln was killed, Surratt claimed to be in New York again on his way to Canada. The prosecution's chief witness, Louis Weichmann, a minor clerk in the Union military who roomed at Mrs. Surratt's establishment on H Street, disputed this, claiming that Surratt was in the capital on the night in question, making last-minute preparations for the assassination; this view was later perpetuated by Lincoln's former secretaries, John G. Nicolay and John Hay, in their ten-volume life of Lincoln published in 1890: a biography that compared Lincoln favourably to Jesus but was also the first important work to deal with the assassination. Time has not proved Weichmann to have been a reliable testator in such matters. In any event, acting on Weichmann's tip, the Washington metropolitan police descended on Mrs. Surratt's boarding house looking for her son, only to be told he was out of the country; instead the police arrested Mrs. Surratt and Lewis Powell, both of whom were later hanged.

On November 24, the war department withdrew its reward for Surratt's capture, because the award was open only to US civilians and Surratt was acknowledged to have slipped out of the country. He was, predictably, in Canada, where he stayed for months, dyeing his beard, affecting spectacles and dressing in what one source calls the style of short coat then favoured by Canadians but less popular in the United States. In August 1866, he was captured on Canadian soil but made a dramatic escape, after which he is thought to have sought asylum with a succession of French Canadian priests. (The Surratts were devout Roman Catholics and the accused, who had once studied for the priesthood, was fluent in French.)

In time, Surratt departed Québec City for Liverpool by steamer, then made his way to Naples, Malta and Alexandria before appearing in Rome. American authorities were aware of his presence in each of these cities but chose merely to observe his movements. Using the name Watson, Surratt enlisted as a private, not in the pope's Swiss Guards as is often claimed (for that he would have needed to be a Swiss national as well as a Catholic), but rather in a papal zouave unit. As luck would have it, another American mercenary, with whom Surratt had been at seminary near Baltimore, recognized him and alerted the local US authorities, who carried on a long and pointless exchange with the Vatican. Long and pointless because the two entities had no extradition treaty with each other at the time and also because, with the hanging or imprisonment of seven other conspirators now complete, the United States had little wish to bring Surratt home to trial. Such action would reopen the never-healed controversy about the hanging of Mrs. Surratt by a military commission that was judge, jury and executioner all in one, even though a majority of the commissioners favoured clemency. In any event, the US Supreme Court ruled in February 1867 that civilians could not be tried by such military commissions. This meant that John Surratt, if put on trial, would be in open court in which he would be free to speak his piece: a prospect dreaded by certain personages deep within the government, according to generations of conspiracy theorists.

Publicity was forcing the government in Washington to act just as a desire to stop living on the run may have been enticing Surratt to surrender. The two impulses met when a Canadian, hoping for a reward, reported that Private Watson was on leave at Veroli, one of the communes of central Italy—far outside the papal state. Surratt was arrested and returned to Washington, where his trial lasted from June 10 to August

10, 1867. During the proceedings, the public learned for the first time of Booth's diary, which was introduced as evidence, its famous missing pages already absent. The jury was composed of four northerners and eight southerners or residents of the border states thought to be pro-southern in their sympathies. The former voted for conviction, the latter for acquittal. Unanimity could not be achieved; the jury was declared hung, and Surratt was released. In 1870, he gave a public lecture on the kidnapping plot and his part in it, but the subject was not well-received, so he abandoned hope of earning a living as a platform speaker. Instead, he worked in a series of clerking jobs, rising to become the auditor in a Baltimore shipping company. Clara Laughlin of *McClure's Magazine* sought him out for what became her important 1909 book, *The Death of Lincoln: The Study of Booth's Plot, His Deed and the Penalty*, the first full-sized work devoted to the assassination; she found his household to be one in which "the pall of tragedy [was] still heavy, stifling."

RESOURCES: *Myths after Lincoln* by Lloyd Lewis (New York, 1929, republished as *The Assassination of Lincoln: History and Myth* [Lincoln, Nebraska, 1994]); *A True History of the Assassination of Abraham Lincoln and of the Conspiracy of 1865* by Louis J. Weichmann, ed. Floyd E. Risvold (New York, 1975); *The Lincoln Murder Conspiracies* by William Hanchett (Urbana, Illinois, 1983); *April '65: Confederate Covert Action in the American Civil War* by William A. Tidwell (Kent, Ohio, 1995). *Confederate Courier* by Helen Jones Campbell (New York, 1964) is a biography of Surratt; *Booth* by the poet David Robertson (New York, 1998) is an excellent novel about Surratt.

SURRATT, Mary Elizabeth Jenkins (1820–1865), the most controversial of the defendants in the conspiracy trial that followed the assassination of US president Abraham Lincoln in 1865, was the first woman in the United States to be executed by hanging. She was born in what is now Clinton, Maryland, previously called Surrattsville after her husband, John H. Surratt, ten years her senior, whom she married in 1840. In 1851, their home was destroyed in a fire rumoured to have been set deliberately by a slave. Rather than rebuild, the Surratts opened a travellers' inn called, then as now, the Surratt House and Tavern. She inherited the property on her husband's death in 1862 and leased it to John M. Lloyd, an alcoholic former police officer, and opened a boarding house in

Washington, about twenty-five kilometres away. The boarding house, at 541 (now 604) H Street NW, between Sixth and Seventh streets, was close to the National Hotel on Sixth (where Booth lived), Herndorn House on Ninth (where some of the conspirators lived and would some-times meet) and Ford's Theater on Eleventh (the scene of the crime, where Booth often performed). When mail service between the Union and the Confederacy was suspended, the Surrattsville hotel became a safe house and pick-up point for Confederate couriers who maintained communication between officials at Richmond and the South's far-flung spies in the North and its diplomats in Canada.

One of these couriers was Mrs. Surratt's younger son, John H. Surratt, Jr. (as proved by his pay records, which survive). He was respon-sible for the decision by Louis Weichmann, a former fellow seminarian, to take lodging at his mother's establishment at $35 a month. Weichmann was a clerk in the Union war department. That Union and Confederate sympathizers should have shared a rooming house was not unusual in wartime Washington. Yet the fact that Weichmann moved in during November 1864 does seem odd timing. A little more than a week after Weichmann's move, Lincoln won re-election, meaning that all hope of ending the war by negotiation was lost, whereupon Booth began scheming to kidnap Lincoln, a plan for which he enlisted his friend John Surratt (or else had Surratt assigned to him as a handler by Confederate intelligence). Booth and Surratt had been introduced originally by Dr. Samuel Mudd. In early 1865, in the middle of his bungled abduction conspiracy, Booth was a frequent visitor to the boarding house; for two months, Mrs. Surratt testified later, he visited regularly, sometimes twice a day. Some students of the assassination contend Booth had an affair of the heart with Mrs. Surratt, others that their bond was religious in nature: Mrs. Surratt was a convert to Catholicism in a time and place when that meant being part of a despised minority, and Booth, who may or may not have made the narrow leap from Episcopalianism to Roman Catholicism, did attend mass with Mrs. Surratt. Whatever the case, the H Street address quickly became a place at which many strange characters appeared. All were friends or acquaintances of John Surratt or of Booth: people such as Lewis Powell, who turned up for the first time on March 13, 1865, calling himself the Reverend Lewis Paine, a Baptist preacher.

The conspiracy to kidnap Lincoln was taking shape and then quickly mutating into one to assassinate him instead—the latter without the approval of the Confederate government, despite the strenuous accusations of Union prosecutors later. The conspirators made use of both the Washington boarding house and the tavern in Surrattsville, even caching weapons at the latter. Mrs. Surratt's role in all of this, except for being the pro-Southern mother of a Confederate operative who worked with Booth to abduct Lincoln and who let her properties be used by conspirators, whether knowingly or not, is, at best, moot.

On April 17, the third day after the assassination, Mrs. Surratt was arrested at her boarding house and confined at the Capitol Prison (where the Supreme Court building now stands) until the end of the month. Then she was transferred to the Old Arsenal Penitentiary, where she and three males were tried in secret by a military commission. The only evidence offered against her came from two of her tenants, Louis Weichmann and John Lloyd. Weichmann testified that on the day of the assassination, Mrs. Surratt asked him to drive her to the Surrattsville tavern, where she left two packages, "things of Booth's," with Lloyd, whose own testimony did not substantially contradict the implication that she was involved in helping to set up Booth's escape route. The chief prosecutor's closing argument ran over six days. The commissioners found all four defendants guilty on June 30, 1865, but five of the officers signed a mercy plea for Mrs. Surratt, not because they doubted their verdict but rather because, like much of the society as it happened, they were horror-struck at the thought that a woman should be executed. President Andrew Johnson, who had the power to accept or refuse the commission's findings and verdict, accepted them and chose to ignore the five commissioners' plea for mercy, which was soon joined by many others. He ordered the executions to take place on July 7, at the Old Arsenal Penitentiary. Today, only one part of the prison—the part where Mrs. Surratt was incarcerated and tried—remains standing. It is known as Quarters 20, a set of residential units for officers at Fort McNair. Like the Washington boarding house and the Surrattsville tavern (both now museums), Quarters 20 is said to be haunted by the spirit of Mrs. Surratt, who has never been granted a posthumous pardon—unlike Dr. Mudd, who was pardoned by President Jimmy Carter in the 1970s.

RESOURCES: *Confederate Courier* by Helen Jones Campbell (New York, 1964); *A True History of the Assassination of Abraham Lincoln and of the Conspiracy of 1865* by Louis J. Weichmann, ed. Floyd E. Risvold (New York, 1975); *The Lincoln Murder Conspiracies* by William Hanchett

(Urbana, Illinois,1983); *Mary Surratt, An American Tragedy* by Elizabeth Steger Trindal (Gretna, Louisiana, 1996).

SUSSMAYER, Gerda (b. 1910?), was a Viennese Jew who, in March 1936, plotted one of the least successful conspiracies against the life of Adolf Hitler (1889–1945). Her plan was to shoot Hitler as he rode in triumph in an open automobile along the Johann Straussgasse, the street in which Sussmayer lived with her brother, Willi, and their tenant of a few days, the prolific English writer Robert Payne (1911–1983). (The previous year, Payne had met Hitler, who had said to him, "I very much admire the English people, and if God is willing, I hope one day to visit England.") The Nazis claimed that a majority of Austrians wished to be brought under Nazi control. To this patently false claim, Kurt von Schuschnigg, a Roman Catholic and a political scientist who was the Austrian chancellor, responded with the promise of a referendum on the question. Knowing that they would lose in the voting, the Nazis invaded; the visit by Hitler himself was intended to symbolize that Austria had become a vassal state.

Gerda Sussmayer had taken part in the unsuccessful anti-German violence of 1934 and, with her brother and perhaps as many as eighteen others, had concealed rifles, pistols and ammunition in anticipation of more such activity in the future. Payne quoted her as saying: "Of course there will be a pogrom. They are already arresting people, mostly Jews. We can't wait! [We must] kill Hitler." Such an act, she said, would mean "the end of the whole rotten Nazi swindle. The whole edifice will come crashing down, because he controls everything. He is an Austrian, and he will meet his fate in Austria." In this atmosphere, many Viennese made plans to escape. French consular officials, for example, spirited to safety the widow of Englebert Dollfuss, the Austrian chancellor assassinated by Otto Planetta in 1934. Individuals, too, were adept at exfiltration, including the Sussmayers, who, though they concocted elaborate plans for escape to Italy, knew that they were unlikely to survive their attempt on the German's life.

When the day arrived, the Sussmayers and others, including Payne, who had willingly joined the conspiracy, were thwarted when the Nazis began a house-to-house search for weapons. To keep theirs from being confiscated, the conspirators carried their guns into the streets under their coats and abandoned them in telephone boxes. Hitler passed unmolested through Vienna, riding along the Ringstrasse. In Payne's words, "He looked curiously small in the huge Mercedes-Benz, and seemed to be in a state of delirium, for he made strange fluttering salutes and his head jerked spasmodically from side to side, so that he resembled a marionette on a string." Sussmayer turned her attention to helping people known to be on Nazi death-lists to escape. A few days later, for example, she persuaded Payne to slip across the Swiss border with Ilse Schott, the leader of the Communist Youth League, posing as her husband. Gerda Sussmayer's fate is unknown.

RESOURCE: *Eyewitness: A Personal Account of a Tumultuous Decade 1937–1946* by Robert Payne (New York, 1972).

TATEKAWA Yoshitsugu (1880–1945), a Japanese agent, arranged the assassination of Chang Tso-lin (1873–1928), the Chinese warlord known as "the Old Marshal," who controlled three provinces in Manchuria. Chang was killed June 4, 1928, aboard his private train while approaching Mukden. He was aware that the Japanese were plotting his assassination, a prospect he had faced as early as 1916 when a Japanese-sponsored team attempted to eliminate him but succeeded only in killing five of his men. Chang's present plan to throw off his attackers included sending on ahead a duplicate of his private train, carrying his number-five wife, in order to draw out the conspirators. Travelling with him that day was a Japanese major, Giga Nobuya, a close friend of Japan's Prince Kanin. Chang felt that the Japanese would never attack a train carrying a Japanese officer with such impeccable connections.

What Chang did not know is that the conspirators had learned of his precautions and had devised solutions. The decoy train was allowed to pass without incident. As the target train approached the station, Giga excused himself from Chang's private salon, explaining that he needed to put his baggage in order. Giga then went to the caboose and lay on the observation deck wrapped in a blanket. Shortly afterwards, the train passed over a section of track under which a Japanese explosives expert, Komoto Daisake, had planted three large drums of blasting powder, which the train ignited, killing Chang. Giga emerged from his hiding place, walked to the front of the train where bodies were being laid out and exclaimed, "How tragic."

General Tatekawa, who was also the mastermind behind the failed attempt on Chang years earlier, was a long-time veteran of Japanese affairs on the Asian mainland. During the Russo-Japanese War in 1904–1905, he led a commando unit behind Russian lines. His exploits were immortalized in the children's book *Tekichū ōdan sambyakuri* (*Seven Hundred Miles into Enemy Territory*) by Yamanaka. Minetaro. Chang had been a thorn in the side of Japan's imperial ambitions. Although the warlord respected foreign rights in China (even supporting the claims of the Soviet Union, despite his virulent anti-communism), he was not accommodating to the Japanese, whom he had never forgiven for the attempt on his life. Accordingly, he pressed for an anti-Japanese stance by China as opposed to the more conciliatory one favoured by Chiang Kai-shek. Japanese military leaders came to believe that the conquest of Manchuria, a region contested by the Chinese and the Soviets, could be achieved only after Chang's death. The conspirators also felt that Chang's assassination would create a state of confusion in Manchuria that would allow the Japanese to proclaim to the world that its military occupation was necessary to stabilize the region.

Tatekawa took a low-level position at the Japanese embassy in Peking to provide him with a cover while he studied Chang's comings and goings. Although Chang's base was in Manchuria, he lived in Peking and regularly travelled to his headquarters in Mukden. When Tatekawa was certain of Chang's travel plans, he enlisted the help of Komoto to booby-trap the tracks.

Although neither Tatekawa nor Komoto was ever punished for killing Chang, the assassination had repercussions in Tokyo. After the explosion, the opposition parties in the Diet pressed the Tanaka government for answers concerning Japanese participation in the killing. Even the emperor insisted that the offenders be punished. The military threatened to take action if the conspirators were arrested but in the end did nothing. The shame of disobeying a direct order from the emperor caused the fall of the Tanaka government, with Tanaka himself dying in disgrace a few months later. Tatekawa Yoshitsugu would later be punished for his support of the attempted military coup in Japan on February 26, 1936. Forced to resign from the army, he moved to the diplomatic corps. In April 1941, as ambassador to the Soviet Union, he negotiated the Soviet-Japanese Neutrality Pact. As for Japanese ambitions in Manchuria, the assassination scandal precluded a military occupation in 1928, but a similar event in 1931 led to Japanese occupation.

RESOURCES: *Stilwell and the American Experience in China, 1911–1945* by Barbara W. Tuchman (New York, 1971); *Chang Tso-lin in Northeast China, 1911–1928* by Gavan McCormack (Folkestone, Kent, 1977).

TEJERA, Luis (1882–1911), assassinated Ramón Cáceres (1866–1911), president of the Dominican Republic, on November 19, 1911, as

Cáceres and his chief-of-staff Colonel Chipi Pèrez were riding to Santo Domingo in the presidential carriage. They had nearly reached the home of Don Francisco Peynado, a friend of the president's, when they were forced to stop because a farmer's wagon and an automobile were blocking the road. A group of armed men emerged from the car and began to shoot at the president. Pèrez returned their fire, striking one of the attackers, but by that time the president had been wounded mortally. Pèrez took his leader to the Peynado home, where he was met by Peynado's wife and his mother; there a second squad of assassins appeared but was driven off by the Peynado women. The Peynado quinta was next door to the American legation. Realizing that the attackers would not pursue their quarry in an American diplomatic building, the women carried him inside the compound through a hole that a machete-wielding servant cut through the fence separating the two properties. As the president was being transferred, he was heard to call out, "My mother"; he died before he could be settled in. The attackers, meanwhile, had sped away, but their car had overturned, fracturing the skull of one of the occupants. The other conspirators, realizing that they would be slowed down by their wounded comrade, left him by the side of the road and escaped to Haiti. The wounded man, Tejera, was picked up by the Guarda Nacional.

Tejera was a career military man, part of the group called "Los Carpinteros," widely admired for his courage and intelligence, particularly so by his commander, Cirilo de los Santos, through whose esteem Tejera acquired power and prestige. Tejera's popularity was enhanced when the US Navy anchored offshore at Santo Domingo with ominous intentions and Tejera immediately formed an army to face down the Americans, with hundreds of Dominican veterans joining his existing unit at Fort Ozama. Later, conflicts with Cáceres caused Tejera to plot against the president. Discovery of these activities led to the execution of Santos, but Tejera was never connected to the conspiracy. Indeed, Tejera was so trusted by the government that he was sent to New York City to sign an agreement with the Americans to consolidate the ruinous loans that had been secured by Ulises Heureaux many years earlier.

After returning home, however, Tejera began secretly plotting against Cáceres with disloyal elements within Los Recortados (the president's office). Cáceres, realizing by now that Tejera might not be entirely loyal, began slandering Tejera. The insults harmed his reputation, causing Tejera to decide that Cáceres must be killed. After the assassination, administration of the government fell to Colonel Alfredo Victoria, commander of the Guarda Nacional. Victoria sent the guard out to capture the assassins, but Tejera was the only one to be found. Victoria ordered his immediate execution without a trial. His body was then mounted on the wall of the Guardia National's barracks.

RESOURCE: *Naboth's Vineyard: The Dominican Republic 1844–1924* by Sumner Welles (Mamaroneck, New York, 1966).

TORAL, José de León (1905–1929), was a young visual artist who on July 17, 1928, shot and killed Alvaro Obregón (1880–1928), the former military leader of the Mexican Revolution who had just been elected president for the second time. Obregón was attending a luncheon in his honour in Mexico City when approached by Toral, a caricaturist who had been sketching him as well as some of the other dignitaries. Obregón's security agents allowed the young artist to show Obregón his work. As Obregón looked at the sketches, Toral produced a pistol and shot him five times in the face and body. Obregón died within seconds and Toral was arrested immediately. Although the revolutionary leaders were popular with many elements in Mexico, such as small landholders and labourers, the revolution had made a dangerous enemy in the Roman Catholic Church. Obregón was considered moderate on the question of diminishing the church's power. By contrast, his associate Plutarco Elias Calles, who followed him as president in 1924, had deported foreign-born nuns and priests, accused the bishops of treason, closed convents and Catholic schools and ordered the registration of all clergy. Obregón, however, was blamed for much of the persecution and had been the target of other assassins, whose attempts he had survived. He thus bolstered his nickname, "Lucky," which was first applied to him during the revolution (despite the fact that he lost an arm to a grenade in 1915). Toral was involved with a group of Catholics who were heavily influenced by a mystical nun known as Madre Conchita. She had recently been arrested, along with twenty-eight other nuns, but quickly released. Toral was suspected of acting against the president-elect in response to this incident, though he insisted that he had acted alone and that Conchita had neither recommended nor even known about the assassination. Nevertheless Madre Conchita was sentenced to twenty years' imprisonment as the "intellectual author" of the crime. For his part, José de León Toral was hanged on February 9, 1929.

RESOURCE: *Y la revolución volvio a San Angel* by *El Instituto Nacional de Estudios Históricos de la Revolución Mexicana* (Mexico City, 1995).

TRESCKOW, Major General Henning von (1901–1944), led an attempt

on the life of Adolf Hitler (1889–1945) on March 13, 1943, when the German chancellor visited the Russian Front to meet with senior officers of Army Group Centre under the command of Field Marshal Hans Gunther von Kluge. Tresckow had set up the visit to facilitate assassination away from familiar surroundings. Tresckow was a career officer who was at first a supporter of the Nazi movement but who, after the Night of the Long Knives and the Kristallnacht pogroms, realized that Hitler was a dangerous demagogue who had to be removed. Hitler's personal magnetism and the loyalty of the average German soldier made a successful coup seem remote; assassination appeared to be the only alternative.

The original plan was for Hitler to be shot while reviewing a cavalry regiment composed of anti-Hitler conspirators. But, though not an actual conspirator, Kluge was aware of the plan and cancelled the attack, reasoning that the war was now going badly enough to stir fatal discontent among the ranks. Therefore arrangements were made to kill Hitler with explosives smuggled aboard his plane, using special British bombs that, unlike the German equivalents, did not emit a telltale hiss. Many such bombs dropped by the British found their way intact to the Abwehr, or German intelligence, which harboured numerous anti-Hitler conspirators, including the Abwehr commander, Wilhelm Canaris. Sympathetic Abwehr agents would smuggle a bomb to Smolensk, where the attempt would be made. The bomb was disguised as a package containing two bottles of Cointreau, a brandy that came in distinctive square bottles, and given to Hitler's aide, Colonel Heinz Brandt, to deliver to a general in Berlin. Brandt took the now-activated bomb onto Hitler's plane, and the conspirators waited for news. When the plane had been in the air for over an hour with no report of a crash, the conspirators knew they had failed. After the aircraft arrived safely back in Germany, another problem arose. Brandt still had in his possession a package that if examined would lead to the arrest and execution of the conspirators. Fabian von Schlabrendorff, a field officer with Army Group Centre and one of the conspirators, flew to Berlin and informed Brandt that he had been given the wrong package; he handed him an identical-looking one that actually did contain brandy. On examining the bomb, von Schlabrendorff discovered that the detonator was defective. The same type of bomb, however, would be used again in the July 20, 1944, attempt on Hitler. Realizing that he would be arrested in the general round-up following the July 20 attempt, Tresckow committed suicide by swallowing poison.

RESOURCE: *The Secret War against Hitler* by Fabian von Schlabrendorff (New York, 1965).

TSAFENDAS, Dimitri (1918–1999), assassinated South African prime minister Hendrik F. Verwoerd (1901–1966) on September 6, 1966, using a long dagger. A lowly messenger in the South African parliament, Tsafendas was born in Mozambique, the child of a Greek father and a mixed-race mother. When his father later married a Greek woman, Dimitri was scorned by his family as a reminder of his father's past. Described as a bitter, frustrated man with few friends, Tsafendas was a drifter, travelling penniless from country to country. His life was a series of short-term work, occasional jail terms and a history of mental illness that was documented in several nations. He killed Verwoerd as the prime minister sat at his desk in his house. F.W. Waring, a member of the cabinet and a former athlete, disarmed and subdued the assassin. Four other members, who had medical backgrounds, attended to Verwoerd immediately. Within minutes Verwoerd was in an ambulance but was declared dead on arrival at hospital.

At Tsafendas's trial, psychiatrists who examined him described him as schizophrenic, mentally deranged and unbalanced. In his own testimony, Tsafendas blamed his life's misfortunes, including Verwoerd's murder, on a huge tapeworm inside him, which he also referred to as a demon, a dragon and a snake. He denied that he had taken the parliamentary job as a way to get close enough to the prime minister to kill him, and the fact that he did not buy the weapon until the day of the assassination seemed to bear this out. The prosecution and the defence were in agreement on Tsafendas's mental state and the judge halted the trial and declared him insane. Dimitri Tsafendas was committed to an asylum, where he died.

Verwoerd was succeeded by B.J. Vorster, and the policy of apartheid, of which Verwoerd was architect, continued. Verwoerd became prime minister in 1958 after first serving as native affairs minister and passed legislation disenfranchising blacks and limiting black rights to education, movement, places of residence, jobs and education. The policies made Verwoerd popular with the white minority, and the National Party was re-elected with a large plurality. Yet his assassination was not politically motivated.

RESOURCE: *Verwoerd* by Alexander Hepple (Middlesex, UK, 1967).

TSUDA Sanzō (1854–1891) was a Japanese police officer in the city of Ōtsu, in the prefecture Shiga, who, on May 11, 1891, attacked Russian Crown Prince Nicholas Alexandrovich (later Czar Nicholas II). The prince (1868–1918), who was touring Japan along with Prince George of Greece, was being guarded by a group of police, including Tsuda, who, without warning, swung a sword at the royal visitor, cutting a gash in his head down to the bone. A second blow was blocked by Prince George with his walking stick before Tsuda was apprehended by the other security men. Tsuda believed that Nicholas was reconnoitring Japan for a Russian invasion. The Japanese government expressed its regret and sorrow. Japan's home minister and foreign minister both resigned after accepting responsibility for what became known as the "Ōtsu Incident." The Russians accepted the apology and the prince recovered from his ordeal. Tsuda was charged with attempted murder and sentenced to life in prison, where he died later that year.

RESOURCE: *The Romanovs* by W. Bruce Lincoln (London, 1991).

TYRRELL, Sir James (d. 1502), a shadowy and disingenuous figure in English history and a supporter of Richard III, the last of the Yorkist kings, was ultimately beheaded but not before confessing to having assassinated "the Princes in the Tower"—the boy-king Edward V (1470–1483) and his brother Richard, Duke of York (1472–1483)—sometime in September 1483. For Richard III (1452–1485, reigned 1483–1485), eliminating the elder youngster (his twelve-year-old nephew) was partic-ularly important in order to preclude any challenge to his own usurpation of the throne. Richard is popularly supposed to have given the grisly assignment to Tyrrell (sometimes spelled Tyrell), the grandson of Sir John Tyrrell (d. 1437), who had fought at Agincourt and been Henry VI's household treasurer. Sir James (as he became, after being knighted for valour at the Battle of Tewkesbury) has long been at the centre of a heated historical controversy that continues to pit rival conspiracy theorists against one another. Tyrrell received many honours and perquisites from Richard both before and after the murders, which figure importantly in Shakespeare's *Richard III*. Indeed, Tyrrell continued to enjoy preferments, including pardons for past crimes, from Richard's successor, Henry VII, the first of the Tudor monarchs. In recent decades, fresh documents contemporaneous with Richard III and the murders have come to light, but most of our knowledge of the cloudy events surrounding the princes' imprisonment and deaths still derives from Sir Thomas More's *The History of the King Richard III*, which was written *c.* 1514–1518 and relies on personal experience and observation. In this account, Tyrrell planned the murders in detail but entrusted the actual killings to men named Miles Forrest and John Dighton. These were two of the prisoners' attendants, who, one midnight, "came into the chamber and suddenly lapped them up among the [bed]clothes, so bewrapped them and entangled them, keeping down by force the feather and pillows hard into their mouths, that within a while [they were] smothered and stifled; their breath failing, they gave up to God their innocent souls unto the joys of Heaven, leaving to the tormentors their bodies dead in the bed." In 1674 the skeletons of two persons of the appropriate ages were unearthed beneath the staircase of what had been a forebuilding of the White Tower, exactly where legend held that the corpses had been dumped; these remains now rest in Westminster Abbey, in an urn designed by Sir Christopher Wren, the architect of St. Paul's Cathedral.

RESOURCES: *The Princes in the Tower* by Alison Weir (London, 1992) is perhaps the most cautious and level-headed of the many books on the subject. Its author threads her way through the various published chronicles and arguments, with a warning: "Nearly all the narrative sources for this period have a partisan bias: most were written in the south of England and reflect anti-northern sentiment, for Richard III was identified very much with northern interests."

U

ULYANOV, Alexandr (1866–1887), conspired to assassinate Czar Alexandr III of Russia (1845–1894). Ulyanov was a prize-winning science student at the University of St. Petersburg when he became politically active as a result of observing police suppression of youth protests. He was one of the founders, and the acknowledged ringleader, of the so-called Terrorist Section of Narodnaya Volya ("the People's Will"), named after the group that had assassinated Alexandr II in 1881.

In January 1887, the cell made its decision to kill Alexandr III on March 1, the anniversary of his predecessor's death. After buying ingredients and pistols with a hundred rubles he raised by pawning a gold medal he had received for outstanding scholastic achievement, Ulyanov began making bombs, though he did not actually throw any. By day, he continued his studies in biology (his specialty was worms) while trying to manufacture explosives at night. The pistols he purchased wouldn't fire and the bombs he developed didn't explode. In any case, the plans never progressed to the point of an actual attempt on the czar. A letter from one of the conspirators found its way to the secret police, who staked out Nevsky Prospekt and eventually arrested several members of the group who were carrying suspicious packages. One of the conspirators, however, managed to conceal his bomb when arrested and attempted to set it off in the police station, only to find that it too was a dud. The arrested terrorists gave up the names of the others, and Ulyanov was apprehended. When the police failed to find a copy of the notice that the group was planning to post after Alexandr's death, Ulyanov rewrote the document from memory. He also instructed the others to assign all blame to him, as he hoped to use his trial as a means of spreading the group's message. But the trial, which lasted four days, was held in secret. Nonetheless the story of it quickly spread by word of mouth, and by the end of the proceedings Ulyanov had won the admiration and respect of the public, the judge, the prosecutors and even the czar. When Alexandr read a transcript of Ulyanov's testimony, he wrote in the margin, "This frankness is touching."

But Ulyanov refused to ask for mercy, which would have resulted in a sentence of exile to Siberia, because he felt that the strength of his message would be lost if he appeared weak. As a result, he and four others were executed in May 1887. Ulyanov's mother, who had attempted to plead for his life and also begged her son to show remorse, was devastated. No less affected was the condemned man's brother, Vladimir Ulyanov (1870–1924), then seventeen. After his brother's execution, some say, the younger Ulyanov was unable to smile or laugh again. Legend also insists that when told of his brother's death, he said, "Another way is necessary." Following his brother's arrest, Vladimir himself became politically active, and within six months was expelled from school for participating in banned demonstrations. He would continue to work for revolution throughout his life. In 1901, Vladimir Ulyanov began using the name Lenin. After the Bolshevik Revolution, the story of Alexandr Ulyanov's bravery and determination would be told and retold to children in the Soviet Union.

RESOURCES: *The Young Lenin* by Leon Trotsky (Garden City, New York, 1972); *Lenin: The Compulsive Revolutionary* by Stefan T. Possony (Chicago, 1964); *Lenin's Childhood* by Isaac Deutscher (London, 1970).

VAILLANT, Auguste (1861–1894), attempted to assassinate Jean Casimir-Périer (1847–1907), prime minister of France, on December 9, 1893, during a Saturday session of the Chamber of Deputies. From the public gallery, Vaillant threw a wooden box containing a bomb towards Casimir-Périer and his associate, Charles-Alexandre Dupuy (1851–1923). In later accounts, Vaillant claimed that a woman jostled his arm just as he was hurling his device, but this is unlikely as women and men sat in separate galleries at the time. In any case, Vaillant's bomb struck a marble pillar where it exploded and rained nails among the deputies—harmlessly for the most part, though ten persons were wounded (so slightly that only one required an overnight stay in hospital). Police seized Vaillant, a frequently unemployed furrier, before he could leave the scene.

In his youth, Vaillant was arrested several times for petty crimes, mainly theft, and served short jail terms, rarely more than thirty days. As he matured, he took an interest in radical politics, first becoming a socialist and later an anarchist. In 1887, he emigrated to Argentina, partly to seek new opportunity in the New World but also to escape his wife and daughter. In Buenos Aires, Vaillant's fortunes did not improve. After a series of petty jobs, he decided to return to France. While en route, he had an affair with a married woman, in the course of which he appropriated her husband's identification and re-entered France under the name Marchal.

By now in his thirties, living a life of near poverty while employed in a leather works, Vaillant discovered that his dislike of those more materially successful than himself had turned to hatred. He decided to vent his rage on Casimir-Périer, who was not only prime minister but also a wealthy conservative from a mine-owning family. Vaillant's bomb consisted of picric acid and prussiate of soda, separated by a piece of cotton soaked in sulfuric acid; on impact, the chemicals combined, creating the explosion. After first claiming to be Marchal, Vaillant quickly broke down and told his entire story to police, who tested his claim by recreating the bomb according to his formula and detonating it amid a pack of chained dogs. When the justice minister met with him and asked why he had tried to kill Casimir-Périer, Vaillant responded, "You are bourgeois, you would not understand."

The day after the attack, Casimir-Périer used the event to enact sweeping anti-anarchist measures. These included restrictions against newspapers, increased funding for police, legislation declaring all anarchists to be criminals and stricter laws on the possession and use of explosives: measures condemned by left-wing deputies; even those wounded in the attack found the proposals were excessive. At his trial, Vaillant's defenders claimed that he had not been trying to kill anyone but rather making a political statement and sending the prime minister a warning. Vaillant's lawyer argued that if his client had intended to kill anyone, he would have filled his box with bullets rather than nails. Vaillant was found guilty and sentenced to death. The decision caused an uproar even among moderates, while socialists took to the streets in spontaneous protest. Appeals for leniency flooded the office of President Sadi Carnot, who refused to commute the sentence. Vaillant was executed by guillotine on February 4, 1894.

In a development that completely surprised the authorities, Vaillant's funeral became an enormous affair attended by so many supporters that police were incapable of arresting everyone. Fresh flowers were laid on his grave along with a crown of thorns. Vaillant had become a martyr, and for years afterwards the anniversary of his execution was a day of protest in certain circles. Vaillant's daughter was often the guest of honour at these gatherings. Casimir-Périer's government did not long outlive Vaillant; the execution and various other draconian measures caused its fall in May 1894. Six months after Vaillant's attack, in June 1894, President Carnot was himself assassinated in Lyons by an Italian, Sante Cesario. The act resulted in widespread anti-Italian rioting in France, and Casimir-Périer succeeded Carnot as president.

RESOURCE: *Paris and the Social Revolution* by Alvan Francis Sanborn (London, 1905).

VILLAIN, Raoul (1885–1936), a rightist student, assassinated Jean Léon Jaurès (1859–1914), leader of France's socialist party, on July 31, 1914, as Jaurès was dining with some associates at a small restaurant near his office in Paris. The evening was warm and all the restaurant's windows were open, although curtains had been drawn to give the diners a certain amount of privacy. At about 9:40 p.m., Villain, holding a revolver, thrust his hand past the curtains and fired on Jaurès, striking him twice in the back of the head. Jaurès was dead by the time his head hit the table. Although Villain's first impulse was to run, he slowed to a walk after only a few steps, and within seconds was swarmed by onlookers determined to tear him apart on the spot. Police took charge, however, and quickly led him away.

A native of Reims, Villain was born to a minor official in the justice system and a mother who was committed to an asylum when her son was still a child. He studied at a Jesuit college in Reims, where he joined the Sillon, a conservative Catholic political movement frowned on by the Jesuits. He left that organization at the same time he left school, after suffering a nervous breakdown; otherwise there is no evidence of any political activity on his part.

Villain travelled extensively and later settled in Paris, where he was a schoolmaster for a time until mental instability forced him to leave the post. A patriot, Villain considered journeying to Germany to assassinate Kaiser Wilhelm II but gave up the idea as being impractical. The years leading up to the First World War were times of intense nationalism and no little hysteria about the war, which was universally regarded as inevitable. Villain read in conservative newspapers, particularly *L'Action Française*, the allegation that Jaurès, a pacifist who was trying to slow the drift into war, was disloyal to France. Socialist attempts to block conscription were particularly irksome to Villain, who decided that killing Jaurès was as patriotic an act as killing the Kaiser would have been. Purchasing a revolver, he began to stalk his prey. A few days before the shooting, Villain literally bumped into him. When Villain was arrested, he declared that his act was one of "patriotic indignation against a traitor and a coward."

The day following the assassination (August 1, 1914), Russia declared war against Germany, thus leading to the mobilization of nations aligned with one country or the other: the Great War had begun. Realizing that an impartial trial of the assassin would be impossible during wartime, the authorities held Villain without trial for the duration of the conflict. French officials believed, as did most experts, that the war would be over within a few weeks; but of course it lasted more than four years.

Not until March 1919 was Villain tried for the murder he had committed almost five years earlier. His lawyers argued that their client, who had been declared mentally unstable but fit to stand trial, had been affected by slanderous articles about Jaurès in the right-wing press. In the days before his death, Jaurès had taken a patriotic stand as he realized that, with war indeed inevitable, to argue for peace and disarmament would be detrimental to France. *L'Action Française* continued to suggest that Jaurès was in the pay of German interests long after Jaurès had abandoned his pacifist stance. The prosecution, although admitting that Villain was unbalanced and should not be executed, advocated life imprisonment; the defence argued for a shorter sentence and reminded the jury that Villain had already served almost five years in prison. The verdict surprised both sides: acquittal. In a decision that was condemned by leftist and rightist papers alike, Villain walked out of court a free man. But his notoriety made him a pariah. Unable to find a job, he was arrested several years later for passing counterfeit money. Realizing that he always would be remembered in France for killing Jaurès, he left the country and later joined the nationalists in the Spanish revolution. In 1936, in a battle near the Spanish town of Minorca, he was killed by Republican troops.

RESOURCE: *L'assassinat de Jean Jaurès* by Marcel Le Clere (Tours, 1969).

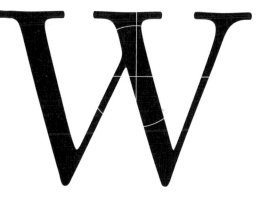

WALUS, Janusz (b. 1953), is the Polish-born South African white supremacist who assassinated Martin Thembisile ("Chris") Hani (1942–1993), the secretary-general of South Africa's Communist Party and leading anti-apartheid activist. On April 10, 1993, Hani, who had given his bodyguards the day off, drove to a local supermarket in Baksburg, an interracial suburb of Johannesburg, to pick up a newspaper. Returning home, he had just left his car when he was accosted by Walus, who shot him four times at point-blank range, killing him instantly.

Nineteen ninety-three was a transitional year between white South African rule under the National Party and full democracy for South Africa's black majority. Walus, a member of South Africa's far-right pro-apartheid Conservative Party, was apparently ordered to assassinate Hani by a party activist, Clive Derby-Lewis. After the shooting, a neighbour called police and gave them the licence plate number of Walus's car; Walus was apprehended within hours. Not only did the police find two pistols, one of which was positively identified as the weapon that had killed Hani, but also a list of prominent South Africans that included Hani, the ANC leader Nelson Mandela and the National Party leader F.W. de Klerk, as well as others who were at the time negotiating the end of white rule in South Africa.

Conspirators hoped that the death of Hani, considered the number-two man, next to Mandela, in the struggle against apartheid, as well as a favourite of South Africa's radical black youth, would set off a series of riots that would stall, or possibly end, talks on eliminating apartheid. The Conservatives even believed that if the county's unrest was severe enough, they might be able to seize power. But Hani in his last days had taken a more moderate stand on change, speaking in favour of a negotiated end to white rule. Mandela appealed for calm, and while there were isolated cases of unrest as a result of the assassination, the country did not experience the widespread rioting that the Conservatives had hoped for. In fact, the number of politically motivated killings decreased in the week following Hani's death. Some argued that Hani's assassination helped to expedite the process of negotiation: mainstream support in South Africa for majority rule increased after Hani's death. Nationalists began negotiating in earnest with the ANC. In October 1993, Nelson Mandela and F.W. de Klerk shared the Nobel Peace Prize for the relatively peaceful transition from white to majority rule in South Africa. Free elections were held for the first time in April 1994, just over a year after Hani's death. Mandela's ANC formed the first black-led government in South African history.

Walus and Derby-Lewis, who had supplied Walus with the pistols used in the assassination, were both charged with murder, but pleaded not guilty and refused to testify. Both were sentenced to death, but these sentences were later commuted to life imprisonment when the ANC abolished capital punishment. In 1999, Walus and Derby-Lewis attempted to apply for amnesty to the South African Truth and Reconciliation Commission. Walus claimed that he had been acting under direct orders from the Conservative Party and that the list police had found was a hit list supplied to him by the party—assertions that had been denied at his trial. Walus, who had fled Poland in 1981, stated that his intention was to kill Hani to prevent a communist takeover of South Africa. The commission ruled that the two men had acted alone and that they did not meet the criteria for pardon.

RESOURCES: *Anatomy of a Miracle: The End of Apartheid and the Birth of the New South Africa* by Patti Waldmeir (London, 1977); *Nelson Mandela: A Biography* by Martin Meredith (New York, 1997).

WALWORTH, Sir William (d. 1385), the lord mayor of London, assassinated Walter Tegheler or Helier, better known as Wat Tyler (d. 1381), leader of the Peasants' Revolt, in which a huge army (some estimates put its strength at more than a hundred thousand) descended on the city demanding redress. Two days later, on June 15, 1381, Tyler, supposedly protected by a flag of truce, met Richard II in Smithfield Market; he approached the king, then only fourteen, in order to vent the rebels' grievances. Accounts of what happened next vary, with some suggesting that Tyler was about to strike the young monarch and others declaring that Tyler presented new and outrageous demands, such as the confiscation of church lands. Still others, however, hold that Tyler's actions or words had no bearing on what was in any event a premeditated assassination by Walworth, possibly aided by an accomplice, Ralph Standish. In any case, Walworth, once a fishmonger's apprentice and the lord mayor since 1381, drew his dagger and struck Tyler. While Tyler was on the ground, one of the king's men ran him through with his sword, killing him.

Wat Tyler was not the rebel leader's real name. He likely had no surname, Tyler being only a description of his profession before the uprising: a tiler of roofs. Probably a native of Kent, he appeared at the head of an army of peasants, skilled tradesmen, small landowners and even some segments of the clergy. The rebellion stemmed from imposition of a poll tax, levied on everyone but beggars. Needed to help finance the Hundred Years' War, the tax was graduated, but in some regions its burden fell more heavily on the poor than in others. As the Black Death had killed an estimated third of England's population, thus reducing revenues proportionately, the new tax, levied after several years in which no taxes at all were collected, led to a spontaneous uprising. By the time the authorities in London apprehended the danger, the ragtag army was descending on the city, with Walworth and his forces holding London Bridge against the onslaught.

With Tyler's killing, the situation could have worsened but for the actions of the young Richard. With Tyler's body still on the ground, and his supporters still stunned by the betrayal, Richard rode into the crowd saying: "Sirs, will you shoot your king? I will be your chief and captain; you will have what you seek. Only follow me to the fields without." Their loyalty to the Crown thus challenged, the rebels turned and followed Richard to the fields of Clerkenwell. Soon afterwards, the peasant army dispersed, though later the king had to send troops (and Walworth) to rebel strongholds in Kent to pacify insurgents there. Walworth was knighted for killing Wat Tyler, whose head was mounted on a pole on London Bridge. Other rebel leaders were drawn and quartered. By December 1381, a general amnesty was declared for the surviving rebels. Today a statue of Walworth may be found at Fishmonger's Hall in London along with a dagger (almost certainly a fake) said to be the weapon he used.

RESOURCE: *The Peasant's Revolt of 1381*, ed. Richard Barry Dobson (London, 1970).

WANG Ching-wei (1883–1944) attempted to assassinate Prince Ch'un (1875?–1950?), prince regent to China's last emperor, Pu-Yi. In winter 1909, Wang and a group of conspirators planted dynamite under a bridge just outside the Imperial Palace in Peking, intending to detonate it as Prince Ch'un returned from a banquet. A stray dog began to bark at the conspirators, and the sound set off other stray dogs; soon the air outside the palace was filled with the sound of yelping. The noise was certain to rouse the guards, so the conspirators fled. When the authorities discovered the dynamite, they began an immediate search of the area. Wang reached a train station but made the mistake of tipping his hat to a lady. This gave him away, because, being a rebel, he had made a point of cutting off his queue, in defiance of the law that made queues mandatory for ethnic Chinese males in Manchu China. He had been wearing a false queue, and when police searching the station noticed someone with a false queue, they knew they had their man.

The son of a minor government official, Wang had excelled in his studies and was a likely candidate to enter government service himself after writing his examinations. With the Ch'ing dynasty beginning to crumble, however, the examination system was abolished. Later, Wang studied abroad, first in France, then in Japan. While in the latter country, he met Dr. Sun Yat-sen. Wang soon joined the Tung Meng Hui (United League) and became an activist for Chinese nationalism, belonging to an extreme fringe known as the Dare-to-dies, a group that believed in direct action rather than political agitation. Wang felt that the assassination of the prince regent would help to revive the spirits of the revolutionaries, who had been suffering reverses of fortune in recent months.

At his trial, Wang took full responsibility for the attempt on Prince Ch'un's life and spent most of his time denouncing the regime; his impassioned defence soon won him support not only from the public but also from the judges. Citing his youth, the court refused to order his execution but sentenced him to life in prison. In 1911, after the Nationalists under Sun Yat-sen overthrew the Ch'ing, Wang was released and offered a cabinet post in Sun's government. Wang declined the position on the grounds that the government was rife with corruption. Shortly after his release, Wang married Chen Pi-chun, the daughter of a wealthy family and, ironically, the very woman to whom he had tipped his hat. Wang was financially secure for the rest of his life.

When Sun's Kuomintang (KMT) government moved to Canton after warlords occupied Peking, Wang joined the KMT and became known as

Sun Yat-sen's "left-hand man." When Sun died, Wang was elected chair of the central executive committee of the KMT, a position regarded as that of party leader. In 1926, a split in the KMT led to the establishment of two parties: one in Nanjing led by Chiang Kai-shek, the other in Wuhan led by Wang. Later that year, Chiang and Wang met to reunite the party but with Chiang rather than Wang as head. Wang spent most of the next several years living abroad.

Although Wang was strongly anti-communist, he was considered leader of the left-leaning faction of the KMT, and even while overseas was looked on as opposition leader within the party. In 1937, when the Japanese invaded China, Wang was elected deputy leader (under Chiang) of the KMT's wartime government. After a year, however, Wang left to establish a peace movement in an attempt to negotiate a truce between China and Japan. In 1940, the Japanese named Wang head of the Japanese-sponsored regime in Nanjing. Although he tried to maintain Chinese rule in the occupied territories, Wang was instantly denounced as a traitor and a puppet of the Japanese invaders. He died in Tokyo where he was receiving medical treatment for wounds suffered at the hands of an assassin.

RESOURCE: *Duel for the Middle Kingdom: The Struggle between Chiang Kai-shek and Mao Tse-tung* by William Morwood (New York, 1968).

WEISS, Carl (1905–1935), is considered the assassin of Huey Long (1893–1935), the US senator from Louisiana and the state's former governor, a charismatic, demagogical and corrupt figure who had achieved national importance as a right-wing populist and was a likely challenger to the re-election of President Franklin D. Roosevelt in the 1936 general election. Like so many other modern political assassinations, the crime is surrounded in mystery, but Weiss does not fit the pattern of America's social-misfit assassins. He was in fact a prominent surgeon in the state capital, Baton Rouge, and a happily married man with one child. His father-in-law, Judge Benjamin Pavy, was an outspoken critic of Long, who intended to deprive him of his judgeship by the sort of redistricting tactic known in the United States as gerrymandering. Long (nicknamed "the Kingfish" after a character from a popular radio show of the time) continued to run the state's political machine even though he had ceased being governor in 1931—as witness the fact that he still worked out of the capitol building. Some believe that Long also planned to start a disinformation campaign that the Pavy family was tainted with "colored blood," a charge considered political poison in Louisiana. There is no evidence, however, that Weiss knew about any impending smears, although he was of course aware of Long's sponsorship of the anti-Pavy bill.

On September 8, 1935, Weiss attended mass and spent a pleasant Sunday with his and his wife's families. On returning home he was summoned to his hospital to confirm a tonsillectomy scheduled for the next day. He departed at about 9:00 p.m., telling his wife that he would return shortly. After a quick visit to the hospital, he drove to the capitol, where Long was working late preparing a press release criticizing Franklin Roosevelt for the deaths, in a Florida hurricane, of three members of the Civilian Conservation Corps, one of Roosevelt's New Deal public-works schemes. Weiss, who wore a white linen suit and was carrying a .32-calibre pistol he had brought back from a trip to Europe, caught up to Long in the corridor. Although Long was surrounded by bodyguards, Weiss managed to approach him and either shoot him once or merely pistol-whip him; accounts vary. In either case, Long's security responded by shooting wildly at Weiss. The bullets ricocheted freely from marble walls and floor, and it is possible that the round that struck Long in the abdomen was one fired by his own men, though the bullet, which exited through the victim's back, was never recovered. The bodyguards finally brought down Weiss, shooting him repeatedly even long after it was obvious that he was dead. Long was quickly ushered outside the building where an aide flagged down a passing car to rush him to hospital. Long, before he died, mentioned only that Weiss had hit him in the mouth. Long might have survived the attempt on his life, but he expired two days later as a result of botched surgery. No autopsy was performed. Many believe that the only surgeon in the city who might have saved Long's life was the very individual who took it. Weiss's funeral was lavish and well-attended, as he was seen as a hero by a large faction of the public.

RESOURCES: *The Day Huey Long Was Shot* by David H. Kinmon (New York, 1963); *The Huey Long Murder Case* by Herman B. Deutsche (Garden City, New York, 1963); and *The Kingfish and His Realm: The Life and Times of Huey P. Long* by William Ivy Hair (Baton Rouge, 1991).

WHELAN, Patrick James (1840?–1869), was the presumed assassin of the Irish-Canadian politician, poet and editor Thomas D'Arcy McGee

(1825–1868). McGee arrived in Montreal in 1857 to edit a radical Irish newspaper, having already performed the same work in Ireland and the United States. He became caught up in the nationalist policies of Sir John A. Macdonald, such as the protective tariffs known as the National Policy, the idea of a transcontinental railway and the notion of a Canadian confederation. He served briefly in the cabinet. McGee was anathema to the Fenian Brotherhood, who favoured Irish independence through invading Canada and holding it hostage to exchange with Britain for their homeland. Whelan was a red-headed Irish-born tailor who immigrated to Canada about 1865 and practised his trade in Montreal, Quebéc City and Ottawa. At about 2:00 a.m. on April 7, 1868, McGee was returning to his rooming house on Sparks Street in Ottawa (the location is now marked by a commemorative plaque) when some-one—Whelan, it is supposed—killed him with the latest in firearm technology, a .32-calibre Smith & Wesson Model 2 Army revolver, serial number 50847. Rumours (never substantiated) that Whelan was a Fenian led to panic in the capital, where forty suspects, including Prime Minister Macdonald's coachman, were detained. Whelan was arrested less than twenty-four hours after the crime and was charged with murder on April 9. Hearing the verdict of guilty pronounced, Whelan said, "Now I am held to be a black assassin. I never took that man's blood." Two appeals were unsuccessful, and on February 11, 1869, Whelan was executed before a crowd of five thousand: the last public hanging in Canada. Among his final words was the statement that he did "know the man who shot Mr. McGee." No one else was convicted of any part in the crime. After being lost for more than a century, Whelan's revolver surfaced on the centenary of the crime in 1968.

RESOURCES: *Trial of Patrick J. Whelan for the Murder of the Hon. Thom. D'Arcy McGee* by George Spaight (Ottawa, 1868); *Ardent Exile* by E.J. Phelan (Toronto, 1951); *The Assassination of D'Arcy McGee* by T.P. Slattery (Toronto, 1968); *"They Got To Find Mee* [sic] *Guilty Yet"* by T.P. Slattery (Toronto, 1972).

WHITE, Daniel James (1946–1985), assassinated San Francisco's mayor George R. Moscone (1930–1978) and city supervisor and gay and lesbian rights leader Harvey Milk (1930–1978) on November 10, 1978, igniting homosexual protests that surpassed those arising from the Stonewall incident in New York City in 1969, from which the present gay rights movement often dates its inception. Dan White was a former city supervisor (equivalent to alderman or city councillor in other municipalities) who arrived at City Hall with a loaded .38-calibre pistol in his pocket, climbing into the building from a cellar window as the main entrances were equipped with metal detectors. White went to the office of Moscone to demand to be reinstated to the supervisor position from which he had resigned a week earlier. When Moscone informed him that he would not be reappointed, White shot Moscone five times. From there, White walked to the office of Milk, reloading his revolver along the way. White felt that Milk was responsible for the mayor's decision; White shot Milk five times as well, putting one bullet into the brain stem from point-blank range. Both victims died instantly. White had been elected from a district that was predominantly conservative Irish-American Roman Catholic. A Vietnam War veteran and a former paratrooper, firefighter and police officer, he was as fair a reflection of his constituency as Milk was of his, which included the heart of the large gay community. At first, relations between White and Milk were cordial, even friendly; they were often featured panelists on TV news shows that attempted to present contrasting views of local issues. But when Milk refused to vote against building a psychiatric treatment centre in White's district, relations between them soured. In retaliation, White voted against Milk's gay-rights bill. White was experiencing financial difficulties, as his political position paid about half of what he had been making with the police department; his wife was compelled to find work in the fast-food industry. White was also a manic-depressive and began consuming great quantities of junk food. After sinking into despair, he resigned from office. When fellow conservatives pointed out that Moscone likely would appoint a fellow liberal to the vacancy, thus tipping the balance of power, White made the decision to try to rescind his resignation.

After the shootings, White turned himself in. Some have argued that White, as a former police officer who had shot a supervisor considered hostile to police interests, was treated with special consideration by the authorities. His taped confession was conducted in such a way as to present him as a sympathetic figure, a depiction that worked to his advantage at his trial. White's lawyers pointed out that junk-food binges could have changed White's body chemistry to a point where, combined with his serious depression, he no longer was fully responsible for his actions. This tactic became known as "the Twinkie defence," after a certain cream-filled American pastry. Using the California statutes of diminished responsibility, the jury, which overrepresented Roman Catholics and included no gays or lesbians, found White innocent of murder but guilty of voluntary manslaughter. He was sentenced to the maximum term of seven years and eight months, of which he served five years and one month before being paroled. On October 21, 1985, he committed suicide by asphyxiating himself in his automobile.

RESOURCES: *The Mayor of Castro Street: The Life and Times of Harvey Milk* by Randy Shilts (New York, 1982); *Gay by the Bay: A History of Queer Culture in the San Francisco Bay Area* by Susan Stryker and James Van Buskirk (San Francisco, 1996). Rob Epstein's film *The Life and Times of Harvey Milk* (1984) also did much to make permanent the legacy of Milk (who is also the subject of an opera, for example).

YAMAGUCHI Otoya (1943–1960) was a seventeen-year-old student and son of an army colonel when he stabbed Japanese Socialist Party leader Asanuma Inejiro on October 12, 1960. Yamaguchi was a member of the ultra-rightist group the Greater Japan Patriotic Party. He had been arrested previously for numerous acts of violence relating to his political activities. Asanuma, known to his supporters as "the human locomotive" on account of his boundless energy and physical stature (he weighed about a hundred kilos), and to his opponents as "the man whose body is too large for his brain," was taking part in a televised election debate in front of a live audience of about three thousand people. As he was speaking, he was heavily heckled by a group of rightist students. Suddenly Yamaguchi burst onto the stage from the wings. Shouting incoherently, he stabbed Asanuma twice in the chest with a short Samurai sword which he had taken from his father. Asanuma died en route to hospital. Yamaguchi was immediately captured by aides from all three political parties (Socialist, Democratic Socialist and the ruling Liberal Democratic). At the time, political experts felt that the assassination could have an adverse effect on the ruling Liberal Democrats as the most right-wing of the major parties as well as create sympathy for the Socialists. But the Liberal Democrats were re-elected with only a small loss of seats. As a minor, Yamaguchi was remanded to the Tokyo family court, which ruled that he should be tried as an adult. Yamaguchi stated that he had acted alone. He further revealed that he had been planning the attack for six months and was also planning to kill the leader of the Communist Party, Sanzo Nozaka, as he felt that Sanzo and Asanuma were intending to establish a communist government. On November 2, 1960, Yamaguchi hanged himself in his cell at the Juvenile Detention Home. Written on the wall, in toothpaste, was the message "To serve one's country for seven lives, 10,000 years to the Emperor."

RESOURCE: *Ningen Kikansha–Asanuma Inejiro* by Toyoda Jo (Tokyo, 1991).

YOUSSOUPOV, Prince Felix (1887–1967), assassinated Grigory Yefimovich Rasputin (1872?–1916), monk, healer, mystic and favourite of Czarina Alexandra of Russia. At midnight December 29/30, 1916, Prince Youssoupov arrived at Rasputin's to take him across St. Petersburg to his own home. Youssoupov informed Rasputin that the visit must take place at such a late hour because they must wait until Youssoupov's father, who hated the monk, was asleep. On arriving, the prince led Rasputin to a room in the cellar. "Yankee Doodle" was playing on a gramophone upstairs, where, Youssoupov explained, his wife was entertaining some guests but would be joining them shortly. Some have suggested that Youssoupov was using his attractive wife as a lure to entice Rasputin, who was well-known for his sexual escapades. But later, when a movie on Rasputin's assassination suggested this possibility, Youssoupov sued the producers to protect his wife's honour. In fact, Youssoupov's wife was not at home that night: the gramophone was playing to drown out any noises below. Youssoupov poured wine and offered Rasputin some chocolate cakes. Both the wine and cakes were laced with potassium cyanide, as were the wine glasses. Rasputin, although not fond of cake, was persuaded to eat some. The wine, of which Rasputin was more than ordinarily fond, he consumed with less prodding. Rasputin is reputed to have ingested several times the fatal dose of cyanide with no effects whatever, except for a burning sensation in the throat: he suffered from dyspepsia, which prevented his stomach from secreting the hydrochloric acid that would have activated the poison. After resting for a time, Rasputin, noticing a guitar in a corner of the room, requested that Youssoupov play and sing for him. Youssoupov, now petrified, did so, but then excused himself and went upstairs to consult with his fellow conspirators. Realizing that the assassination must take place even though the poison had failed, one of the other conspirators gave Youssoupov his Browning pistol and sent him back downstairs. Fearing the monk's supposed mystical powers, Youssoupov tried to trick him into making the sign of a cross, an act he felt would negate his evil powers. Youssoupov directed Rasputin's attention to an ornate crystal crucifix. As Rasputin turned to look at it, Youssoupov revealed the pistol and told Rasputin to cross himself as he was about to die. The prince fired and the monk screamed and fell to the floor.

When the other conspirators heard the shot they raced down. Dr. Stanislaus Lazovert, who had prepared the poison, examined the body and declared Rasputin dead. The conspirators then went upstairs to celebrate their deed. One of them left Youssoupov's in Rasputin's coat and boots, impersonating the victim. A few minutes later, Youssoupov, returning to the cellar, saw Rasputin's motionless form, and began kicking and pummelling the corpse. Suddenly, Rasputin opened his eyes and attacked Youssoupov, ripping one of the epaulets from the prince's tunic. Youssoupov ran upstairs and Rasputin followed, crawling on all fours and roaring like a wounded animal. The prince burst into the room where the other conspirators were still celebrating and told them that Rasputin was alive and was trying to escape. By this time, Rasputin had dragged himself out the front door into the snow-covered courtyard. Vladimir Purishkevich, another of the conspirators, fired four shots from a revolver, two of them missing but one hitting Rasputin in the back and the other in the head. Purishkevich found two soldiers sympathetic to the conspiracy and ordered them to take Rasputin's body back to the cellar. To explain the gunfire and blood in the courtyard, a dog was shot. When the monk's remains were once again indoors, Youssoupov took a steel club and beat the body about the face and chest. The soldiers then wrapped Rasputin in a heavy blue curtain tied with ropes. The body was taken to the Neva and dumped in the icy water.

Youssoupov had been a spoiled, sickly child who distressed physicians with his susceptibility to disease; the nurses and governesses who took care of him seem to have become either alcoholics or inmates of asylums. Youssoupov was sent to the Goureievich Secondary School in St. Petersburg, a common choice for unruly sons of Russian nobility. By eighteen, Youssoupov's existence was little more than an endless spree of whoring and drinking with one unusual diversion: from an early age, he displayed an interest in transvestitism, sometimes going out for an evening with his brother Nicholas while dressed as a woman. The prince's escapades reached their peak when he was hired by the Aquarium Club in St. Petersburg as a female vocalist, but his parents ended his career there after one of the club's patrons recognized some of Youssoupov's mother's jewellery. Youssoupov continued to dress as a woman whenever he was away from Russia. While so attired in Paris, he attracted the attention of Edward Prince of Wales.

After the death of his older brother in a duel in 1908, Felix Youssoupov inherited the immense wealth of the Youssoupov family, and he married and attempted to produce an heir. He was on his honeymoon in Berlin when the First World War erupted; only the intervention of Spanish diplomats prevented him from being interned in Germany for the duration. Once home, Youssoupov converted the ground floor of his mansion into a hospital for wounded soldiers. He had no desire to actually enter the war himself, so he enrolled in officers' school and consistently failed his examinations in order to avoid being commissioned.

By this time, Rasputin already was an influential figure at court. While wandering men of God were a familiar feature of Russian culture, and were often the guests of aristocrats seeking novelty, Rasputin was different. His charisma was legendary. Upper-class women were enthralled by his personal magnetism and begged his sexual favours; men sought him out for religious and personal advice. In 1905, Rasputin was presented to Nicholas II and Alexandra. Although he seemed not to have created a deep impression on the czar, he had a strong effect on the czarina.

Nicholas and Alexandra had four daughters before a son was born, but their joy soon turned to dismay when their son was diagnosed as a hemophiliac. Any cut or even a simple bump was dangerous. When the czarevich bled, the Romanov court would sink into despair. Rasputin, however, had the ability to make the bleeding stop, though there is no reason to believe that he possessed medical knowledge but only superficial training in hypnosis. To Alexandra, the explanation for her son's cure was that Rasputin was born with the ability to perform miracles. Although it was commonly believed that Rasputin was regularly consulted on matters of state, an assertion of which he boasted many times, his influence lay less with the czar than with the czar's wife, and then only in matters pertaining to their son, Alexi. The belief that Rasputin had too much power was nonetheless the cause of his assassination.

During the First World War, Russia suffered both at home and abroad. At home, the czar and czarina's insistence that the monarchy be absolute led to rebellion; in the field, Russian offensives against Germany and Austria-Hungary led to nothing but appalling casualties. One did not need mystical powers to see that the Romanov dynasty was in peril. Among the nobility, the blame for Russia's misfortunes was laid at Rasputin's door. The assassins felt themselves patriots who were trying to save the czar. Rasputin was also widely believed to be either an agent of Germany or in the pay of others who were. In the case of Felix Youssoupov, however, killing Rasputin had a more personal element. Youssoupov's father had been governor general of Moscow. When anti-German riots broke out against the czarina and her sister the Grand Duchess Elizabeth (both German-born), the elder Youssoupov was blamed for failing to keep order in the city. When confronted by the czar, the senior Youssoupov used the opportunity to criticize Rasputin and his alleged influence in the czar's decisions and was fired on the spot—a disgrace to the Youssoupov family.

Felix Youssoupov decided to try to ingratiate himself with Rasputin, to gain his confidence, in order to make killing him easier. He consulted Rasputin professionally, getting the monk to pray for him and possibly hypnotize him. Rasputin's abilities as a hypnotist are difficult to judge, but in many cases the subjects would seem to have hypnotized themselves due to their own superstition and Rasputin's reputation. Youssoupov soon became a favourite of Rasputin, partly because the monk found him amusing, partly because Rasputin felt that the meek, effeminate prince was perfectly safe and trustworthy. In any event, as Rasputin did not feel threatened by Youssoupov, the prince easily wrote the scenario that led to Rasputin's death.

The monk's disappearance, combined with the fact that shooting had been reported at Rasputin's last known whereabouts, quickly led the authorities to conclude that Youssoupov had been involved in foul play. After first confessing to the crime, Youssoupov attempted to recant. Police soon found the spot where Rasputin had been thrown into the river, and the body was discovered the following day about ninety metres downstream. Examination of the corpse revealed the startling fact that Rasputin had not been dead when he was hurled into the water; he had managed to untie one of his arms while in the river. The fact that his lungs were full of water indicated that, after the poisoning, beating and shooting, Rasputin actually had died by drowning. The czarina intervened on hearing that an autopsy was underway and had the procedure stopped. Rumours have circulated that the conspirators castrated Rasputin before dumping him in the river. This supposed fact is one of the story elements in John Berendt's 1994 novel *Midnight in the Garden of Good and Evil* and the subsequent film of the same title. But the fact that castration was not mentioned in the report of the incomplete autopsy would indicate that the story is untrue.

Reaction to Rasputin's death was mixed. Among the urban poor, who regarded Rasputin as one of their own, his death was another act of oppression. Among intellectuals, cosmopolites and officials of the Duma, the death was seen as the possible salvation of Russia. To the czar and czarina, the attack on Rasputin was an attack on the royal family itself. Nonetheless Youssoupov's punishment was not especially harsh. He was banished to his estate in Rakitnoe in central Russia, and even that sentence did not stand long, for after the Bolshevik Revolution, in November 1917, he no longer felt bound by the czar's sentence and returned to Petrograd. When he realized that the new Russia was no place for the old aristocracy, he fled his homeland with little more than the clothes on his back, two paintings by Rembrandt, a string of black pearls once owned by Catherine the Great and several hundred precious gems. Like many Russian refugees, he settled in Paris, where he soon found himself impoverished. His fortunes took an upturn, however, with the release in 1934 of the Hollywood film *Rasputin and the Empress* (retitled *Rasputin the Mad Monk* for European distribution). The film implied that a woman, obviously based on Irina Youssoupov, was the lure that made Rasputin come to Youssoupov's home that fateful night and that he had raped her. The Youssoupovs sued MGM for defamation. The case was tried in England and resulted in a settlement, considered the largest of its type at the time, of an undisclosed figure greater than £25,000 but probably less than £100,000. This windfall, along with the profits from a book Youssoupov wrote about the assassination, allowed the couple to pursue a comfortable existence for the rest of their lives.

RESOURCES: *Rasputin and the Fall of the Romanovs* by Colin Wilson (London, 1964); *The Man Who Killed Rasputin: Prince Felix Youssoupov and the Murder That Helped Bring Down the Russian Empire* by Greg King (New York, 1995); *Rasputin: The Saint Who Sinned* by Brian Moynahan (London, 1999); *The Rasputin File* by Edvard Radzinsky (London, 1999).

ZANGARA, Giuseppe (1900–1933), tried to assassinate US president-elect Franklin D. Roosevelt on the evening of February 14, 1933, but instead killed Anton Cermak (1873–1933), the mayor of Chicago.

A native of Ferruzzano in southern Italy and an unsuccessful Italian soldier, Zangara first planned to travel to Washington, DC, to kill Roosevelt's predecessor, Herbert Hoover. Then he learned that Roosevelt (1882–1945) was coming to Miami with Cermak. Zangara purchased a .32-calibre revolver at a Miami pawnshop for eight dollars. Standing on a chair, the assassin, who stood less than 1.5 metres tall, fired five times, wounding Cermak in the lung and four others less seriously. Cermak, whose animation of the Democratic vote in Chicago had been instrumental in Roosevelt's election, died nineteen days later. Zangara was immediately apprehended by police, who probably saved him from being beaten to death by the angry crowd. A bricklayer by trade, Zangara had immigrated to America in his teens and first worked in Philadelphia before relocating to Miami in 1932. Stories immediately after the event suggested that Zangara was in the pay of the Chicago underworld, but this allegation has never been substantiated or even maintained plausibly. Throughout his adult life, Zangara suffered from stomach pains, which were never properly diagnosed but which he attributed to the existence of the capitalist classes. A doctor had removed his appendix, but this did not alleviate his suffering. He felt that only death could end his agony. Perhaps this is why he showed neither fear nor remorse when sentenced to die in the electric chair, which he did on March 19. His grave in a prison cemetery was unmarked. An autopsy revealed that Zangara's supposed stomach problems actually had been due to a damaged gallbladder.

RESOURCE: *The Five Weeks of Giuseppe Zangara: The Man Who Would Assassinate* FDR by Blaise Picchi (Chicago 1998).

ZASULICH, Vera Ivanovna (1849–1919), was the Russian revolutionary heroine who, on January 19, 1878, twice shot General Dimitry Trepov (1855–1906), chief of police of St. Petersburg, who, though seriously wounded, survived the attempt. Zasulich, who had gone to his office on the pretext of interviewing him, was immediately arrested and put on public trial, during which her lawyer changed the focus of the case from attempted murder to police brutality. In 1877, a political prisoner named Boglubov was publicly flogged for refusing to remove his hat in Trepov's presence. Flogging of prisoners had been expressly prohibited as one of the reforms of Czar Alexandr II. By the end of the trial, Zasulich had become an idol to the public as well as the jurors. When the jury ruled that Zasulich was not guilty, observers in the court set off "a hurricane of applause."

Naturally the St. Petersburg police disagreed with the finding, and as Zasulich and her throng of admirers left the courthouse, they were besieged by police determined to rearrest her. Her supporters surrounded her and fought off the police. Shots rang out from both sides, and although several people were killed in the clash, Zasulich was hustled away before she could be apprehended. When Alexandr learned of the verdict, he immediately ordered Zasulich's re-incarceration. Before the order could be carried out, however, Zasulich fled to Switzerland. Her actions made her a major figure to the revolutionary movement in Russia and inspired numerous terrorist activities including Alexandr's assassination in 1881. Zasulich was a pacifistic personality who deplored the acts committed in her name. And yet her shooting of Trepov was neither the first nor the most notable of her activities.

She had been a dedicated member of the revolutionary underground for several years before shooting Trepov. In 1869, she had been a courier for Sergei Nechaev while he was living in exile in Switzerland, and as such had been arrested and imprisoned for two years. Following this she herself spent several years in exile. Returning to Russia in 1875, she joined the Southern Mutineers, a radical group in Kiev. In 1876, she moved to St. Petersburg, where she worked on the underground newspaper *Land and Liberty*. This credential is what allowed her to gain admittance to Trepov's office. After the assassination attempt, Zasulich travelled abroad extensively, but also revisited Russia on several occasions before returning to stay in 1905. While outside Russia, she began corresponding with Karl Marx and befriended Eleanor Marx, his daughter. She also met Friederich Engels in England. In the late 1890s, Zasulich edited two publications for the exile group known as the Union of Social Democrats

Abroad. She was equally active within Russia. In 1884, by now a committed Marxist, she helped found the Emancipation of Labour Group, the first Russian Marxist organization. Zasulich was not, however, a revolutionary leader. Her role was more that of a supporter. She showed no skill at organization and her writing was not of a particularly high calibre. But she was hard-working and diligent. In short, she was considered a loyal disciple. Similarly, her deeds inspired many feministic women, but she was not herself a feminist, her actions being in support of proletarian revolution rather than the emancipation of women.

In 1900, Vera Zasulich met Lenin for the first time. He was impressed enough by her that he asked her to join the editorial board of *Iskra* (*The Spark*), his new party newspaper. By 1903, however, he was calling for her removal from the board. She had been attacking Lenin's approach of building a small party of revolutionaries rather than a broad-based political alliance. As time passed Zasulich became increasingly critical of the Bolsheviks. She not only advocated alliances with other revolutionary groups but also supported Russia's war with Germany in 1914. She condemned the Bolshevik Revolution in 1917 on orthodox Marxist grounds, as she believed that the proletariat was not large enough for the revolution to be consistent with Marx's theories. In 1919, the seventy-year-old Zasulich was evicted from the Writers' Home for her anti-Soviet stance. She died of pneumonia in May of that year.

RESOURCES: Official Soviet biographers of Zasulich praise her contributions to the movement before 1903 but become quite critical after her clash with Lenin. See her posthumous autobiography, *Vospominaniia* (Moscow, 1931).

INDEX OF VICTIMS